The Underground Railroad
in DeKalb County, Illinois

The Underground Railroad in DeKalb County, Illinois

Nancy M. Beasley

McFarland & Company, Inc., Publishers
Jefferson, North Carolina, and London

Library of Congress Cataloguing-in-Publication Data

Beasley, Nancy M., 1942–
The underground railroad in DeKalb County, Illinois / Nancy M. Beasley.
        p.   cm.
Includes bibliographical references and index.

ISBN 978-0-7864-7200-0
softcover : acid free paper ∞

1. Underground Railroad — Illinois — DeKalb County.   2. Fugitive slaves — Illinois — History — 19th century.   3. DeKalb County (Ill.) — History — 19th century.   I. Title.
F547.D3B43 2013   975.8'22503 — dc23   2012051478

British Library cataloguing data are available

© 2013 Nancy M. Beasley. All rights reserved

No part of this book may be reproduced or transmitted in any form or by any means, electronic or mechanical, including photocopying or recording, or by any information storage and retrieval system, without permission in writing from the publisher.

On the cover: artwork *The Underground Railroad*, 1893 (© 2013 PicturesNOW); lantern (© 2013 Shutterstock); background letter Sycamore Congregationalist 1852 Resolution outlining displeasure with slavery

Manufactured in the United States of America

*McFarland & Company, Inc., Publishers
Box 611, Jefferson, North Carolina 28640
www.mcfarlandpub.com*

To my husband,
George Franklin Beasley

Acknowledgments

My profound gratitude and praise:

To Phyllis Kelley (1924–2011), DeKalb County historian (1989–2011), with whom I shared a love of local history and who provided clues for research and details for the narrative. She read this manuscript before she died; her concise comment was, "It's all there."

To the many anonymous volunteers at the Joiner History Room, in Sycamore, DeKalb County, Illinois, who checked county archives for obituaries and historical references.

To Francis O'Donnell, archivist, Andover-Harvard Theological Library, with whom I had several enlightening telephone calls and who supplied photocopies of archival materials.

To Pat Michel, for her initial editing assistance and narrative suggestions.

To Jim Womack, professional photographer, for his invaluable assistance in the preparation of educational slides for public presentations of the subject matter.

To George Beasley, Bonita DeVale, Judy Eulburg, David Hankins, Virginia McComb, Lynne Miller, Jane Ann Moore, William Moore, Carole Murphy, Fay Stone, Nancy Wehlage and Gary Wehlage, who read all or part of the draft manuscript, for their questions and suggestions.

To my contemporary friends who endured the several years of my obsession with my old friends, the Abolitionists of DeKalb County, Illinois, the antislavery movement and its byproduct, the ever mysterious and still elusive Underground Railroad.

And to my husband, George. You believed in the project and provided encouragement during the long research and creative process. As the years of research and writing continued, you asked the ultimate motivational question, "When are you going to finish?"

I extend my humble thanks to you all.

Nancy M. Beasley

Table of Contents

Acknowledgments vi
Preface 1
Introduction 3
Chronology of Events 6

1. An Abolitionist's Milestone   11
2. Remember the Underground Railroad   17
3. Illinois: A Burned-Over Reunion   25
4. The Abolitionists! Thank God!   36
5. First, the Church   54
6. No Apologists for Slavery: The Congregationalists   59
7. Resolute and Unwavering   76
8. All Brethren: The Universalists   90
9. Seceders and Covenanters: The Presbyterians   102
10. Evangelistic Lawbreakers: The Wesleyan Methodists   113
11. The Western Citizen Reads the *Western Citizen*   123
12. God Will Thank the Republican Party   131
13. Lincoln Knew the *True Republican*   150
14. Reasons to Be Unreasonable   161
15. Hail and Farewell!   171

Antislavery Advocates: A Biographical Dictionary 175
Notes 207
Bibliography 215
Index 221

Preface

Several years ago I discovered the original 1840s handwritten minutes book of the First Congregational Church and Church Society in Sycamore, Illinois. The Congregationalists merged with the local Universalists in 1927 to become the Federated Church. What a treasure trove! Here were accounts of the public accusations and ecclesiastic trials of church members who had transgressed stated church rules of conduct. Occasionally a notation would direct the reader to a paper file, which unfortunately no longer exists. Evidence of America's early Puritan ethics abounded in the flowing cursive. As various names were repeated throughout the record, this resident historian asked questions. Who was Deacon David West, alleged to be active in the Underground Railroad? From what region did he come? In what state had he lived previously? What was his background?

My curiosity increased when I read about the Rev. Oliver W. Norton, who voluntarily ended his ministry at the First Congregational Church following several consecutive Church Society meetings at which his opinions about slavery were discussed. Norton was obviously antislavery. How did he happen to be in Sycamore, Illinois? Where did he go next?

The historian separates fact from fiction. This study, however, compiles current known information, both facts and area folklore, regarding the antislavery movement and the Abolitionists in DeKalb County, Illinois. A preponderance of evidence combined with additional reading created background for the narrative. When the truth becomes legend, then the legends are what you recount. This includes regional beliefs pertaining to the Underground Railroad and has drawn on various written and oral historical sources. With the addition of information from previously unpublished documents, a clearer picture of the area's antislavery movement emerges.

Some of what was initially recorded may have been romanticized by the aging memories of those original Abolitionists. However, I cannot ignore the prevalent strong local oral traditions. Neither do I seek to create an alternative history.[1] To neglect the fact that only white people were helping the fugitive slaves flee through DeKalb County would be to disregard the truth. This does not mean that I am overlooking any contemporary research about the brave African Americans who aided the thousands escaping slavery. It simply means that in the mid–1800s in DeKalb County, Illinois, that avenue of assistance and guidance did not exist.

Because local sites and individuals can be connected to Underground Railroad activities through primary sources, the myths and legends surrounding DeKalb County activists acquire credibility.[2] It is my purpose to present the collected information in one book. Research utilized long overlooked sources, together with newly-discovered data regarding DeKalb County Abolitionists, their involvement in the antislavery movement and their activities locally in the Underground Railroad. The conclusions independently reached by this local historian about the antislavery movement and the Abolitionists in one county in Illinois are the same conclusions now being reached by noted professors of history as they re-examine the subject matter.[3]

To learn more about the antislavery advocates, it was necessary to research those individuals. Where did they come from? Why did they move to DeKalb County? Who were their family members? An appendix lists and describes the people in DeKalb County who were either active as Abolitionists, in the antislavery movement and/or in the Underground Railroad. Much of the information pertaining to vital statistics was drawn from census records plus secondary printed information, including obituaries and historical works. Subscriber lists for the antislavery newspaper *Western Citizen* and church membership rolls yielded valuable data. Family genealogists should treat the information as clue material only, and continue to research original documents containing vital statistics for verification.

The word "Abolitionist" used as a noun is purposely capitalized throughout when referring to the active antislavery citizenry of DeKalb County. They personally considered being an Abolitionist a badge of honor, akin to belonging to a church or a political party, and much deserved the elevated status. Unlike other geographical areas in both the Northern and Southern United States, DeKalb County Abolitionists were neither openly persecuted, nor publicly prosecuted. There are no reports of mob action by anti-abolitionists. There are no reports of proslavery riots. And there are no recorded incidents of civil action against the locals who disobeyed the Fugitive Slave Law. Privately, there may possibly have been subtle criticisms against the antislavery voices. However, the overriding factor was that the good citizens who were the church members, the antislavery activists, and the elected county officials were one and the same. There was no room for discord.

Let the reader enjoy the story of this part of our nation's history as it occurred in Northern Illinois.

Introduction

DeKalb County, Illinois, was a forgotten county; forgotten throughout the annals of history whenever an author wrote about the Underground Railroad. Maybe it was forgotten because it was exclusively agrarian in its beginnings. The county seat in the city of Sycamore sits squarely at the north end of thousands of mostly flat acres of fertile prairie, where glaciers deposited rich nutrients in the black soil which is still cultivated for cash crops. Early commentary on the area indicates that DeKalb County was populated with wealthy farmers.[1] Because of its extremely productive soil, agriculture continues to play a lead role in the economics of the county. Yet hundreds of other counties in the new states on the western frontier were also grounded in agriculture, and farming by itself was not unique.

Maybe DeKalb County was forgotten because the northern end of Illinois was settled years after the southern and central parts of the state. Perhaps contemporary writers in the late 19th and early 20th centuries stereotyped the farmers and assumed that no one in the western frontier in Northern Illinois was sophisticated enough to concern himself with issues of national importance. Though the transformation from an agrarian to an industrialized and perhaps more gentrified society had not yet occurred in this part of the nation, the population was not unintelligent. It was a misjudgment on the part of historical researchers and writers in the late 1800s to think otherwise. In their quiet manner those early farmers, together with informed citizens in other occupational pursuits, persevered in their quest to make their newly settled homeland a better place to live. They hoped to bring about a peaceful change in the treatment of their fellow human beings.

Whatever the reasons for the omission, with the exception of a couple of locally printed and distributed histories, DeKalb County was neither recognized nor thoroughly discussed by authors exploring the Underground Railroad across the northern part of the United States.

A comprehensive history of the Underground Railroad in the United States was attempted in 1898 when history professor Wilbur H. Siebert of Ohio State University wrote his pioneer tome, *The Underground Railroad from Slavery to Freedom*. The author accomplished an amazing job of gathering scarce documentation pertaining to the well-guarded system used to aid fugitive slaves. Written only a little more than three decades after the close of the Civil War, the book remains one of the definitive resources regarding the activities of this most secretive activity. In his first chapter, Siebert commented that "the participants in underground operations were quiet persons, little known outside of the localities where they lived, and were therefore members of a class which historians find it exceedingly difficult to bring within their field of view."[2]

Siebert also acknowledged the lack of primary evidence on which to base the history of the legendary assistance given to fugitive slaves. Using independent verbal interviews with people contemporary to the events, he recreated the story and was himself "content with the materials discovered without making additions of his own." Siebert also let his "conclusions be defined by the facts, rather than seek to cast these 'in the mould of [his] hypothesis.'"[3] The work is frequently footnoted and as a printed source certainly offers the reader numerous additional clues for further research.

In trying to create a comprehensive work, an author runs the risk of not being comprehensive enough and as a result not satisfying expectations. The greater narrative of antislavery, Abolitionists and the Underground Railroad in the northern United States is influenced by religion, politics, geography and economics. In DeKalb County, religion was the major force that energized the entire antislavery movement. Politics played a secondary, although powerful, role. The influence of Protestant Christian denominations inspired and supported a new confidence that the government could correct the wrong committed in allowing slavery.

Siebert's published research does not reach into every individual county in each state considered. DeKalb County was one of those excluded. Consequently, important facts were perhaps inadvertently omitted from the final work and the end result is not as comprehensive as the author would have the reader believe. His oft-heralded published study is a good example of such omissions.

Illinois had its full complement of 102 counties by 1859. Yet only 38 of those counties are represented by the abolitionists listed by Siebert as active participants in the state's antislavery movement. In reality, a large majority of the counties were involved, but most of the two northern tiers of Illinois counties are missing entirely from Siebert's text. Some letters to Siebert from aging Illinois abolitionists exist in scrapbooks he compiled and are now located in the Ohio Historical Society. The memories related to Siebert by those former Abolitionists reflect geographic areas mostly in central and southern Illinois, which all had differing histories regarding aid to fugitive slaves. Any information relating to the antislavery movement in DeKalb County, however, is not discussed in his book. In fact, the data Siebert collected, which was not included in his book, mentions only the Beveridge family in Somonauk in southern DeKalb County and no others.[4]

According to his bibliography, Siebert relied on very few sources to augment the oral interviews. There are no more than six Illinois local and/or county histories which represent only four counties for his complete Illinois Underground Railroad history pertaining to the 38 counties he discussed. These references included two sources for Chicago, two histories on Will County, one history for McDonough County, and one for Knox County. How can this be representative of the entire state of Illinois?

Those six Illinois books all postdate the locally well-known Henry L. Boies' 1868 *History of DeKalb County, Illinois*. This volume, published only three years after the close of the Civil War, is especially conspicuous by its absence from Siebert's research. Two other historical retrospectives, *Voters and Tax-payers of DeKalb County, Illinois*, and *Portrait and Biographical Album of DeKalb*, were written in 1876 and 1885, respectively, again well before Seibert's publication date of 1898, yet these books were not cited. Some credit for historical data was given to several individual Illinois newspaper articles, as well as a handful of personal letters and one obituary pamphlet. The consequence is that as comprehensive as Siebert's book may appear at the outset, DeKalb County was indeed forgotten in his study of the Underground Railroad. Perhaps Siebert was unaware that anything of consequence occurred there.

When Boies wrote his 1868 county history he commented that the county had a "quiet and uneventful ... career."[5] The recent Great Rebellion was over and his work sought to explore the story of DeKalb County's participation in the effort to save the Union. Boies said, "Few knew, or adequately appreciate, the extent of the service that our brave boys rendered in that grand struggle for the preservation of the life of the Nation."[6]

We can say with conviction that few know or adequately appreciate today the extent of the service that our common citizens—ministers, farmers, merchants, clerks—rendered prior to the Civil War in aiding those fugitive slaves who passed through DeKalb County on their way to freedom in Canada.

This book was initiated with an interest in uncovering why so many residents in DeKalb County were avowed Abolitionists. The result is not a treatise on the entire antislavery movement, nor is it intended to be a comprehensive sociological or genealogical reference about local Abolitionists. The goal here is to identify those local individuals who supported the antislavery cause.

The Underground Railroad in DeKalb County, Illinois, focuses on the influence of Protestant Christian denominations in the antislavery movement and the fact that they dominated the thinking on the Northern Illinois frontier. As a result of their efforts, the local antislavery movement was fostered and Abolitionists were oftentimes created because of their religious associations and membership in the churches in DeKalb County. The recipient of their impassioned beliefs was the famed Underground Railroad. It was a familiar part of their daily lives. Abolitionist fever may have come later to DeKalb County, compared to those counties in central and southern Illinois, yet it burned with a quiet intensity.

During the 1840s there were no free blacks living in DeKalb County. Neither were there any slaves in DeKalb County. Consequently, no African American churches existed in the area. There also were no resident Quakers, who for decades already had a reputation for helping runaway slaves in the eastern United States. There only existed white evangelical Christians who sincerely felt that they were the only ones who comprehended the gravity of slavery. They believed they had "seen the light" and understood that slavery needed to be abolished. The majority of people in DeKalb County were not initially motivated by politics; they were motivated by their own moral refusal to tolerate man's inhumanity to man. They thought that their republican form of government, operating with the consent of its citizens, could eventually correct the wrong. But their overriding motivation was spiritual, supported by their chosen religious denominations, which inspired them to actively participate in the Underground Railroad. Unlike Eastern Abolitionists, whose ministers only preached to the South to release the enslaved, DeKalb County church members did what they knew was right in the eyes of God. They could do no less.

Here are the stories of who they were, where they came from, and why they did what they did. To paraphrase Boies, this book seeks to rescue the facts about the antislavery movement in DeKalb County, Illinois, from an undeserved oblivion; to gather and fix these ephemeral incidents before they are gone forever; to give our citizens a knowledge of these events and to give to the world some information about its history.[7]

Chronology of Events

1787 • Northwest Ordinance created the Northwest Territory which included Illinois and prohibited the introduction of slaves into that territory west of the Ohio River

1818 • Illinois admitted to the Union as a slavery-free state; indentured system is permitted

1820 • Federal Missouri Compromise passed; Missouri admitted as slave state and Maine as a free state, which maintained balance in the Senate between free and slave states

1824 • Illinois voters defeated call for a convention to amend the Constitution to legalize slavery

1824 • Illinois Governor Coles was prosecuted for freeing his own slaves in violation of state's existing Black Codes; Coles found guilty but the verdict later overturned

1831 • Illinois passes stronger law forbidding black or mulatto people to reside in the state unless they first provided a bond and security

1837 • DeKalb County created out of Kane County

1837 • Illinois General Assembly designated Sycamore as county seat of DeKalb County; charter for City of Chicago also approved

Oct. 26, 1837 • Illinois State Anti-Slavery Society formed under leadership of Elijah Lovejoy

Nov. 1837 • Abolitionist newspaper editor Elijah Lovejoy murdered by proslavery mob in Alton, Illinois; his brother, Congregational minister Owen Lovejoy, became outspoken antislavery activist

1838 • Dr. Horatio F. Page arrived in DeKalb County; settled first in Genoa, then Sycamore

before 1840 • Jesse C. Kellogg arrived in Sycamore

before 1840 • John Maxfield hosted first county Abolitionist meeting in Sycamore Township

1840 • Per U.S. Census, Illinois had 331 slaves and 3,598 free persons of color; the majority of African Americans resided in southern half of the state

1840 • Reuben Pritchard of Clinton Township hosted Abolitionist meeting at which Owen Lovejoy spoke; proslavery antagonists set fire to Pritchard's barn housing Lovejoy's horse and carriage

1840 • Sycamore First Congregational Church organized; congregants required to affirm antislavery belief as a membership requirement

1840 • James G. Birney was first antislavery candidate for U.S. president under the Liberty Party banner; Whig William Henry Harrison, with no party platform, was elected over both Birney and incumbent Martin Van Buren, a Democrat who had opposed federal interference with slavery

Feb. 1841 • Illinois' first antislavery convention held in Lowell, Illinois

1841 • Whig John Tyler was the first vice-president to succeed to presidency upon death of a president, William Henry Harrison

1842 • George Beveridge family arrived in Somonauk from Washington County, New York

May 1842 • Antislavery "Liberty State Convention" held in Chicago, Illinois; this founded the Illinois Liberty Party

July 1842 • Advent of antislavery newspaper *Western Citizen* by Zebina Eastman before July 1843 • DeKalb County Anti-Slavery Society formed; Kane, DuPage and Lake counties antislavery societies also formed between July 1842 and July 1843

1843 • David West and family arrived in DeKalb County from Erie County, New York, and witnessed their first fugitive slaves in Illinois

1844 • Antislavery songbook, *The Liberty Minstrel*, compiled by George W. Clark; used by DeKalb County Abolitionists

Feb. 24, 1844 • David West and family joined Sycamore First Congregational Church

Feb. 24, 1844 • Antislavery resolutions first introduced and tabled at Sycamore First Congregational Church

March 23, 1844 • First annual meeting of DeKalb County Anti-Slavery Society at courthouse; First Congregational minister Edwin E. Wells spoke

March 30, 1844 • Temperance resolutions passed at Sycamore First Congregational Church; antislavery resolutions tabled a second time

April 13, 1844 • Antislavery resolutions tabled a third time at Sycamore First Congregational Church

June 21, 1844 • Resolutions on Slavery adopted in the convention of the General Congregational Association of Illinois

June 30, 1844 • Antislavery resolutions passed at Sycamore First Congregational Church

Summer 1844 • Sycamore First Congregational Church banned from DeKalb County courthouse as a result of their public profession of antislavery beliefs

Sept. 16, 1844 • The Liberty Party convened at the DeKalb County courthouse

Nov. 1844 • Liberty Party presidential candidate, James G. Birney, loses to dark-horse Democrat nominee James Polk; favored candidate Whig Henry Clay also defeated because of spoilers Birney and a fourth independent candidate, Mormon Joseph Smith. Polk supported annexation of Texas, a proslavery viewpoint; Clay was anti-annexation, but was undercut by Birney in the North; Birney received 146 votes in DeKalb County, Polk 273 and Clay 132

1845 • Universalist Church in Sycamore first met in DeKalb County courthouse

May 4, 1845 • First recorded minutes for Mayfield Wesleyan Methodist Church

June 18, 1845 • Mayfield Wesleyan Methodist camp meeting; all "anti-slavery brethren" invited

July 4, 1845 • Annual meeting of DeKalb County Anti-Slavery Society

1846 • Somonauk United Presbyterian Church officially organized by the Rev. Rensselaer W. French

1847 • Extra effort by Illinois state Liberty Party organization to elect local Liberty candidates in DeKalb and six other northern counties

March 1848 • Illinois voters approved new state constitution: free persons of color prohibited from immigrating to Illinois; slave owners could no longer bring slaves into the state specifically to set them free

April 12, 1848 • Sycamore First Congregational Church conducted a "desultory conversation with regard to the propriety of modifying or defining the Term 'Apologist' contained in the standing rule of the Church on American Slavery"

March 1848 • Minister Oliver W. Norton resigned from Sycamore First Congregational Church, as a result of the divided vote over his views on antislavery, temperance and war

Aug. 1848 • Formation of the Free-Soil Party; opposed extension of slavery into territories

Oct. 23, 1848 • Sycamore First Congregational Church special assessment inventory taken of members' personal property; David West owned 40 wagons and carts; at least one was used as transportation for fugitive slaves in Underground Railroad

Nov. 1848 • Whig Zachary Taylor elected president; campaign issue was the antislavery Wilmot Proviso, a bill to ban slavery in territories acquired during Mexican War; former President Martin Van Buren ran as third-party candidate under antislavery Free-Soil Party

1850 • *Uncle Tom's Cabin* by Harriet Beecher Stowe published in New York

1850 • John Shepherd, 17-year-old black male, enumerated in household of Horatio F. Page

July 10, 1850 • Vice-President Millard Fillmore sworn in as president after death of President Taylor; Fillmore had presided over the Senate debate re: the Compromise of 1850

Sept. 18, 1850 • Compromise of 1850 passed; included a more restrictive Fugitive Slave Law making it a federal offense to aid a runaway slave

Oct. 30, 1850 • "Indignation Meeting" in Somonauk resulted in the passage of antislavery resolutions in direct response to the new Fugitive Slave Law

1852 • Democrat Franklin Pierce elected president over Whig candidate Winfield Scott; Pierce was nominated as a compromise candidate on the 49th ballot. Both party platforms supported the Compromise of 1850, but "cotton" Whigs and "conscience" Whigs (South vs. North) divided their support for their candidate

Nov. 27, 1852 • In response to political atmosphere, Sycamore First Congregational Church passed additional, stronger antislavery resolutions

1853 • The Rev. Thomas J. Carney officially organized Sycamore Universalist Church Society

1853 • Illinois legislature passed more restrictive "Black Laws" which existed until after the Civil War

1853 • Sandwich Congregational Church organized

Feb. 28, 1854 • Antislavery men in Ripon, Wisconsin, declared intent to form Republican Party if Congress passed the Kansas-Nebraska Bill

May 30, 1854 • Passage of the federal Kansas-Nebraska Act sponsored by Sen. Stephen A. Douglas; called "popular sovereignty," Kansas and Nebraska territories could decide whether or not to allow slavery within their boundaries; effectively repealed Missouri Compromise of 1820

July 31, 1854 • "Anti-Nebraska" antislavery meeting held in courthouse in Sycamore

Sept. 14, 1854 • DeKalb County Republican Party organized in Sycamore

1854 • Delegates from DeKalb County Democrat, Free-Soil and Whig parties sent to convention in Aurora, Illinois, to help organize State of Illinois Republican Party

1854 • William Parker Dutton lost his appointed federal job as Sycamore Postmaster over his anti-slavery views opposing the Fugitive Slave Law in the Compromise of 1850

1854 • First Congregational Church in DeKalb organized; members affirmed as "equal brethren ... irrespective of Color"

1854 • Former slave Stephen Depp delivered lecture in DeKalb County

1856 • Sycamore First Congregational Church withdrew from American Home Missionary Society; affiliated with new antislavery American Missionary Association

1856 • Antislavery proponent John C. Fremont was first Republican Party candidate for president with slogan "Free soil, free labor, free speech, free men, Fremont"; Democrat James Buchanan, opposed federal interference with slavery, and won over Fremont and former president Millard Fillmore, who was the anti-immigration/anti–Catholic Know-Nothing/American Party candidate

1857 • Dred Scott decision in Illinois declared that African Americans are not considered as "full citizens" and therefore cannot sue for their freedom; decision stated that Congress has no authority to prohibit slavery in the states and territories

1857 • The antislavery newspaper *True Republican* established in Sycamore, Illinois, by Campbell W. Waite, to counterbalance the local proslavery Democrat *Republican Sentinel*

March 30, 1858 • Campbell W. Waite sold the *True Republican* to James H. Beveridge, Caleb M. Brown, and Daniel B. James; Waite retained as editor

1858 • The *True Republican* publisher, O.P. Bassett, printed first separate printing of Abraham Lincoln's "House Divided" speech

Sept. 15, 1858 • Abraham Lincoln, following debate with Stephen A. Douglas in Jonesboro, Illinois, commented publicly on article in the *DeKalb County Sentinel*, formerly the *Republican Sentinel*

Oct. 2, 1858 • County Republican Party convention held in DeKalb County courthouse

1860 • U.S. Census listed mulatto Mary A. Wadgen and daughter in home of Horatio F. Page; Edward Freeman, black man living in own home; 14-year-old Matilda Dublin, black female servant in home of Abraham Ellwood; mulatto Joseph Roe, servant in home of John C. Waterman; mulatto John Wilson, a barber in Sycamore

1860 • Per U.S. Census, 7,628 African Americans lived in State of Illinois

1860 • Abraham Lincoln elected president on Republican platform which called for end to slavery in the territories, but upheld slavery in southern states; defeated were Democrat Stephen A. Douglas, National (Southern) Democrat John C. Breckinridge, and John Bell, who ran under the Constitutional Union party consisting of old-line Whigs and remnants of the Know-Nothing/American party.

1861 • Advent of the American Civil War; in theory, Underground Railroad no longer necessary

1862 • Civil War in progress; thousands from DeKalb County answer President Lincoln's call for volunteers for the Union Army

1862 • Sycamore First Congregational Church continued to support fugitives with $3.00 contribution to "Mr. Browning, Black Man"

Jan. 1, 1863 • President Lincoln signed the Emancipation Proclamation, nominally freeing those slaves residing in areas of the South not under federal control

Feb. 1, 1865 • Illinois first state to ratify the 13th Amendment to U.S. Constitution, abolishing slavery

The reasonable man adapts himself to the world;
the unreasonable one persists to adapt the world to himself.
Therefore all progress depends on the unreasonable man.
— George Bernard Shaw (1856–1950, Nobel Laureate)

Chapter 1

An Abolitionist's Milestone

If a man does not keep pace with his companions, perhaps it is because he hears a different drummer. Let him step to the music which he hears, however measured or far away.—Henry David Thoreau (1817–1862), author, philosopher

His Special Day

On the morning of his 80th birthday, Deacon David West may have awakened to a serenade of soft coos from mourning doves and the raucous crows of barnyard roosters. He probably stretched his long legs, no longer limber, and may have silently thanked God for awakening him to yet another day. His aging eyesight could have made it difficult to groom the beard which elongated his weather-beaten face. The day was a milestone day for him and he probably expected to spend it quietly with no particular fanfare. Eighty years was a long time to live in 1886. As he completed his morning ablutions, if West paused to glance out the window of the two-story frame house built with his own hands, his farsighted eyes could have lingered on the dirt road he had so often traveled.

It was easy to envision

> that venerable carriage used by David West of this place ... it was one of the passenger coaches on the underground railroad which ran through this place, and as late as 1859, Elias West and Hiram Kellogg, then boys in their teens, used it to aid a half-dozen dusky fugitive slaves from Missouri to Canada. These were the last but not the first of them by hundreds.[1]

God had watched over West and his unique passengers — all runaway slaves — too many times to count when he drove his specially-built wagon down that particular road. Such memories can flood one's thoughts. The fierce determination that carried him over that road and caused him to debate publicly in defiance of the then existing fugitive slave laws still burned in his heart, even with the passage of time.

This glorious morning of July 16, 1886, dawned hot and humid, with temperatures guessed to be hovering in the 80s, typical for July in DeKalb County, Illinois. Two days previous, severe thunderstorms blew across Minnesota and threatened the plains of Northern Illinois with similar weather patterns. As the temperature rose by mid-afternoon, a caravan of horse-drawn wagons and buggies clip-clopped along that same road, the dusty Sycamore to St. Charles State Road heading east out of town, once a familiar route in the area Underground Railroad. The con-

Elias Collins West, son of David West, is seated center, surrounded by members of his family at the West family home. The house and adjacent corn crib, located west of Sycamore, served as a "station" to shelter fugitive slaves on the Underground Railroad.

veyances were laden with a different purpose from that of forty years ago as the entourage slowly made its way to West's country farm home. All occupants were intent on celebrating the day's special occasion. Unknown to the Deacon himself, invited guests included David's six children, Alice, Orrin, Asa (sometimes called by his middle name of Porter), Elias, Sarah Louise and Minerva, only four of whom were able to attend that Friday afternoon. West's wives, Sarah and Lucinda, had predeceased him in 1849 and 1883, respectively. Other eager guests were seven of West's grandchildren and 11 of his 15 great-grandchildren. They undoubtedly expected a joyous event.

Occupants of the slow-moving carriages either carried personal gifts for David West or carted containers of prepared food for the "sumptuous repast" to come. The birthday party was planned to astonish the celebrant. Unbeknownst to anyone, the festive commemoration would evolve into a local antislavery reunion.

Upon arrival, hungry men immediately set up to accommodate the surprise summer picnic. They placed makeshift tables outside on the grounds of West's "pleasant home," under the "shade of trees planted by the Deacon long years since on the then bare prairie." West's son Elias readied the stakes in the sand pits for his favorite game of horseshoes. Later in the day when the gathered group finished eating, the Honorable Henry Wood, himself a professed antislavery advocate, arose to speak. Using "appropriate congratulatory remarks," Wood presented West with "a beautiful easy chair for his advancing years." David West was speechless. The man, who in 1844 spoke so eloquently about the evils of slavery, had no "fluent words in reply." The event caught him unawares and he was overcome with gratitude. All present agreed that the birthday surprise was a huge success.[2]

Among the close friends in attendance that day were other local aging Abolitionists: Agrippa Dow, now 93 years old; West's brother-in-law Dr. Ellsworth Rose, 75 years old; and Deacon Charles Smith, a younger 69. As the afternoon festivities progressed, someone produced a "well preserved copy of *The Liberty Minstrel*,"[3] the antislavery songbook compiled in 1844 by George W. Clark and published a year later. When Clark originally disseminated his collection of abolitionist and antislavery songs and poems, he admonished the singer to "enter into the sentiment of the piece ... that they may impress it upon their hearers."[4] The compiler stated that his collection of antislavery music would both "affect and improve the heart."[5] Assembled guests at David West's birthday party appropriately joined together to sing those particular songs in commemoration of this milestone occasion. Deacon West, this specific aging Abolitionist, was instrumental in the success of the antislavery cause in DeKalb County through his personal involvement in the Sycamore's First Congregational Church, and through his frequent travels on the local rails of the Underground Railroad.

Arising from the assembled group, an improvised choir "sang again gleefully the same songs of freedom sung by the same voices forty years ago." As they raised their voices to the heavens, the words and melody of "The Fugitive" resounded once again. "A noble man of sable brow / Came to my humble cottage door ... / He begged if I had ought to give / To help the panting fugitive."[6] The words in each verse conveyed the progression of the antislavery movement from an evangelical perspective, beginning with the initial response of the stranger to the fugitive: "I told him ... he was black — a slave astray / And should return as he had come / That I would to his master give / The straying villain fugitive."[7]

In the rhyme, through his actions and entreaties, the escapee argues for his place among mankind: "He fell upon his trembling knee and claimed he was a brother man / That I was bound to set him free according to the gospel plan / And if I would God's grace receive / That I must help the fugitive."

Six stanzas recount the story of the lone fugitive slave seeking help from strangers, and conclude with the Abolitionist agreeing to help. "I bowed and took the stranger in, and gave him meat, and drink, and rest / I hope that God forgave my sin, and made me with that brother blest / I am resolved, long as I live, to help the panting fugitive."[8]

Many years before, the stirring songs sung at antislavery meetings rallied the supporters to action, creating a bravado which shielded them from harm as they sometimes risked their lives to save a fellow human being. Singing together bonded the choristers and created a loyalty to a common cause. They now no longer needed to take such risks, yet raising their voices in song revived the fervor and passion that had once boosted their enthusiasm.[9] Recalling the supplications of the slave, they sang, "Am I not a Man and a Brother?" a question which is followed with, "Sell me not one to another / Ought I not, then, to be free? / Take not thus my liberty. / Christ our Saviour, Died for me as well as thee.[10]

Another musical rendition from *The Liberty Minstrel* is "Ye Heralds of Freedom," which encouraged the Abolitionists to "go onward, go onward, your cause is of God / And he will soon sever the oppressor's strong rod."[11] After the rousing songs, the old friends joined in "pleasant raillery of Deacons West and Smith," a royal roasting of sorts. Laughing about their many exploits, they reminisced freely. Speaking of their own brazen conduct as active conductors on the Underground Railroad, they remembered how they defied the law of the land "contrary to statutes in such cases" when they helped "fugitives from service in the South on their way to Canada."[12]

Like their fellow Abolitionist, John Hossack, in neighboring LaSalle County, the DeKalb

THE LIBERTY MINSTREL.

"When the striving of surges
Is mad on the main,
Like the charge of a column
Of plumes on the plain,
When the thunder is up
From his cloud cradled sleep
And the tempest is treading
The paths of the deep—
There is beauty. But where is the beauty to see,
Like the sun-brilliant brow of a nation when free?"

BY

GEO. W. CLARK.

NEW-YORK:
LEAVITT & ALDEN, 7 CORNHILL, BOSTON: SAXTON & MILES, 205
BROADWAY, N. Y.: MYRON FINCH, 120 NASSAU ST., N. Y.:
JACKSON & CHAPLIN, 38 DEAN ST., ALBANY, N. Y.:
JACKSON & CHAPLIN, CORNER GENESSEE AND
MAIN ST., UTICA, N. Y.

1845.

The Liberty Minstrel, a songbook used by Abolitionists for an impromptu songfest at David West's 80th birthday party.

County conductors never traveled to southern states in order to transport slaves back to the north. Their thoughts and actions echoed Hossack's comment to the court after he was later convicted of harboring fugitives: "I go not to Missouri to relieve oppressed humanity," he proclaimed, "but when He that directs the steps of men, conducts a poor, oppressed, panting fugitive to my door, and there I hear his bitter cry, I dare not close my ear against it."[13] DeKalb County Abolitionists followed the same creed.

A physical reminder of Deacon West's days as an Underground Railroad conductor was the weathered wood carriage still standing on the West property. West personally constructed the "car" by hand, incorporating a hidden bottom which was large enough to hold seven people. The wagon, still used by the West family in 1886, could tell many stories of midnight travels smuggling fugitives on the underground path to freedom. That afternoon on West's 80th birthday, the assembled men recounted tales about carrying fugitives from West's Underground Railroad station on his own farm to the next station in St. Charles, Kane County, Illinois. "David West's [farm] of Sycamore was well known as a home and place of refuge for the fugitive Negroes; and many an interesting story of their experience in aiding and secreting these oppressed people are now told with a freedom, that before the downfall of American slavery would have been dangerous."[14] In a special assessment inventory performed by the First Congregational Church in 1848, West declared ownership of 40 carts and wagons, which was more than most landowners in the county. With that many options for transportation, the well-known false-bottomed carriage may not have been the only conveyance he used to carry fugitives.

Visualize a small campfire in the country clearing as the late summer sun settled towards the western horizon. The lingering twilight sky showed broad paintbrush strokes in shades of pink and blue. Maybe a humid haze still lingered in the air while the elderly Abolitionists contemplated their accomplishments, retelling the stories for the next generation. They remembered one occasion when

> seven fugitives, man, wife, and children, came to the house of Deacon West when he was away. Mrs. West felt some hesitancy in taking them in, in the absence of her husband, but the children urged her to do so. They found one of the seven a white girl. At supper time the old folks were allowed to eat first and the pretty white girl and the children had to wait with the other members of the family. Supper over, the problem arose as to how they would keep so large a number, but by making beds on the floor all were comfortably entertained for the night. Morning came, but Mr. West did not, and she sent her son [Elias C. West] over to Deacon [Jesse] Kellogg, who was also friendly to the cause, and told him how they were situated. He said he would let his eldest son [Hiram Jesse Kellogg] go and take his team and Mr. West's wagon, so the seven were loaded up and started for the next station near St. Charles, reaching Dr. [Joseph P.] Bartlett's soon after midnight and went to the door and knocked. He came and asked what was wanted and was told that he had seven fugitives. Mr. Bartlett said that he understood they were coming and had made provision for them. After putting up the team he remained all night at the home of Mr. Bartlett, who took the party on to Chicago, where they were placed on a boat and taken to Canada. About a year later a letter was received from the young lady, who was then about 20 yrs. old. In the meantime she had learned to read and write quite intelligently. She said they were happy in their new Canadian home and could not thank us enough for helping them on their way to freedom. The exact date cannot be remembered, but it was sometime in the early '50s.[15]

The raconteurs inserted other details into this narrative. In 1852 West's sons Asa and Elias were 15 and 13 years old, respectively. Jesse Kellogg's son, Hiram, who was one of the first white children born to settlers in DeKalb County, was also then only 13 years old. These three young friends aided their fathers frequently in their locally known quest to end slavery until the onset of the Civil War.[16] Years later, Elias West recounted this same story while visiting in Ottawa, Kansas, in 1910. He commented that the "only evidence of Negro blood about [the white female fugitive slave] were the delightful curls in her hair."[17]

Other memories ebbed and flowed in the soft fading sunlight. The jubilant old Abolitionists raised their voices once again and concluded their pleasant evening of reminiscences with such songs as "Shall We Gather at the River" and "Sweet By and By."[18] The familiar music once sounded different to them, reminding them of the human oneness of black and white with God, and the melodies called them to rally 'round the cause for personal liberty. Forty years before, these songs and others with similar lyrics caused their blood pressure to elevate in response to their naked enthusiasm to assist fugitive slaves. The Abolitionist's birthday gathering was a fitting tribute to the man who dreamed of a land free from human bondage and who allied himself with the great reform for emancipation in his country. When Deacon David West lifted his voice in the songs of liberty, he undoubtedly heard a different drummer and stepped well to the music he heard. And now forty years later, while listening to the inspired melodies, West's sleepy great-grandchildren may have lingered comfortably on their mothers' laps and all seemed right with the world.

Deacon David West, c. 1885, Congregationalist and foremost Abolitionist and conductor on the Underground Railroad in DeKalb County, Illinois.

CHAPTER 2

Remember the Underground Railroad

> The [Abolitionists] have given the American slaves their freedom, and the American people the possibility of a country. Until they appeared, the slave dragged his heavy chains without pity and without hope.[1]—Frederick Douglass (1818–1895), freed slave and Abolitionist speaker

The Well-Kept Secret

All was not right with the world forty years before David West's 80th birthday party. In 1846 the United States was in the midst of intense internal arguments regarding human slavery and the enslaving of Negroes. Certain people began to aid fugitive slaves who were fleeing for freedom to Canada. Those people became part of what is known as the Underground Railroad.

But what was the Underground Railroad? Was it only a legend? Was it a myth? As contemporary author Larry Gara writes, "Legends are usually compounded of both fact and fancy, and the legend of the underground railroad is no exception."[2] Legends exist because at some point in time an event occurred which created a story. That narrative is perhaps embellished in the retelling over the years, but the basic facts remain.

In an interpretive publication, the National Park Service describes the covert Underground Railroad, saying that it was

> like nothing else in American history: a secret enterprise that today is famous, an association many claim but few can document, an illegal activity now regarded as noble, a network that was neither underground nor a railroad, yet a system that operated not with force or high finance but through the committed and often spontaneous acts of courage and kindness of individuals unknown to each other.[3]

There was no real organization, even though what was accomplished worked and was actually quite effective.

While the Underground Railroad itself may have been in existence since the 1700s, speculation exists regarding the terms associated with this clandestine activity. Scholars do not agree about exactly where or when the term "underground railroad" began. The generally accepted legend tells us that a Kentucky farmer was mystified when his runaway slave, Tice Davids, disappeared after crossing the Ohio River to Ripley, Ohio. Unable to discover a hiding place, the slaveowner returned to Kentucky and informed others that his slave must have disappeared on an underground road.

It was not a literal mechanical railroad and it did not run under the ground. The phrase apparently came into use during the 1800s when actual steam railroads were being constructed. Subsequently, railroad terms such as "conductors," "stations" and "depots," "routes," "cargo," "passengers," and other related words became familiar "Underground Railroad" phrases. The conductors were those people who transported fugitive slaves from one point to another. Stations were the resting places, usually the homes or barns of antislavery sympathizers, along the way. A station might be utilized for longer than one night's stay, depending on care needed for fatigued individuals. The line was the route traveled, small portions of which were only known by key individuals as they traveled to the next station. Cargo, of course, included the runaway slaves themselves, sometimes stowed away under bags of grain in a common wagon. Those same wagons were referred to as the cars of the Underground Railroad. The metaphor equating the mechanical cross-country railroad system with a secret fugitive slave transportation method was perpetuated in the Abolitionist print media as seen, for example, in the *Western Citizen*, published in Chicago, Illinois.

Why was it covert? Why was secrecy so important? The answer lay in the fugitive slave laws. According to the fugitive slave law of 1793, slaveholders had a right to claim their property. In order to avoid the slave catchers, those professional bounty hunters coming north to hunt for runaways, the conductors in the Underground Railroad needed to act covertly. The same overland route was not often traveled in succession. It was necessary to be circumspect and not draw attention to the illegal activity. In DeKalb County, the people living in the town of Somonauk knew that "to ask for a map of the routes of the 'railroad' is to ask for a map of the routes by which the wily fox evades the hounds."[4] Yet, with so many people involved, especially in rural areas, the routes taken could be extremely varied as they traveled across any given county. The goal was always the same: Go north! Freedom lay in that direction.

When the new 1850 Fugitive Slave Law was passed, the slaveholders' rights became even stronger. Northerners were required to return slaves to their owners and they could be punished for not doing so. Because of the necessary secrecy involved in the Underground Railroad, very few written records were kept. Much of the known contemporary information comes from autobiographical accounts written after the events of the mid–1800s occurred. Many years after the Civil War ended, accounts about the Underground Railroad appeared in local history books, as well as newspapers and magazines. Of course, elderly Abolitionists were the source for these stories, which were sometimes inflated by eager writers.

Consequently, because people contemporaneous to the events were afraid to talk about it and rarely wrote about it, we do not have any consolidated or detailed written records about the process. We are indebted to the people who through the years have saved and retold their stories about the activities of family members active in the antislavery movement. We accept that these local legends and "oral tradition [fill] a great void in the largely unwritten history of the Underground Railroad."[5]

The Antislavery Movement

In order to understand the Underground Railroad, a brief history of the antislavery movement is important.

1775: Before the Revolutionary War, Quakers formed the first Antislavery Society in America in Philadelphia.[6] This was later incorporated in Pennsylvania as the Pennsylvania Society for Promoting the Abolition of Slavery, and Relief of Free Negroes Unlawfully Held in Bondage, and for Improving the Condition of the African Race. During the years preceding the Civil

War, numerous antislavery and abolitionist societies were formed throughout the northern states, with many counties and towns creating their very own organizations.

1787: The Second Continental Congress passed the Northwest Ordinance, which created the Northwest Territory. Article VI of the ordinance prohibited the introduction of slaves into that territory west of the Ohio River: "There shall be neither slavery nor involuntary servitude in the said territory, otherwise than in the punishment of crimes, whereof the party shall have been duly convicted."[7] This large geographic area, comprising the future states of Ohio, Indiana, Illinois, Michigan and Wisconsin, was deemed permanently free. A provision allowed fugitives found in the territory to be returned to their rightful owners.

However, in Illinois the first territorial governor, Arthur St. Clair, and his successor territorial governors, interpreted the 1787 Ordinance as not affecting the status of the blacks who were already held as slaves in the Northwest Territory prior to the passage of this regulation. Blacks were still slaves in the governors' eyes, and it would take the civil courts 58 years, until 1845, to reverse this position.

1793: The Second Congress of the United States passed "an Act respecting fugitives from justice, and persons escaping from the service of their masters."[8] This was the first Fugitive Slave Law, affirming the constitutional rights of slaveholders to their property. This required the return of runaway slaves to their owners.

1808: During this very early period in our nation's history, Congress also passed the Act to Prohibit the Importation of Slaves. This law included the extremely significant provision "that from and after the first day of January, One thousand eight hundred and eight, it shall not be lawful to import or bring into the United States or the territories thereof from any foreign kingdom, place, or country, any Negro, mulatto, or person of colour, as a slave, or to be held to service or labour."[9] This law, in keeping with Article I, Section 9 of the U.S. Constitution, effectively abolished the African slave trade in the United States and "was the first attempt on a national scale to curb the rising tide of slavery."[10] The illegal importation of slaves continued in spite of the new law, but on a greatly diminished basis, owing to the large number of slaves already present in the United States.

1818: An interesting collateral story occurred in 1818 when Illinois petitioned Congress to be admitted into the Union as a new state. The original northern boundary was to have been a line drawn straight westward from the bottom of Lake Michigan to the Mississippi River. Judge Nathaniel Pope, father of the future Civil War General John Pope, was a representative in Congress from the Illinois territory at that time and he well understood that Illinois would be more powerful if it were attached to the navigation system of the Great Lakes in the north. If the only ports for Illinois were at its southern border along the Ohio and Mississippi Rivers as originally planned, the state would surely identify with the southern states. Moving the boundary line between Illinois and Wisconsin northward served to neutralize the river navigation system and helped keep Illinois' sympathies with the Union. Congress was already keenly aware of the extensive philosophical divisions between the North and the South.

> It was also deemed important that the Illinois and Michigan canal ... should have its entire course in one State. Urged by these considerations, Congress consented to move the northern boundary line fifty miles to the north; and so it happens that a love of the Union caused that section of the country which is now [the] County of DeKalb, to be a part of the State of Illinois instead of Wisconsin.[11]

1820: When slaveholding Missouri, adjacent to Illinois, wanted to be admitted to the Union, Congress forged the Missouri Compromise. The free-state faction in Congress adamantly sought to maintain a balance between slave and free states. There were then 11 states represented by each bloc. The compromise allowed Maine to be admitted as a free state and Missouri admitted as a slave state, which sustained the balance. Additionally, slave states would not be created out of territories north of Missouri. This congressional action served to galvanize and motivate the eastern United States' antislavery defenders.

1831: William Lloyd Garrison published the first issue of the Abolitionist newspaper, *The Liberator.* Garrison was perhaps "America's foremost agitator and Abolitionist."[12] He was considered unreasonable, a radical who originally was a gradualist. He once supported the slow elimination of slavery, but changed direction and through his newspaper publication advocated for immediate emancipation.[13] In his first issue of the newspaper, Garrison demanded the immediate, unconditional elimination of American slavery: "On this subject I do not wish to think or speak, or write, with moderation. No! No! Tell a man whose house is on fire to give a moderate alarm ... but urge me not to use moderation in a cause like the present."[14] The publication of *The Liberator* marks the traditional beginning of the Abolitionist era and the beginning of angry and defensive responses from the slaveholding South. All of this rising activity and reaction pertaining to slavery and the fledgling antislavery movement occurred well before the organization of DeKalb County in 1837.

1833: Garrison established the American Anti-Slavery Society with the help of his good friends and fellow Abolitionists, brothers Lewis and Arthur Tappen. Philadelphia was the site chosen for this organization, which included prominent black and white antislavery activists. The Society considered slavery a moral evil and their goal was to completely eliminate slavery throughout the United States. They called for immediate elimination, accomplished by using all possible means, which soon incorporated both moral persuasion and political methods.

1850: On the surface, when the Compromise of 1850 was passed by the U.S. Congress, it allowed California to be admitted as a free state. Utah and New Mexico territories could decide to be free or slave states. Included in this compromise, however, was a much stronger federal Fugitive Slave Law which required that escapees be returned to their masters. It expanded federal powers to protect the interests of slaveowners and made it illegal to aid a runaway slave. Additionally, it became legal for slaveholders to pursue runaways into states where slavery was illegal. If someone aided a slave fugitive, he could be fined and punished. This played straight into the necessity for the creation, use and secrecy of the Underground Railroad and its activists.

1854: The Kansas-Nebraska Act effectively created a bloody geographic warfare when the two territories were allowed to decide by "popular sovereignty" whether to be free or slave states. This congressional act gravely affected Northern Illinois and drove many to become activists in the movement to free the slaves.

The Abolitionists did not deviate from their behavior in the antislavery movement because of newly enacted federal laws. In direct response to the stronger 1850 act, they increased their activity as an act of rebellion against the new law. Siebert described their response succinctly:

> In aiding fugitive slaves the Abolitionist was making the most effective protest against the continuance of slavery; but he was also doing something more tangible; he was helping the oppressed, he was eluding the oppressor; and at the same time he was enjoying the most romantic and exciting amusement open to men who had high moral standards. He was taking risks, defying the laws, and making himself liable to punishment, and yet could glow with the healthful pleasure of duty done.[15]

The entire antislavery movement became intertwined with religion, politics and economics. In studying the subsequent War Between the States, it might initially seem difficult to come to one single conclusion as to what actually caused the Civil War. Scholars still debate the several causes and rank the importance of economics, politics and slavery itself, with its attendant moral issues. However, no one can deny that slavery drove the Southern states' economics through their labor force and gave the southern states more political power emanating from the 1787 constitutional system which designated that ⅗ of the number of slaves held by a state could be counted for the purposes of representation and taxation. Every state had allowed overriding economic and political concerns to supersede the moral issues of slavery. Slavery was indeed the basic issue. And the Abolitionists, through pressure placed on churches and political leaders, brought that issue to the forefront. In doing so, they helped to create the demand to end slavery. They opposed slavery initially on moral and religious grounds, but soon realized there was political power in their position. The antislavery stalwart, Wendell Phillips, defined this position concisely in 1848 when he said, "The Abolitionist ... looks upon the institutions of his country, religious and political, as forming the character of her great men.... [W]hen we have pronounced these two words [religion and politics], we have expressed every thing that gives pressure to American thought."[16]

Abolitionists and Antislavery

By definition, there was a basic difference between antislavery supporters and Abolitionists. Many antislavery advocates merely opposed the expansion of slavery. They proposed mitigation of the conditions of the slaves, or gradual liberation of the slaves, or their removal through colonization. Scores of governmental officials who in truth did not want to "rock the boat" held that viewpoint. By taking the middle road, those elected officials carefully held the opinion that slavery would probably die a natural death and end in due course without any help from anyone.

All Abolitionists were antislavery. However, not all antislavery advocates were Abolitionists.

True, active Abolitionists were more vocal and physically worked to help slaves escape. Many Abolitionists advocated or demanded an immediate end to slavery. Through that belief, they became "immediatists," although some Abolitionists might interpret this as "immediate emancipation gradually accomplished." "On the political plane Abolitionists imperiled the Federal Union itself; at the religious level they proscribed slaveholding brethren and their defenders as sinners no less than murderers and adulterers and asked churches to discipline them accordingly."[17] But the definitions of Abolitionists and antislavery advocates overlap and become very blurred through their usage in various geographic areas, even through the magnifying glass of historical research. This was especially true in DeKalb County, Illinois.

Throughout the nation, religiously motivated Abolitionists constituted a very large group. DeKalb County was no exception. In the eastern United States, some religious activists even organized loosely into the William Lloyd Garrison–inspired American and Foreign Anti-Slavery Society from 1840 until the mid–1850s, which comprised both black and white Abolitionists. DeKalb County's religious activists followed suit.

An organized annual meeting of the DeKalb County Anti-Slavery Society scheduled for early June in 1845 was postponed until July 4 that year so that attendees could have time to return from Alton. Alton, Illinois, was the June site for the seventh annual meeting of the Illinois Anti-Slavery Society, and local participants wanted to be able to take full advantage of new information and excitement expected to be generated at that meeting.

Political Abolitionists were motivated by their chosen religion and were themselves divided into three provincial factions: (1) In New York, the philanthropic Abolitionist, Gerrit Smith, served as a catalyst for organization. These radicals urged political action against slavery. James G. Birney aligned himself with Smith to form the antislavery political party called the Liberty Party. Birney was their candidate for president in 1840. (2) Cincinnati served as the center for a political offshoot of the Liberty Party, which was succeeded by the Free-Soil Party. These partisan movements sought to force the major Whig and Democrat parties to end slavery. (3) Abolitionists in the Boston vicinity who could not support Garrison constituted yet another group.[18]

Nationwide, the majority of political Abolitionists joined the new Republican Party upon its organization, with antislavery as its primary platform. Again, this was true in DeKalb County as well, when delegates from the Whigs, the Free-Soilers, and the Democrats all attended the Republican organizational convention in Aurora in 1854.[19] The Liberty Party was represented through its previous absorption into the Free-Soil Party.

The debates among Abolitionists were obvious: religion vs. politics, overt action vs. secrecy, and diplomacy vs. violence. "The argument over which set of tactics was more productive sometimes obscures the fact that the Abolitionist movement, with all its divisions, was extremely effective. It did much to bring the nation to a confrontation over slavery within thirty years."[20] As a result, the fact remains that the Underground Railroad, as a proactive arm of the antislavery and Abolitionist movement, became "one of history's finest symbols of the struggle against oppression."[21]

Abolitionists Come to Northern Illinois

By 1834 Yankee settlers began to drift out to DeKalb County, Illinois. Like an oncoming tidal wave, these new settlers landed upon the shores of Lake Michigan in overwhelming numbers, bearing their dreams for the future. The federal census of 1850 indicates that 64 percent of the heads of households in Sycamore Township were born either in the state of New York or in New England.[22] Why did the majority come from New York and other eastern states? It was simple. There was affordable government land available — with wonderful open prairies ready to cultivate, together with abundant stands of forest for building houses and barns. Transportation was accessible. They could use the new Erie Canal and the Great Lakes for access and easier transport to Chicago and westward. Once in Northern Illinois, they often encouraged relatives and neighbors from their native states to come west.

Henrietta Norton, the wife of the Congregational and Presbyterian minister Oliver Norton, was one who frequently tried to persuade family members to move west. In 1844, she wrote to her sister, Augusta, from her new home in Roscoe, Illinois. Her sister's husband, David Marvin, was a physician in New York.

> I know that it must take a young physician almost a lifetime to get established in a large city. I am going to try again to get you out here or into the country somewhere, where you will not have to spend anything to keep up appearances and (if you will come West) where provisions, &c., are so cheap and sickness so plenty that doctors are pretty sure to have plenty of business. You need not hesitate on account of sickness, as I have noticed that our physicians and their families are remarkably exempt, probably because they know how to guard against it.... I think there is a good opening at Rockford [and] we have [no physicians] in Rosco[e] and have to send four or six miles for one. If you will come out here you ... will be most welcome to a home with me (and I have a very good one) ... while Dr. rides about to find a place to locate.[23]

After her husband accepted the call to minister to the First Congregational Church and they were settled in Sycamore, Illinois, Henrietta Norton cheerfully wrote about her new home.

> [Sycamore] is like many of our Western villages, pleasantly situated and rapidly growing, and presenting an interesting field to a humble, self-denying missionary.... We have a snug little house and I am heartily glad to get away from the farm and live where the children can attend school and church without walking a mile or two.[24]

How did some settlers on the Western Frontier receive their information about antislavery? The answer lay in one line of one of Henrietta's numerous letters: "I received the Evangelist,"[25] she wrote in 1842. The *New York Evangelist* recounted the activities of antislavery societies and published reports from churches throughout the United States. Mr. and Mrs. Oliver W. Norton either subscribed to the antislavery publication, or read it secondhand when it was mailed to them from family members. The same was true of other Midwestern settlers. Their knowledge and opinions generated encouragement to friends and family in the East and consequently affected the growing antislavery thinking in Northern Illinois.

This does not mean that everyone in Illinois accepted the prevailing ideas. They were not all in agreement with the antislavery thoughts expounded by the influx of New Englanders. There was no dominant public antislavery policy or philosophy. Differing views were presented in various geographic areas. However, in Northern Illinois, because the majority of the initial DeKalb County founders came from New York with a similar regional and cultural heritage, they tended to be of one mind.

After the territory became a state in 1818, the Illinois legislature created statutes that included the now infamous Black Laws, which as characterized by Boies, "ever after disgraced the statute book and the State"[26]:

> This code permitted immigrants to bring their slaves with them; and if the signatures of the slaves could be obtained to an agreement to that effect, it compelled their continual service as slaves — or registered servants, as they were called. It forbid any free negro to reside in the State without giving bonds for his good behavior and that he would not become a county charge. Any negro found without a certificate of freedom could be arrested and sold for a specified time. Any negroes assembled for a dance or revelry were to be committed to jail and whipped by the sheriff, not to exceed thirty-nine lashes on the bare back.[27]

The severe "Black Laws" were originally copied from Virginia and Kentucky during the territorial status of Illinois. When re-enacted by the legislature in the new state of Illinois, a Negro had basically no protection or recourse. These extremely restrictive laws were not officially repealed until after the Civil War.

In spite of political actions elsewhere in the state, DeKalb County, from the first settlement in 1834, was "the home of a strong, active, zealous party of anti-slavery men." The people who lived there were "men who were avowed Abolitionists, who gloried in that name when it was a term of reproach; who not only voted for, but labored and expended their money for the freedom of the slave." After the end of the Civil War in 1868, author Boies described the area: "Scattered here and there over the whole county, were numerous well-known stations on the 'under-ground railroad'; homes of thrifty, hard-working, God-fearing haters of oppression, in which, it was well understood, the panting fugitive escaping from Southern Slavery, would be sure of finding rest, refreshment, a safe shelter, a warm welcome."[28] The common citizens of this vast prairie provided the means to help thousands of fugitive slaves on to other stations northward on the route to freedom in Canada.

Why escape to Canada? Slavery had ceased to exist in that country, a former British colony, as early as 1833 when Britain abolished slavery in all its colonies. Canada consequently became the geographic goal for an untold number of fugitive slaves seeking a better life. The minds of runaways seeking freedom contained a mythical image of a roadmap to Canada. Amos Rogers of Pampas Township in DeKalb County often repeated these fugitive slave song words to his granddaughter: "I'm on my way to Can-a-day, that cold and dreary land / The dire effects of slavery, I can no longer stand."[29]

The song is recognized by Vicki L. Eaklor in her documentary reference *American Antislavery Songs: A Collection and Analysis*. It is attributed to author Joshua Simpson, complete with seven more verses plus variations, and sung to the tune of the old familiar folksong, "O, Susannah!" The words remembered by the 90-year-old DeKalb County resident were followed with the chorus of: "O righteous Father, wilt thou not pity me? / And aid me on to Canada, where colored men are free."[30]

Canada is the place where the freedom seekers coming through DeKalb County wanted to go. Canada is where they were headed if they just followed the North Star. And following the North Star, with the aid of numerous Underground Railroad conductors, is how they managed to find their way to DeKalb County and beyond. The self-appointed obligation of the antislavery believers in this Northern Illinois county was first to keep the fugitives safe from capture and second to aid them to the next stop in their long journey. They believed it was their God-given task to help the downtrodden.

Foremost among the Underground Railroad conductors was Deacon David West, who along with other Abolitionists in DeKalb County provided a successful link in nonviolent action.

Gara refers to the legendary "inherent yearning for freedom" and writes that people thought that the slave's role "was largely passive." "In this legendary melodrama — the villains are the slave catchers; and the Abolitionists ... are idealists of fortitude and courage."[31] Gara contends, "[Even] some of the most uncompromising opponents of slavery considered such activity useless or even immoral."[32] Yet to the Abolitionists in DeKalb County, thoughts of immorality in connection with aiding someone seeking liberty were not prevalent. David West was one of those uncompromising opponents of slavery who did not consider such activity as immoral. To him, each fugitive he assisted became a profound personal moral victory. David West was Shaw's "unreasonable man."

For an undercover operation like the Underground Railroad to even exist, there had to be people willing to help in numerous and diverse capacities. Who were those thrifty, hard-working, God-fearing haters of oppression? Who were the forgotten individuals who gave to the African American people the possibility of a country? Among thousands across the nation, they were the unknown antislavery proponents bringing hope to those in chains. These quiet heroes, the unreasonable men and women who called themselves Abolitionists, worked together without notoriety in DeKalb County, Illinois.

CHAPTER 3

Illinois: A Burned-Over Reunion

> Let us therefore animate and encourage each other, and show the whole world that a Freeman, contending for liberty on his own ground, is superior to any slavish mercenary on earth.—George Washington (1732–1799, first president of the United States, General Orders, Headquarters in New York, July 2, 1776)

A Freewoman

She rode across the colorful Mayfield Township prairie peppered with native wildflowers, nearly flying over the fields from farm to farm as she distributed handbills with information about the church. Separating the fields were dense forests through which meandered the Kishwaukee River. She continued on, surely excited to spread the news to the nearest neighbors. The rumors were true: the Methodists planned to organize a new Wesleyan Methodist antislavery church. Astride her father's well-trained horse, her hair trailing in the wind, at age 18 Armena Jackman must have relished the opportunity to be part of a cause. Women in the 1800s did not normally play a role in the prevailing political culture, but it is highly likely that the Jackman family encouraged participation in social concerns. Armena was nurtured to be an unreasonable woman.

Raised in a Methodist Episcopal environment, the Jackman children together with their parents regularly attended Methodist study classes held in neighbor's homes. Although both were born in Vermont, Abner and Louisa "Mary" Jackman soon moved to New York, and by 1834, "before the Indians had left,"[1] they arrived with other pioneer settlers on the Illinois frontier. The Jackmans raised their three sons and five daughters to be self-sufficient and to think for themselves.

Armena's father was a "strong Abolitionist"[2], a lumber and coal dealer who also farmed his land to sustain his family. Active in local affairs, Abner Jackman became one of the first petit jurors for DeKalb County and served as a justice of the peace in Sycamore Township. Not only did he subscribe to the antislavery newspaper *Western Citizen*, but significantly, when he died in 1851, his wife Mary continued the subscription in her own name. Both parents were stalwart examples of independent thinking. For their daughter to volunteer to hand-deliver information about the organization of a new antislavery church was completely within the norm of what they expected and anticipated their children to do.

The Jackman family provides a good illustration of the strength inadvertently achieved in the antislavery movement through marriages between Abolitionist families. Armena married Latin Nichols of the well-known antislavery Mayfield Township family; Eliza Jackman married Jeremiah Libby Brown of Genoa; and sister Louisa Jackman married Caleb Marshall Brown of Sycamore. These men, with the support of their wives, were all prominent Abolitionists in DeKalb County. Over 130 years later, the Mayfield church still remembered that "Armena Nichols rode horseback, soliciting for the church, promising all denominations could use it."[3] The vision of a woman on horseback with her horse-haired petticoats billowing in the breeze was implanted in the collective mind. She was a Freewoman overtly supporting a cause both personal and public.

In 1845 the antislavery advocate Armena supported freeing Negro slaves, at a time when she did not even have the same rights as the men around her. The slaves were officially freed by the Thirteenth Amendment of 1865, but it would be another 55 years before another important 19th century cause supported by women like Armena Jackman Nichols gave women the right to vote. Yet this Freewoman worked to give a larger freedom to less fortunate men and women.

Freemen and Freewomen Leading the Way

They came from New York in search of their own ground, these Freemen and Freewomen whose ancestors contended for liberty. Some emigrated from Vermont and other New England states, but the overwhelming majority of early DeKalb County settlers left their more comfortable homes in New York in search of more land, better opportunities, a future for their children — all the same objectives sought by immigrants to the New World one hundred years before them. These pioneers whose grandfathers and great-grandfathers fought in the Revolutionary War for the freedom of an entire nation blazed new trails across the vast land. Northern Illinois was often a direct target for the internal migration of Yankees in the westward expansion of the United States because of its proximity to the Great Lakes. Transportation was afforded straight west through the Erie Canal from western New York, through the Great Lakes, then overland west from Chicago to DeKalb County.

The migration from New York of a group of people with like characteristics is highly significant in light of the events that transpired in the Empire State during the 1830s and 1840s. From Buffalo to Albany, the narrow stretch of western New York State was in the midst of the Second Great Awakening. The First Great Awakening had occurred during the colonial period when immigrant Protestants experienced religious upheavals. This new Second Great Awakening was a religious revival of such magnitude that it spawned several new denominations, including the Church of Jesus Christ of Latter-day Saints (or Mormons) and the Seventh-day Adventists. By re-examining their relationship with God, adherents of the new faiths created new directions for the expression of moral and social values.

More than a few spiritual leaders placed themselves as heads of entirely new religious denominations. Flamboyant evangelists rejected teachings no longer in favor and created new theologies in their place. Religious revivals blazed over western New York with the intensity of frequent prairie fires, creating such heated spiritual fervor that the area became known as the "Burned-over" District. Evangelical Protestantism evolved into social reform, led appropriately by the fiery Congregationalist minister Charles Finney, the antislavery organizer Theodore Weld, and Harriet Beecher Stowe's father, Lyman Beecher, among others. Education was embodied in religious revivalism. The abolition of slavery in the United States became a logical extension of the new evangelical social reform, and the flames were further fanned by preachers across the northern United States. The Abolitionist's fire slowly burned westward.

It is ironic that emigrants from the mountainous "Burned-over" district in New York would settle on an expanse of Northern Illinois flat land which itself was literally, physically "burned over" as a result of the all-too-common prairie fires. Historians writing about northern DeKalb County note, "In the early days of the pioneers prairie fires were common. Beginning in the township of South Grove they would generally sweep over the prairie, much of which was uninhabitable."[4]

> On one occasion while Mr. J.H. Dick, a pioneer of the early '40s, was lying ill and unconscious with typhoid fever, being attended alone at night by his wife, a prairie fire broke out, which threatened to destroy their home. This being sometime after midnight we can easily realize the terror felt by the one woman in the care of her sick husband. A catastrophe was only evaded by the prompt assistance of the neighbors, who, knowing of her helpless condition, responded and thus saved their lives and property.[5]

John H. Dick was born in Scotland, but after living in New York for a while, he headed westward to Northern Illinois. An avowed antislavery man, Dick joined hundreds of transplanted easterners in DeKalb County, and allowed his home to become a station on the Underground Railroad.[6] In fact, there were so many Abolitionists from New York in Illinois that the antislavery society meetings in Illinois were characterized "to a considerable extent [as] reunions of alumni of the Burned-over District."[7]

During the 1840s, DeKalb County became a microcosm of western New York State. The sociological trends from five and ten years earlier in the western part of the Empire State were duplicated again in DeKalb County. As both the rural and urban people of that part of New York migrated to Northern Illinois, they created similar leadership patterns within their newly formed communities. Professional and political alliances remained the same. It was familiar; it was home.

Expanding Illinois

Congress carved the original Northwest Territory into the five areas that would eventually become the states of Illinois, Wisconsin, Indiana, Michigan and Ohio, but even after Illinois officially gained statehood, there was no rush to develop and settle the entire state. Geographically, the state of Illinois was populated and developed from the south upwards. Kaskaskia was the first capital in the southern part of the Illinois territory. In 1818, after Illinois became the 21st state, the capital was moved to Vandalia, still in southern Illinois. Growth stalled because the Sac (also known as Sauk) Indian Chief Black Hawk controlled the majority of the lands in the northern part of the fledgling state. There were major territorial disagreements with Chief Black Hawk and his loyal Sac Indian disciples. An earlier treaty between the Sac and Mesquakie, also known as Fox, tribes with the United States caused the Indians to cede all of their lands east of the Mississippi river and moved the tribes to Iowa. Black Hawk, however, determined that the treaty was not valid and shifted his band of followers back into Illinois.

Consequently, very few people ventured into Northern Illinois until after 1832, following the Black Hawk War. The bloody events of that summer ended with Black Hawk's surrender and arrest. By then the Sac and Fox tribes had been driven from Illinois. Prior to that time, the Potawatomie and Winnebago tribes had also ceded their lands to the state, which opened up the northern prairie and forests to settlement. Finally, people believed it was safe enough to bring their families to that part of the United States. A full eighteen years after Illinois attained statehood, the danger of an Indian raid was no longer an issue. Remaining in the area were the Potawatomie Indians and their friendly Chief Shabbona, and they were not a threat. When it was considered safe for the white pioneers to settle in that part of the state, many adventurous New Englanders came directly west to seek their fortunes and found their way beyond the swamp called Chicago to the prairies of DeKalb County.

Consequently, although the growth of the state was from the south upwards, initial development for DeKalb County did not come from the south. During the 1840s, the county's growth was entirely nurtured from the east. Virgin prairies waited to be tilled for crops and acres of timber stood in readiness to build houses and places of business. Plus there existed a small meandering river running north through the land.

An Unconventional Settler

"The term 'Pioneer Settlers' ... stands in the forefront of our country's history; it has won its way to that honor because it means 'brave men and self-denying.'"[8] But they were not always men. One of those early pioneers was a gutsy young woman named Charlotte Waterman. Charlotte was born in 1812 in Fairfield, Herkimer County, New York. Her father, John Dean Waterman, was also from New York; her mother, Mary Graves (Waldo) Waterman, was born in Massachusetts. One of ten children, she had six brothers and three sisters who all grew to adulthood.

By the time she was 28 years old, Charlotte Waterman must have wanted a change, perhaps seeking novelty and a chance to do something different. She sought the experience of living in a completely different locale in unfamiliar surroundings. Was she afraid? Of course she was. Afraid and maybe a little apprehensive at first, but her desperation for that challenge created a passion for something beyond New York, even though it seemed it might be difficult to achieve.

Charlotte apparently yearned for the excitement of the unknown. It was not enough to live vicariously through her adventurous brothers; she needed to experience the western frontier for herself. And Charlotte Judith Waterman echoed all who had come before her and all who would arrive after her. For the pioneers coming to DeKalb County, there was no natural disaster with a life-altering catastrophe which caused them to pick up their Atlantic roots and head west. There was no famine or war in the eastern United States forcing them out. These were not criminals or Native Americans who relocated to a different geographic area under force or duress.

New settlers excitedly urged their families and friends to join them in the new West. In December of 1840, Charlotte J. Waterman wrote from DeKalb County to her friend, Phocion Hoffman in New York, that there was a "fine opening for a young lawyer" in Sycamore. Alluding to his friendship with Miss Waterman, Mr. Hoffman responded with a gentlemanly reply: "Your hint is not lost. It shall be seriously considered. I intend to push my fortune somewhere in the great west; and what could be more agreeable than to cast my lot where I would still, at times, enjoy that society which has constituted so large a share of the happiness of my past life."[9]

His letter to Charlotte continues and expresses his concern for the long trip west that Miss Waterman had recently undertaken:

> I'll confess you are a woman of true courage. Who would have believed that you would have dared to push off into woods in such an independent manner? I was scared when I heard you had started without an escort, and it was a great relief to me when I heard you had performed your journey in safety. The woman who can accomplish such an undertaking is worth a dozen heroines. She would do for the wife of a hunter. The next time I hear from you I expect to be informed that you have gone beyond the Mississippi on a trading expedition or as a missionary among the Hot-heads [Indians].[10]

Charlotte must have written a glowing description of her new home to her friend Phocion, for he deduced from her correspondence that Sycamore was "quite as large & thriving a place as Fairfield,"[11] New York, where she previously lived in Herkimer County. Although, he further commented, "It must seem odd enough to you [to] find yourself so suddenly transplanted into a country where scenery is so strange to your eye, to see your brothers [James, John and Charles] looking so unlike the spruced up fellows who visit N[ew] York, and to join in a society so novel [and] little in accordance with your tastes."[12]

Phocion Hoffman, however, never came to visit Charlotte in DeKalb County. He ultimately found his true love back East and chose not to "push [his] fortune somewhere in the Great West." Hoffman never ventured from New York State.

The courage and independence exhibited by Charlotte Waterman was not surprising. With Revolutionary War ancestors, these Yankee settlers were a people for whom it was entirely natural to have an impassioned cause. Taking action based on one's beliefs and principles was commonplace. Following a recognizable pattern, over the next few years the remainder of the Waterman family reunited in Illinois. They created their own "burned-over reunion" in 1843 when her mother and her sister Mary joined Charlotte and her brothers in Sycamore. Her oldest brother Henry was already married, living in New York, but also removed to Sycamore in 1857. Her brother Robert settled first in Boone, then Will County, ultimately emigrating from Illinois westward, and was later elected governor of California. Philanthropist brother James soon endowed Sycamore's St. Peter's Episcopal Church, while Charlotte, her mother and brother John maintained their membership at Sycamore's antislavery First Congregational Church. John was a "zealous Republican"[13] who was a member of the appointed political subcommittee at the 1854 DeKalb County Anti-Nebraska (antislavery) Meeting.[14] James and John Waterman, and sister Mary who married Timothy Wells, were also Congregationalists and became well-rooted in the area, contributing much to the future of the community. Charlotte's brothers and sisters all found spouses in the new western frontier. The unreasonable Charlotte never married, living as a "lady," as designated in the 1860 census record. Her death occurred in San Diego, California, one month following the death of her brother, Robert, former governor of California.

Why They Came

Here were ordinary people following the paths of their friends and family. As the tales of opportunities and future prosperity in the west proved to be irresistible lures, they left their civilized homes in New York and Vermont and set aside thoughts of possible difficult living conditions ahead. Scattered throughout were the men who were not first sons in their birthright, who would not inherit land and wealth in the East, and who decided to strike out on their own, bringing their young families with them.

Here, too, were the New England immigrants for whom the financial panic of 1837 provided the impetus to send them west. Their forefathers originally came to the United States to seek their fortune. Now these inexperienced pioneers were blazing newer trails, perhaps to build on their grandfathers' accomplishments, but more likely to create their own. They followed their fortunes to find and claim open land in the new Northwest Territory to create a new future for themselves and their families.

Among the easterners emigrating from New York were missionaries from several Protestant denominations with plans to spread the gospel throughout the western frontier. They did not initially come to DeKalb County because of religious or ethnic persecution, but they carried with them the strong desire for the freedom to exercise their own religious beliefs. Like their

Puritan ancestors, these Northern Illinois settlers fervently believed in the freedom of religious expression. Itinerant preachers like the Universalist minister the Rev. William Roundsville soon realized that "most of the population in the 1830s consisted of emigrants from New England and New York. None was wealthy, but the majority was liberal in social and religious views."[15] Roundsville himself headed for Sycamore in his quest to create footholds for the Universalist Church on the prairies west of Chicago. Did they come because they were drawn to an area already known for being populated with antislavery advocates? Maybe, but these unreasonable settlers created an atmosphere of freedom after they arrived.

The practice of slaveholding did not exist in the villages of DeKalb County. The county never had a community of Quakers, who were known to be sympathetic to fugitive slaves. Although the Quakers were an especially strong antislavery religious group in Pennsylvania, they never aggressively pushed further west during the 1840s. The county's founding Christian congregations were forthright in their own views regarding slavery and simply brought those same views westward. Four religious denominations with strong antislavery proclivities — Congregationalist, Wesleyan Methodist and Presbyterian, joined by the Universalists — were the most prominent in the area. These churches with similar Christian theology, yet different administrative backgrounds, were geographically located in three different areas of the county.

The communities in the county which seemed to have the greatest concentration of a strongly-held sense of the injustice of slavery were Brush Point in Mayfield Township in the north, Freeland Corners in Somonauk Township in the south, and Sycamore in the north central part of the county. Mayfield Township was home to a group of loosely organized Methodists who later became the Wesleyan Methodist Church; Somonauk saw the beginning of the Somonauk Presbyterian Church; and Sycamore gave birth to the First Congregational and Universalist Churches. Each of these geographical areas enjoyed common factors, including their ardent local church membership and strong family ties. The families who were members of these denominations completely dominated the religious, social, and political life in their communities. They were the obvious founders of the settlements. These same people were the original members of the major local churches. Some individuals, like Deacon David West, were the products of the New York Great Revival — not with the oratory or militancy of the famed Abolitionist William Lloyd Garrison, but with their own fervent belief in the immediate elimination of slavery in America.

Life on the Prairie

An observant journalist described the 1839 DeKalb County countryside: "For miles about as far as the eye could reach, nothing was visible but the beautiful prairie covered with tall rich grass, sprinkled with bright colored flowers, except that along the Kishwaukee creek, which was quite a river in those days, dense forests stretched for miles. The nearest neighbor was miles away."[16] Once ensconced on the plains of Northern Illinois, settlers fresh from New York and New England awoke at dawn to the strange sounds emanating from large flocks of sandhill cranes. Their loud musical honking call heralded the morning sunrises on the prairie, reminiscent of roosters crowing to awaken the barnyard. At four feet tall, with a wingspan of seven feet, the elegant sandhill cranes are no longer common in DeKalb County, but in the early 1800s they were found in abundance throughout the interior United States. On the frontiers these cranes were often hunted to put sustenance on the table, the meat considered a delicacy. Strutting proudly across the grain fields and marshes, sandhill cranes always displayed a confident attitude which paralleled the settlers in their quest to find food and shelter. Other wildlife abounded.

Wolves were plentiful, rattlesnakes were common, and over 100 deer could be found "in a drove."[17]

As the earth came to life in the wee hours of the morning, the singing of numerous birds and other sounds of wildlife surrounded the 1840s family. Such clamor was accompanied by the fresh, outdoor scents of the fields and prairies, combined with an occasional marsh or pine stand. One scent especially was always prevalent and remained constantly in the air. The aroma of open wood fires lingered in the atmosphere from small tended fires used for heating homes and cooking meals. From the time settlers awoke in the morning until the sun set, the priority of each waking moment was to perform tasks designed to help feed and clothe themselves. This included tending gardens, caring for animals, chopping wood, hunting for game, preparing and cooking foods for that day, as well as preserving food to store for the winter months.

Leisure time was rare. It is a wonder that the populace had any spare moments to read a newspaper, when available, or to discuss world or national events with a neighbor, but surprisingly enough, they did. During a visit to the local post office, or to the Sycamore store owned by Charlotte Waterman's brothers, or at local church services on Sunday, the adults in DeKalb County, Illinois, were very much attuned to what was happening in their own towns and state, as well as in the larger United States. Charged with the self-appointed responsibility of creating new governments locally and statewide, these immigrants from the East paid attention to events occurring around them. Their well-being depended on it.

Stories about a frontier pioneer's trek from the East could easily be written once and then repeated verbatim with reference to each family traveling westward. A narrative begins with families leaving their comfortable homes in the East, and then traveling for many days filled with hardship to reach their destination in Northern Illinois. Usually they traveled with one or two oxen-pulled wagons, loaded with family members, maybe some friends, and all their worldly goods. The trip was inordinately long compared to 21st century travel, taking weeks or sometimes over a month to journey from New York, to Northern Illinois. Upon their arrival, the story again is always the same. They resided with another relative or friend in a small, crowded log cabin while they cleared land nearby to prepare for the erection of their own log house. Anyone who longs for the "good old days" should spend some time reading about those early pioneers whose daily existence was all about survival. The first settlers desperately needed each other for physical assistance to accomplish the necessary tasks of building a house, or to plant and harvest a crop. In tandem with the nation's development they were an agrarian society, being almost entirely self-sufficient for their food, clothing and shelter. At a time when more civilized villages like Fairfield, New York and Ripley, Ohio, had stately brick homes and buildings for commerce, DeKalb County was still very rugged, untamed land dotted with log cabins.

A former New York merchant named Moses Dean relocated his family to Illinois around 1848. Dean would later be elected mayor of Sycamore. Of necessity, he became a farmer in his chosen promised land and easily recounted firsthand a "vivid sketch of the life of the farmer, especially of the pioneer farmer ... how he started into the wild woods with his ox team, felled trees, rolled up the logs into a log cabin, cleared an acre or two by chopping, made a rude plow of wood and a drag of a crotch of a tree, got in a little rye for bread, reaped it by hand sickle, sowed flax for linen, pulled it, hatchelled it and spun it for clothing and so on through the toils, privations, labors and joys of the poor farmer."[18] Wood was used for everything: houses, tools, wagons, fences and firewood for heat and cooking. Pickling, salting and drying were the common methods of food preservation. From Sycamore it was 30 miles south to Ottawa in LaSalle County or 25 miles east to St. Charles to the nearest mill to grind the wheat into flour. Chicago was the closest market in which to sell any grain or flour. This meant a minimum two-day trip, with an overnight stay at an establishment like Garfield's Tavern west of St. Charles for 37½ cents per night. A team of horses could be stabled for the night and the traveler would receive a light meal and a place to sleep, although perhaps with a stranger or two in the same bed.

For Hearth and Home

Henry Wood was only 11 years old in 1836 when his parents, Zechariah and Sarah, set out from Vermont to Illinois with six of their ten children traveling with them. Three of their offspring had already died in Vermont and Zechariah felt "the narrow valleys of the Green Mountain State and the limited opportunities of crowded New England afforded small outlook for the prosperous and useful future of his children."[19] Their goal was to reach the home of Henry's sister and brother-in-law, Phoebe and Jesse Kellogg, who recently settled in Plainfield in Will County, Illinois.

Henry Wood, Congregationalist, Abolitionist, Republican, Illinois State Representative; arrived in Illinois in 1836 as a child.

Over the years an older Henry Wood still remembered the impressions of that long, arduous trip to their new home. One incident in particular stands out in his mind. The Wood youngsters, Henry and his sister Sarah Emily, were "walking some distance in advance of the wagons ... when a train of cars came rushing toward them. Darkness was coming on, and in the dim light the wholly new experience presented a terrific appearance — the blinding headlight, the unearthly mixture of sounds and the unparalleled speed of the approaching monster conveyed the impression that the fabled horrors of the lower pit had broken bounds and was abroad for prey. The youngsters precipitated a retreat and paused not until they were once more with the wagons."[20]

The approaching monster was a locomotive. To the Wood children, it was a scary, yet awesome sight. As they traveled, the family prepared their meals over an open fire "by the roadside" during the entire journey, arriving in DeKalb County fully two months after departing Middlebury, Vermont. Wolves, lynx and bear were commonly seen in the countryside, and the quail or fish caught along the way provided nourishment for the pioneer family.

By the next year the Wood family unit moved from Will to DeKalb County and built a house of logs on Zechariah's land claim in Sycamore Township:

> The structure was 14 × 14 feet in dimension and covered with "shakes," a variety of substitute for shingles riven from oak, three feet long, from four to six inches wide and bound in place with poles, no nails being obtainable, and if they had been, each pound was worth a pound of butter. The floor

of the upper apartment was of shakes and that of the room below of puncheons made from basswood logs. Bedsteads were made by boring holes in a log on one side of the house, in which were driven poles, and with poles for cross-pieces a frame was constructed on which a straw mattress was placed. Two of them were on the lower floor, the upper not being sufficiently high for the purpose. The boys were required to sleep in the room above, and it was a frequent thing for them to wake in the morning and find their beds covered with snow from one to three inches in thickness, which drifted in between the shakes.[21]

The summer of 1837 was described as a "hard one" with few crops surviving, and Henry Wood, a future Illinois state representative, endured all the privations of pioneer life. During that season, Wood's family existed on "potatoes and samp with milk. The samp was homemade, and was obtained with the aid of a carpenter's plane, which was held in place with the cutting side upward. Pushing the ears of corn over the bit reduced the grain to hominy, which made wholesome and palatable food."[22] In addition to deteriorated growing conditions for produce, the prices for necessary household provisions during the previous winter were considered to be high. They paid the market price in Chicago for essential items. "Butter was 50 cents a pound, flour $25 a barrel, and pork and lard were 37½ cents a pound."[23]

Antislavery farmer Solomon Wells reported that he often killed more than 100 deer "and at times counted 125 in a drove."[24] Such numbers together roaming the Midwest are not found today. In the mid–1800s the thick forests provided ample food and cover for their numbers. Those dense woods would later be depleted when whole groves were harvested to help rebuild Chicago after its devastating 1871 fire. Mayfield *Western Citizen* subscriber John Mullen "tells how he and his son, Phillip, killed seven deer before breakfast in the early 1850s."[25] Such events were a regular occurrence.

The two Wood boys, Henry and his older brother Thomas, grew up to become Abolitionists and Republicans. They were both members of the Congregationalist church. Thomas subscribed to the *Western Citizen* and Henry would later present Deacon David West with his 80th birthday present. The energetic little boys who walked part of the way west to Illinois and who hunted deer and game for food matured into unreasonable men.

The Route to Chicago

No one would have thought that an obscure Northern Illinois county had any special appeal as a gateway from the South to freedom in the North. The area provided a point of access to a grand funnel emptying into Chicago, Lake Michigan and ultimately Canada. Geographically, Sycamore in northern DeKalb County, and the towns of Somonauk and sometimes Paw Paw in the southern end of the county, were all means of entrance to that conduit. From these towns, freedom seekers were escorted to the Fox River Valley area. Fugitives traveling from Sycamore usually continued directly east to St. Charles and Elgin, or occasionally northeast through Dundee in Kane County. Research indicates that escapees reaching Somonauk, about 25 miles south of Sycamore, more likely chose a main line east running through Sugar Grove, Aurora and Hinsdale to arrive at Lake Michigan. To avoid detection and the pursuit of slavecatchers, there were always exceptions to the routes followed. Fugitives were known to travel overland directly north, as well, always keeping the Great Lakes and Canada as their objective.

Runaways who traveled closer to Chicago were soon in the narrow neck of the imaginary funnel's cone shape, with fewer choices for diverse escape routes. There it was no longer necessary to crisscross diagonally over the countryside. These so-called fugitives from justice needed to continue in a straight line east in order to reach their crucial goal: a dependable boat sailing north to Canada.

William Nickerson of Mayfield Township remembered, "Some of the lake captains were very strong anti-slavery men. We knew who they were, and our friends on the lake shore knew what vessels would take them in safety to Canada."[26] Canada was the land of freedom. The closer they were to Chicago, the closer they were to the goal. It was more important than ever to connect with the trusted Underground Railroad conductors and safe stations along the way. Wilbur H. Seibert, in his history *The Underground Railroad from Slavery to Freedom*, reiterates that as early as 1815 there were fugitives already crossing the Ohio Western Reserve with assistance from "regular stations of the Underground Railroad."[27] They, too, were headed to Canada. He further states that by 1860 the journey was reversed, with approximately five hundred former slaves annually making the trip from Canada back to the southern United States to "rescue their fellows"[28] and family members. Canada remained the ultimate goal.

During the operation of the Underground Railroad, DeKalb County was never the final destination for fugitives; it was a brief stop along the way, a very long route which had its beginnings in any Southern state along the Mississippi River. Fugitive slaves entered Illinois by crossing the Mississippi River at three main points: Chester, Alton and Quincy, all in the southern half of the state. There were also a few smaller river towns further north which provided access to the overland routes, such as Rock Island and Moline, Port Byron and Albany, but they never achieved the notoriety gained by the southern entry points. From the point of entry into Illinois, the only choice for an escapee was to somehow travel overland, mostly at night for safer passage. They were at the mercy of the many anonymous volunteers along their route.

The majority of runaways traveling through DeKalb County came via the Princeton route which began at Quincy. According to an 1883 letter written to Zebina Eastman, editor of the antislavery newspaper, the *Western Citizen*: "The Underground R.R. was laid out from Quincy to Chicago through Princeton in the spring of 1839. Rev. John Cross ... engineered it through and it very soon commenced business and continued to pay good dividends until Lincoln's Proclamation of Emancipation [1863]."[29] From Princeton, sometimes the fugitives were brought to Somonauk, Sycamore or Mayfield, depending on the need to divert their route in order to avoid detection. From Sycamore, the next stations were in Elgin or St. Charles in Kane County. Anyone knowledgeable about the Underground Railroad knew that "John Cross ... was the leader in the work here ... he laid out the route, selected the depots & the agents, and seemed to be trusted with all affairs in relation to the route."[30] The Rev. John Cross was legendary in his work as an Abolitionist with the Underground Railroad. "Stations were established at proper distances, and agents in readiness to convey fugitives forward as soon as they arrived. It was almost an everyday occurrence for slaves to pass through on this line, while their masters followed after by the ordinary means of conveyance, and were surprised to find how fast their chattels had traveled."[31]

Mayfield Township's William Nickerson knew John Cross personally. He remembered an "incident of another character which was amusing," involving the well-known Presbyterian minister. Cross lived in Knox County when the incident occurred, though he later moved to Bureau County. The story is told in several history books;[32] here is Nickerson's rendition:

> Mr. Cross, an underground railway man, was suspected of carrying Negroes by the sheriff and he was arrested. The road over which [the sheriff] must travel with his prisoner was through a Quaker [usually antislavery] settlement, and he was sure he would have trouble with the Quakers if they knew he had John Cross in custody. Cross told him that [the sheriff] might lie down in the wagon and [Cross] would drive through the settlement and there would be no suspicion on the part of the Quakers that [Cross] had been arrested. He did so, covered up, and Mr. Cross drove slowly through the Quaker town. The sheriff delivered Mr. Cross to jail, but they failed to prove anything against him.[33]

It is obvious from the various accounts of the same story that because "Mr. Cross made no secret of his principles ... accordingly [he] became game for his enemies."[34] Although Cross was indicted for harboring fugitives, he was not convicted.

Siebert thought that "the mass of the people of the free states were by no means abolitionists; they cherished an intense prejudice against the Negro and permitted it to extend to all antislavery advocates."[35] DeKalb County, Illinois, did not fit that description, nor did it contain a mass of people with intense prejudice against the Negro. The area consisted of neighboring towns equally sympathetic to the antislavery cause. There was no open friction between local communities over the slavery issue and there was very little sympathy for slaveholding states. The atmosphere was almost one of an isolated island in a sea of turmoil. The calm that pervaded DeKalb County did not prevail everywhere across the northern United States. Elsewhere Abolitionists were often reviled, tarred and feathered, subjected to rotten eggs thrown at them, and run out of town.

Years later the Wesleyan Methodist minister George Young reflected on the county Abolitionists and commented about one of Mayfield Township's esteemed residents, Stephen Townsend. He could have been writing about all the antislavery proponents in all of DeKalb County.

> From his home on the prairie [Townsend] ever extended a helping hand to the black man fleeing from the chains of slavery to freedom from bondage, then only secure upon reaching Canada. Mr. Townsend advocated emancipation of slavery when ministers behind pulpits denounced it. He had courage to defy an unjust law and say to the slave catchers, that never by his help would he return a slave to the chains of a cruel master.[36]

Stephen and Ann (Denman) Townsend worked their farm property in Mayfield Township which they purchased through a land patent. Along with Stephen's parents, Joshua and Phebe Townsend, they were longtime residents of the area. Townsend was born in New York in 1807 and fathered ten children before he died in Illinois in 1882. He faithfully subscribed to the *Western Citizen*, was a Wesleyan Methodist acting as one of the church's first trustees, and became a Free-Soil party delegate to the 1854 organizing convention for the Republican Party.[37]

When his wife Ann died in 1902, the Townsends' antislavery legacy was still remembered: "They early allied themselves with the cause of human freedom. They were firm friends of the slave, and their home was one of the depots of the famous underground railway."[38]

To paraphrase the chapter-opening quote by President George Washington, while living their laborious, everyday lives, these ordinary pioneers, if pioneers can ever be called ordinary, both animated and encouraged each other in their antislavery activities, and discreetly showed the whole world that Freemen and Freewomen contending for liberty on their own ground in DeKalb County, Illinois, were superior to any proslavery person on earth. The unplanned but highly successful reunion of New York's Burned-over District fanned the quiet blaze of antislavery convictions in Northern Illinois.

Chapter 4

The Abolitionists! Thank God!

> No class of the American people can look toward the sunset of life with a larger measure of satisfaction than the Abolitionists.... They have done a great work — the great work of the century.[1] — Frederick Douglass (1818–1895), freed slave and Abolitionist speaker

The Work of the Century

What Frederick Douglass called the "great work of the century" silently gained a foothold in rural Northern Illinois. Of necessity, the adult transplanted New Yorkers were mute about their nocturnal behavior as they performed their secret work of the Underground Railroad. They quietly continued to create hiding places in houses, barns, and sometimes, yes, actually underground, yet they never revealed exactly where those places existed to people who they thought had no right to know. Two inquisitive little boys, however, uncovered one of the area Abolitionists' secrets, a cleverly concealed space used to hide runaway slaves.

When John Vetch Henry was born in 1844 in Lakeville, New York, no one could have predicted that his family would be involved in clandestine activities. The boy was a grandson of George Beveridge, the upright Scot Presbyterian who emigrated from Washington County, New York, to Somonauk, Illinois, in southern DeKalb County. Together with their immediate family and close friends, the Beveridges established the Presbyterian Church in Somonauk and interpreted their high moral beliefs as support for antislavery. This translated into actively maintaining the southern DeKalb County route of the Underground Railroad, as chronicled in grandson John's "intimate view of the Beveridge [Underground Railroad] station."[2] At age 9, young John V., as he was called, was curious, but did not receive any answers to the many questions he asked.

John V. and his seven-year-old brother, George, "were allowed to gather eggs and sell them for whatever they could get."[3] The boys periodically collected freshly laid eggs from under the hens and received payment in the form of "candy for their eggs"[4] at their Uncle Alexander Patten's store. It constituted a good rural barter system for the youthful entrepreneurs. John related the story about their interesting adventure one summer day: "after our egg-hunting expedition, we were playing on top of a straw stack when suddenly the straw gave way."[5] They abruptly landed in a dark, underground hole. Unexpectedly, "we found ourselves in a rather circular room about eighteen feet in diameter, with upright posts about seven feet." The sides were constructed "with old rails and brush behind to keep the straw like a wall, and overhead poles running upward to the center pole for a roof."[6] What a surprising discovery for two small boys! They had no idea of where they were or how they might escape.

John V. Henry further relates, "Though we searched for a long time, we could find no way of exit, and finally managed to climb the dead tree and make our escape from this 'Underground Station.'" He and his brother "told of our escapade at the house, but the family did not enlighten us as to the uses made of the straw-stack room."[7] When they questioned their parents and their aunts and uncles about the meaning of the secret underground room, they received no answers. With the childhood memory behind them, the two small boys forgot about the room until many years later.

Henry served in Co. H of the 105th Illinois Infantry during the Civil War, and in 1865 at the close of the war, he and the other Somonauk volunteers made their way back home. His story continues, "After my return from the army, when secrecy was no longer required, I learned that had we searched the room closely on the ground, exactly in the north center (toward the 'North Star') we would have found an exit." The only way out of the "Underground Station" was "packed with straw and that straw was thinly lain on top where we fell through, for the purpose of ventilation."[8] Throughout his 96 years, John V. Henry often remembered his personal experience when two small boys fell through the rudimentary opening originally created to be an air passage. Back in 1853, though, not one adult would explain why that opening even existed. The work of the century performed by the Beveridge adults was a systematic, peaceful undertaking.

In one published county history, we read the comment, "Strange as it seems to us now, nine-tenths of the people of DeKalb County in the early '50s [1850s] were opposed to the plan of the underground railway."[9] This was written in 1907 when it was finally considered very safe to report the activities of previous prominent citizens who were active in the Underground Railroad. However, there is no documented basis for the given statistic of "nine-tenths" of the residents' disagreeing with antislavery methods, and the statement is undoubtedly the opinion of that writer. There were no proslavery demonstrations, no violence against antislavery activists, no arrests, and only casual mention of any dissenting opinions. The nine-tenths claim has no supporting evidence; the number is simply not true. Perhaps that was a statistic that might have been valid for a different geographic area, but DeKalb County history, recorded closer to the actual events than the incorrect 1907 account, reflects an exact opposite truth.

Abolitionists Gather

DeKalb County's "first Abolition meeting held in this county,"[10] mentioned in the *Portrait and Biographical Album of DeKalb County, Illinois*, was the earliest instance when area men were invited to a neighborly gathering with the express purpose of discussing the matter of slavery issues gaining prominence in the national news. Should slavery be abolished? Should Negroes be granted rights equal to those of the Caucasians? They were unconcerned that their discussion was considered radical by some.

This first so-called Abolition meeting ever convened in DeKalb County took place before 1840 at John Maxfield's country log cabin north of Sycamore, with no public fanfare. The nonviolent Civil War against slavery wrought by unreasonable men and women in this Northern Illinois area began here. Knox and Bureau Counties to the southwest were also populated with quiet Abolitionists who worked side by side with the more outspoken Lovejoy brothers. These silent partners had met a year or two earlier to lay out what became the unwritten Underground

Railroad routes coming from the Mississippi through Galesburg and Princeton and on through DeKalb County.

We now know that nationwide, this peaceful war against slavery was fought on different fronts long before 1861. And initially it was a very *civil* war. People were still polite for the most part, even though they adhered to their own personal beliefs with regard to slavery. An essential civility pervaded state and federal government, as well as in growing municipalities even though the participants disagreed regarding the issue of human bondage. Tolerance combined with a laissez-faire attitude permeated attitudes towards the "peculiar institution" called slavery. And sometimes tolerance, and more oftentimes laissez-faire, lulled thinking men and women to opt to maintain the status quo rather than to agitate for change. Only as time passed did people ultimately begin to realize that there was nothing "civil" about the slavery disagreement. As the national situation deteriorated and in reality became less civil, the bloody War of the Rebellion began in earnest.

Why Abolitionists?

What dynamics produced the Abolitionists in DeKalb County? As expressed previously, certainly some influences prevalent in the eastern geographic areas were also present on the western frontier. Writing about the Underground Railroad in the state of Pennsylvania, a contemporary author commented that "antislavery legislation, the abolitionist societies, and the publications [created] an atmosphere in which many people could see the evils of slavery."[11] However, in newly settled areas, people were more concerned with their own day-to-day existence. They were no longer citified, and, new to the western frontier, they became country folk of necessity. The edicts of state and federal governments seemed to be merely declarations affecting only people living outside of the frontier daily environment. Abolitionist societies were new entities, and publications that preached against slavery were in scarce supply. Overriding outside influences was the fact that the original settlers in DeKalb County arrived there with their personal social causes intact. Theirs was not a profound shift from basic survival to one of social causes as their new settlements matured. They were already opinionated and entrenched in their social concerns. The cultural and ethnic backgrounds rooted in their Scot, Irish and English heritages influenced them beyond their immediate comprehension.

For these transplanted New Yorkers and New Englanders, what then were the determining factors that tugged at the edges of their hearts, ultimately pushing and shoving them into action? At the top of the list were their religious beliefs. Their religious convictions were paramount in guiding their primary thought that slavery should be abolished.

Politics held the position of second place in the minds of these trailblazers. Their Northern Illinois political theories, first as Whigs, Democrat Republicans, then later as Liberty Party men and Free-Soilers, held a subordinate position to a strong religious ideology. By 1854 a majority became rooted in the newly formed antislavery Republican Party.

Additionally, immediatist abolitionism, which encompassed the idea of ending slavery immediately rather than gradually, combined with their religious fervor to create thousands of activists throughout the northern United States. Illinois was home to many hundreds of those self-proclaimed reformers. One writer describes "abolition as a sacred vocation."[12]

Abolitionists were often labeled as agitators or radicals in the eastern United States, but in DeKalb County, they were not a disruptive element of society. They were the quiet reformers. In DeKalb County, being an antislavery sympathizer was akin to being an Abolitionist. Various notices published in the *Western Citizen* in 1845 speak of both Abolitionists and antislavery people in the same paragraph. There is support for the theory that the populace considered Abolitionists and antislavery sympathizers to be one and the same.

If you were an antislavery sympathizer living in DeKalb County, it was highly probable that you were an Abolitionist. There was no difference in their minds. In spite of the fact that later historians prefer to delineate a difference between the two, in 1845 in DeKalb County, Illinois, they were identical. Varying degrees of zealousness translated into participation (or not) in the area Underground Railroad.

Obituaries in local newspapers, as well as narratives in printed county histories, proclaimed the fact that the individual being discussed perceived himself as being an Abolitionist, with a capital "A." In later years people would mention being an Abolitionist prior to joining the Republican Party, as though it was a natural progression. Being an Abolitionist in DeKalb County was equivalent to simultaneous membership in a denominational church, a political party, a fraternal organization and a neighborhood watch group.

The Compromise of 1850, which admitted California to the Union as a free state and allowed any newly acquired territories the right to make their own decisions on the slavery question, also included the new strict fugitive slave law. Any runaway slave could be arrested "on demand" and returned to his or her owner. Additionally, a federal marshal could be fined $1,000 for refusing to apprehend suspected fugitives. Northerners were expected to adhere to that new law. A flaw in the statute became evident when a fugitive was brought before a magistrate: it was far more lucrative for the judge or magistrate to return the slave to the person claiming to be his or her owner, because doing so netted the magistrate a fee of ten dollars. If the judge determined that the alleged slave was actually a free black person, then he only earned the lesser fee of five dollars. It paid twice as much to rule a black person a fugitive, regardless of the facts.

Abolitionists adhered to the belief that the Fugitive Slave Law of 1850 was a deviant, unjust law that did not deserve to be observed. This strong belief provided further impetus for their need to take action.

Such action was illegal, certainly. Helping a fugitive slave on the path to his or her freedom was definitely illegal. One could be punished severely — maybe even shot or hanged, depending on the state in which he lived. In direct opposition to the Fugitive Slave Law, the New England states passed personal liberty laws pertaining to free blacks to hopefully protect them from unlawful seizure by slave catchers. The Illinois legislature, however, aligned itself with the philosophies of border state Kentucky and its ally, the state of Virginia. It sharply contrasted with eastern states by imposing a fine of $500 on all persons "who shall harbor, hire, or in any way give sustenance to any negro or mulatto" who did not have a "certificate of freedom duly authenticated."[13] These provisions constituted part of the Illinois Slave Code, sometimes referred to as "Black Laws," which were in effect from the time Illinois became a state in 1818 until they were repealed in 1866 after the end of the Civil War.

According to the publishers of the *Genius of Liberty*, the original print arm of the Illinois Anti-Slavery Society, "To Illinois is due the honor of first enacting a law which makes it a crime to feed the hungry, clothe the naked, and shelter the stranger and punishes with fine and imprisonment the individual who does those acts which Christ has said he will approbate in the great day of account."[14] Editors Hooper Warren and Zebina Eastman spoke out strongly against the Illinois state Black Laws and characterized the laws unfavorably in their antislavery publication.

DeKalb County Abolitionists were so strongly entrenched in their antislavery beliefs that they were willing to quietly risk punishment or possibly even their lives in order to help the fugitive slaves. They precisely modified the adage: if a law is unjust, *change* it. The axiom became: if a law is unjust, *ignore* it. Well over 100 years later, speaking on the rights of the black race in America, a United States civil rights leader would again declare, "An unjust law is a human law that is not rooted in eternal and natural law."[15] That man, the Rev. Martin Luther King, Jr., championed the art of peaceful, nonviolent protest. The big problem in the 1800s was that slavery was tied into an economic system that helped to support the entire nation — and too many people could not understand or ascribe any value to dismantling a system that benefited so many others in society.

One could opine that, for those in the North who did not own slaves and whose livelihood did not directly depend on plantation slave labor to create their wealth, it was easier for them to be antislavery. But the beliefs of antislavery advocates went much deeper than that. Theirs was an inherent belief that, simply put, slavery was wrong. The majority of the people in early DeKalb County, Illinois, were of a mind that slavery was unjust and against the natural laws of God. It was inhuman. The economics of the nation was not the priority, when helping to free a slave might ensure the abettor an ultimate seat on the right hand of God on Judgment Day. And being on the right hand of God was a daily dominant thought to the pioneer in the 1800s. Consequently, unacknowledged individual self-interests played an unknown role.

When the strengthened Fugitive Slave Law passed in September of 1850, it strengthened the Underground Railroad activities already in motion. According to Siebert, the Fugitive Slave Law did not "check or diminish in any way the number of underground rescues." In fact, "The decade from 1850–1860 was the period of the Road's greatest activity in all sections of the North."[16] Although in some geographic areas of the northern United States the new law may have had a discouraging effect on the very active Underground Railroad, that effect was certainly not the case in DeKalb County, Illinois, which exemplified Siebert's observations of increased activity.

Why would someone deliberately want to create major problems for himself with the civil authorities? Why commit an act that could possibly cause the local law enforcement officials to scrutinize your activities? Why draw the attention of any traveling bounty hunters?

The logic and reason came from the church. God's law was above any laws that man could write, and God's laws must be followed faithfully or else one might not ultimately enter the gates of heaven. If you truly believed in God's laws, then the Puritan ethics paramount in the denominational churches would take precedence over a mere civic rule designed to prevent you from doing what you knew in your heart to be right.

Who Were the Abolitionists?

DeKalb County was settled by Abolitionists. Indeed, the earliest settlers were already antislavery sympathizers. A developed profile of the antislavery supporters in DeKalb County indicates the following: they were mostly Caucasian men and women, the majority being 30 to 49 years old. A high percentage (79 percent) of the men were farmers, and the remainder included laborers, doctors, lawyers, merchants and clerks. Most were landowners, but the size and value of their acreage did not differ from that of the general population.[17]

The majority of the DeKalb County antislavery advocates subscribed individually to the abolitionist newspapers, the *Western Citizen* and later the *Free West*. Others undoubtedly read copies loaned to them by their neighbors and family members. Many are identified in printed historical sources as claiming to be Abolitionists or being active in the Underground Railroad. Others are identified by aligning themselves with the antislavery movement through their own comments in original manuscript sources.

These people were all strong participating members of local churches espousing antislavery beliefs, either the First Congregational or Universalist in Sycamore, the Somonauk Presbyterian, or the Wesleyan Methodist in Brush Point. Membership at the Sycamore First Congregational Church was especially important as prospective members were required to subscribe to an antislavery covenant affirming their belief that slaveholding was against the laws of God. Additionally, each time communion was served, in order to partake of the sacraments, those in attendance were required to publicly affirm their belief that slaveholding was a sin.

They participated in the county Antislavery Society. Some men whose names were not on the *Western Citizen* subscription list were identified in newspaper accounts as officers of the Antislavery Society. Most likely, they read their neighbor's copy of the antislavery newspaper.

They lived in Sycamore, the county seat, and they were the elected county officials who "looked the other way" when Underground Railroad activity occurred. We cannot assume that everyone living in Sycamore was antislavery, but those who subscribed to the *Western Citizen* abolitionist newspaper certainly held those viewpoints. Neither can we assume that everyone living in Somonauk held antislavery views, but the townspeople did create antislavery resolutions at an open town meeting. Any combination of two or more of the given criteria for DeKalb County activists only adds further credibility to an individual's designation as antislavery and/or Abolitionist.

When the government said it was against the law to help a fugitive slave, and when some churches elsewhere in the United States were preaching tolerance for the institution of slavery and patience with regard to its elimination, these were the people who persisted in changing the world. Together they became part of the quiet, enormous number of abolitionism's forgotten heroes.

These Abolitionists are Shaw's unreasonable men and women.

A Peaceful Convener

As the convener of the first Abolition meeting held in DeKalb County, John Maxfield was among the first unreasonable men. He arrived in 1837, an early settler from New England who lived and farmed north of Sycamore. After seven years, he was finally able to purchase the Sycamore Township acreage from the United States government at the Land Office in Chicago. Born in Vermont in 1791, by 1816 he met his wife, Joanna Pond, known simply as "Anna." They were married in Crawford County, Ohio, and arrived in Sycamore about 21 years later. Following the typical pioneer pattern, an early DeKalb County history book briefly chronicled the familiar trip west: "He sold his property in the Buckeye State, and, equipped with five yokes of oxen, two wagons, a horse and carriage and the household goods, the family came to DeKalb County, camping at night while on their way hither."[18]

The family consisted of John and his wife, plus children William Munson, who was then 20 years old; John, called "Nelson," 13; and Gilbert, age 9. William probably drove one wagon while the horse and carriage trailed behind. Anna Maxfield and even young Nelson also likely took their turns at the reins through the long, hard trip overland. According to his son, Gilbert, John Maxfield used much forethought when he purchased the lumber with which to build their new home as they passed through Chicago on their way to DeKalb County. After he laid claim to his 160 acres, his son William purchased an additional 40 acres slightly southeast of John's acreage.[19] Living in tents and wagons, the family managed to survive until "a log house was built for their accommodation."[20]

In 1838 pioneer John Maxfield distinguished himself when he was selected to sit on the first grand jury for the newly created DeKalb County during the term of the first circuit court. If this pioneer family classified themselves at all, they would have considered themselves as being

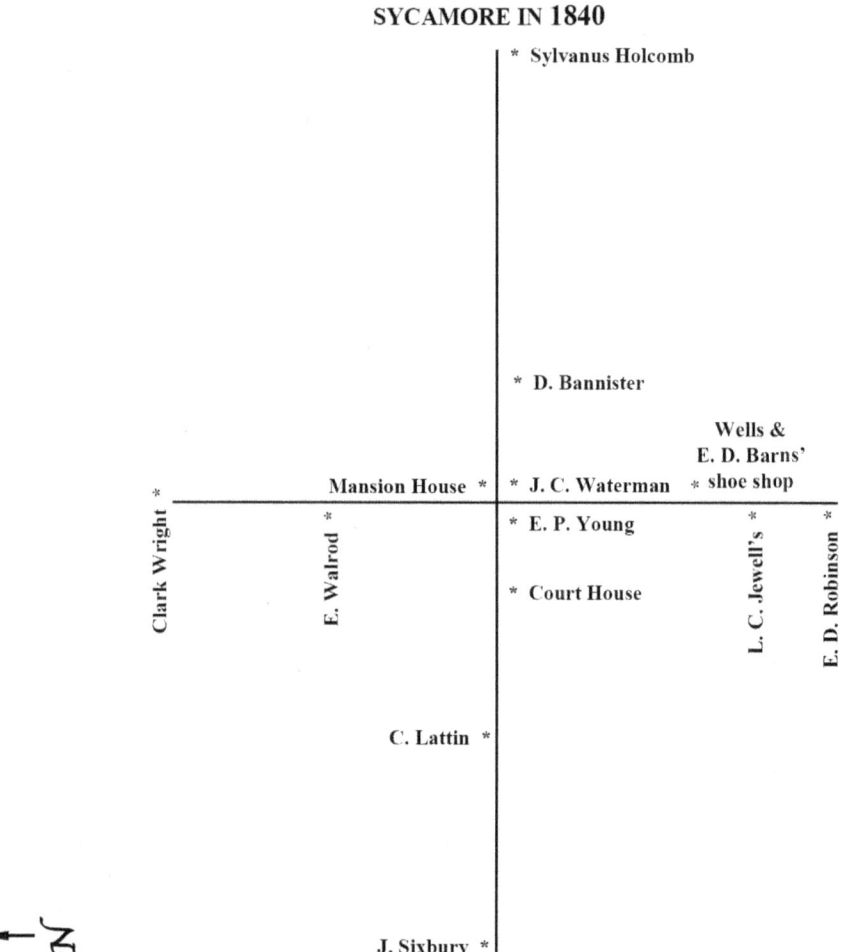

1840 map of Sycamore (arrow added) showing locations of residences and businesses. Orientation is east at the top of map and north on the left, as originally printed (Boies, *History of DeKalb County, Illinois*, 1868).

only farmers. Yet almost 40 years later, the renowned escaped slave, Frederick Douglass, would categorize them as a special "class of American people," for they were Abolitionists.

We do not know the precise month and day the DeKalb County Abolitionists met for their first informal meeting at the Maxfield home. We only know it was before 1840, which was when Reuben Pritchard hosted a similar meeting in Waterman. It was also well before the first public antislavery meeting of 1845 published in the *Western Citizen*. There is no recorded attendance list for that very first secret assembly at Maxfield's home. By comparing the *Western Citizen* mailbooks (subscription lists) with the 1840 U.S. Census and other historical sources, we know who certainly could have been invited to attend.

In 1840 there were already numerous individuals living in DeKalb County who openly expressed their antislavery views and would soon subscribe to the *Western Citizen*. Among those men were: Joseph Arbuckle, Daniel Bannister, Erastus Barnes, Henry and Levi Barber, George Beveridge, Charles Branch, Thomas Brooks, Arnold Brown, Benjamin Brown and his brother Jeremiah, William Brown, James Cartwright, Zenus Churchill and his sons Castle and David,

Rufus and Calvin Colton, Alexander Crawford, William Davis, Major Dennis, Ira Douglass, Levias Dow, Henry Durham, Decatur and John Eastabrooks, Wells Fay, Moses Foster, John Freeman, George and Henry Gandy, Houten and Robert Graham, Ezra Gregory, Ephraim and Marcenus Hall, Erastus Hamblin, Elias Hartman, Sylvanus Holcomb, Burage Hough, Luman Huntley, Alvin Hyatt, Harvey Ide, and Abner Jackman. Jackman was John Maxfield's closest neighbor, living on the next farm down the road. Given the proximity of his residence to Maxfield, he was undoubtedly among the original Abolitionists to attend that evening meeting at Maxfield's home.

The compiled list continues with Phineas Joslyn, John Judd, Jesse Kellogg, Gideon King, Joseph Landers, William Lattemore, Carlos Lattin, Samuel Lay, the Rev. James Mackie, William "Harrison" Mackey, Dr. Henry Madden, Harry Martin, John Maxfield and his sons William and John ("Nelson"). William and Nelson Maxfield are not listed individually in the 1840 U.S. Census because they were not yet heads of households. Nelson, however, later subscribed to the *Western Citizen* and most certainly attended the meeting, for "like his father, he was a staunch and true friend of the black man."[21]

Other openly antislavery men among the original settlers were Sam Miller, William Miller, Emory Moore, John Mullen, Peter Nichols and his son Ephraim P., as well as Peter's father Reuben, and his brothers John, Ira and Latin Nichols, Winslow Norcutt, John Orput, Horatio Page, William Phelps, William Poplin, Chester Potter, Almus Pratt, Justin Preston, Almon Robinson (husband to Mercy), Andrew Shepard, Joseph Sixbury, Joseph Sly, Curtis Smith and his brother Spafford, Moses Stafford, John Snow, Marshall Stark, Samuel Stevens, Neil Sweeney, Joshua Townsend and his sons Charles and Stephen, Morris Walrod, John Waterman, Solomon Wells, Timothy Wells, William White, Cyrus Whitford, Benjamin Whitmore, George Willson, Thomas Woolsey, Clark Wright and Ralph Wyman.

These 102 named individuals comprise a total of twenty-five percent of the men who were heads of households in DeKalb County in 1840. As the research shows, there were many other antislavery advocates who moved to the county before 1840 but were not enumerated in that first census. And there were hundreds more who settled in this area of Northern Illinois in the early 1840s. This esteemed group, however, was the initial local antislavery vanguard. They were open about their views and actively worked to change the course of history. These neighbors, farmers, tradesmen, retail merchants and various learned professionals, together with their wives, had as their common denominator an extreme dislike of slavery. As unreasonable men and women they were the first Abolitionists in the county and their numbers grew as DeKalb County's population increased. By the time the shots were fired at Fort Sumter marking the beginning of the Civil War, there were over 1,000 antislavery supporters in DeKalb County.

All of the above-named 1840 residents became subscribers to the antislavery newspaper, the *Western Citizen*. They increasingly found local support for their cause to help fugitive slaves. When the *Western Citizen* made its debut during the summer of 1842, it was an overwhelming regional success. Its editor, Zebina Eastman of Chicago, created a thorough distribution system throughout Illinois via direct household delivery. He solicited local agents to handle distribution of the newspaper and named Ezra Starr Gregory as agent in DeKalb County.

The Lovejoy Brothers

Rumblings of discontent with the tradition of slavery were also heard slightly farther southwest in Illinois. About the same time that people in DeKalb County adopted the cause to abolish slavery, a man named Owen Lovejoy arrived in the town of Princeton, in Bureau County southwest of DeKalb County. It was 1838, the year Lovejoy accepted a position as minister at the local Hampshire Colony Congregational Church. Based on his own personal experiences, this man already had the fire in his belly regarding the peculiar institution of slavery. Owen's older brother, Elijah Lovejoy, was a Presbyterian minister and the editor of the newspaper, the *St. Louis Observer*, in St. Louis, Missouri. Elijah was not simply an ordinary newspaper editor, reporting daily gossip published with the daily news. He wrote anti–Catholic and fiery antislavery opinions which he persisted in printing in his publication. After repeated antislavery editorials created an untenable situation for the proslavery people of St. Louis, they destroyed one of his presses and essentially ran him out of town. Elijah was determined to continue his abolitionist preaching and moved his family and newspaper business from Missouri across the Mississippi River to Alton, Illinois, southwest of Princeton.

The proslavery population in Illinois, which existed to a greater degree in the southern half of the state, frowned upon the distribution of antislavery documents of any type. Anyone who possessed antislavery pamphlets or newspapers, even if only passing through a town, could be liable to punishment from local vigilante groups. The reality was that the existing 1793 Fugitive Slave Law already gave slaveholders the right to reclaim their "fugitives from labor." Slaves were definitely considered to be real property and by law were to be returned to their rightful owner. A person thus transgressed upon the slaveholder's rights through the distribution of any information or ideas to the contrary which might give any slaves the idea that they could enjoy a free life of their own. Proslavery defenders were concerned that dissemination of information directly to either ordinary citizens, or slaves themselves, regarding the word "freedom," or even the suggestion that slaves might also have rights, was a threat and would only cause agitation.

On July 20, 1837, Lovejoy's *Alton Observer* editorial invoked language directly from the Declaration of Independence and stated Elijah's interpretation of a creed for Abolitionists:

> Abolitionists hold that "all men are born free and equal, endowed by their Creator with certain inalienable rights, among which are life, LIBERTY, and the pursuit of happiness."
> They do not believe that these rights are abrogated, or at all modified by the colour of the skin, but that they extend alike to every individual of the human family.
> As the above-mentioned rights are in their nature inalienable, it is not possible that one man can convert another into a piece of property, thus at once annihilating all his personal rights, without the most flagrant injustice and usurpation....
> Abolitionists, therefore, hold American Slavery to be a <u>wrong</u>, a legalized system of inconceivable injustice, and a <u>sin</u> ... against God.[22]

As a direct result of his activities which encouraged antislavery thinking, Elijah Lovejoy again became a victim of violent mob action in Alton. In November of 1837 an angry group of proslavery ruffians, thought to be from Missouri, attacked Elijah and killed him. Characterized as a "drunken posse,"[23] a similar group had destroyed his printing presses on an earlier occasion by crushing and throwing them into the Mississippi River. Undiscouraged by that previous action, Elijah was in the process of replacing the lost printing presses so he could continue to publish the *Alton Observer*. Lovejoy's perseverance so angered the mob that they set his building on fire, dumped his press once again into the Mississippi River, and murdered him with a flurry of bullets. That was their prompt answer to this clergyman who was a consummate champion of antislavery. When Lovejoy's corpse was carried through the streets of Alton the next day, the proslavery men jeered from the sidewalks. Illinois gave the antislavery movement its first martyr for the cause of liberty.

Abolitionists in the United States were simultaneously both outraged and energized by the martyrdom of Elijah Lovejoy. The people in DeKalb County quietly absorbed the news of the event. They were not apathetic, but in 1837 they did not fully realize that they were destined to become willing assistants on the path to freedom. The news of Lovejoy's murder was undoubtedly the tinder for their fire in the antislavery battle.

A similar incident had occurred eighteen months earlier in Cincinnati, Ohio, when a proslavery mob destroyed the printing presses of James G. Birney. Birney published the abolitionist newspaper *The Philanthropist*. Anti-abolitionist protesters sometimes traveled from place to place to wreak havoc wherever they could. However, unlike Lovejoy, Birney was not killed in that action, and later went on to become a candidate for president on the Liberty Party ticket. It was obvious that "such riotous and atrocious acts did not augment the cause of slavery; rather they furthered the anti-slavery cause and made it more open, outspoken, and aggressive."[24]

Elijah Lovejoy's brother, Owen Lovejoy, determined to defend his martyred brother's life's work and antislavery philosophy. His "deep conviction that slavery was wrong and that it was a Christian's duty not only to oppose it, but to be active in trying to abolish it"[25] led him to become a Congregational minister in Princeton, Illinois. There, as pastor of the Hampshire Colony Congregational Church, the Rev. Lovejoy confidently used his outstanding oratorical skills to witness against slavery both in the pulpit and later as an exceptionally outspoken member of Congress. In addition, his home and farmstead in Princeton became a well-known station on the Underground Railroad. Before Elijah's death, Owen Lovejoy was involved with his brother in the 1837 formation of the Illinois State Antislavery Society. He was also instrumental in the creation of the Illinois Congregational General Association, a loose organization of member Congregational churches. People in DeKalb County who were aware of the antislavery movement were certainly aware of the Rev. Owen Lovejoy and his activities. They could read in the *Western Citizen* about Lovejoy's arrest and subsequent lawsuit in 1843 for aiding slaves. He was a frequent correspondent contributor to the weekly abolitionist newspaper.

The route traveled to Sycamore on the Underground Railroad came straight through Princeton, Illinois, most probably directly from the home of Owen Lovejoy. The unreasonable Lovejoy is credited with helping countless numbers of fugitives on their way to freedom.

A Hint of Opposition

Although warned in Princeton that he, too, would be mobbed and killed for his antislavery beliefs, Owen Lovejoy continued to ride his horse in public. One fine evening in 1840, Lovejoy journeyed to DeKalb County to speak to a group of loyal antislavery proponents. He traveled with his own horse and carriage all the way from Princeton, a distance of about 50 miles. The DeKalb County antislavery assemblage gathered in Pritchard's Grove at the farm and home belonging to Reuben and Celestia Pritchard, sited in Clinton Township near where the town of Waterman exists today. Centrally positioned in the county, the location was accessible from either the north or south without too much trouble.

This was an enlightening event for area citizens. Lovejoy was carrying out the oath he took when proslavery men murdered his brother and he "swore he would do, as preacher and man, all he could against slavery."[26] Sympathetic listeners watched Lovejoy roll up his shirtsleeves readying himself to present an emotional antislavery tirade. They were undoubtedly reminded that "The constitution of the United States was [not] ... ordained to hunt men and women, for this is ... degrading to us as American citizens."[27] "Lovejoy spent much time connecting political antislavery language with patriotic love of the Union."[28]

Local Abolitionists and antislavery people listened firsthand to the man talk about his martyred brother. They heard this eloquent speaker bestow further authority to their already staunch antislavery position. Venues such as this were proving grounds for later fiery speeches in the

United States Congress. Owen Lovejoy may have even tested certain phrases on his live audience. As he later bravely proclaimed:

> Anyone who chooses may transform himself into a bloodhound, sniff, and scent, and howl along the path of the fugitive.... I would not have the guilt of causing the wail of a man's despair, or that wild shriek of a woman's agony, as one or the other is captured, for all the diadems of all the stars in heaven....[29]

Lovejoy always wanted his message to "echo through all the arches of heaven, and reverberate and bellow along the deep gorges of hell, where slave-catchers will be very likely to hear it."[30]

While the 1840s audience listened to Owen Lovejoy's fiery abolition speech, a ragtag faction of proslavery people set fire to Pritchard's barn, where Lovejoy's horse and buggy were sequestered. The animal and conveyance were both "consumed in the flames."[31] That evening, Pierpont Edwards of Paw Paw kindly loaned the Rev. Mr. Lovejoy the use of a horse and buggy for his trip home to Princeton. Perhaps Lovejoy dropped Edwards off at Edwards's own home on his way further southwest. Reports are that Lovejoy returned the carriage "a fortnight later."[32] Yet, in spite of this hint of brief local opposition to the antislavery movement, DeKalb County remained an island of calm amidst the rolling sea of changing attitudes towards slavery.

In the District of Columbia, Congress imposed a gag rule in order to avoid considering the Abolitionists' petitions against slavery. Southerners burned antislavery pamphlets published by the American Anti-Slavery Society. Northern Abolitionists were attacked by angry mobs like the one that murdered Elijah Lovejoy. But violence either by antislavery proponents or by avowed radical Abolitionists did not exist in this Northern Illinois area. The single act of arson reported in the *True Republican* was the only recorded aggressive incident in DeKalb County for the duration of the entire antislavery movement. No one was arrested and convicted for the crime, and if there were ever any other incidents, they apparently were not of sufficient importance to warrant mention in the published newspapers of the day.

He Was Called by the Name — Abolitionist

Deacon David West undoubtedly had heard of Owen Lovejoy and his passionate speeches, but West did not arrive in DeKalb County in time to meet him personally at the 1840 antislavery meeting held at Reuben Pritchard's farm. Neither had West been in Northern Illinois in time to be present at the earlier antislavery organizational meeting at the home of John Maxfield. Pritchard, Maxfield, Jackman and others laid the very important foundation upon which David West would build.

West was a true stereotypical pioneer, born in Oneida County, New York, in 1806, one of nine children. By age 15 his father was dead and he lived with his sister and brother-in-law, Polly and Daniel Hurd, in Madison County, New York. By the time he was 20 years old, he was already a contractor clearing land in the enormous forests out east.[33] West "was a man of gigantic physical strength, his strong arm felling hundreds of acres of the forests of western New York and making them fruitful fields."[34] His father, Asa West, was an avid Seventh Day Baptist in New York, yet when David was 25 years old, David joined the Congregational church in Collins, Erie County, New York. Both denominations were exceptionally strong in their antislavery viewpoints. West's physical prowess, however, "was but a counter part of his great efforts in conquering the spiritual wastes of the world to make them bear fruits to the glory of our God."[35] That comment subtly refers to David West's efforts as an Abolitionist in the Underground Railroad, where he helped to conquer the spiritual waste caused by slavery.

"Deacon" was an ecclesiastical title conferred upon West by the Congregational Church and was a title he very much enjoyed. This deacon was a direct product of the familiar geographical area known as the Burned-over District in western New York State. This 1830s center for antislavery and abolitionist thought and activity simultaneously spawned several new Protestant denominations. An extreme dislike of slavery intensified a sense of benevolence toward slaves, and the transplanted Northeasterners compassionately incorporated antislavery convictions into their belief system. The Abolitionists gravitated together in Illinois and created true reunions of alumni of the Burned-over District.

During the next 14 years, David West's own Congregational antislavery and religious beliefs became clear to him and ultimately drove him to go west. By 1843, at age 37, he sold his farm in Evans, New York, and together with his wife, Sarah Chapin West, and five young children, started for Illinois, making the journey with a pair of horses, a wagon and a few household goods.[36] Their youngest child at the time was only 18 months old. With the fortitude born of a self-sufficient life, West figured that he had tamed virgin timber in the Northeast and he would do it again on the Midwest prairies.

This was not easy travel. They traversed dirt trails across the countryside until they reached the Erie Canal, loaded their possessions onto a canal barge, and traveled the canal as far as they could go. At the end of the canal, rather than travel by steamship through the Great Lakes, they off-loaded their belongings and started to make their way west again in the covered wagon. After 23 days of horse and wagon travel, including 15 days of snowy weather conditions, "exclusive of Sundays,"[37] the West family arrived in Sycamore in the later part of the year. They stayed the winter with David's brother and sister-in-law, Aaron and Emily (Adams) West, who owned a tract of land in Section 34 east of the town center. Like others before him, West brought his New York antislavery sentiments to the Northwest Territory with expanded confidence. It did not take long for a runaway slave escaping oppression to find the West family.

In 1843 the eldest West child was 13-year-old Alice, and her next oldest sibling was Orrin, age 11. One early November morning, "shortly after their arrival ... the West children had their first sight of a colored person." Imagine their innocent wide eyes observing someone who looked so different from anyone they knew. Porter, who was seven years old, and Elias, then four years old, were probably shocked into silence at the appearance of so strange a sight in their house. Their mother and Aunt Emily West fed the hungry man in their own kitchen. "He was in the house only long enough for his meals," and the conversation they overheard informed the children that this was his second escape attempt. They noticed that the runaway was "on the alert every moment."[38]

> During the day he hid in the cornfields and slept in the barn at night. Finally Mr. West took his wagon and put in some bags of wheat, [and] covering them up, with the Negro hidden somewhere in the load, started for the next station near St. Charles. On the way he was stopped and asked to see what he had in his load. He told them that was his business and whipped up his horse, soon turned in a new road and heard nothing more from the man following him.[39]

In the middle of the night, Deacon David West saw the growing national debate appear in his family's farm yard. The lone black man, a human personification of the sad racial conflict, needed assistance and West was not afraid to assist him. Whether confronted by a curious neighbor or a slave bounty hunter, West was undaunted. We have the image of a confident man using a self-assured clear voice to inform the questioner that as he could plainly see, there was nothing but bags of wheat in West's wagon! West might also have politely informed him to mind his own business, then quickly applied a whip to the horse to hasten his departure.

With careful preparations, he arranged to transport the fugitive to further safety. His younger brother, Aaron, was aware of local Underground Railroad nocturnal activities and undoubtedly offered advice on where the next station existed. Aaron was also already a subscriber to the *Western Citizen* and regularly read about the antislavery movement.

David West's well-known handmade "car" used to transport fugitive slaves on the Underground Railroad from Sycamore to St. Charles, Illinois. His son, Elias West, is right, with West family members posing in blackface for illustrative purposes in the 1907 photograph (Gross, *Past and Present of DeKalb County*, Vol. 1).

Shortly after arriving in Sycamore, before he cleared any land for himself or built his own house, David West joined the First Congregational Church where his brother Aaron was already a member. Deacon David West undeniably knew that the local fledgling antislavery movement was ripe and ready for someone with his vision and quiet, yet ardent, leadership.

An anonymous writer later observed about West, "In his youth, while in spiritual darkness and somewhat in despair about ever finding the way of life, he went alone to the woods, and there in the solitude of the forests, alone with God, he made the firm resolve that whether he ever found the light of life or not, he would never neglect any known duty. From that moment [the] light grew brighter and brighter."[40] Like many people who lived during the spiritual Great Awakening in western New York, David West experienced a religious conversion. His duties were clear to him.

"In the days when Sycamore was in its incipiency his house was the home of the clergy who came hither in the practice of their calling, and it was also a depot on the 'Underground Railroad,' Mr. West often being called on to aid the refugees from the South and help them on their way to a land of freedom."[41] Repeatedly, West reached out to help freedom seekers traveling through Sycamore. It was well known that at the West home the "latchstring was always out, especially to the poor slaves of the south." Deacon David West was one of those early pioneers who "came to be known as one of the most ardent abolitionists in this section of the country."[42]

Primary evidence exists to support the stories about the West family harboring fugitive slaves. Elizabeth Wood wrote firsthand about the benevolence of David's wife, Sarah. Her original handwritten account about the women's work in the early years of the First Congregational Church was discovered in 2001. Wood was the daughter of First Congregational Church member Emily Rose, and stepdaughter of Dr. Ellsworth Rose, one of the first physicians in Sycamore, who is identified as an antislavery sympathizer. Her husband, Henry Wood, another Abolitionist, was the brother of Phoebe (Wood) Kellogg, wife of Deacon Jesse C. Kellogg, first DeKalb County clerk and one of the founding members of the First Congregational Church. She was therefore surrounded by a family of Abolitionists through her husband, her stepfather and her brother-in-law. Her sympathies for the antislavery movement are evident.

Elizabeth Wood wrote, "Mrs. David West shared with her husband the extra labor of sheltering and feeding the homeless and destitute wanderers fleeing northward for life and liberty. Many and many a time were they good Samaritans to these friendless people, exemplifying the scripture text — 'Bear ye one another's burdens.'"[43]

When "these friendless people" needed a hiding place in Sycamore, the West barn, which was purposely constructed over a secret underground room, was a logical resting place — a known Underground Railroad station. Later owners of the farm razed the barn in about 1918, uncovering an eight-foot-square underground room, which had been completely unknown to the 20th century proprietors. Stories about the hiding places in both the house and barn abound. The corncrib also contained a "secret dugout hiding place," and "slaves stayed [in the house itself] in a little room connected to an outside door by a narrow hall."[44] Also inside the house was a room with no windows concealed in the center of the structure. Two stairways led to the upstairs and it was impossible to go from any one of the three different upstairs locations to another.[45] According to a 1947 owner, four adults could stand behind a false wall in a downstairs bedroom. It is presumed that West purposely built the house with "unusual features" to hide fugitive slaves.[46]

Deacon David West "sometimes stood for a while almost alone among his fellows. He was called by a name which was then a stigma but in the increase of light and growth of liberty has become a crown of glory." West was an unreasonable man; he was called an "Abolitionist."[47]

A Doctor Named Page

Horatio Page, the son of Phinehas and Lynthia (Macomber) Page, came from a well-established New England family in Hawley, Franklin County, Massachusetts. Prior to the Revolutionary War, King George III deeded land to Horatio's grandfather, Theopolis Page. Page experienced the Christian life through the practices of the Congregational Church; it was ingrained in the Page household. East Hawley had an established Congregational church as early as 1778, before the incorporation of the town, and another Congregational church organized in West Hawley before 1825.[48] It was inevitable that Horatio Page grew up in the Congregational Church.

After studying medicine with a doctor in Charlemont, Massachusetts, and advanced studies at Williamstown, Page decided in 1838 to seek his fortunes in the west. His home town of Hawley was growing too slowly for him, and he was anxious to make his way in life. Younger brother Phinehas was a lawyer, and brothers Joel and Bradford Page were both farmers. Their widowed mother is listed in the 1850 Census for Pittsfield, Massachusetts, as still living with the unmarried brothers. Horatio Page arrived in Genoa, Illinois, in 1838 and "commenced practice of medicine."[49] He was the first physician in DeKalb County, and when he later settled a few miles south of Genoa, he immediately acquired the title of first resident physician in Sycamore. As a leader in the young community, Page was easily chosen assessor for the Kishwaukee District when the county commissioners' court divided newly formed DeKalb County into three assessment districts.[50] Neither did he waste any time in continuing his inbred religious antislavery practices, which included becoming a charter member of the First Congregational Church of Sycamore in 1840.

Because he was a physician, Page inherently tried to help people through diagnosis of diseases and the administration of medicines. It was a natural transition to aid people through other avenues. Horatio and Eliza's only son, also named Horatio, died in 1854 when only 11 months old, and they never had any more children. Even as an experienced physician, Page was helpless to save the infant. For a short time the Pages raised Horatio's nephew, his brother Austin's son, who was also named Horatio Franklin. However, without children of their own to raise, they both had the time and energy to reach out to others. It became a natural extension of their unselfish personal kindness to help the downtrodden fugitive slaves.

By 1860 in the U.S. Census, Horatio and Elizabeth Page are enumerated with a mulatto, Mary A. Wadgen, and her two-year-old daughter living in their home. The suspicion is that they were fugitive slaves. Ten years earlier, Horatio Page harbored a young black man in his home, listing him as a student. Page undoubtedly attended the Abolition meeting at John Maxfield's log cabin.

Another Medical Practitioner

There is one man who, on the surface, seems to have no record of direct involvement with the antislavery cause, yet he knew intimately all the active participants in DeKalb County abolitionism. That man was another physician, Dr. Rufus Hopkins, who, like so many others, was born in New York. Hopkins is listed in the DeKalb County Medical Society archival information among the first ten early doctors to practice in this frontier region. He officially served as the Society's first treasurer, as well as being one of two "censors." His practice apparently covered Coltonville, Sycamore and DeKalb in the northern end of the county.[51] Through Dr. Hopkins's journal, which is a daily record of his medical visits and dispensation of drugs to local patients, we read that he attended a large number of the identified Abolitionists. The 400-page journal covers several years, beginning in 1848, and lists patients' names and the service rendered to them. Were they only "visited" or did they receive any medication? Was the contact to attend to a family member, a wife or child? The information is all cataloged in Hopkins's own handwriting in very precise order, listed on a daily basis according to the man's name, or the head of the household, as was the custom. The question arises, if Dr. Rufus Hopkins was not known to be overtly involved in the Abolitionists' cause, why did many of them gravitate towards him for medical attention when necessary? Part of the answer may lie in the fact that one of the known Abolitionists who practiced medicine, Dr. Horatio Page, was out of the state during 1848-49. He began his practice in 1839 when he first arrived in DeKalb County, but later went back to Massachusetts for about a year to claim and marry his wife, Elizabeth "Eliza" Pratt. Although they returned to Sycamore, where he continued his profession, anyone ailing in the meantime needed to turn to someone else, and Dr. Hopkins was available. Additionally, there is a suggestion that perhaps Hopkins knew that the Underground Railroad existed in the environs, but chose not to mention it to anyone. The possibility of being labeled "antislavery" could have had a negative effect on his medical practice, and staying in business was a stronger personal motivation to him than the antislavery cause itself. He was in business to practice medicine, not to give slaves their freedom. Yet Rufus Hopkins could keep secrets, and by never mentioning to anyone that he personally knew who the antislavery people were, he indirectly helped to free the slaves.

An Old Soldier

Horace Wright Fay was "old and grey [when] he early enlisted in the war for the Union."[52] At the time, in 1861, he was 60 years old. Fay was born the third of seven children to Jonathan and Rhoda (White) Fay, one of four boys and three girls. His youngest brother, Wells, arrived in DeKalb County about 1836, and when Horace came to DeKalb County a year later he and Wells purchased land together in Squaw Grove Township. By 1850 they had land patents documenting ownership of 480 acres.

All told, Fay was a father figure to twelve children. Fay and his first wife, Roxanna Eaton, were the parents of five; then, after Roxanna's death, Horace married Alida Adams and fathered another daughter. When Alida died, Fay married a third time to Margaret Stipp, and they became parents of four more children, plus Margaret's two children from her previous marriage.

His farming apparently did not keep him busy enough, so Fay became active in the local political arena. In 1848 he was elected as only the second representative to the Illinois state legislature from DeKalb County. By 1853 he was elected an official surveyor for DeKalb County and is credited for platting the villages of Malta and Sandwich, as well as many other parts of the county. He was also involved in the creation of the Illinois and Michigan Canal as one of the civil engineers.

Then in 1854, Horace Wright Fay became one of the delegates chosen at a Sycamore gathering to attend an upcoming antislavery meeting in Aurora, Illinois. The Aurora meeting was one of the organizing conventions for the Republican Party.

Throughout his life he acted as an itinerant minister when called upon and maintained his interest in music. Those two attributes played an important part in what became of him.

Horace Wright Fay, farmer, Illinois state representative, minister, oldest man from DeKalb County to enlist in the Union Army; buried at Vicksburg, Mississippi.

When civil strife became a reality, although he was already considered old, Fay was sufficiently passionate about the antislavery movement to enroll in the Union Army. He "answered his country's call in 1861,"[53] enlisting for three years in the 8th Regiment of the Illinois Volunteer Infantry.

Fay was discharged as a drum major in December 1863, specifically to accept an appointment in the 5th Regiment, 1st Mississippi, U.S. Colored Troops Heavy Artillery. This time he served as an officer, a commissioned chaplain. Horace was not black; it was common practice for a white person to serve as an officer in the Colored Troops. A love of music and a spiritual calling for the ministry united with Fay's antislavery sentiments and led him to Vicksburg, Mississippi.

The Vicksburg campaign lasted for 46 days during the spring and summer of 1863. It officially ended on July 4, 1863, when Confederate General John C. Pemberton surrendered to Union General Ulysses S. Grant. Our national Independence Day would not be celebrated again in Vicksburg, Mississippi, until during World War II.

Horace W. Fay observed that Union victory, only to be killed at Vicksburg almost a year later on Saturday, April 16, 1864. He was one of four soldiers from his regiment mortally wounded. The exact circumstances of his death are unknown. He may have died from a gunshot wound from a stray sniper in the area. Although there is a grave marker for Fay in Oak Mound Cemetery in Somonauk, Illinois, he was actually interred at Vicksburg, Mississippi, and is one of 16,822 Union soldiers killed near that city.

The idea that a person was too old to serve in the military was unacceptable to Horace Fay. He surmounted the perceived impediment of old age, and at age 60 was likely the oldest soldier from DeKalb County to defend the Union.

Compelling Examples

We sometimes think of those early pioneers as being completely cut off from the rest of civilization, and in the early days of the remote Northern Illinois frontier they were indeed isolated. They were without a daily newspaper; the telephone was not yet invented; the first telegraph message was not sent until 1844, and the telegraph system was not readily available until some years later. Yet, like people everywhere, the locals hungered for information about what was happening in their world. On the Illinois frontier, the main method of communication, besides personal exchanges at the general store or post office, was letters to and from home — that is, wherever home used to be in the eastern United States. When Charlotte Waterman heard from her friend Phocion Hoffman in New York, when the Universalist minister Thomas Carney received a letter from his beloved Julia Fletcher in Boston, and when Henrietta Norton, wife of Congregational minister Oliver W. Norton, wrote from Illinois to her family in Connecticut, they were all creating a narrative about life on the western frontier. They did not know that they were also quietly creating a chronicle about the subtleties of the antislavery movement. They were only living their everyday lives as best they could.

The peaceful citizens in DeKalb County made a conscious choice to pursue the avenues of abolitionism in spite of their common knowledge regarding the treatment of Abolitionists elsewhere. They were not radical Abolitionists, yet they carefully nurtured their antislavery sentiments. Whatever they may have heard about the anti-abolitionist mob that killed Elijah Lovejoy in Illinois, or about his brother Owen Lovejoy in nearby Bureau County charged with harboring fugitive slaves; whatever they read about an Abolitionist in Ohio being extradited to Kentucky for trial, they were unafraid. Nothing created a fear in their hearts strong enough to cause them to cease their activities to aid the fugitive slave. Nothing deterred them from their self-appointed task of doing what they could to help end slavery.

What they did know were the stories they heard from those liberty-seeking pilgrims describing the dogs chasing them at night. They caught a glimpse of the runaways' backs scarred from whippings. They knew the rudimentary fundamentals of escape, such as the value of onions, used by runaways to rub on the bottoms of their feet to mask a human scent and thwart the hounds that pursued them. They learned about the need to wade in the shallow waters of rivers and streams to avoid detection. As each escapee passed through DeKalb County, in the minds of these quiet reformers, that runaway was one more free person.

And they also personally knew and were inspired by people like John Hossack in neighboring LaSalle County. Hossack began his extensive work with the Underground Railroad in 1844 when renowned Underground Railroad conductor Ichabod Codding brought a fugitive to his house. Later, in 1860, after being found guilty for aiding in the escape of Jim Grey, another runaway, Scottish-born Hossack addressed the open court in a speech that clearly rings with an Abolitionist's passion. He greatly loved his adopted country and was adamantly opposed "to carrying out wicked and ungodly laws."[54]

Hossack told the court that he should not be sentenced simply because he was an Abolitionist. "I have no apologies to make for being an Abolitionist. As a man who had fled from the crushing aristocracy of my native land [Scotland], how can I support a worse aristocracy in this land?"[55]

He further charged that the Fugitive Slave Law "is at variance with both the spirit and letter of the constitution. The parties who prostituted the constitution to the support of slavery, are traitors; traitors not only to the liberties of millions of enslaved countrymen, but traitors to the constitution itself, which they have sworn to support."[56]

Invoking the Bible, Hossack insisted that he should not be sentenced "for raising my hand to rescue a fellow-man from a mob that would strip him of his liberty and life-long toil without due process of law, without trial by jury. [The Fugitive Slave Law] is so obviously at variance with the law of God ... that the path of duty is plain to me."[57]

The jury found Hossack guilty under the prevailing Fugitive Slave Law. In his statement to Judge Drummond, Hossack agreed with the jury that he was guilty only of "carrying out the great principles of the Declaration of Independence."[58] His impassioned plea continued:

> What country is this? Can it be that I live in a land boasting of freedom, of morality, of Christianity? ... Yes, the Jury say guilty, but recommend me to the mercy of the Court. Mercy, sir, is kindness to the guilty. I am guilty of no crime; I, therefore, ask for no mercy. No, sir, I ask for no mercy; I ask for justice. Mercy is what I ask of my God. Justice in the courts of my adopted country is all I ask. It is the inhuman and infamous law that is wrong, not me.[59]

The words of John Hossack fearlessly echoed the thoughts of Abolitionists throughout both LaSalle and DeKalb counties, as well as throughout the entire northern United States. Hossack was ready to die for the cause of the Abolitionists and insisted that slavery must also die.

His final request to Judge Drummond of the U.S. District Court in Chicago is recorded:

> I have, sir, endeavored to obey the divine law, and all the laws of my country that do not conflict with the laws of my God. My humble wish is that it may then appear that I have done my duty; all I wish to be written on my tomb-stone, "he feared God and loved his fellow men."[60]

The jury recommended that the court show mercy. Hossack's very lenient sentence constituted ten days in jail and a fine of $100 plus court costs. During his incarceration, Mayor John Wentworth of Chicago visited Hossack and even took him out to lunch, while Hossack's supporters in Cook and LaSalle counties raised enough money to pay all of his fines. DeKalb County Abolitionists did well to emulate the powerful example of their fellow Abolitionist in neighboring LaSalle County.

Thank God for the brave people who refused to tolerate man's inhumanity to man. Thank God for the "people who did a great work — the great work of the century."[61] Thank God for unreasonable men and women, the Abolitionists!

CHAPTER 5

First, the Church

> For, while politicians contend, and men are swerved this way and that by conflicting tides of interest and passion, the great cause of human liberty is in the hands of One.[1] — Harriet Beecher Stowe (1811–1896), Abolitionist, author of *Uncle Tom's Cabin*

It Was Always the Church

The church came first. A man could love and cherish his family, toiling hard to provide shelter and food to sustain them. A man could have faith in his country and defend the values proclaimed by his ancestors in creating a free nation. Yet the church told him how to live his daily life within the confines of the young democracy, and generally, the majority of church members accepted edicts from the church and its leadership. After all, even through years of conflicting tides of individual passions and interests, the church leadership was in "the hands of One," and that One was the One God to whom they would listen.

The church came first. How to conduct oneself each day within a family or community was of far more importance than whatever was happening in the outside world. The seat of government seemed so far away and news of any action at the federal level only reached small rural communities a week or two after their occurrence through the sometimes irregular printing of area newspapers or gleaned from letters from friends and family on the eastern seaboard. On the western frontier, rural communities relied on the church as their central social structure, as well as their obvious spiritual core. Consequently, the church dictated to its members not only how to interpret the Bible's teachings throughout everyday life, but also how to understand and abide by the laws of the civil government. And when the government's laws seemed to go against the laws of God, the church could and would overlook those civil transgressions in favor of the redeeming grace which would ultimately be received by the brethren from an act of compassion or contrition by one of its members.

The church came first. It was more important to the church to determine if each and every member of its body followed the internal rules as set forth in their denomination's particular covenants, articles of faith, or any subsequent adopted standing rules, than to address a perceived general wrong in society. What might appear to be a seemingly trivial infraction of the standing rules was often given an intense internal investigation by the governing body of the church and its appointed committees. This was true across several different denominations. Members perceived that the county and local ordinances would govern the ne'er-do-wells in the public domain outside the church. The church needed to take care of its own within its membership.

Americans during the mid–1800s believed "that God actively intervened in everyday affairs." One old-timer recalled, "It was God who sent you children, made the potatoes turn out well, put the blight on the orchard trees, and caused the roan mare to sicken and die."[2] If you attended church, were married or owned real estate, then you were respectable and perhaps honorable as well. Your acceptance as a creditable member of the community depended wholly on these factors. If you were single, being gainfully employed was expected. If you were a widow or a spinster school teacher, you had a suitable designation for a single woman. Since motherhood and teaching were regarded as comparable occupations, any other roles were completely below those two vocations on an acceptability scale.

This was the Calvinistic view of how to live one's life; it was the foundation of the theology in the Presbyterian and Congregational churches. The conviction was that God was at work in all realms of existence; God would govern all things; God's will was the cause of anything that happened. And, if you followed the teachings of the Bible, you would reap the rewards of the righteous. Consequently, when the Bible beseeched the Christian reader to "bring the poor that are cast out to thy house," the believer knew that "then shall thy light break forth as the morning, and thine health shall spring forth speedily ... the glory of the Lord shall be thy reward."[3] It followed that it was spiritually good for the church member to aid or harbor a fugitive slave.

Health was yet another issue, and the church used a moral approach to weigh in on that subject as well. There is a vast difference in America today regarding attitudes towards the value of good health compared to the beliefs of the mid-nineteenth century. For example, through both public education and consumer marketing campaigns, we are well aware that the use of alcohol and tobacco can lead to diseases and a possible early death.

Over 150 years ago, however, the argument against imbibing or smoking focused on a person's spiritual life, not his physical condition. If you smoked or drank, you were condemned by your fellow church members. "Opinion holders kept in mind the view of the long-term: They argued that these habits were evil vices which led down the path to hell. Everlasting damnation was a far more compelling argument than the threat of physical illness."[4]

By 1835, out on the western prairie, "almost before the new comers had got a roof over their heads; before the Indians had removed; before the first semblance of civil government had been established; the devoted missionaries of the Methodist church made their way into the country."[5] These tireless transient religious missionaries would gather "little audiences of eight or ten, wherever in grove, hut or shanty, they could be found, preached, prayed, sang hymns, and exhorted the new comers to found a community of Christian people, and amid the pressing cares of this, not to forget to prepare for ... immortal life."[6] Worship services had the effect of helping to keep the peace and promoting tranquility on the plains. Another added benefit was life after death.

In DeKalb County, Illinois, there existed a religious and philosophical backdrop on which was painted an overlay of the stigma of slavery — or maybe the atrocity of slavery was the backdrop on which was painted the overlay of religion. The sister sin of alcohol usage, no matter how infrequent, was the second pressing topic of the day. The subjects of temperance, the avoidance of or abstinence from alcohol, and slavery were often discussed together. They were each viewed by many as being evil and certainly anyone who partook in either activity would be eternally damned.

Across the nation, the temperance movement continued to grow as a cause célèbre. In her letter of February 23, 1842, Mary Hadley of Geneva, New York, writes to her friend Charlotte

F. Waterman in Sycamore, Illinois, about the thrill of a temperance demonstration in honor of George Washington's birthday:

> Day before yesterday the anniversary of Washington's birth, was a great day here — the TeeTotal Temperance Society & Societies of reformed inebriates from a number of the neighboring towns met the Societies of this place & after marching in long procession through most principal streets, with banner, & music, they assembled at several of the churches where they heard addresses appropriate to the occasion. A new movement is making [its way] in our eastern world in behalf of Temperance. The sweat of the effort in behalf of that class hitherto considered beyond all hope, is truly astonishing — Societies of reformed drunkards exist in almost every place — Very great changes in regard to the character of the people for Temperance ... is said to have recently taken place....[7]

A public exhibition of excitement among the citizenry pertaining to either the temperance or the antislavery movements was not yet evident in Northern Illinois, although in a religious setting under the auspices of a worship service, temperance and slavery were both matters for discussion. The local First Congregational Church in Sycamore recorded several such discussions during their meetings in 1844. They repeatedly used the words "temperance" and "slavery" in the same sentence, indicating the gravity of both subjects. Church members were concerned about the possibility of any member selling or drinking "intoxicating liquor as a beverage." They were equally concerned about "American slavery,"[8] although for several months temperance seemed to take precedence and slavery was sometimes mentioned as an afterthought.

Intemperance was considered a heinous sin of self-gratification. It was obvious to even the casual observer that a man could ruin his reputation, his family and his life by over-imbibing. By being intemperate, a person put his own needs before anyone else's. The entire antislavery movement further expanded the accepted view of the nature of sin. "Slavery, even more than intemperance, exemplified self-gratification — beyond sacrificing the needs of others, it appropriated the whole human being and turned the slave into an object whose whole purpose was to serve the desires of the master."[9] Therefore, slavery, like drinking intoxicating beverages, by association with self-indulgence was considered to be exceedingly sinful.

At First Congregational Church, Brother Asahel Stowe quickly learned about temperance and the folly of imbibing too much alcohol. Stowe was the father of Louisa (Stowe) Rose, and father-in-law to the esteemed Judge Jesse Rose of DeKalb County. An antislavery sympathizer, Jesse Rose subscribed to the *Western Citizen*. Asahel Stowe lived with Jesse and Louisa in their Sycamore home, along with his younger daughter, Louisa's sister Martha, and consequently may have been indebted to Judge Rose for his shelter in the frontier town. To his credit, Stowe enjoyed his own subscription to the same antislavery newspaper, which he undoubtedly read in the company of his extended family. He was one of 11 men who voluntarily consented to an 1848 tax assessment on his personal property to construct the new Congregational house of worship, which gave him a respected position in the community.

During the winter of 1844 the First Congregational Church appointed Asahel Stowe as a delegate to the Fox River Union, scheduled to meet in Elgin, Illinois, in January. The Fox River Union represented a loose association of member Congregational churches in the Fox River Valley area of northeastern Illinois. As an organization, it had no jurisdictional authority over the member churches, but provided an entity which would list member ministers and create opportunities for sharing ideas and problems. Another church member, Chauncey Rose, brother to Jesse Rose, was appointed as the alternate delegate.

Asahel may have attended the area meeting alone, or maybe Chauncey Rose accompanied him. No matter what the circumstances were on that particular trip in 1844, over the years, Asahel had occasion to make other similar sojourns, and somewhere along the way, someone witnessed Asahel partaking of alcohol. In December of 1849, the church minutes show this entry:

> The following communication was read to the Church, to wit "To the 1st Congregational Church in Sycamore Ill, Whereas it appears by common fame that our Brother Asahel Stowe has at different times, drank intoxicating liquors on the road to Chicago from this place — He is therefore requested to attend the next meeting of this Church & answer said charges."[10]

After presenting the communication, church Brothers Jesse C. Kellogg and David West quoted New Testament scripture: "For he shall be great in the sight of the Lord, and shall drink neither wine nor strong drink."[11] The two deacons then vouched for the fact that appropriate church procedures were being followed in addressing their "offending brother" Stowe.

> It was Voted, that Brethren C.M. Brown & Harry Martin be appointed a Committee to visit Brother Stowe & deliver him a copy of the above communication giving him reasonable time to prepare & make his defense at the next Church meeting.[12]

Caleb Marshall "Jersey" Brown and fellow church Brother Harry Martin, who were both antislavery men, comprised the committee of two and visited Asahel Stowe within the week. They personally delivered to Stowe a copy of the charges professed by the church body.

Instead of taking weeks or months to bring the issue to a conclusion, by the following Sunday, a repentant Stowe appeared at the worship service, ready to be relieved and forgiven of his sin: "Thereupon he arose in the meeting — admitted said charges to be true, expressed a penitential sorrow for having violated the Temperance rules of the Church, and his willingness to confess his error publickly [sic] as well as to the Church."[13]

> At the request of Brother Stowe, Voted, that the following be read in the public Congregation on the morrow by our Pastor: Viz "I hereby acknowledge that last summer I did make use of intoxicating liquor on the road to Chicago as has been commonly reported. That it was a violation of my covenant obligations to the Church of which I am a member, & that it was itself morrally [sic] wrong. I have no excuse to urge, but wish thus publickly [sic] to express my sincere regret & my determination to avoid the like offence in future.
> (Signed) Asahel Stowe"[14]

The Congregational members in attendance then "Voted that in consideration of the above confession that it is the duty of the Church to forgive the trespass of Brother Stowe & that he be discharged from further answering the charges herein preferred before the Church."[15] The entire incident all happened very swiftly. There was no room for further discussion or admonitions. Being the brother-in-law of a prominent judge in the county carried with it the burden of having to be above reproach in the administration of his own affairs. Judge Rose's political advice to Asahel to admit the wrong, apologize and move on allowed the congregation to quickly forgive and forget. Of course, we do not know what threats, if any, Judge Rose imparted to Stowe had he not confessed and asked for forgiveness immediately, but he was undoubtedly persuaded to publicly express the folly of his ways so as not to embarrass his own daughter and son-in-law.

In various printed historical biographies and obituaries, a deceased person was often touted as never having used tobacco or alcohol in his entire life. It was a badge of honor to have forever abstained from drinking alcohol. In contrast, the honor of public recognition for being antislavery was given only after the Civil War was over. Only then do we see included in biographical commentaries that the deceased was Republican and antislavery in his political beliefs.

Why did the people in DeKalb County abhor slavery? Why were they repulsed by the thought of someone among them, one of their neighbors perhaps, condoning slaveholding? They read the Bible. Antislavery sympathizers well understood the Biblical admonition, "Thou shalt not deliver unto his master the servant which is escaped from his master unto thee: He shall dwell with thee, even among you, in that place which he shall choose in one of thy gates, where it liketh him best; thou shalt not oppress him."[16]

The people of DeKalb County had no slaves of their own. Nor were there any freed slaves living among them. The answer lay in the churches. In this Northern Illinois county, their quiet practice of the abolition of slavery soon became a motivating force behind their religion, if not a religion in itself. Abolition did not initially drive the church; religious convictions were the primary force behind abolition. As the undercurrents of conflicting tides of interest and passion regarding slavery expanded, these unreasonable men and women — Abolitionists and antislavery advocates all — steadfastly believed that the hands of the Almighty One would guide them and their churches to act for the greater cause of human liberty.

CHAPTER 6

No Apologists for Slavery: The Congregationalists

We consider American Slavery a gross violation of the great laws of love, leading to an infraction of all the commandments.[1] — Minutes of June 30, 1844, First Congregational Church, Sycamore, Illinois

Practicing Puritanism

Congregationalists never strayed far from their Puritan roots in the mid–1800s. As practicing Puritans, they vehemently enforced the moral rules of greatest priority to their community. Consequently, the matter of temperance was initially a more demanding subject than that of American slavery. It affected them where they lived and it was a perceived moral issue over which they could exert a modicum of control. The problem of over imbibing was usually addressed directly with the people they already knew — their friends and neighbors; their fellow church members who subscribed to the same moral tenets. During the early years of its existence, the members of the First Congregational Church in Sycamore went about their business disciplining themselves to follow the edicts and code as they were taught by the fledgling religious society. They did not question the wisdom of their church elders; they knew that if they adhered to pure thoughts and acts, the way to heaven would be open to them. However, increasingly the problems inherent with drinking intoxicating beverages demanded further attention.

When Jabez H. Simons and his wife, Thurza, were accepted into membership at First Congregational in May of 1845, Mrs. Simons was "examined in relation to [her] religious experience [and] doctrinal views."[2] Jabez, however, was received as a member in good standing through a letter of transfer from the Presbyterian Church in Springville, Pennsylvania. Nothing was mentioned again about them in the minute books until a little over a year later in August of 1846. At that time, "The case of Brother J.H. Simons — who was reported to have purchased a quantity of Whiskey & to have dealt it out to persons in his employ during harvest, was brought before the Church for investigation."[3] A committee of three esteemed church members, consisting of Harry Martin, Aaron West and Charles Robinson, was appointed "to converse with Brother Simons with regard to this violation of our temperance rules & report at our next meeting."[4]

At some point during the fall or winter of 1846–47, the appointed committee met with

Simons to discuss the matter. Simons had perhaps already decided that there were too many rules to be followed and must have responded to the interrogation with comments similar to, "Yes, I gave my hired hands whisky during the fall harvest. After working all day in fields under the blazing sun, the men were hot and thirsty. What's wrong with a little cold beverage to sooth [sic] the tongue?" The church membership thought that plenty was amiss with that perceived irresponsible, immoral action.

Several months elapsed until the next meeting of the First Congregational Church Society, which occurred the following February 6, 1847, when the investigative committee reported the following: The Messrs. Martin, West and Robinson "visited Brother Simons & endeavored in Christian faithfulness to point out to him his error. He admits the charge as correct but thinks he has done no wrong. [He believes he] has done nothing which ought to offend his brethren in the Church."[5]

However, Puritanical forces were at work, and the Congregational Society voted to send a letter to Jabez:

> Dear Brother:
> Whereas it has been represented to the Church, that you are reported to have purchased a quantity of whiskey and to have dealt it out to persons in your employ during the last harvest; And Whereas Brethren Harry Martin A.C. West & Charles Robinson, have been appointed a Committee to converse with you in relation to this alleged violation of our temperance Rules who have Reported, that they have visited you and endeavored in Christian faithfulness to point out to you your Error that you admitted that the Report as correct, but thought you had done no wrong — had done nothing which ought to offend your brethren in the Church; And Whereas the Church, upon the adoption of the Report of this Committee, unanimously expressed a desire to extend to [you] further opportunity & every reasonable facility for exculpating yourself from blame, in the premises, according to your own admission;
> Therefore, you are earnestly requested to attend the next monthly meeting of the Church ... for that purpose[6]

The church members also voted unanimously that Jabez Simons make a public confession of his transgression and admit that he committed a grievous wrongdoing by offering alcoholic beverages to employees. Because he was steadfast in his sin against the church regulations, he would be punished.

But Jabez H. Simons did not think he had sinned. In his estimation, he had done nothing wrong. Simons stood against the rules of the local church and in doing so, he demonstrated that he would think for himself to decide if a regulation or law was appropriate to govern his own behavior. He was an unreasonable man.

The Simons issue was not an isolated incident within church communities during the mid–1800s. Jabez Simons personified the mental toughness of those men who were hardened in their convictions of right and wrong; of what could and could not be tolerated in society. This raises a puzzling question: was organized religion itself no more tolerant in the New World than in Europe? The Puritans fled from the Old World religious persecution against them and slowly evolved into Bible-toting rule-makers, with the reformation of a new nation as their objective.

Puritan Evolution

Congregationalism in the United States traces its beginnings to the Pilgrims, who brought Puritanism to the New World during the mid–1600s. One group of Protestant reformers, called

Separatists, was especially radical in their approach to religion, acknowledging equal rights and equal responsibilities for members of their congregation. By 1620, a group of these Separatists were among the passengers who sailed on the *Mayflower* from Plymouth, England, to America, where they founded Plymouth Colony. It was an organized religious community with a democratic form of self-government.

Although all Pilgrims were not Puritans, Puritan congregations in New England molded the entire organization of each community, both socially and politically. Puritans dominated the religious and political life of the communities. Town meetings only allowed male church members to vote. In order to become a church member, one first needed the minister's consent. The same precepts of Puritanism prevailed as the population grew westward and later became dominant in Northern Illinois.

Preferring the idea of no church hierarchy, with each individual congregation being self-governing, the Puritans eventually adopted Congregationalism. "Congregationalism ... [regarded] church authority as inherent in each group."[7]

"If an individual did not conform [to the rules of the local church], he was at liberty to go elsewhere."[8] And go elsewhere they did. Jabez and Thurza Simons were unlike their fellow church member, Asahel Stowe, who had familial and political ties to other members. Stowe quickly repented his wrongdoing so as not to embarrass his brother-in-law, Judge Jesse Rose. Mr. and Mrs. Simons, however, never again attended a worship service at the First Congregational Church in Sycamore and were officially excommunicated by the end of 1849. By the next Census in 1850, the Simons and their six children had moved to neighboring Lee County, Illinois, and so did not completely disappear from the local scene. Both Jabez and Thurza are buried in East Paw Paw Cemetery in Paw Paw Township, DeKalb County.

When one church did not satisfy, the pioneers required and sought another. Across the new West, a patchwork of Congregational and various other denominational churches emerged as the population increased and moved to the newly opened western frontier, sometimes called the "Middle West" of the United States.

Beginning in Ohio in 1788, Congregational churches were organized throughout the old Northwest Territory as settlers moved westward. Unlike other denominations, the Congregationalists never established a foothold in the southern United States. This alone became extremely important with increasing support for antislavery thinking. As a result of their geographic growth throughout the North, the Congregationalists never experienced a split in the church over the slavery issue. From the beginning, there was never a strong proslavery faction within the national denomination. They were fundamentally of one mind on the subject; they were definitively antislavery and believed that God was on their side.

The denomination's absence of a proslavery attitude can be traced to economics and politics, as well as its strong Puritan background. In the Midwestern United States, Congregational settlements "lay in areas adjacent to the Lakes rather than to the Mississippi and Ohio rivers." Consequently, according to Congregational historians, "their strongest economic ties were developed by wheat and flour with the East rather than by corn and pork to the South. Congregational concentration was coincident with the portions of these states where Republicanism first became strong."[9]

In fact, "of all the major denominations, Congregationalism alone was confined to the area north of the Mason-Dixon Line."[10] Congregationalism, therefore, "did not have to deal with the sin of slavery among its own communicants, and could therefore well afford to be more ruthless in its condemnation of the evil."[11] They mercilessly condemned the sin of slavery, not only through their state church associations, but within the local membership, as we shall see.

Congregationalists Organize

After 1834, Easterners who were impatient to seek their fortunes in the great Northwest Territory began to arrive in Northern Illinois via the Erie Canal to the Great Lakes, as well as by overland passage with wagons and oxen or horses. They passed through Chicago, which was only a cluster of log houses situated around Ft. Dearborn, to claim the land farther west for their own. This was the frontier where wolves routinely killed domestic poultry. As one travels from the East, Sycamore is more directly in line on the route from Chicago, whereas the city of DeKalb is slightly south and farther west. Consequently, Sycamore was settled first and became more heavily populated than DeKalb. In 1840, the entire population of DeKalb County, Illinois, was 1,697. By 1850, Sycamore Township alone had a total population of 978. In contrast, DeKalb Township had only about half as many people, with a total population of 486.[12] There were no slaves listed in either the 1840 or the 1850 Census for DeKalb County. Because the center of the population growth was in Sycamore, it was logical that the seat of government and commerce begin there. DeKalb was not even considered originally when the local leaders argued about where the center of government should be. Other areas in contention included Coltonville (at the present intersection of North First Street and Coltonville Road), Brush Point (at the intersection of Five Points and Pleasant Hill Roads in Mayfield Township) and Sycamore. Situated at the north end of DeKalb Township, the residents in the small settlement of Coltonville tended to gravitate towards Sycamore for commerce and society. Coltonville ceased to be a viable town shortly after the Civil War, and Brush Point never grew into an established area. Neither was DeKalb in the running for the organization of a Congregational church. Only Sycamore achieved that honor at the time.

The First Congregational Church in Sycamore, Illinois, was the vanguard in the local antislavery movement. Specific actions by the Congregationalists soon sounded the antislavery call to Abolitionists in DeKalb County and blatantly ignored the governing civil law of the time. Twenty-five years after the end of the Civil War, when the First Congregational Church in Sycamore celebrated 50 years of its existence, a longtime member was given the task of reviewing the original minutes. That anonymous person wrote that those recorded minutes were "as devoid of interest as a potato field."[13] A contemporary examination of those same recorded minutes reveals the exact opposite.

The Federated Church in Sycamore today is the successor to that original First Congregational Church. Research in the church archives clearly illustrates the early church's interpretation of its own theology and is rife with examples of how perceived sins against the church were handled. Judgments on the sins of intemperance, infidelity, profanity and Sabbath desecration were delivered promptly. Rising to a prominent place above all sins was the heinous sin of slaveholding.

On April 11, 1840, a small group of eleven dedicated people met in Sycamore together with a four-man ecclesiastical committee.[14] There were four men and seven women, including the 70-year-old organizing minister, James Mackie, and his wife, Susan. The potential new members were Jesse C. Kellogg; Jesse Rose; Erastus Hamlin and his wife, Harriet, plus three of the Hamlin's daughters, Harriet Hamlin Williams, Caroline Hamlin and Mary Ann Hamlin; Mrs. Rebecca McCollum; and Mrs. Caroline Colton. Original church record books add Dr. Horatio F. Page to the list, creating a total of 12 original members. As the clerk of the Church Society, Jesse Kellogg charitably listed his wife, Phoebe, as well as Louisa Rose, wife of new member Judge Jesse Rose, as being charter affiliates of the group. Other church records, however, indicate that the two women did not officially join until 1853 and 1855, respectively.[15] Kellogg's intentions were admirable and the ladies may have wished to be included, but perhaps their official letters of transfer from their previous churches were not received in time. The total number of original members stands at twelve.

Members of the organizing ecclesiastical council included the Rev. Nathaniel C. Clark from Elgin, who was often called "the father of Congregationalism in Northern Illinois,"[16] and was himself an original member of the Kane County Antislavery Society. Clark was responsible for organizing thirty-four churches throughout the Fox River area. Other members of this specially appointed committee were the Rev. Ebenezer Brown, Hamilton Norton, who was a delegate from the Byron Congregational Church, and the Rev. James Mackie, who became the occasional preacher for the new church until their first official minister was hired. Foreshadowing the times to come, three of the five new male church members would soon be subscribers to the new abolitionist newspaper, the *Western Citizen*: Jesse C. Kellogg, Horatio F. Page and Jesse Rose. In addition to being among the first settlers in town, these men already enjoyed local prominence in the small community. Kellogg was the first clerk of the County Court, Page was the first physician in town, and Rose was a county judge. Consequently, the newly formed religious group was easily given permission to convene regularly in the new DeKalb County courthouse. This unassuming wood frame building stood on the south side of the muddy road named State Street, facing what is today the permanent courthouse square. Their sole intent and common purpose was to organize a Congregational church and church society in Sycamore. Dividing the ecclesiastical responsibilities from the administrative duties, the church oversaw the worship service and other religious activities, and the church society was the governing business body with officers and committees. The same people were members of both entities.

According to Henry Boies in his *History of DeKalb County*, when the First Congregational Church initially organized in 1840, Sycamore was considered a "dreary, little village [which] consisted of a dozen houses, scattered over considerable land,"[17] with no fences and only one well. Church members lived in "log cabins with shake roof and puncheon [rough timber] floors, heated from the fireplace and lighted with the tallow candle."[18] In her memoirs of Women's Fellowship at the First Congregational Church, Elizabeth Wood, wrote, "Coming from Eastern homes of beauty and comfort the contrast was startling and often disheartening. Their dwellings were small and poor."[19] Rhoda "Elizabeth" (Richards) Wood was the stepdaughter of church member and antislavery proponent Dr. Ellsworth Rose. As the wife of Abolitionist Henry Wood, she was also a sister-in-law to one of the church founders, Jesse C. Kellogg, whose wife was Henry's sister, the former Phoebe Wood.

Nationally, Congregationalists already had a reputation for being antislavery. As early as November 1836, Illinois Congregationalists went on record at their own state association meeting, where they condemned slavery as a sin, called for its speedy abolition, and "commended those who despite persecution and obloquy [verbal abuse against them] devoted their entire energies to the cause of emancipation."[20] Further, the Illinois Congregational Association resolved that if a minister or church member was a slaveholder, he could not be admitted "to our Pulpits and communion tables."[21]

Strangely, when they created their original Articles of Faith for the new Sycamore church, the small self-appointed committee did not mention any condemnation of slavery. The cause of human liberty was indeed in the hands of God and was expected to work through the hands of man. One of the men who helped guide the early church was the Rev. David I. Perry, who was its first resident minister and "commenced laboring with the church as a gospel Minister"[22] in 1841, continuing until 1843.

The original Articles of Faith written by the organizing members of the First Congregational Church were quite basic and included a belief in one God, in the Bible as the word of God, and in the Trinity, as laid out in the first three articles:

1. We believe, that there is but one God, the Creator, Preserver, and moral Governor of the universe; a Being of infinite power, Knowledge, wisdom, justice, goodness, and truth; the Self existent, independent and immutable Fountain of good.
2. We believe, that the Scriptures of the Old and New Testaments were given by inspiration of God; that they are profitable for doctrine, for correction, for reproof, and for instruction in righteousness; and that they are our only rule of doctrinal belief, and religious practice.
3. We believe, that the mode of Divine existence is such, as lays a foundation for a distinction into three persons, the Father, the Son, and the Holy Ghost, and that these three are one in essence, and equal in power and glory.[23]

Article No. 2 hints at the very reasons why the church was so adamantly antislavery in its beliefs and opinions. The scriptures which constitute the Holy Bible were considered as "given by inspiration of God," and as such were "the only rule of doctrinal belief and religious practice." The Congregationalists' antislavery foundation came from the Bible. They resolutely recited, "And he that stealeth a man and selleth him, or if he be found in his hand, he shall surely be put to death."[24] The Bible was God's law. Congregationalism "had its birth in the conviction which seized upon a number of conscientious, sincere, and zealous souls, that slavery was forbidden by the Bible, and therefore a sin."[25]

Additionally, Article No. 16 revealed one of the primary differences between the Congregationalists and the soon-to-arrive Universalists: "We believe, that all mankind must one day stand before the judgment seat of Christ to receive a just and final sentence of retribution, according to the deeds done in the body; and that at the day of judgment the state of all will be unalterably fixed; and that the punishment of the wicked, and the happiness of the righteous will be endless."[26]

A professed belief in the endless "punishment of the wicked" hinted at the Congregationalist belief in a hell. In contrast, the Universalist denomination, with whom the Congregationalists would eventually merge locally, did not believe hell existed.

Church membership increased as the young settlement continued to grow. By 1844, the local citizens were thriving and built more comfortable homes. There was less discussion of returning to their old homes in the eastern states. By this time, seven years after the first pioneers came to Sycamore, people thought of DeKalb County as home. More enthusiastic settlers arrived each month in Northern Illinois, and the open prairie and dense forests of the old Northwest Territory were tamed.

David West Reaches His Destination

The First Congregational Church minutes record book reflects that a certain enthusiastic settler, one Deacon David West, his wife Sarah, and daughter Alice, presented a letter of transfer from Evans Centre Congregational Church, Erie County, New York on February 24, 1844.[27]

Joining the Congregational Church in Sycamore was of primary importance. The church was West's reason for being. The church was a personal vehicle for his own fervent belief to correct the wrongs he saw in society. David West was definitely a man who viewed "abolition as a sacred vocation."[28] Antislavery as a moral issue was an important focus in his life, and the task of raising the consciousness regarding slavery in his beloved Congregational church was an equally important outgrowth of that focus.

Deacon David West knew that other members of the fledgling church came from New York and Vermont, and he was aware of the predominant feelings of those individuals against slavery. Many had already been exposed to a type of evangelicalism which provided that "salvation demands not merely faith and divine grace, but also good works."[29] The "good works" included activity in the Underground Railroad.

The area in Western New York where West had lived was home to numerous well-known Abolitionists. "Of the fifteen top and high-ranking abolitionist leaders, all resided either in the 'burned-over' district or in other areas which experienced major revivals; all were intensely and actively religious."[30] West was a product of the evangelical Second Great Awakening. His own personal experiences as a young adult in New York State were the foundation for his passion. The time was ripe. The time was now. West could not wait until the next year to begin his work for the downtrodden. Slavery must end now! Immediate emancipation! This was the cry of a true immediatist abolitionist, and David West was indeed that. He was compelled to physically help the fugitive slave escape from bondage. He remembered the words of Isaiah: "Make thy shadow as the night in the midst of the noonday; hide the outcasts; betray not him that wandereth."[31] Deacon David West resolved to be an Underground Railroad conductor.

People in DeKalb County eagerly learned about the antislavery movement with each issue of the *Western Citizen*. Over 500 subscribed regularly to the abolitionist paper and its successor, the *Free West*. They devoured the antislavery editorials and participated vicariously in the experiences of other Abolitionists. This was the largest concentration of readers in the entire state of Illinois. And the DeKalb County antislavery advocates were not content to stand on the sidelines and merely read about abolition activities. What they perceived as a moral issue deserved more than cursory attention. Initially these self-made friends of freedom were motivated by their profound religious antislavery beliefs, exhibited in their choice of Christian church membership in the local Congregational or Presbyterian denominations. Soon, they publicly sought political change, as witnessed by their involvement in the Liberty and Free-Soil political parties. They were very active members in the religious bodies that did not tolerate slavery. And privately, the good citizens of DeKalb County turned their houses and barns into safehouses for runaway slaves. Isaiah's words echoed through their minds.

Historians are sometimes quick to place people and events into neat little categories years after the fact. Scholars are careful to note a technical difference between antislavery sympathizers and true abolitionists. To reiterate, all Abolitionists were antislavery, but all antislavery defenders were not Abolitionists. However, in researching the Sycamore people involved, there is the distinct impression that the terms "antislavery" and "abolition" were oftentimes used interchangeably. They thought that if they were against slavery, it followed logically that they were Abolitionists. When they advertised their antislavery meetings in the *Western Citizen*, they publicly put out a call for all Abolitionists to attend.[32] This could be why so many people were listed as Abolitionists in both printed historical biographical sources and later in their own obituaries. If you were antislavery and lived in DeKalb County, then you were an Abolitionist.

The DeKalb County Abolitionists were not of the militant type as personified by the fiery William Lloyd Garrison or the sometimes violent John Brown. Minus the rough fury, it was easier for them to consider "antislavery" and "abolition" as being the same. Some individuals simply read the abolitionist newspapers, the *Western Citizen* or the *New York Evangelist*, Charles Finney's publication which reported the activities of antislavery societies. Still, they considered themselves Abolitionists and not merely antislavery sympathizers. At this time, David West maintained membership in the Free-Soil Party that postulated there should be no further expansion of slavery into any new territories acquired by the United States. Politically, that would have initially classified him only as an anti-expansionist. However, his growing abolitionist thinking created an internal turmoil that ultimately caused him to renounce the Free-Soil Party platform in favor of the emerging Republican Party's policy of antislavery. Ten years later, when that new political group organized, he was one of the official delegates from the Free-Soil Party to the convention that created the Republican Party in Illinois.

Yet, the first overt act Deacon David West committed in Illinois as an antislavery sympathizer and Abolitionist was to join the First Congregational Church. The pervading feeling among religious evangelicals during this period was to always place the church as a top priority. What does the Bible say about a man's actions? How would God interpret your innermost thoughts? What is the minister going to say on Sunday at the worship service to address the issues of the day? A large amount of personal guilt entered into the assessment. Am I going to get into heaven? What if I believe it is legal to hold slaves? For good Christians, what the church taught and thought always came first.

Early Church Services

In 1844, the church body did not meet every week. Sometimes, depending on the weather, worship services were not even held every month. This was true in most rural churches served by an itinerant circuit rider minister, no matter what the denominational affiliation. Changing weather sometimes made it difficult for a man to travel on horseback to each of his appointed mission stations on a timely basis.

It was not easy for church members living on scattered farms to physically make the trip into a town center for the worship services. In Sycamore, Illinois, the Kishwaukee River, was occasionally too high and church members themselves were unable to traverse into town at the appointed time. The South Branch of the Kishwaukee River, meandering through the entire county, has always created seasonal problems. The original center of the town of Sycamore was just north of where it exists today, next to the Kishwaukee River. Of course, the river was important to the early pioneers, as well as to the Potawatomie Indians who camped near the river. Of necessity, the founding fathers determined to find the highest elevation, and in 1837 abandoned the river site and moved the town to where the courthouse square still exists. A hickory pole stuck into the ground in the center of the platted town indicated the center of Sycamore and the site of the seat of justice.[33]

Unlike towns bordering major rivers in downstate Illinois, DeKalb County did not have the advantage of being close to the great Mississippi or Ohio Rivers. As a result, it was not immediately considered an obvious gateway to freedom for the fugitive slave. However, the geographic proximity of DeKalb County to Lake Michigan and available water transportation through the Great Lakes to Canada gave this mid–northern Illinois area an inherent value in the run for liberty. It became part of the funnel through which unknown numbers of runaway slaves traveled, following the overland route from the Mississippi River border town of Alton to Princeton in Bureau County, through DeKalb County and points east. Sometimes of necessity the route varied, coming from the south up through LaSalle County. Unusually, the Kishwaukee River in DeKalb County actually runs north. Most rivers in the entire Northern Hemisphere run south to the equator. But the Kishwaukee runs north. What a symbol! What better place to become a catalyst for the area antislavery movement? Unfortunately there is no proof that the DeKalb branch of the northern-flowing Kishwaukee was used as a means of transportation in the Underground Railroad. All anecdotal evidence points to overland routes as the mode of choice. And David West's house and barn were located on the main road heading east towards

Opposite: **Map of 1860 Underground Railroad showing routes funneling to Lake Michigan at Chicago, originally used in 1898 by William H. Siebert.**

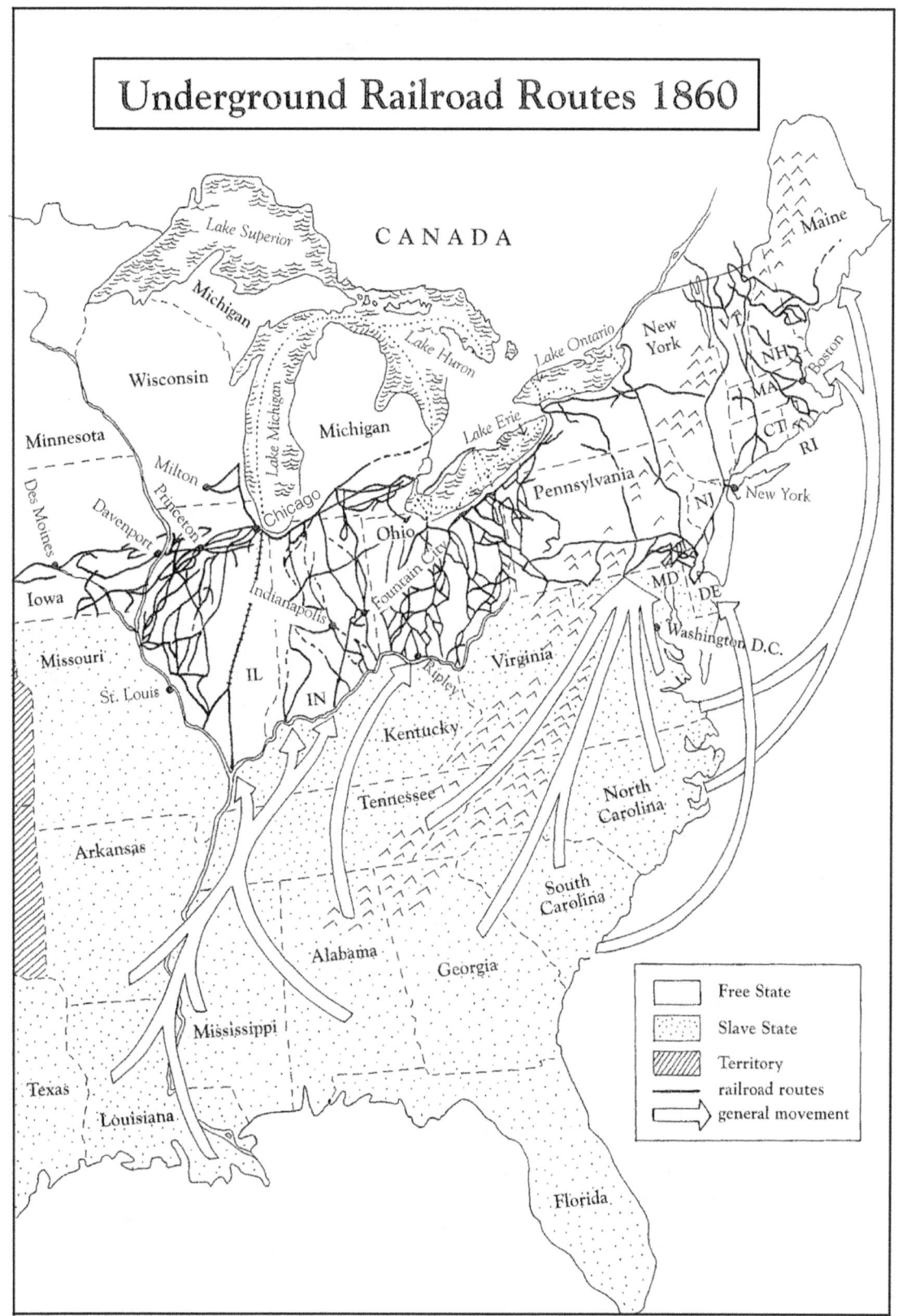

Chicago. It is likely that David West created the actual Underground Railroad route between DeKalb and Kane counties, between Sycamore and St. Charles.

First Antislavery Resolution Introduced

David West's brother Aaron was already a member of the First Congregational Church. According to the minute books, at that same February 1844 meeting of the church body, his brother Aaron West "presented certain Resolutions in relation to the vending and use of intoxicating liquor as a beverage." And, almost as an afterthought, the church's clerk added to his report, "also concerning American Slavery."[34] "After some discussion [they] Voted to defer further consideration of said Resolutions until the next Meeting of the Church."[35] The church members apparently wanted to thoroughly weigh the importance of the temperance and slavery resolutions.

David West arrived from New York embodying the revivalism of the religious Great Awakening recently experienced in the Burned-over District. He was an open admirer of the extreme Abolitionist and Congregational minister, Vermont's own Beriah Green. Green lectured widely in western New York, and David West possibly heard him present his 1836 sermon in Whitesboro, only a few miles from West's home. Green spoke about "Things for Northern Men to Do" about slavery. This was Green's "most widely disseminated antislavery essay" and directed an "accusatory finger at northerners themselves."[36] Green admonished his audience to first of all "thoroughly examine and freely discuss the whole subject of American Slavery." Second, "regard the enslaved as the children of our common Father, Saviour, and Sanctifier." The Rev. Green continued by suggesting that people "become familiar with the history of emancipation" and "entreat and rebuke the South." And lastly, "petition to abolish slavery in the District of Columbia" and "dissolve connections with pro-slavery churches."[37] All these items could not be accomplished at once, but David West started at the beginning of Green's list by helping to raise the subject of slavery as a discussion issue within the Sycamore First Congregational Church.

And so it was during the church society meeting where David West was accepted into membership at the Congregational Church, that West's brother Aaron, already a trusted and respected member of the congregation, introduced the subject of slavery. Had they discussed their proposed action over dinner the previous evening? Was there a predetermined design in this action on the part of David and Aaron West? Were they purposefully introducing a New York antislavery position into DeKalb County, Illinois? The answers seem obviously affirmative.

The Colonization of Illinois

The identical New England Congregational and Presbyterian influences which transformed David West in New York were now having their affect in Illinois. Back in Oneida County, New York, the foremost Presbyterian minister, Dr. George Washington Gale, founded the Oneida Institute. Gale had persuaded the Oneida Presbytery of the "New School" [antislavery] Presbyterians to "embark upon an educational enterprise."[38] The Oneida Institute's goal was to educate young men of limited financial means who intended to become evangelistic ministers. They were required to perform manual labor at the institute to help support their education. What began as the simple education of ministers became, during the evangelistic Great Revival, the education of radical abolitionists.

From the Oneida Institute, groups of three or four men purposefully headed to the Illinois frontier specifically to "colonize" the land. With money supplied by New York philanthropists sympathetic to the education of ministers and the abolitionist cause, they would purchase an entire township of land at the government price of $1.25 per acre. Five acres would be set aside for an educational institution. After the lots in the township were sold to incoming settlers intending to live in the colony, part of the profit would be given to start the new college, and the remainder would be used to start yet another colony, "until the whole western country was supplied with the means of obtaining a good Christian education."[39] Within a seventy-mile radius of Galesburg, Illinois, there were approximately 15 such colonies, plus numerous "missionary stations."[40]

Today Knox College and Monmouth College in Illinois still exist as monuments to this colonization plan. Both were products of the colonization resulting from the eastern Abolitionist master plan. Like the others, the Geneseo Colony north of Galesburg, in Geneseo, Illinois, was charged to "go to Illinois for the sake of Christ, establish a manual labor school and foster temperance and the principle of antislavery."[41] There was another colony even closer to DeKalb County, at the junction of the Kishwaukee and Rock Rivers just south of Rockford, Illinois, but it did not prosper. Interestingly, the city of Sycamore and greater DeKalb County were never chosen as a place for a "manual labor school." Next to Sycamore, neighboring DeKalb Center, as it was called, was not as well populated in 1844 and would have to wait until 1895 to become the site for the Northern Illinois State Normal School, which today is Northern Illinois University.

West's Perseverance

David and Aaron West were undeterred by the lack of a manual labor school in DeKalb County. It mattered not to them that they did not have an official charge from either the Presbyterians or the Congregationalists to foster temperance and the principle of antislavery. What mattered to David West was how he felt personally about the evils of slavery, and he convinced brother Aaron to think and act accordingly. Subsequent to the introduction of the initial resolution supported by the West brothers, the First Congregational Church Society met again in March 1844, and decided to first adopt a major standing rule which included their belief that the church was the final adjudicator in deciding what was right and wrong. They passed an extreme omnibus rule which gave themselves the right to create any future rules on whatever subject they deemed appropriate: "Resolved: That the position of every church in a community should be right & well defined on all great moral questions that agitate the public."[42] Even card-playing and dancing would later come under the official jurisdiction of the local church edicts.

The second rule passed that day was a temperance resolution. They resolved that selling intoxicating liquor or using it as a beverage was considered a "public sin against God, and consequently a disciplinable offence when committed by a church member."[43] This was the first step in convincing the membership to publicly acknowledge the gravity of the various sins being committed throughout the land. The other two remaining resolutions pertaining to slavery were tabled a second time.

Congregationalists have always been a grassroots organization, with church polity allowing members to have full control over what they do and say within the local churches. Then, as now, edicts did not come from a higher authority or church government to be subsequently passed down to the community churches. Local congregations always retained control and voted on each matter. In fact, during the 1800s they voted on everything! Were you rude to someone in public? They voted that you must make a public confession of your sins. Did you neglect your duty to worship regularly? They voted to suspend you from membership. "The congregation's elders and ministers [had] the power to sit in judgment on the character and faith of their neighbors."[44] No further discussion was allowed.

There was a proscribed procedure to follow regarding any infraction of the church's rules. First, the charges were made in writing and brought before the church society. Following the written charges, a committee was appointed to "enquire into the propriety of the church's taking further action in a matter."[45] If that committee found that the charges warranted a full investigation, then an additional committee was appointed to conduct the investigation or "trial." The accused and the accuser could testify and present witnesses on their behalf, after which the investigating committee reported back to the church society and made their recommendations.

That is the way it happened for the independent Dr. Page.

The Matter of Dr. Horatio Franklin Page

After practicing medicine in Genoa for about a year, Dr. Horatio Franklin Page moved in 1839 to Sycamore, where he lived in the new Mansion House. Built by Captain Eli Barnes, the edifice was the first stick construction building erected in the village. All previous structures were of the log cabin type of construction. The Mansion House served as a tavern and hotel and was the "great center of population" and "crowded with occupants"[46] John and Charles Waterman, both brothers to local pioneer woman Charlotte Waterman, kept a sort of general

The "Mansion House," a tavern and hotel for travelers and boarders, was the first stick construction in Sycamore, Illinois. Located on the northeast corner of current State Route 64 and Route 23 (State Street and Main Street) on the site of the present Sycamore Public Library.

store in one corner of the building. Their business was originally located north of the center of Sycamore on the north side of the Kishwaukee River. When the center of town was officially moved south of the river, the Watermans moved with it. Many young men hoping to make their fortunes in the new West boarded at the Mansion House. They were characterized as being a carefree group

> as full of pranks and fun, and practical jokes, as ever a dozen wild fellows could have been. For some [unknown] reason the hotel came to be called the Nunnery, and went by that name for many years. It was a most inappropriate title as there was nothing more like a nun about it than the one hired girl in the kitchen. Indeed, there were but three marriageable women in the place, and when dances and parties were made, the country for twenty miles around was scoured in search of lady partners.[47]

With no marriageable women available, Horatio Page soon went back to Massachusetts to claim a wife. He married Eliza A. Pratt in Pittsfield in 1849. They subsequently returned to Sycamore, where he continued to practice medicine for a total of 34 years until three months before his death in 1873.

We know that Horatio and Eliza Page were always ready to accept wayfaring strangers and runaway slaves into their home at any time of the day or night. Evidence exists of one instance sometime during 1850. As the first physician to practice medicine in Sycamore and first president of the DeKalb County Medical Society, Dr. Page had a certain degree of public credibility and recognition. On November 5, 1850, the Federal Census enumerator knocked at his door. The Page home was located in town, at approximately 307 N. Main Street. Page owned several lots in that area and constructed a small house on the property where the historic Charles O. Boynton mansion was later built.

The census taker elicited the usual information about the head of the household, which shows that H.F. Page was a 38-year-old white male physician, born in Massachusetts, with $2,000 worth of real estate. Eliza Page, age 29, was a white female also born in Massachusetts. Then the inquirer asked the questions about any other members of the household. After hearing "No" to the query "Do you have any children?," the census taker would have asked, "Does anyone else live with you?" Imagine the enumerator's surprise when the Pages responded in the affirmative with, "John Shepherd, a black male." When asked to supply information about whether or not the 17-year-old Shepherd attended school during the past year, the Pages would have answered that Shepherd was a student. They blatantly included Shepherd within their family group in order to give him some legitimacy in the eyes of the government. Horatio Page was deliberately open and apparently unashamed of his participation in the Underground Railroad movement.

In Sycamore, Illinois, and in all of DeKalb County, there was no fugitive slave community or free black population. The entire 1850 Federal Census shows only one black in DeKalb County, and that person is John Shepherd, the youthful "student" living with Dr. Horatio F. Page and his wife in Sycamore. Dr. Page is one of the identified Abolitionists. He, along with hundreds of others in DeKalb County, subscribed to the *Western Citizen*. The possibility that Shepherd may have been a runaway slave was thereby publicly acknowledged. When the census taker returned in 1860, Shepherd was no longer listed in DeKalb County. He would have been 27 years old. One cannot help but wonder if Shepherd indeed followed the underground path to freedom. We do not know where he went, but ten years previous he was openly included by the Pages in their family unit for census purposes, which provided the black teen some measure of safety from exposure.

Before his antislavery views became so barefaced, five years before his marriage to Eliza, Dr. Page personally endured the indignation of the Puritan philosophies within his chosen

Christian denomination. In March 1844, he was openly charged in front of the First Congregational Church Society with several counts, including lying about being asked to invite another physician to consult with a patient. The accusing physician, Dr. Ellsworth Rose, was also a member of the First Congregational Church, and it was Rose who personally alleged the charges against Page.

The second charge against Horatio Page was "unchristian conduct" based on allegedly "collaring Dr. Rose in a public place and threatening personal violence — using at the same time language unbecoming a Christian."[48] One wonders exactly what the esteemed doctor said.

Another charge claimed that the medicine Dr. Rose administered to a sick boy in Sycamore was different from what was originally prescribed by Dr. Page. The church committee decided that they were "not prepared intelligently to decide whether there was what would be called by medical men a change in the treatment."[49]

Why did Dr. Rose bring these grievances against Dr. Page? On the surface, they seemed to have a lot in common. They were colleagues; they were both physicians. They were both antislavery men and both subscribed to the abolitionist newspaper, the *Western Citizen.* They were members of a local denomination with exceptionally strong antislavery sentiment. In 1843, Dr. Rose was only the second doctor after Dr. Page to begin practicing medicine in DeKalb County, and Rose became the second president of the DeKalb County Medical Society after Page's tenure. Rose was just one year older than Page, so the possibility that Rose felt wiser because of his age seems unlikely. Maybe Ellsworth Rose felt that his education at Willoughby Medical College in Ohio and subsequent practice in Erie County, New York, was superior to Page's training in Massachusetts. Perhaps their individual egos collided with Puritan Congregational ethics, thereby creating the impasse.

A month later, in April 1844, it was determined by the investigating committee, and voted upon by the congregation, that the nature of Horatio Page's offense (lying and unchristian conduct) required a public confession which could be done either orally or in writing. The lying charge was ultimately not sustained.[50] Curiously enough, at that same meeting, Horatio's older brother, Austin Page, was received into membership. Dr. Page understood the internal church political battle confronting him and wanted to stack the deck by securing yet another member willing to vote in his favor. After a year, brother Austin Page's membership would be terminated "for absenting himself from our meetings and communions for the year past."[51] He served his familial purpose and probably wanted no further obligation to the church.

Additionally, at that same previous meeting in March 1844, the "Resolutions concerning American slavery"[52] were brought forward for a vote and tabled to be considered at the next church meeting. It is material to recognize that even in a professed antislavery church, it was of greater local importance to address the perceived pressing personal sins of congregation members, rather than to immediately consider the much larger sin of slavery that affected the entire nation. The Horatio Page matter took precedence and the slavery resolutions did not receive much attention in the transcribed minutes, appearing almost as an afterthought. The matter of unchristian conduct involving an errant member was of far more provincial significance than a discussion of slavery or the church's position relative to slavery. The West brothers, David and Aaron, were possibly having some difficulty convincing the membership of the immediacy of addressing the slavery issue. Abolitionism was not always an easy sale, even to professed Christians.

Brother Page's infractions were duly adjudicated. According to the church minutes from June 1844, we read:

> Whereas, the church having patiently & impartially investigated the case decided that the said charge be sustained: And that Bro Page be required to make a public confession, either verbally or in writing; and Whereas, Bro. Page having been duly lectured with, has refused to comply with

this reasonable decision, although he admits the wrong, Therefore Resolved: that Bro Page be & he hereby is suspended from Church communion & privileges, till he give satisfactory evidence of repentance by a public confession.[53]

The Congregational Church Society gave him a year to repent, but by April 1845, Horatio Page was excommunicated. Church members said that because

> he has not only refused to make a public confession of his fault but has also continuously absented himself from our stated and occasional meetings and neglected his Covenant duties for more than a year, therefore resolved: that he be excluded from our church Communion & fellowship as a disorder by member — And that this resolution be publickly [sic] read by our pastor on the coming Sabbath.[54]

And that is how they handled a transgression of church ordinances in the mid–1800s. Strange that the same Puritans, who originally left their European homeland because they believed they had a right to dissent from the church's beliefs, were now passing judgment on someone who would challenge an individual's right to dissent from a church's rules. The Puritan ethic was alive and well in the First Congregational Church in Sycamore, Illinois, and although ten years later Horatio F. Page moved his church membership to St. Peter's Episcopal Church in Sycamore when it organized in 1855, in his heart he must have remained a Congregationalist. Almost 25 years after his death, he was still credited with being a member of the Congregational Church, Republican in politics, and "a straightforward man."[55]

No Apologists for Slavery

According to the minutes of church meetings of the First Congregational Church in Sycamore, "Owing to a storm of rain and the state of the roads, church did not meet on the last Sabbath in May," 1844.[56] After the determination in the Horatio Page matter, church members assembled again on June 30, and through the courtesy of fellow member and DeKalb County recorder Deacon Jesse Churchill Kellogg, they once again met in the DeKalb County courthouse. Both the Congregationalists and the Universalists "held alternate or occasional services there."[57] Later, the Methodists were also given permission to use the courthouse, and each denomination paid $15.00 per year for that privilege. The two-story frame building was 20' by 30' and enclosed according to the building specifications. It did have a "roof and some siding upon it, but there are no doors or windows and the only floor consists of some loose boards covering one half of the upper story."[58] The building was later referred to as a "little old hovel of a courthouse."[59]

The second-floor courtroom had loose plank flooring and church members of necessity sat on uncomfortable wood plank benches with no supporting backs. There were no windows, and the only light for the meeting, which began at 2:00 P.M., was provided by kerosene oil lanterns.

The afternoon of June 30, 1844, was only four months after David West joined the First Congregational Church of Sycamore. The four months that saw winter become spring and then summer also saw the antislavery resolution brought forward and tabled at three successive

Dr. Horatio Franklin Page, the first physician in Sycamore, was openly antislavery. He and his wife harbored several runaway slaves in their home, a known "station" on the Underground Railroad.

> 30.
>
> voted, also that the Moderator make this decision public at the next Sabbath Meeting.
>
> The remaining resolutions before the Church No's 3 & 4 — were then unanimously adopted — as a standing rule of this church. As follows —
>
> Resolved, That we consider American Slavery a gross violation of the great law of love, leading to an infraction of all the commandments in the decalogue. Therefore —
>
> Resolved, That we cannot have fellowship in any way with this "unfruitful work of darkness" — and consequently will not receive to our communion any Slave Holder, or apologist for slavery knowing him to be such —

Resolution of June 30, 1844, outlining opposition to slavery in the original handwritten minute book of the Sycamore First Congregational Church Society.

meetings. The meeting opened with prayer, followed by opening remarks by the moderator. Due to the congregation's meager finances, they owned no musical instruments to enhance the worship service. Soon they heard the lone voice of a member singing a hymn, "Amazing Grace, how sweet the sound / That saved a wretch like me," and all joined in solemnly. Coincidentally, the familiar hymn, first published in 1779, was written by the English slave trader turned Puritan minister, John Newton.[60]

This particular summer meeting proceeded according to form. In the First Congregational Church, the "business exercises are interspersed with frequent devotional exercises, as prayer, singing and reading the scriptures with exhortation."[61]

The meeting continued in a very businesslike manner. Having dispensed with Dr. Page's transgressions, the congregation was now ready to tackle national moral issues. There was no fanfare indicated to announce the passage of their monumental antislavery decision. It was reported in a very matter-of-fact style on Saturday, June 30, 1844:

> The remaining resolutions before the Church were then unanimously adopted as a standing rule of this church as follows:
>
> <u>Resolved</u>: That we consider Am[erican] Slavery a gross violation of the great laws of love, leading to an infraction of all the commandments....
>
> Therefore —
>
> <u>Resolved</u>: That we cannot have fellowship in any way with this "unfruitful work of darkness"— and consequently will not receive to our communion any slave holder, or apologist for slavery knowing him to be such.[62]

No apologist for slavery would be tolerated at the First Congregational Church in Sycamore, Illinois. After four months of discussion, they publicly voiced their opposition to "Am[erican] Slavery" and put that belief into a written resolution.

David West's spiritual mentor, Beriah Green, had used the term "American Slavery" in his 1836 sermon in Whitesboro, New York. According to Green, "American Slavery" also included the sins of fraud, adultery and murder. The Sycamore congregation concluded that the practice of enslaving another human being was indeed "a gross violation of the great laws of love." The admonition "Thou shalt love thy neighbor as thyself,"[63] in Christianity considered the second greatest commandment, was paramount in their rationale. The great fear was that if someone sanctioned slavery, and did not love his neighbor, then it followed logically that they would also break the very sacred Ten Commandments. As a safeguard in maintaining their antislavery stance, they refused to permit anyone to join their church or even to participate in the holy sacrament of communion during a worship service if he apologized for slavery. They refused to condone slavery anywhere in the United States. They refused to apologize for their point of view.

CHAPTER 7

Resolute and Unwavering

No one [had] the slightest doubt as to the fact that Congregationalists of Illinois were among the staunchest anti-slavery elements.[1] — Mathew Spinka (author)

A Leader in the Movement

Nine days prior to the final passage of the Sycamore First Congregational antislavery resolution, a group of church people assembled at the Congregational Church of Farmington, in west-central Fulton County, Illinois. The express purpose of this June 21, 1844, gathering was to organize a General Congregational Association in Illinois.

The stated Business Committee presented a "lengthy report on the subject of slavery," and it was noted that "surprisingly vigorous — if not violent — language" was used when addressing the slavery issue. Illinois Congregationalists were indeed among the "staunchest anti-slavery elements."[2]

In order to be a Congregational minister, a man had to be antislavery. Additionally, punishing those who helped fugitive slaves was wrong, regardless of any laws demanding punishment. Such a law was "a wicked interference with the rights of conscience."[3] Confident members of the First Congregational Church in Sycamore echoed the frame of mind of the new General Association of the Illinois Congregational churches.

Led by Jesse Kellogg and David West, the congregation in Sycamore voted that their new slavery resolutions, together with the temperance declaration, be sent to the *Western Citizen* and *New York Evangelist* for publication. It was important to proclaim to the public how they felt about slavery. This was the fourth time the congregation addressed antislavery resolutions, and all within the first four months of David West's appearance in Sycamore. In those short months, West's steady perseverance prevailed. By spreading the gospel of Abolitionist Beriah Green, the doctrine of abolition from the Burned-over District channeled through the Congregationalists, West provided necessary leadership to the frontier.

At this same meeting in Sycamore on June 30, church members discussed electing another deacon, and not surprisingly, the outspoken newest member, David West, was elected. When he earlier presented his letter of transfer from the Evans Centre Congregational Church in Erie County, New York, he was already referred to as "Deacon." Presumably because he had been previously elected to this esteemed church position, it was logical that the First Congregational

Church in Sycamore reaffirm that position. Note that this 1844 worship service and church meeting at the First Congregational Church predates the passage of the second and much stronger federal Fugitive Slave Act. That law was not passed by Congress until September 18, 1850.

Even in DeKalb County, where antislavery sentiments ran high, some unrest and strong opinions existed on both sides of the slavery issue.

Civil Law Prevails

As reported in the *Sycamore True Republican*, "This public building [the courthouse] was finally practically denied [the Congregationalists] because of the strong antislavery and temperance principles of the church."[4] The local public officials ultimately decided that there was too much discussion regarding the slavery and temperance issues among the members of the First Congregational Church. Their unwavering abolitionist stance was perceived as meddling. Community sentiment among resident anti-expansionists and tavern owners prompted them to join forces and pressure civil authorities. This group considered itself to be antislavery, not proslavery, but did not categorize themselves as immediatist Abolitionists. Immediatists, by definition, insisted that "slavery was sin and that immediate emancipation was the starting point of any genuine antislavery program."[5]

The Congregationalists' problem was that they made a public pronouncement of their antislavery and abolitionist position. When also combined with their temperance attitude, they quickly became an irritant, and the local tavern owners, bolstered by the anti-expansionists, sensed that the church might have interfered with their livelihood. The Congregationalists could talk and agitate all they wanted, but they would no longer be allowed to do it within the confines of taxpayer-supported public property. They were effectively evicted from their regular meeting place.

Stirring Days

No minutes exist for worship services or church society meetings for the next four months. This is significant because it was at that meeting in June, when minutes were last recorded, that the passage of the antislavery resolutions occurred. The next meeting, recorded on November 9, 1844, took place at the home of their pastor, the Rev. Edwin E. Wells, who was the second minister called to serve this congregation in its early history. Wells graduated from Auburn Theological Seminary and moved his wife and four young children to Sycamore to minister there.

According to newspaper accounts, when the church services were no longer held in the old courthouse, sometimes the meetings were held in the homes of their ministers, Deacon Kellogg's kitchen, or the homes of Harry Martin or Dr. Ellsworth Rose.

Deacon Jesse C. Kellogg's house still stands on the northwest corner of Main and High Streets in Sycamore. The original structure was built by Kellogg in 1842, and although a subsequent addition substantially altered the home, a portion of the existing house remains the oldest residential building in the city. That part of the structure was also used as the very first post office in town when Kellogg was the postmaster.[6]

"Those were stirring days. The church was poor and struggling, but courage was not lacking."[7] Throughout the years, when new members joined the church, they were required to be examined with regard to doctrinal views and sentiments on the subjects of temperance and slavery before the congregation voted to admit the new people into membership.

Jesse C. Kellogg's house was the scene of acrimonious discussion by the Congregationalists. Built in 1842, it is the oldest home in Sycamore, located at the northeast corner of South Main Street and High Street.

The leaders forming the majority within the First Congregational Church in Sycamore were all subscribers to the *Western Citizen* and supported its antislavery philosophy. Those mentioned already—Deacon Jesse C. Kellogg, Deacon David West and his brother Aaron West, the Doctors Horatio Page and Ellsworth Rose, the Rev. Edwin Wells—all regularly read publisher Zebina Eastman's essays pertaining to the evils of slavery in America. Almost two-thirds of the 49 male members of the First Congregational Church subscribed to the *Western Citizen* between 1843 and 1855. Over half of those same men are further identified in historical sources as Abolitionists, plus one who is described colorfully as a "zealous Republican."[8] Because the Republican Party was founded as an antislavery political party, within that context it is accurate to consider a zealous Republican as someone who espoused antislavery. However, all members, male and female, are considered to be antislavery advocates by virtue of the fact that they gave their oath to the church's antislavery affirmation statement.

The Determination of Oliver Norton

Henrietta Norton, wife of the third resident First Congregational minister, Oliver W. Norton, wrote to her sister Augusta in January 1848. In her letter she referred to anonymous county government officials, commenting that "the wicked rule" in the decision to "shut out" the church membership from worship services at the courthouse. Four years after being evicted from the courthouse, Henrietta reported, "They have no place to meet except in the Methodist Church when it is not occupied. We are praying for a revival and there are some glimmerings of hope."[9]

They continued to hope and pray for two more years until their very own first church building was finally completed at the end of 1849. Although the Congregationalists began construction on their own house of worship prior to the Methodists, the inopportune death of their contractor prevented it from being finished on a timely basis. "Delay was inevitable."[10] Consequently, by 1847 the Methodists had already completed a structure at the northwest corner of Somonauk and Elm Streets and were kind enough to let the Congregationalists utilize their building periodically.

It would be misleading, however, to purport that the entire congregation was always in complete agreement on the issue of slavery. Although a majority of parishioners strongly objected to slavery, they were sometimes hesitant when it came to total abolition. In the eastern United States, even stronger attitudes prevailed. There, people developed a hatred for slavery while they simultaneously detested Abolitionists. Luckily, the Rev. Norton was not in the East; he resided in Sycamore, Illinois.

Indications are that the church body in 1847 was only slightly divided on the matter of whether or not to retain their minister, Oliver Norton, because of his specific views on slavery and war. Norton was decidedly antislavery and subscribed regularly to the *New York Evangelist* to read about the proceedings of various antislavery associations and recently passed antislavery resolutions. He kept abreast of what occurred at other church meetings and considered himself to be an Abolitionist.

Oliver William Norton in his wildest dreams could never have envisioned that he would someday be dropped into the middle of a disagreement about slavery. Born in 1811, probably in East Bloomfield, New York, he was the third child of eight born to Sereno and Harriet (Morse) Norton.[11] By age 23, he enrolled in the College of New Jersey, now Princeton University, and after leaving that school continued his education for the ministry at Union Theological Seminary, in New York. Records indicate that he was ordained as a Congregational minister in 1840. During this time he met and married his wife, Henrietta Willcox, who was three years younger. Henrietta, the granddaughter of the locally well-known Adam Stanton of Clinton, Connecticut, grew up in New York City, one of seven children, born to Oliver and Sally (Stanton) Willcox. It must have been a trial only true love and commitment could have survived for the daughter of a financially secure, emotionally close family from New York City to marry an indigent young man who chose a career as an itinerant rural preacher.

Henrietta Norton's experiences as a minister's wife during the early 1800s are recorded in letters written from 1838 to 1849 and saved by her descendants. Together, they moved their growing family from one small town in the state of New York to another, following the Rev. Norton's chosen missionary calling, and were ultimately directed to Northern Illinois in 1842. It was during the period in Rockford, Illinois, that Norton changed his denominational affiliation to Presbyterian, to which he remained devoted the rest of his life. Perhaps he enjoyed the Presbyterian order of a church polity which interpreted theology and created policy at a higher level, with binding authority on the local churches. This obviated the need for local churches to construct their own resolutions to express viewpoints on a particular issue, such as slavery.

However, in keeping with the American Home Missionary Society's accord to help support missionaries supplied to both Presbyterian and Congregational churches, the Rev. Norton, now Presbyterian, was called to serve the First Congregational Church in Sycamore, Illinois. His wife, Henrietta, and five young children remained a few months in Rockford, pending Norton's finding a house suitable for them in Sycamore.

The first mention of O.W. Norton in the church minutes is in May 1847, and concisely describes the business meeting and worship service. These are typical, matter-of-fact references pertaining to regular church business:

> Saturday May 8th 1847.
> Church met, and, after Prayer and singing, heard a preparatory lecture from Rev. O.W. Norton — Adjourned to meet on the morrow.
> Lords day May 9th 1847.
> Church met — had a communion season which was solemn & interesting. Baptism was administered by Rev. O.W. Norton to Cyrus Aaron son of Aaron C. and Emily West.
> Adjourned,
> Jesse C. Kellogg Ch Clk[12]

The business meeting of the church society was usually conducted on a Saturday, followed by the formal worship service on the next day, the Sabbath. Typical business conducted by the local congregation continued in a calm and customary fashion for the next several months, according to the recorded minutes.

However, nine months later, which was four years after passage of the church's first antislavery resolution, the antislavery discussions within the church heated up once again, and it was evident that there were hidden feelings beneath the surface of the written record.

> Saturday Feb 12th A.D. 1848
> Church met according to previous appointment at the house of Jesse C. Kellogg — Meeting opened by prayer by Rev. O.W. Norton Moderator — After singing, a desultory conversation with regard to the propriety of modifying or defining the Term "Apologist" contained in the standing rule of the Church on American Slavery, ensued.
> It was then moved and seconded that a construction be placed upon the rule of this Church in relation to Am[erican] Slavery. After a lengthy and somewhat acrimonious discussion it was voted that the further discussion and action on the aforesaid motion be postponed until the next regular meeting of the church, after which the Church separated.
> Jesse C. Kellogg, Clerk[13]

It was extremely unusual to use negative adjectives in the official report of the church business or worship. A "desultory conversation" and an "acrimonious discussion" indicate a lengthy and probably very heated controversy. One can envision the church members standing to compete for recognition to be heard in Jesse Kellogg's kitchen, or perhaps the parlor to accommodate a larger group, as they loudly proclaimed their viewpoints regarding slavery and the local church's assertions in their longstanding stated antislavery resolutions.

The next meeting of the congregation occurred February 26, 1848, again at the home of Jesse Kellogg.

> Deac. Hamlin opened the meeting by prayer. Rev. O.W. Norton officiated as Moderator. The unfinished business of the last meeting was taken up and discussion had with regard to the propriety of placing a construction on the rule of the Church in relation to Am[erican] Slavery and thereupon it was Voted that the motion now pending be dismissed.[14]

Abolitionist thinking regarding antislavery prevailed over the more moderate anti-expansionist attitude and the original wording of the first antislavery resolution was left in place. Church members would continue their practice of not apologizing for being antislavery.

They went on to discuss the retention of O.W. Norton as their minister. This was usually an annual formality to be verified with written notification to the American Home Missionary Society.

> The supply of the Pulpit of the Church and Society the ensuing year was presented for the consideration of the Church. A part of the Church expressed themselves satisfied with the views and ministerial course of Rev. Mr. Norton on the Subject of Slavery Temperance, War, etc. and desirous of retaining him as our Minister another year. A part of the Church expressed themselves as dissatisfied with the views and ministerial course of Mr. Norton in relation to Slavery, Temperance, War, etc, and thereupon Rev. Mr. Norton declined being a candidate for the Pulpit another Year.[15]

> 52   *Saturday Feb. 12th A.D. 1848.*
>
> Church met according to previous appointment at the house of Jesse C. Kellogg – Meeting opened by prayer by Revd O. W. Norton Moderator – After singing, a desultory conversation with regard to the propriety of modifying or defining the term "Apologist" contained in the standing rule of the Church on American Slavery, ensued.
>
> It was then moved and seconded that a construction be placed upon the rule of this Church in relation to Am. Slavery. After a lengthy and somewhat acrimonious discussion It was voted that the further discussion and action on the aforesaid motion be postponed until the next regular meeting of the Church, after which the Church separated.
>
>   Jesse C. Kellogg Clerk

In 1848, the Sycamore First Congregational Church Society continued to discuss American slavery and the definition of the word "apologist."

The strikeout of the word "Temperance" in the minutes indicates that upon a rereading of the minutes, the congregation agreed that Norton's views on temperance were apparently not an issue. Most likely Norton's views on temperance were tolerable to the congregation at large and the minutes were corrected accordingly. But his views pertaining to slavery and war agitated some of the members. In 1848 a possible civil war already loomed on the American horizon. Norton was decidedly antislavery, an Abolitionist, and not simply anti-expansion of slavery.

    The indication is that the Reverend Norton undoubtedly expressed his own antislavery views at the previous meeting of the church society, and perhaps again from the pulpit during the following worship service. Most likely, he utilized Biblical references such as, "Thou shalt not deliver unto his master the servant which hath escaped unto thee; he shall dwell with thee, even among you, in that place which he shall choose in one of thy gates where it liketh him best; thou shalt not oppress him."[16] This also hints of his support of covert activities in the Underground Railroad. His opinions were probably passionate and as a result, "a part of the church expressed themselves as dissatisfied." Notice that the minutes indicate only a "part of the church" was not in agreement with the Rev. Norton. It does not indicate that a majority was against his antislavery viewpoints. Unfortunately, we do not know the exact element regarding slavery or slaveholding that created the disagreement. Probably there were some members who could be classified as "apologists for slavery" if they held only the opposition of expansion of slavery into territories as their viewpoint. They still considered themselves as being antislavery, as long as the institution of slavery itself did not interfere with their particular way of life in Northern Illinois. But others accused the anti-expansionists of being "apologists." Those anti-expansionist church members may have wanted the word "apologist" removed from the earlier resolution. The situation became a stalemate.

The minutes of that February meeting concluded with a completely different topic: a discussion of ways and means to relieve the church debt incurred for lumber and material in the planned building of their first church meeting house. On paper, the group discussion moved from the emotional to the practical very easily. In reality, the members simmered underneath the businesslike façade and struggled to maintain a civil approach to the business at hand.

By the next business meeting of the church society two weeks later, Jesse Kellogg and the other church leaders determined to once again bring up the notion of extending the invitation to Oliver W. Norton to remain as pastor at the First Congregational Church.

Saturday March 11th 1848
Church met at the house of Jesse C. Kellogg. Prayer by Deac. West. Rev. O.W. Norton Moderator. The Supply of the Pulpit of the Church and Society the ensuing year was brought up for consideration and after much desultory conversation as to the position of Mr. Norton on the Slavery Temperance and War questions. Voted that the Church endeavour to retain Mr. Norton as our Minister another Year and thereupon the Rev. Mr. Norton again declined being a candidate for our Pulpit. The attention of the Church was next called to the case of those who had, after paying their own Subscriptions become individually responsible to pay for work lumber & materials for meeting house — but the day was now far spent. The night was at hand, on the morrow was the Sabbath, and brethren seemed disposed to "go hence without delay"—
Jesse C. Kellogg, Clerk[17]

Again, the descriptive word "desultory" is used to describe the tenor of the discussion. Some members were not happy with Norton's views on slavery and potential war, and they continued to voice their viewpoints.

The last mention of the Rev. Oliver William Norton in any church minutes occurred on March 18, 1848.[18] Because the congregation was not unanimous in their convictions regarding their varying degrees of antislavery opinion, they could not give their minister a unanimous vote of support. Although a majority did approve of the good reverend's views and extended the offer of employment to him, Norton firmly refused to remain in an atmosphere where every single member did not support his opposition to slavery. Oliver William Norton expected his congregation to be in accord on the matters of slavery and abolition.

As a result, Norton chose to move his wife, pregnant with their sixth child, and their young family to Jefferson, in the southern wilderness of the new state of Wisconsin. His own strong personal beliefs guided his life and drove him further away from their extended family back in New York State. Norton's sons attained recognition in fields other than the ministry. Firstborn Oliver Willcox Norton was the famous Union bugler who, in 1862, at the request of Brigadier

General Daniel Butterfield, first played the tune that became known as "Taps."[19] In an ironic twist, when Oliver Willcox Norton later married Lucy Fanning in 1870, the presiding minister was none other than the Reverend Henry Ward Beecher. Beecher, an inexhaustible antislavery preacher and orator in New York, was the brother of Harriet Beecher Stowe, who authored *Uncle Tom's Cabin.*

Note that once again, the recorded 1848 congregational disagreement within the First Congregational Church predated the more stringent 1850 federal Fugitive Slave Act. However, ostensibly church members knew that some of their brethren were active in the Underground Railroad. There were some parishioners who felt that any openly expressed opposition to a civil law, if only against the largely unenforced 1793 Fugitive Slave Law, was unconscionable, even by a church body purporting to obey only God's laws. Still, they all chose to look the other way. If members did not actively assist in the Underground Railroad, by default they were supportive when they disregarded and did not report any clandestine activities. No First Congregational Church members, nor any members of any other antislavery church in DeKalb County, were ever charged with transgressions of the Fugitive Slave Act. In fact, no one in all of DeKalb County was ever arrested for aiding and abetting runaway slaves.

Antislavery Sentiment Prevails

The First Congregational church survived the loss of the Rev. O.W. Norton. Church leaders and the greater membership who comprised the majority were undeterred in their efforts to enact an even stronger antislavery resolution on the part of the congregation. For the next couple of years they were consumed with the details of the completion of their new church building, as well as monitoring ongoing discipline matters pertaining to the infraction of church rules and sins committed against the church on the part of their members. In spite of their preoccupation with these seemingly mundane and practical matters, antislavery and abolition were still topics of conversation, and there continued to be some dissension on the part of a small group of members, as exhibited in 1850. On the "Lords Day June 30 1850," as always preceding the sacrament of communion, the church minute book reports: "The Standing Rules on Temperance & Slavery were also read before receiving the Bread and the Cup." Deacon Jesse Kellogg, who after six years was still the church clerk, wrote, "The Congregation who did not partake of the sacred emblems was large, solemn and attentive."[20]

Clerk Kellogg was not happy that some members could not agree with the standing rules on slavery and consequently did not participate in the communion service. He further editorialized, almost as a postscript comment at the end of the official church minutes, where he wrote, "O Lord! How long: may salvation soon come out of this branch of thy Zion."[21] Kellogg's frustration was evident.

Ten days after the passage of the Fugitive Slave Act in September 1850, the First Congregational Church calmly accepted into membership yet another family who affirmed their antislavery beliefs in front of the church body. Deacon Erastus Hamlin, his wife Harriet, and their daughters Caroline and Mary Ann were part of the original group of people who organized the church in 1840. In 1848 they moved their residence and subsequently their church membership to Byron, Illinois, and its Congregational Church, then two years later returned to Sycamore.

Many churches regularly issued membership transfer certificates for members moving from one church to another in order to assure a congregation that the new arrivals were members in good standing. Even though they were previous members in that same church body, the Hamlin family needed to once again affirm their beliefs in the antislavery standing rules before being readmitted to membership. By this time, almost two weeks after the passage of the new restrictive 1850 law pertaining to fugitive slaves, the citizens in Sycamore had read about that law in their newspapers. Knowing about the new law did not deter church members from their practice of affirming antislavery beliefs. Was the action by the church in continuing to assert their antislavery beliefs a direct affront to the prevailing law of the land? Members knew, of course, that many within their own congregation were regularly aiding fugitive slaves. Any local agitation pertaining to the passage of the stronger law did not seem evident in the regular reports of their traditional church meetings.

It is curious that Deacon David West tendered his resignation from the esteemed office of deacon in 1850 at the second recorded church meeting following the passage of the Fugitive Slave Act. Although there is no obvious stated correlation in the church minutes, the possible connection may be that West was understandably opposed to the constraints of this new law. If caught, he would be more personally liable to punishment for his activities in the Underground Railroad. Why, then, resign from an office in the church body that was apparently so supportive of the Underground Railroad activities? The answer may lie in David West's sense of immediatism with regard to slavery. He may have felt that the church was not acting fast enough to further encourage activism in its approach to ending slavery. Why was it taking so long? Why did slavery still exist? If the church was against it, what would have to happen before believing Christians realized that they must act overtly to end slavery? Enough of this secretive business requiring them to transport people from place to place during the dark hours of night! David West continued to be a part of that "greatest activity."[22]

Second Antislavery Resolution Introduced

After the resignation of Oliver Norton from the pulpit, the Rev. C.F. Hudson was invited to participate as moderator of the church society and became the fourth resident minister of the First Congregational Church. Charles Frederick Hudson was unmarried while living in Sycamore. His parents, Timothy and Catherine Hudson, moved from Indiana to Lyons Township in Cook County, Illinois, sometime prior to 1860. Hudson appears in the 1850 DeKalb County census as a 30-year-old Congregational minister born in Ohio and living with the family of Jesse Rose, a prominent member of the congregation. There are references to a C.F. Hudson, a Congregational minister, who was the author of the book *Debt and Grace*. There is also a record of a C.F. Hudson, teaching in Medina County, Ohio, and later of a Congregational minister, Professor C.F. Hudson, teaching at Cambridge, Massachusetts. Whether or not either of these is the same person who ministered to the First Congregational Church in Sycamore is a mystery. However, while Hudson lived in Sycamore, his contract was renewed each succeeding year for the next five years and the church family continued to prosper. During this period his two younger sisters, Amelia and Cornelia, who were 24 and 18 at the time, attended the Dow Academy, Roswell Dow's private school in Sycamore.

The first new church structure for worship was finally completed during Hudson's tenure, with the congregation pledging their financial support to defray the mounting debts incurred during construction. Two non-member citizens were requested to audit the congregation to determine the members' individual assets and conclude how much money each member should be assessed and taxed to cover the financial obligation. It is not odd that the two people chosen as the auditors were Carlos Lattin and Stephen Townsend. They were both Methodists, thus fulfilling the requirement of being non–Congregational. But Lattin and Townsend were also fellow antislavery supporters and subscribers to the *Western Citizen*, as well as known active par-

Sycamore Congregationalists passed a more assertive resolution in 1852 outlining their extreme displeasure with slavery issues and the "State of bondage."

ticipants in the Underground Railroad. They would have been good friends of the Congregational members.

Antislavery sentiment continued to prosper and grow within the congregation. One year before the end of C.F. Hudson's tenure, the First Congregational Church in Sycamore passed yet another, stronger antislavery resolution, which they forwarded to the American Home Missionary Society:

November 27, 1852
  Resolved. That we view with deep concern the fact that in many of the churches of our land the practice of slaveholding is tolerated and that no bar exists to the admission of those who hold their fellow men as property, denied the avails of their own labour & receiving the light of the gospel as a favor & not as a right, liable to purchase & sale, to the sundering of family ties, to cruelty & dishonor & all the other evils that pertain to a State of bondage.

> Resolved. That we believe such a system, so essentially unjust and wrong, ought to find no place in the Church of God; and that the separation of it from the Church, is our only hope, so far as moral means can go, of its being done away from our land.[23]

The resolution continued with the First Congregational Church entreating the American Home Missionary Society to not support those churches that still tolerated slaveholding:

> Resolved, That in our opinion in the work of the gospel where slavery exists, such churches ought to be aided, and such only, as will entertain the subject of a speedy disconnexion [sic] with Slavery, and that whatever course may be advisable with slaveholders now embraced in their communion, the number of such members should not be allowed to increase: That we hail with pleasure the tokens of a conscience in the Church at large which demands this of our brethren at the South and that it is our earnest hope that this demand of the Christian conscience will be speedily expressed in the counsels given by the American Home Missionary Societies to the men whom they send to the Churches in which slavery now exists.[24]

Frontier Missionary Societies

Delegates from the Congregational and Presbyterian churches organized the American Home Missionary Society in 1826 as their common agency in domestic missions. Their theological compatibility created the 1801 Plan of Union, allowing the two denominations to exchange clergy, and the new society helped provide financial support to assist those western congregations unable to support themselves. When a new congregation requested the services of a minister through the American Home Missionary Society, they needed to guarantee a share of that person's wages. As a result of this historic administrative business arrangement, if a Presbyterian church was initiated in one town, then the Congregationalists would voluntarily bypass it and go to the next town, and vice versa. This way they were not duplicating manpower and financial resources in the exact same town. We see that pattern in DeKalb County, where there is a Presbyterian church in Somonauk in the southern part of the county and one in Waterman in the central part of the county. Additionally, there was a Congregational church in Paw Paw, which today is Presbyterian. The ministers in Northern Illinois considered themselves to be western frontier missionaries, and the area was ripe for an evangelical process to begin. The two denominations never existed in the same town in DeKalb County for over 120 years, until 1964, when a Presbyterian study group, begun in the city of DeKalb three years earlier, formally organized into a governing church. There is still no Presbyterian church in Sycamore. The individual ministers to the congregations were given some financial support from the American Home Missionary Society, based in part on the antislavery views held by the local congregations.

However, the American Home Missionary Society itself seemed to be having problems casting off all taint of slavery associations. They continued to support ministers who were not entirely antislavery and also supported some churches which still allowed slaveholders as members. Finally, in 1846, Jonathan Blanchard, President of Knox College in Galesburg, Illinois, together with other impatient agitators formed the new American Missionary Association to support and represent only the churches which were adamant in their antislavery opinions.

Shortly after the 1852 passage of the First Congregational Church Society's second antislavery Resolution, the Rev. Darius Gore became their fifth minister in Sycamore. He was an 1839 graduate of Amherst College, a bastion of Congregational teaching, and was ordained "as an evangelist."[25] After serving in Sycamore for a couple of years, the Rev. Gore encouraged the local congregation to break its financial and spiritual ties with the American Home Missionary Society and affiliate thereafter with the American Missionary Association. His Christian conscience, and that of his congregation, dictated that their demands for "disconnexion with Slavery" be paramount. Gore's reasons are explained in his letter of December 15, 1856, to the A.M.A.:

> During all this period I have been under the care of the A.H.M.S., & have received its liberal & cordial patronage.... But for reasons growing out of the subject of slavery we preferred to change our Missionary relations & cooperate here-after with a society one of whose principles is to treat slaveholding like any other sin. We hold that this sin is the sin of our nation, & the sooner individuals as Christians, & the sooner churches as bodies get wholly clear of it the better.[26]

The Rev. Gore was grateful for his past association with the American Home Missionary Society, but the issue of slavery as a sin was overriding and he preferred to no longer associate with an entity that either partially condoned slavery or forgave those who did. From this time forward, his personal ministry and that of the First Congregational Church were associated with the new, completely antislavery American Missionary Association.

Area Congregational Church Differences

Even though they came from the same New England religious background, the time lapse between the advent of the First Congregational Church in Sycamore and the First Congregational Church in DeKalb helped to create some differences between the two congregations as related to the subject of slavery. Although their stated philosophies indicated both congregations were antislavery, the differences became apparent on the issue of abolition. At one end of the spectrum were those who were solely against the expansion of slavery into any new territories or states. In other words, slavery was tolerated where it currently existed, as long as the system was not expanded elsewhere. Those at the opposite end of the slavery issue were termed Abolitionists because they demanded that slavery end immediately everywhere across the United States. The extreme Abolitionists were occasionally quite militant.

In between were people whose only obvious antislavery act was to subscribe to and read the abolitionist newspaper, the *Western Citizen*, and other similar publications. They were helping the cause in subtle ways, by paying for the subscription to the newspaper, by attending a church with pronounced antislavery views, and by ignoring a neighbor traveling with a load of "cargo" suspected to be fugitive slaves.

The fact remains that the Sycamore First Congregational Church was organized fourteen years prior to the DeKalb First Congregational Church — and it was organized by people whose strong New England background indoctrinated them with an antislavery and abolitionist mentality.

We have seen that the emigrants from New England transported their Puritan heritage and religious beliefs with them. In Sycamore, the same Abolitionists who first settled in the area were also the same people who organized the First Congregational Church. In 1844, when the Congregational Church passed their first antislavery resolution, they were at the forefront of social action in the county. In 1852, with the passage of the more fervent second antislavery resolution, the First Congregational Church in Sycamore restated their position and publicly made it clear how strongly they felt about the issue. Ongoing antislavery discussions occurred, and these resolutions were passed in Sycamore years before the formation of a Congregational church elsewhere in the county was even a consideration.

By 1853 a second Congregational church organized in the city of Sandwich, situated in the southern end of DeKalb County. At their organizational meeting they passed a resolution which refused admission to any person who owned slaves or who did not abstain from alcoholic beverages. The Sandwich church followed well the example set by Sycamore and other Illinois Congregational churches in addressing the slavery issue. They obviously thought it important to simultaneously include the matter of temperance.

The DeKalb Congregationalists, however, took a more moderate approach. During the mid–1800s, the eight miles between the town centers of Sycamore and DeKalb amounted to a long trip on horseback or with a horse and buggy over rutted or muddy roads. The trip could take a couple of hours to complete. By 1853 the railroad arrived in DeKalb, which made travel much easier for incoming settlers. And so in 1854, fourteen years after the founding of the church in Sycamore, the Congregationalists in the area decided that it was time to create another Congregational church. The First Congregational Church in DeKalb was organized with only eight members. Joseph and Hannah Hiland were two who transferred from the Sycamore First Congregational Church. For the Hiland family, it was far more convenient to worship closer to where they lived.

The original covenant of the First Congregational Church in DeKalb affirmed by members included the instruction: "You receive all true Christians as your equal brethren in Christ, & his friends as your friends irrespective of Color or condition in life and promise to watch over them in all Christian fidelity and tenderness."[27] This directive hinted at antislavery, but did not mention slavery directly, nor did it have the passion and emotion expressed in the Sycamore resolution.

Another factor was the strong movement, early in the state's history, for Illinois to become a slave state. The southern half of the state was very proslavery. Even though Illinois became a state in 1818, it was not until 1824 that the slave state issue was finally settled with the defeat of the proslavery constitutional amendment. As a result, some of the people moving northward within Illinois were not definitively antislavery. DeKalb Center also succeeded in attracting a larger ethnic community, along with the settlers from southern Illinois. Historically, new immigrant groups often divided into two basic categories. Some, like the Irish and Germans in the eastern United States, quickly expressed their sympathies with the antislavery groups, later joining the Union forces in large numbers during the Civil War. Other ethnic groups, however, were sometimes more interested in their own survival — getting a job, providing food and shelter for their families — than in the domestic civil problems in their newly adopted country. They were poor and persecuted in their homelands and wanted to be left alone to persevere as best they could. Neither the national slavery problem nor the regional Northern Illinois and DeKalb County antislavery movement appealed to them.

The timing and manner in which the two neighboring communities were settled and populated, combined with the religious, ethnic and geographic backgrounds of the immigrants, had an enormous effect on the development of the antislavery movement. In spite of the very strong antislavery sentiment in the loose Illinois Congregational Church organization, the city of DeKalb as a whole and the First Congregational Church in DeKalb in particular never acquired the feeling of urgency attached to the antislavery movement. Sycamore alone exhibited such enthusiasm for the cause. With the passionate leadership of its early settlers, Sycamore's early character rapidly developed into a hotbed of religious and political Abolitionists. Sycamore neither tolerated nor condoned apologists for slavery.

The myth that only white people assisted black fugitives was more recently debunked in regional studies about Pennsylvania,[28] Ohio,[29] and Indiana.[30] However, sometimes myths linger because they are true. The truth in DeKalb County, Illinois, was that there was no free black community to help runaways. There were no Quakers who historically were known to help fugitive slaves in other states. There were no fugitive slaves settled in the DeKalb County environs who could offer assistance to others on their journey to freedom. Although several black Americans elsewhere may have been active in various antislavery societies, as well as through their respective churches, in DeKalb County black activists did not exist.

There was no one in DeKalb County who would aid a fugitive slave except white evangelical Christians. An outsider could have observed that these transplanted New Englander Congregationalists were fanatical, but since the majority already belonged in the same Yankee category, no one complained. Apologize for those who were slaveholders anywhere in the United States? Apologize for the existence of slavery? Slavery apologists were not tolerated. These were unreasonable men and women. In the First Congregational Church in Sycamore, Illinois, there were no apologists for slavery!

CHAPTER 8

All Brethren: The Universalists

> None of us will ever accomplish anything excellent or commanding except when he listens to this whisper which is heard by him alone.— Ralph Waldo Emerson (1803–1882), minister, antislavery advocate and essayist

Harsh Allegations

"Curtis Smith is a Black Republican,"[1] the whisperers asserted. Smith heard the whispers meant for him alone and knew that those murmurs behind his back were the voices of small-minded people. To this forthright, opinionated farmer born in Vermont, being called a "Black Republican" mattered not. He listened to the soft intonations and was motivated to sustain his strong opinions. Even if it meant ostracism by some members of the so-called elite society, he would befriend the fugitive slave and remain "conscientiously opposed to the institution of negro slavery."[2]

Aligning himself with others in DeKalb County, Smith held religious beliefs that formed the foundation for his views on slavery. Universalism was the constant in his life and in the vein of fellow believers, he was "confident that slavery would eventually be abolished."[3] How and when that would happen was beyond his understanding and vision. The Universalist belief that all people have divine rights sustained Smith, and he knew when "[the people] had suffered enough from the slave oligarchy they would right the wrong."[4] Smith belonged to the Sycamore Universalist church; Smith was an unreasonable man.

Murmurs of Universalism

The first whispers of Universalism heard by people in DeKalb County came from a Universalist preacher, the Rev. William Roundsville. He visited St. Charles, in Kane County, Illinois, as early as 1836 and decided to settle in the Northern Illinois area.[5] The U.S. 1840 Census shows Roundsville living in Kane County, and by 1850 he and his wife Elvira, and their two daughters Felicia and Letitia, are enumerated in that county living in St. Charles. According to a brief history of towns included in a later directory of Kane County, he preached the first Universalist sermon heard in Aurora, Illinois, in 1838,[6] and subsequently organized the Universalist society in St. Charles in 1839.[7] Traveling by horseback the 25 miles one way from St. Charles to Sycamore, Roundsville spread the Universalist gospel. Roundsville became the first itinerant Universalist minister to preach in that young city.

These dedicated and daring frontier ministers deserve the entire credit historians heap upon them. Through their personal persistence as front-line missionaries, they rarely wavered from their goal to bring Christ to the West. Additionally, the settlers benefited through the strengthening of moral standards. "These frontier preachers helped to shape a society, and we are much in their debt."[8]

As a Universalist religious pioneer and member of the frontier missionary fraternity, Roundsville "affirmed the 'Universal Fatherhood of God' and its logical corollary the 'Final Salvation of All Souls.'"[9] The small frame county courthouse in Sycamore had served the Congregationalists and Methodists before, and by 1845 became the setting for occasional Universalist meetings and worship services. According to church records, there followed a succession of various itinerant preachers after Roundsville, including the Reverends Van Olstine (or Alstyne) and J.M. Day, about whom nothing is known.

A New England Organizer

Eventually the handsome Rev. Carney found his way to the Western frontier and settled in Sycamore in January 1853. He was the minister exclusively responsible for forming the local Universalist Society comprising ten local families.

Thomas Johnson Carney was born June 10, 1818, in Dresden, Maine. He pursued his theological education through studies with the Rev. J.P. Weston of Gardiner, Maine, and was ordained in Philadelphia in 1848.[10] Weston was an acquaintance of both Carney and his soon-to-be wife, Julia. Her personal journal entry for August 30, 1846, mentions that she spent a leisurely Sunday afternoon reading a sermon by "Brother Weston."[11] Thomas Carney was already a Universalist minister when he married the more famous Julia Abigail Fletcher of Lancaster, Massachusetts. An employed teacher at age 21, Julia also wrote many articles and poems for the religious periodicals of the Universalist denomination. In fact, during the entire nine years prior to the Carneys' arrival in Sycamore, the citizens of DeKalb County, Illinois, were already reading Fletcher's short stories published regularly in the *Western Citizen*.[12] She also wrote a series of Sabbath-school instruction books that were used for many years in the liberal churches,[13] and attained world fame for the composition of her 1845 poem titled "Little Things," which espoused the respect and love for nature as captured in Universalist teachings. The poem, sometimes familiarly called "Little Drops of Water," was reflective of Universalist theology. It praised the land and the sea and extolled the virtues of love and kindness. Later, the poem was set to music and was also included in the McGuffey Reader used in many American school classrooms.

Julia Fletcher was intrigued with the antislavery cause long before her marriage to Tom Carney. On May 20, 1846, she wrote in her journal that she had attended a "conference in the evening, quite interesting."[14] According to Martin Litvin, an Illinois journalist who researched and compiled Julia Fletcher Carney's writings, Julia did not specify exactly where the evening meeting occurred or what the subject matter was. Perhaps she was being purposely secretive and did not want to write about current controversial subjects. However, because Julia was an educator, she was well aware of the racial segregation in schools in Boston, where she lived. Litvin writes "a great many of the white women teaching in the Boston schools were strongly religious, and insisted that their Christianity could not subscribe to a program of racial segregation."[15] These same female teachers sought an end to slavery and considered themselves to be Abolitionists. And Julia Fletcher Carney was one of them. Julia continues in her journal, "There was quite an excitement after the meeting in consequence of an article in *The Daily Bee* [Boston newspaper], reflecting upon the conduct of our former pastor. Much indignation was very properly manifested."[16]

Showing her support of antislavery, Julia wrote another poem titled "Think Gently of the Erring," which rings true to the Universalist philosophy about slaveholders. In the verse, Carney conveyed the thought that God's teachings would win over the errant ways of the slaveholders.

The Universalists always held fast to the thought that the Southern plantation owners would someday see the error of their ways and set their slaves free. Like Sycamore's Curtis Smith, Julia Fletcher was hopeful of leading both slaves and slaveholders to the Universalist fold with soft tones of love combined with holy words.

Thomas and Julia Carney ultimately parented nine children: Amanda JoAnna, William Thomas, Julian ("Fletcher"), Illinois and Maine (twins), Julia Louisa, Charles Henry, James Weston, and Eugene Francis. Four of their children died in infancy. After brief stints as a Universalist minister in Maine and New York, Carney moved his wife and family to Sycamore, Illinois, where he diligently worked to organize the Universalist Society and became the first official paid minister for the local Universalist congregation. Before they were married in 1848, Julia responded to Tom's questions regarding a potential ministerial position. In referring to a new congregation, she wrote, "To have a fair understanding with them at once that you are willing to be to them a pastor if they will be to you a people, but if they want your time and strength spent for them, they must pay you sufficient for a support. They would not ask the merchant for his goods, or the mechanic for his services gratuitously."[17] This advice from his future wife perhaps served him well throughout his pastoral career.

His last service to God was performed in Galesburg, Illinois, which was a known a bastion for Abolitionists in the Midwest area. Galesburg was the Carneys' home for their remaining careers. Thomas Johnson Carney died in 1871 and is buried alongside his wife, Julia, and oldest son, William, in Hope Cemetery, Galesburg, Illinois.[18]

The original minutes from the early Universalist Society meetings did not survive. We cannot know, therefore, what transpired verbatim at those initial gatherings. Only by learning about the early beliefs and theology of the Universalist Church and by knowing who the founding Sycamore members were can we deduce that the Universalist Church in Sycamore was antislavery in sentiment. We know that many of those members by their own admission were antislavery people, some avowed Abolitionists, and were involved in local Underground Railroad activities. Those listed in DeKalb County history books and Universalist Church record books as the first new members and heads of families in the congregation included Phineas Joslyn, his son Harry A. Joslyn, George Weeden, Curtis Smith, Hosea Willard, Kimball Dow, his brother Lavias F. Dow, John Waterman, Henry H. Gandy and George G. Spring.[19] Nathan H. Peck is also listed as a charter member in the earliest existing Universalist Church record book.[20] Both Peck and Sylvanus Holcomb are named as trustees for the church, along with Smith, Spring and Weeden.

The majority of the Universalist charter member families came from Vermont and New York. A list of the charter member names is very important because once again, we see antislavery sympathizers who are also active church members in the Sycamore community. Six of the twelve men, namely both Joslyn men, Weeden, Smith, K. Dow, and Holcomb, subscribed to the abolitionist newspaper the *Western Citizen* for several years, and the abolitionist activities of four of them are mentioned in printed historical sources. Both Henry Gandy's brother, George Gandy, and Hosea Willard's father, Oliver Willard, also subscribed to the *Western Citizen*. Member John Waterman, who was born in 1794 in Rhode Island, may be distantly related to the other, more prominent John Calvin Waterman of Sycamore, who was born in 1814 in New York.

The earliest Sycamore Universalist Church house of worship was built in 1854 on South Main Street. By 1875 a more imposing structure replaced it, and this building was sold as a residence (courtesy of the Joiner History Room, DeKalb County Archive, Sycamore, Illinois).

John Waterman and all the other original Universalist members were suspected antislavery men by virtue of their affiliation with a known antislavery church.

Like Curtis Smith, Kimball Dow openly shared his antislavery opinions. Dow served as the first secretary for the DeKalb County Antislavery Society, organized in 1843. In the county elections of August 1845, the Liberty Party ticket shows Kimball Dow as a candidate for county school commissioner and Curtis Smith on the ballot for county treasurer. Unfortunately for the Friends of Liberty, as the Liberty party ticket candidates were sometimes called, Democrats Harrington and Waterman defeated them. However, these particular Democrats did not project the rigid proslavery stance held by the Democrat Party of the time. They were already leaning towards an antislavery philosophy. James Harrington was later one of the delegates to the organizational convention of the new antislavery Republican Party in 1854, and John Calvin Waterman actively participated in the Anti-Nebraska meetings.

Under the Rev. Carney's tutelage, the formal Universalist church organization in Sycamore prospered, and by 1854 the congregation built their first permanent church structure on Main Street, a brick building with Gothic windows. Church member George Weeden was presumably instrumental in the construction of the initial house of worship. He was a local mason who earlier laid bricks in 1849-50 for the very first masonry building in Sycamore. It was a private school built on South Main Street named the Dow Academy after its founding teacher, Roswell Dow, son of Agrippa and cousin to Kimball Dow. As a member of the congregation, Weeden's masonry proficiency provided leadership in erecting the first Universalist Church building. The building is one of the oldest remaining brick buildings in Sycamore. Local folklore suggests that this first Universalist structure on South Main Street was used to hide occasional runaways en route to points north. Documented physical proof does not exist, but one can imagine a congregation with strong antislavery proclivities opening their own house of worship for the greater cause.

Over the next 20 years, members soon felt that their once fine church home was not as grand an edifice as local society expected. Consequently, by 1875 they decided to build a more imposing structure on West State Street. A local Sycamore man, Arthur Stark, purchased the older church building and remodeled it into a private residence, which it remains today.

Universalist Doctrine

As a matter of conviction, members of the Universalist Church adhered to the idea of having religious choices. One of those choices was the belief that "no person would be condemned by God to eternal damnation in a fiery pit."[21] The belief that all people will be saved was their doctrine of universal salvation, and universal salvation was applied without distinguishing between races. In more temporal matters, it was impossible for them to be any more effective at bringing about immediate abolition of slavery than any other denomination.

The Universalists operated from the premise of the "fatherhood of God and the brotherhood of man."[22] Consequently, one might expect that they would "immediately condemn the institution of slavery, take appropriate action to further its abolition, speak as one voice, and become the pioneers in a great effort to further the cause of humanity."[23] Not so. The Universalists encountered the same difficulties as other contemporary denominations and were completely unable to translate their high ideals regarding slavery into immediate effective action. Slavery, from the viewpoint of the church, had become an institution that was "inextricably interwoven into the fabric of the entire nation."[24]

New England was home to the very first Universalist church in the United States, in Gloucester, Massachusetts. From its origin, "Universalism challenged its members to reach out and embrace people whom society often marginalized."[25] They believed that "dignity and worth is innate to all people regardless of sex, color, race or class." Universalists translated their principles into social action, which included being staunch abolitionists.[26] However, an overwhelming majority of Universalists within the abolition movement were moderates rather than extremists. They preferred to apply a quieter rationale to the slavery issue.

The abolitionist politics and radical thinking of the militant William Lloyd Garrison did not appeal to Universalists. They rejected the idea of immediatism, or abolishing slavery immediately, much preferring the abolition of slavery through "gradual and peaceable means based on moral persuasion, example, and enlightenment through education. Patience, forbearance and tolerance" was their call as they tried to exert pressure to "transform the American conscience."[27]

Perhaps Universalists could have been at the forefront of the abolition movement during the mid–1800s if they had heeded their own teachings from the previous century. Their Articles of Faith and Plan of Church Government, adopted by the delegates at a 1790 Philadelphia convention, are very clear about slaveholding: "We recommend a total refraining from the African trade and the adoption of prudent measures for the gradual abolition of the slavery of the negroes in our country."[28] This antislavery resolution passed by a religious body even predated the 1793 federal Fugitive Slave Act. The problem was that, although this was an admirable position to espouse, the resolution had no binding authority. It was essentially a suggestion to the Universalist Church members at large for a humanitarian approach to the slave issue. In 1790, they did not see the need for immediacy and were content with gradual abolition. Additionally, and maybe more importantly, there was no contemporary political action in the nation at that time to support this important ecclesiastical resolution.

It was evident that the Universalists wanted to philosophize and verbalize their ideals about the elemental wrongs built into slavery, but that was where the discussion ended. No overt action was ever taken on the part of the greater church.

Universalists were also considered to be heretics by other, more traditionally orthodox Protestant denominations. They did not believe in the everlasting damnation or eternal hell that Puritan churches proposed. In fact, "the genius of Universalism in earlier years seemed to find expression in healing the wounds inflicted in serious and sincere hearts by the fear of hell rather than in building up an ecclesiastical body."[29]

William Paine Dutton, who was the son of Sycamore's Civil War General Everell F. Dutton, explained this position in a letter to his sister-in-law, Jane. Dutton firmly commented on the Universalist philosophy, "The Hell Fire which laid in wait for the careless of other faiths was not for us. Our final redemption was fairly certain and this conviction, (which I personally thought to be a very comforting one) divided us sharply from the other Protestant Churches."[30] Universalists believed in the good inherent within everyone, including the Negro race. Therefore, it was an easy transition for the Sycamore Universalists to serve their beliefs by helping fugitive slaves through the local Underground Railroad.

During the 1830s, although the Universalists bristled against the idea of any organized antislavery movement, they clearly recognized that the antislavery forces were fueled by a combination of politics and religion. As a religious phenomenon, they perceived that the antislavery movement "was largely Presbyterian and Congregational in makeup, although ostensibly interdenominational."[31] Universalists often refused to join any of the antislavery organizations because they had a distinct distaste for the political orientation of such activist groups. Secondly, they thought the antislavery movement was dominated by the so-called orthodox denominations. Those two perceptions were anathema to the Universalists. They needed to maintain the idea of having their own religious and political choices.

It was during the 1830s and 1840s that the Universalist Church struggled to pass a national resolution within the society pertaining to the "existence of American slavery or expressing a desire for its abolition."[32] The church was much divided on whether or not the question of slavery should even actually be discussed within the structure of the religious organization. This position worked to their advantage in DeKalb County, Illinois. Because of their public silence on the issue of slavery, the Universalist Church in Sycamore, unlike their Congregationalist friends, were allowed to continue to hold their worship services in the courthouse. The Congregationalists were quite vocal about their antislavery position; the Universalists were not. Regardless of what the rank and file members did individually, as a group they did not openly agitate either against slavery or against the prevailing civil laws.

When slavery was discussed, no mention was made of such discussions in the minutes reporting the meetings, and even Universalist owners and editors of various church publications in both the Northern and the Southern parts of the country refused to print any proposed slavery resolutions in their newspapers.[33] Universalists hoped that by spreading their doctrine of universal salvation, the Southern slaveholders would simply renounce their evil ways and voluntarily free their slaves. After freeing the slaves, "the ex-slaveholders would admit that they had been wrong all along, and in a fit of remorse, buttressed by economic need, would promptly hire their ex-slaves; then all would be well."[34] This was the overwhelming belief that Sycamore Universalist residents like Julia Fletcher Carney and Curtis Smith always held close to their hearts.

An 1841 resolution passed by the Danvers, Massachusetts, Universalist Church was "typical of many to follow within the denomination."[35] It exhorted Universalist members to exert their utmost influence for the immediate overthrow of slavery. But in reality, what were they supposed to do? Were they truly advocating war? How should they approach their Southern religious counterparts? The result was that each local Universalist Society treated the idea of slavery as they saw fit within the confines of their particular community. The Sycamore Universalists may have passed a similar antislavery resolution condemning slavery, as did the local members of the First Congregational Church. Appropriate documentation is nonexistent. The personal actions of Universalist members, however, indicate firm determination in their resolve against slavery.

When Universalist preacher William Roundsville first came to DeKalb County, he, too, understood the mindset of the emigrants from New England and New York. The New England state of mind included their strong antislavery attitudes. According to the 1850 and 1860 Federal Census, all the founding Universalist members in Sycamore were from New York and Vermont, except Henry Gandy, who hailed from Ohio.

A Patriot and Christian Recants

William Parker Dutton, grandfather to William Paine Dutton, and member of the Sycamore Universalist Church, was born in New Hampshire in 1817, the son of a New England farmer. He was educated in a public "common school," and married when he was 18 years old. By 1844, he decided to move his family to Illinois, first settling in St. Charles in Kane County before moving to Sycamore. This was the same year that the Congregationalists were evicted from the DeKalb County Courthouse as their place of worship for taking an antislavery stand.

At a time when the majority of people in Sycamore were antislavery, William Parker Dutton was adamantly proslavery. He considered himself a strong Democrat, adopted a stance of proslavery, and supported the extension of slavery into new states being admitted into the Union. Dutton's wife, Mary Turner Dutton, is described as being an "intelligent, amiable and industrious woman"[36] who probably acquiesced to the viewpoints of her husband. His outspoken views in support of slavery, however, may well have invoked the ire of his daughter-in-law, Rose (Paine) Dutton. Rose married Dutton's son, Everell F. Dutton, who attained fame as a General in the 105th Illinois Infantry during the Civil War. Rose Dutton was also a member of the Universalist Church with its antislavery philosophy.

William Parker Dutton showed interested in the Kansas-Nebraska free soil issue when the newly created territory of Kansas preoccupied itself with the slavery question. Congress erroneously thought they were avoiding any federal discussion of slavery in 1854 when they formed the Kansas and Nebraska territories. Sponsored by Illinois' own Senator Stephen A. Douglas, and using his favorite theory of popular sovereignty, under the Kansas-Nebraska Act, territories could decide for themselves whether or not they would allow slavery. This negated provisions of the 1820 Missouri Compromise, and Douglas underestimated the Northern outrage that would ensue.

Back in Sycamore, William Parker Dutton recognized that his friends and fellow church members all possessed a more compassionate view of the runaway slaves coming through town than he did. In his position as Sycamore's postmaster, he had a professional obligation to uphold the federal Fugitive Slave Law enacted in 1850, because he was an employee of the United States government. He could not legitimately aid a fugitive Negro in opposition to the new law. Yet his conscience must have continued to gnaw around the edges of his resolve.

Every Sunday at the Universalist Church where Dutton attended worship services, the Rev. Thomas Carney sermonized about the brotherhood of man. Some of the hymns Dutton sang with the congregation were even composed by Carney's wife, Julia, the quiet Bostonian antislavery activist. Dutton may have wondered, could the slave could possibly be his "brother"? Slavery had always existed. Leave it alone and ultimately, as other Universalists prophesied, the goodness of man would prevail and slavery would disappear on its own. That was the way to end slavery.

Daily, his position as local U.S. postmaster allowed Dutton to be aware of the pronouncements and moods of other Sycamore citizens. He kept his ear to the ground. As a result, he readily learned that many good Samaritans in Sycamore were actually helping those itinerant runaway slaves by hiding them in their barns or giving them rides to somewhere outside of town. Recently, though, he read in the weekly *Western Citizen* about the upcoming "Anti-Nebraska Convention" to be held in Sycamore. With Missouri a bordering slave state to Kansas, many assumed that Kansas would vote to allow slavery. But there was still a chance to keep slavery out of Nebraska. The local "Anti-Nebraska Convention" was theoretically convened to discuss whether Nebraska should allow slavery in its new territory. However, local town gossip indicated that the main subject to be discussed at the meeting would be the issue of slavery itself, more than the idea of statehood for a western territory. The Kansas-Nebraska Act had passed in Congress in May 1854, and antislavery organizers in DeKalb County planned their Anti-Nebraska Convention meeting for July 31, 1854, at the courthouse in Sycamore.

Enough already! First Dutton must endure endless talk of antislavery in his own church and now the entire issue was becoming political. The people who were against slavery in the territories of Kansas and Nebraska now seemed to be against slavery everywhere in the United States. It became obvious that this local gathering was not totally an Anti-Nebraska Convention; in actuality it was a DeKalb County antislavery convention commingled with a political motivation to organize the new Republican Party.

And so, "with the expectation of making a truthful report to that effect for the benefit of the Democratic party,"[37] Dutton decided to personally travel west to Kansas specifically to denounce the antislavery views firsthand. He expected to lend his hand physically to help the cause in Kansas and Nebraska to allow slavery in their territories. Antislavery people in Kansas had formed a political group called the Free State Party, and Dutton was "in full belief that the free-state people were entirely at fault."[38]

However, once there, he witnessed the atrocities of slavery and experienced firsthand the "outrages against the free-state men."[39] William Parker Dutton rapidly reversed his position on the issue. "When he saw with his own eyes the terrible and sad condition of the [black] people of that distracted country, he experienced a complete change of opinion, and there openly and unhesitatingly declared himself in favor of the free state idea, which he previously so vigorously condemned."[40] This unreasonable man promptly declared himself a free-state man and returned to Sycamore "denouncing the conduct of the 'border-ruffians' as infamous."[41] The term "border ruffians" described individuals who crossed into Kansas and through sometimes violent and illegal means sought to influence political decisions in the new territory. They advocated the establishment of slavery in Kansas. The physical disputes over the slavery question in Kansas caused the territory to quickly become a national battleground in the struggle against slavery. Kansas rightly earned the designation of "bleeding Kansas."

Dutton was now an Abolitionist. A true Universalist answering the call of a patriot and a Christian, he recanted his proslavery position and adopted the philosophy of abolitionism. As a result, "the Democratic ax fell upon the head of that postmaster,"[42] and he lost his job. Dutton crossed the line when he openly vocalized his new ideas and his course of action cost him his politically appointed government position as postmaster of Sycamore, Illinois.

This local decision to relieve Dutton of his postmaster duties paralleled the earlier 1844 decision to prohibit the Congregationalists from using the courthouse as a meeting place. Some government officials felt that they needed to uphold the existing fugitive slave law as written in the Compromise of 1850, and anyone holding an opposite opinion or engaging in activities to aid fugitive slaves was subject to scrutiny. William Parker Dutton left Sycamore in 1857 and moved to Kansas permanently. He carried his new abolitionist thought process into elected civic positions, where a year later he was elected the first treasurer of Lykens County. After serving as a delegate to the Wyandotte Constitutional Convention in 1859 for the state of Kansas, Dutton was elected to two terms as Miami County (formerly Lykens County) sheriff. During the Civil War "he was a conspicuous figure in Kansas affairs, and a strong supporter of the government."[43] Dutton personally "organized and commanded a military company for the protection of the border"[44] and served on the staff of Kansas' governor as an aide-de-camp. After the Civil War he divided his time between his farm in Sycamore, Illinois, and Paola, Kansas, where he died in 1888.

It seems strange that William P. Dutton was fired from his government employment in Sycamore because he followed his imperative duty as patriot and Christian at a time when Universalists were still considered to be Christians. County Clerk Jesse C. Kellogg, who also had an antislavery attitude, remained in his post. The difference is that Kellogg's position was an elected county post, rather than a federal appointment, and consequently gave him the necessary insulation against being suddenly ousted from office. He was not an employee of any government, state, federal or municipal, and could not be fired from his job because of his personal views. Additionally, because Kellogg's was not a federal position, it was easier for him to ignore prevailing federal laws which did not affect the day-to-day operation of his office. Upholding the Fugitive Slave Law ran against local sentiment, and favorable local sentiment towards Kellogg as a candidate was what first elected him.

Sylvanus Holcomb Aids David West

As one of the trustees and later a deacon in the Sycamore Universalist Church, Sylvanus Holcomb was characterized as a man "of many sturdy traits of character [with] unquestioned integrity."[45] He was a person who acted on his Universalist beliefs. Holcomb lived on the state road going east towards the county line between DeKalb and Kane Counties. Like Deacon David West, Holcomb was also born in Oneida County, New York. In 1826 he married Julia B. Joslyn and by 1839 decided to leave New York. The young family included his wife and six children, ages 2 through 11, who were all packed into a wagon and with a team of horses they headed to Illinois "for a home in the West."[46] Holcomb settled in Section 34 in Sycamore Township, where he built a log house of 18' × 24' in the middle of the unbroken prairie. The life of a settler was fraught with uncertainty. "One night the fire went out and as they were without matches, Mr. Holcomb was obliged to go more than a mile to obtain fire."[47] The first map drawn of Sycamore in 1840 shows Sylvanus Holcomb's residence as the last house at the eastern edge of Sycamore Township.[48] "There was but one house in sight [probably belonging to David West's brother, Aaron], and the neighbors were the deer and wolves, which then were in abundance."[49] Holcomb fit the profile of the New Yorker who brought his antislavery beliefs with him to the new Northwest Territory.

When David West and his family arrived on the scene four years later, he became Holcomb's nearest neighbor across the road and slightly to the west. The two pioneers, coming from the same geographic area in the state of New York and both with antislavery ideas, were now neighboring farmers along the same country road in Illinois. Holcomb and West often worked together in aiding fugitive slaves. The following anecdote demonstrates this shared sentiment.

Sometime after 1844 an unidentified Southern sheriff arrived in town to post a disturbing sign in Sycamore. The sign indicated that there was a reward of ten thousand dollars for the apprehension of two fugitive slaves. The large reward of $5,000 per slave was higher than the then current national average, but local written and oral history supports the amount. There followed a description of the two runaways and instructions to the public that they could claim the reward upon the return of the slaves.

Such signs had never appeared in Sycamore previously, and the posting of this particular handbill surprised the local citizens. With the strong antislavery sentiment in and around DeKalb County, it was unusual for any slavery supporters to rear their heads. People in Sycamore were not particularly eager to give slavecatchers information on how or where to find a fugitive slave. They were more concerned with how and where to keep black men and women safely hidden.

The out-of-town sheriff had heard of David West's prowess in aiding runaways and was determined to be confrontational regarding these particular individuals and "make it more than usually interesting for Mr. West." When the sheriff arrived to question West at his family home on the state road east of town, he soon "went away no wiser than when he came." David West, it seemed, "had grown skillful in giving evasive answers if he chose."[50] In truth, the fugitives were actually hiding on West's property, perhaps in the underground room under the corn crib, and they were later transported to points east in their quest for freedom.

In the meantime, there were a few unnamed "prominent men of Sycamore [who] were anxious to receive part of the ten thousand dollars reward offered and tried in every way possible to assist in the capture of the two valuable negroes."[51] West's good friend and neighbor, Sylvanus Holcomb, intervened and informed the bounty hunters that "Deacon West was skillful with a rifle and could hit the eye of a deer at long range." The area proslavery men, along with the Southern sheriff, "thought best to return to Sycamore and give up the matter of securing the ten thousand dollars for the capture of the negroes."[52] Even the prospect of securing an unusually large prize did not convince the out-of-towners to confront David West.

This story further supports the thought that everyone in Sycamore was not necessarily antislavery. Someone in town was willing to help the Southern sheriff to enforce the law in his pursuit of the slaves — though perhaps their only objective was their own financial gain. The inhabitants of this small Midwestern town were not all Abolitionists, yet those who professed to be antislavery like Holcomb, were not afraid to act on their beliefs. Sylvanus Holcomb was an unreasonable man.

A New Voice Labors On

While the Rev. Thomas Carney was its pastor, the Universalist Church became an active influence in the community. Other local denominations felt the competition. The Rev. Darius Gore of the First Congregational Church saw the makings of a rivalry and complained to the American Missionary Association, "As obstacles to contend with, we have here [in Sycamore] a Universalist Society which has preaching all the time."[53] Gore was feeling the pressure to vie for a growing church membership. He further reflected on a perceived "coldness and indifference ... some infidelity, intemperance, Sabbath desecration and profanity"[54] on the part of the Universalists. Clearly in 1856 the two congregations were not as compatible as they would become with their local merger in the next century.

When Thomas and Julia Carney left Sycamore for Galesburg, Illinois, in 1857, the Rev. Rufus Sanborn arrived on the scene. He was undoubtedly encouraged to come to Sycamore by Carney and his wife. The Carneys knew Sanborn when they lived in New England. Ten years earlier Julia wrote to Thomas from Dresden, Maine, and mentioned Sanborn's preaching from the text "Let your light so shine." Ever the sweet diplomat and colored by her love for Thomas, she commented, "It was a more finished and labored essay than yours upon the same, but did not contain half as much of original thought."[55] Sanborn was more inclined towards pure academia.

An intellectual whose writings can still be found in the Andover-Harvard Library at Harvard Divinity School, the Rev. Rufus Slocum Sanborn was not thwarted in his academic pursuits upon moving to the Midwest. Born in Epsom, New Hampshire, in 1819, Sanborn was one of 14 siblings, including the four natural children of his own mother and father, plus eight half-brothers and sisters from his father's first marriage, and two more children from a third marriage. In 1841 he married Emily F. Howard in Hinsdale, New Hampshire, where he also became the pastor to his first Universalist congregation.

The Sanborns reared five children, Susan, Albert, Clarence, Rufus and Frank. After pastorates at several towns in Vermont and Provincetown, Massachusetts, they moved their family to Sycamore, Illinois. Sanborn purchased a comfortable frame house plus the empty lot adjacent to it at the northwest corner of Elm and Governor Streets for $1,200 and lived there until 1862. Sanborn eagerly supported the antislavery agenda of the local church, while he simultaneously proclaimed the Universalist brand of religion. Church members and townspeople held him in great esteem for his "public enterprise and social spirit."[56]

At some point during the late 1850s, Elder Sanborn was "summoned" to "uphold salvation" at an open forum public debate. Various Universalist church members attended to give support to Sanborn's argument.

> There was no daily paper then. The *Chicago Democrat* once a week and the *DeKalb County Sentinel* comprised the literary outfit of most houses, but religious discussion was rampant in every shoe shop, store, and on the street. People were long on doctrine in [the 1850s] and had decided opinions on the question of universal salvation and everlasting damnation. The tension finally got so high that an arrangement was made to have an exhaustive discussion of the whole subject in Champlin's Hall by the leading champions of the two sides in this section of the country. The Universalists summoned Elder Sanborn, a Sycamore preacher, to uphold salvation. Eldred Coltrin, a powerful Freewill Baptist preacher from Blackberry, was chosen to refute the arguments of this adroit and plausible emissary of Satan. The school, which was held in the hall with a daily attendance of seventy-five pupils was dismissed, a time keeper and referee were agreed upon and the champions, each finally idolized by their supporters, went at it. Hod Champlin, old Uncle John Waterman, old Uncle Phin Joslyn, Nathan Peck and others giving aid and comfort to Sanborn; Deacon A.V.L. Smith, Dave Champlin, John Eaton, Edwin Burr and a score of others standing grim and determined by the heavy Baptist; nor did they lack for an audience. The hall was filled to suffocation morning, afternoon and evening for the larger part of a week, many coming ten or twelve miles, and still these champions kept hurling text and argument, hour and hour about, the audience excited to a high pitch throughout. Both sides won, and it could have been proven at any time twenty-five years after the discussion took place.[57]

By his own admission, Elder Sanborn "preached constantly for 27 years,"[58] and may have been slightly bored with it all.

He also had "a genius for mechanical invention."[59] In 1866, at age 47, Rufus Sanborn invented the first steam fireproof safe, deemed one of the great inventions of the age. Patented in both the United States and Great Britain, the safe was welded iron and steel and contained "water vessels having steam valves for the purpose of affording additional security to the contents of the safe in case of fire, by filling it with the steam generated by the boiling of the water in the vessels."[60] By that point in his life, he had made his fortune and purchased a palatial home in Rockford, Illinois.

"I have not preached since I invented the Steam fire proof Safe, now manufactured by the American Steam Safe Company of Boston," he wrote. "I have lived in Rockford, Ills, without any pastoral charge."[61] There is a sadness in his own personal comments which is reflected in his obituaries. Apparently he gradually lost much of his money, and allegedly "had a care-worn, troubled life and seemed far from a happy man."[62] Rufus Slocum Sanborn died at the Elgin Insane Asylum, Elgin, Illinois, from "softening of the brain," which was most likely dementia.

Like many people in DeKalb County, the Rev. Sanborn's affiliation with abolitionism is inferred from his profound association with a local antislavery church. Being a Northern Universalist minister at a church in a town known to be antislavery, and through his association with the Carneys, who defended an antislavery position, Sanborn's support of the antislavery movement is correctly assumed. The Universalist Church in Sycamore would not have called a minister to their congregation who was not antislavery. As the congregation grew and prospered during the 1850s, the local antislavery movement included many of its members. With the unreasonable Sanborn, the Universalists, along with their friends and neighbors, the Congregationalists, all white evangelical Christians, quietly did what they could and would not let go of the idea that slavery should be abolished.

A Black Republican's Theories

The Black Republican and Universalist Curtis Smith privately advanced two theories to abolish Negro slavery. The first hypothesis focused on education. Smith felt strongly that education of the Negro race was paramount to help solve the dilemma. He commented that "no innocent person with a proper education can be retained in slavery."[63]

Second, he advocated an exceptionally radical opinion for the mid–1800s: Intermarriage should be allowed and encouraged between the white and black races. His thought was that "in time the colored strain might be eliminated [thus causing everyone to be born more white than black], then it would be very difficult to enslave a white person in this country."[64]

But on April 12, 1861, when that first cannon shot surprised the federal military at Fort Sumter, Curtis Smith remarked, "The problem is solved. Slavery has received its death blow."[65] This unreasonable man who was called a "Black Republican" knew that with the beginning of the Civil War, his peaceful protests, once heard only by a few, would finally be heard by the multitudes. And the Universalist dream of all people everywhere becoming brethren would possibly be realized.

CHAPTER 9

Seceders and Covenanters: The Presbyterians

> I first saw the light among the rugged and free hills of Scotland; a land, sir, that never was conquered, and where a slave never breathed. Let a slave set foot on that shore, and his chains fall off forever, and he becomes what God made him — a man.[1] — John Hossack of LaSalle County, Illinois (1806–1891), Abolitionist convicted of violating the Fugitive Slave Law

Let a Slave Set Foot on That Shore

The year was sometime in the mid–1850s. It was a summer Sunday in Somonauk, Illinois, the special day of the week when everyone who was physically able either walked, saddled his horse, or rode in a carriage or wagon pulled by horses or oxen over dusty or muddy trails to make his way to Sabbath worship services. You dared not miss. If you were sick, you had a good excuse, but if the weather was inclement, too bad. Unpleasant weather was not a legitimate reason for missing Sunday church. The Associate Presbyterian Church was still the primary catalyst in this place. Church members emigrated from New York as a group and remained here together. The local Presbyterian Church was the sturdy glue holding the pieces of the community together.

This particular Sunday saw the small congregation filling up the pews in their recently built house of worship. The Rev. Mr. Rensselaer W. French stretched his tall frame as he rose to take his place at the pulpit in the chancel area in front of the sanctuary. Although the transplanted New York Presbyterians held their first worship service in 1842, they were not officially organized until four years later. In 1846 French officiated as the organizing minister for the young congregation, and three years later accepted a call to the permanent Somonauk position. The good Reverend divided his time initially ministering to both Somonauk and Ross Grove, near Paw Paw, as well as Wheatland Presbyterian Church in Will County. However, because he and his wife Nancy owned land and lived in Clinton Township close to Somonauk, the Somonauk area was their home.

The feeling of being truly home came not only from French's new professional affiliation with the Associate Presbyterian Church, but also from his sense of kinship with local doctrines. Somonauk was a place where the "great majority of citizens were of one mind on the subject of slavery."[2] It was a pleasure for the French family to live and work in that kind of environment. They followed the example set by New York's congressman William H. Seward, who in the previous year had informed Congress that there was a "higher law than the Constitution."[3] Somonauk's citizenry agreed that there was a higher law than the 1850 Fugitive Slave Law requiring people to return runaway slaves to their masters. In Somonauk, the "friends of the [Underground Rail]road declared its charter came from God," and the Rev. French was "in full accord with the activities of this institution."[4]

Always a formidable figure, as French moved to the pulpit that summer Sunday, he looked out at his congregation with those piercing eyes above his clipped beard and clerical collar. The antislavery congregation, which included the Rev. French's friends and relatives, entered the church that warm morning and perhaps noticed the seven or eight Negroes sitting near the pulpit in the corner pews. All who saw them would have silently realized that the small cluster of ragged, tired people were runaway slaves finding momentary refuge among the church people of Somonauk. They may even have learned prior to the worship service that the runaways would be in attendance. Either French himself or their friend and community leader, George Beveridge, brought them to church and seated them where they would be observed.

On the preceding Saturday evening, these fugitives had arrived at an Underground Railroad station in the Somonauk area. According to Albert French, Rensselaer's youngest son, the runaway group stayed the night at George and Ann Beveridge's home, a known Underground Railroad location. The Beveridge cabin was "generally known throughout the state as one of the main stations on the Underground Railroad."[5]

Even though there was a rumor that slavecatchers might be in the vicinity looking for the renegades, the entire congregation maintained their decorum and overcame any anxiety about the circumstances. The Sabbath worship service began. Scripture was read; psalms were sung according to prescribed psalmody with no musical instruments, and the Rev. French then requested that a special collection be taken to assist these scared, courageous children of God who were seated in the church corner. From his vantage point in the pulpit French could see out the sanctuary door and, unbeknownst to the congregation facing him, he quickly realized that several strange men had stopped outside. They could only be the dreaded slavecatchers, and when one man hurriedly approached the church building, Pastor French abruptly stopped in the middle of his sermon and admonished his flock to pray. In response, the congregation "immediately rose to its feet, as was its custom."[6] And what became of the fugitives? When the congregation stood, the quick-thinking minister gestured to the fugitives to stay seated. The stage was set.

An unfamiliar man entered the sanctuary and was greeted by either David Miller Dobbin or William Patten. They were the two first elected ruling elders in the Somonauk Associate Presbyterian Church and assisted at morning worship services. The stranger asked of the elder, "Have you any runaway niggers in there?"[7]

Dobbin or Patten replied "blandly with a wave of his hand, 'You can look for yourself.' The man looked, saw the congregation standing, and a parson vigorously praying, couldn't see any 'niggers' and turned around and went off."[8] The seated fugitives were safe.

As in the rugged, free hills of Scotland, the prairies of Somonauk, populated with first- and second-generation immigrant Scotsmen, were a place where a slave never breathed. This small group of fugitive slaves set foot on the shores of Somonauk Creek and their chains fell off forever. They were bound for Canada and freedom.

The Spirit of Freedom

Scots are legendary; they are celebrated for their resolve in battle. Authors repeatedly highlight the strong Scot cultural and ethnic characteristics — their sense of right and wrong that first pervaded clan disputes, then carried them over the Atlantic Ocean to a new world and bolstered their determination when they chased their dreams to the western frontier. These same Scots, as Christians, adhered to the Presbyterian denomination.

Members of the Church of Scotland signed a national covenant in 1638 whereby they pledged to uphold the autonomy of the church. When England tried to impose an Anglican Episcopal system upon the Scots, they rebelled and many were killed. Presbyterianism was eventually restored in Scotland some 50 years later, but this group refused to accept the new Presbyterian Church. They wanted to keep the old National Covenant and therefore were called "covenanters." Their action created the Reformed Presbyterian Church.

Protestants may have questioned the connections between the state and the church, but there was never a deviation from their Christian faith. The Presbyterians were very strong-willed people. Once again, during the middle 1700s, a group of like-thinking men determined to leave the Church of Scotland. This group seceded from the parent church, became identified as "seceders," and was known openly as the Associate Presbyterian Church. Over the course of history, the Presbyterian Church would sustain additional divisions as free-thinking men and women re-interpreted theological doctrines anew.

Descending from the strong Calvinistic and Puritan rationale that prevailed at that time, the Presbyterian quest was to become what God made them: a stalwart alliance that never wavered from their belief that all men were free. For these seceders, members of the Associate Presbyterian Church, Washington County in mid–eastern New York was their first home in the United States.

Following the pattern of their forefathers who came to America as a religious group, the first Presbyterians who settled the community of Somonauk, Illinois, also came as a group from Washington County, New York. Once again they sought to continue the same freedoms hard won by their ancestors. As descendants of that same immigrant group, their relationships intertwined through marriages, they encouraged other friends and family to follow them. The rolling prairie land was beautiful; the timber was plentiful; the water was pure; and there was obvious opportunity for growth in this new western frontier. For the Presbyterians, the Scottish spirit of freedom flourished.

Become What God Made You

One of those stalwart Presbyterians was George Beveridge, whose wife Ann was unlike some women in the mid–1800s. Ann actually encouraged her husband to go west to seek out fertile land for a new farm. George was so stalwart that he professed to dislike all Catholics, preferring the Orange Men of Scotland to anyone under the Pope's purview. Beveridge's resolute piety was always evident and even once caused him to stay home from church, which was unthinkable. His own son, Andrew, was an ordained minister who came to preach at the Somonauk Presbyterian Church. Apparently Andrew's theology did not quite match with his father's, and rather than hear his accomplished son speak, George chose not to attend the worship service. He did not want to subject himself to viewpoints differing from his own.

In 1838 the steadfast Scotsman Beveridge began his thousand-mile journey west to Illinois with his wagon and a team of horses. His youngest son, John Lourie Beveridge, who later became governor of Illinois, accompanied him. From Chicago's Fort Dearborn he followed the new road leading to the Galena lead mines, the Chicago-Galena Road. This same trail would be utilized for years by wagon trains, those prairie schooners heading west with the California gold rush.

When George Beveridge arrived at Somonauk Creek, his first order of business was to secure a shelter — a home for his family. He wanted to buy land, with an eye to his future and that of his wife and children. Very soon Beveridge met John Eastabrooks and purchased from him an existing old log cabin and a tract of land. George and his son John spent the next four years refurbishing the cabin structure and working the land. At the end of the four years he decided it was time to go back to New York to gather his family for the return trip to their new home. Accompanying Mr. and Mrs. Beveridge to Illinois were five of their seven living children, James Hoy, Thomas, John Lourie and Agnes, plus their daughter Isabel, her husband William French, and their infant daughter, Ellen. These Beveridge children plus one grandchild ranged in age from 1 to 27. Another daughter Jennett, who was 29 years old and married to James Henry, remained in New York, coming to Somonauk at a later date. At that time, George and Ann's son, Andrew, was studying for the ministry in New York and so stayed behind. Following the example set by their Scot forefathers, the Beveridges moved ensemble to a new land in the west.

The Beveridge family was characterized as "sturdy Presbyterians in religious [faith], and strongly anti-slavery in political faith."[9] Being antislavery was a political faith which they practiced as fervently as their religious faith, never deviating from the pathway of righteousness and justice. A story about the family involvement in the Underground Railroad, recorded in Boies' 1868 *History of DeKalb County*, is repeated verbatim in both *The History of the Somonauk United Presbyterian Church* and its sequel, *The Church of the Pioneers*.

For many years the Beveridge home was well known as a station on the Underground Railroad. George and Ann unquestioningly welcomed any fugitive slaves passing through the Somonauk area. The friendly couple readily offered a hot meal with a place to hide and sleep for the night. Such notoriety about their activities came with a price. They frequently ran the risk of slavecatchers discovering their hideaways, and after the passage of the Fugitive Slave Law, they accepted the greater risk of a government representative or proslavery person turning them in to Federal agents for illegally harboring a runaway.

According to a published story, one evening in 1852 there was a knock at the door and a "gentlemanly stranger," a white man, stood on the threshold "begging shelter for the night." Because the Beveridges' original log cabin had once been a tavern stopover on the stagecoach trail from Chicago to Galena, in the early years it was never unusual for someone to seek shelter overnight. However, this particular evening, neither George nor Ann had a good feeling about the unfamiliar person who appeared on their doorstep. Their indications from the outsider led them to believe that he "was a detective, searching for evidence of their connection with the crime of aiding slaves to their freedom."[10]

The stranger, though, must have felt comfortable with the tenor and direction of his conversation with the Beveridges, because he pointedly asked Ann Hoy Beveridge if she had ever secretly hidden fugitive Negroes.

She knew she could possibly go to prison for such a crime, but her response was quick and succinct, with a simple "Yes." And then, with her Scottish ire aroused and perhaps her hands on her hips, Ann rose and faced her interrogator and continued, "In spite of your oppressive laws, I will do it again whenever I have an opportunity."[11]

The older Beveridge couple awaited the presumed officer of the law to announce that they were under arrest. However, the stranger laughed heartily. He quickly explained that he was a physician from Quincy, Illinois, with the express purpose to establish stations on the Underground Railroad. From that time on, there was "a frequent stoppage of trains at this station, and much time and money was spent in forwarding the flying Negroes on to Plano and other places of refuge."[12] It is quite possible that the physician was Dr. Richard Eells, a prominent Quincy Abolitionist who was known to be openly active in the Underground Railroad. However,

Dr. Eells died in 1846, before the reported 1852 visit occurred. Therefore, if the person was Dr. Eells, the date given in Boies' *History of DeKalb County* for the doctor's visit may be incorrect. The accurate date for Eells' unannounced visit to the Beveridge home would have been prior to 1846. Or the visitor may have been a business associate of Eells.

The Scotsman George Beveridge and his wife Ann easily became what God made them, an unreasonable man and woman.

Presbyterians Flourish

A comment printed about the original Scot colonists equally applied to the Somonauk flock: "They had lost nothing of their austerity of life, stern purpose and steadfast Christian faith by their migration to America nor by their subsequent freedom from Britain"[13] through the American Revolutionary War. The Presbyterians persevered. For four years the Somonauk Presbyterian Church was a mission church served by a succession of occasional ministers supplied by the Associate Presbyterian Church Board of Home Missions. Between ministers, they met regularly as a "cottage prayer" and study group in the Beveridge log cabin. That family home became, in fact, the first church building. Always considering themselves as a "church," they eagerly welcomed a succession of occasional supply ministers from the greater church body until the Rev. Rensselaer W. French officially organized the new congregation in 1846. Finally, after a new log schoolhouse was constructed in 1849, the religious settlers relocated their meetings to the public space.

The newly organized congregants were 20 strong in number and included George and Ann (Hoy) Beveridge; their daughter Isabel (Beveridge) French, who was married to William French; David and Mary (French) Dobbin; Mary's parents Jonathan and Ann (Edgar) French; their son and daughter, Alexander and Sarah French; Margaret (Brown) Howison, wife of William; William and Elizabeth (Pratt) Patten and his mother, Mary (Robertson) Patten; William and Isabel (Williamson) Robertson; Dr. John Shankland; Ann (Dobbin) Telford, married to Francis Telford and cousin to David Miller Dobbin; John and Nancy (Walls) Walker and John's father, James Walker. Although George Beveridge is credited with being the original pioneer leader in the new Somonauk Associate Presbyterian Church, the French family was initially better represented in the list of charter church members with four family members, plus a daughter-in-law, who just happened to be George and Ann Beveridge's daughter.

New members were quickly added when they moved into the Somonauk area: Robert and Alexander Patten, who were both sons of Mary and brothers to William Patten; and Agnes Beveridge, another daughter of George and Ann. Agnes later married Alexander Patten. Additional new members showed their undeniable heritage through their obvious Scot surnames: Ferguson, Graham, Boyd, Stewart, McClellan, McAllister and McCleery. It is important to note that these identical Scotsmen during that same time period were all also subscribers to the antislavery newspaper *Western Citizen*. They were keenly aware of antislavery activities in the Northern Illinois area, as well as in the rest of the United States.

One of Pastor French's first tasks as the organizing minister was to assist the fledgling group to tender a call to a minister whom they hoped would serve them on a part-time basis. However, that man, the Rev. Pollock, declined the Somonauk responsibility. Soon afterwards, French himself was asked to accept a call to minister to the newly organized congregation. It was a perfect fit in more ways than one. Being a Presbyterian minister and being antislavery created a match that suited both French and the Somonauk Presbyterians for the next ten years.

Rensselaer W. was the son of John Blair and Robena (McMicken) French. Like the majority of the Somonauk immigrants, he was born in New York. When he was 25 years old, he married

Nancy Pollock. Nancy was the daughter of a John Pollock, but it is unclear whether or not she was related to the Rev. R.H. Pollock, who previously ministered occasionally to the Somonauk Presbyterians. Their children were John Pollock, Robena Jane, Mary Anne and Albert Collins. Unlike most clergymen of his day, he owned property. He secured a land patent for acreage in Clinton Township, near Somonauk, and enjoyed farming. And like most of his flock, he subscribed to the *Western Citizen*.

His son Albert French, also known as "A.C.," wrote about "Father's unceasing fight against negro slavery."[14] Albert talked about the fact that in some other communities everyone was not always strongly antislavery. In all of DeKalb County, however, and in the little hamlet of Somonauk, "the predominating sentiment was with him."[15] He could stand straight on Sunday mornings and expound about the sin of slavery and encourage his flock to work tirelessly on behalf of the downtrodden. Under the tutelage of this unreasonable man, the Presbyterians flourished. Rensselaer W. French was right at home.

"Without Distinction of Party or Sex"[16]

On October 30, 1850, the unreasonable men and women of Somonauk could stay quiet no longer. They determined to be vocal about their antislavery philosophy, which instantly made them politically active and ultimately gave them a large degree of notoriety. In the minds of Somonauk residents, the federal government had gone too far in creating the recently passed Fugitive Slave Law, and they were obligated to object and be certain that a protest was heard. Their remedy was to call an assembly of the citizenry with the specific goal to agree upon certain antislavery resolutions. Women did not yet have the right to vote in the United States, but the Somonauk people solicited men and women alike to contribute to the discussion. Additionally, because the traditional political factions of Democrats and Whigs had been further splintered into the Liberty Party, then the Free-Soilers, and the Antislavery-Democrats, organizers wanted to be certain that everyone "without distinction of party or sex"[17] was welcome to attend this important meeting. One month after the public meeting the entire report of their proceedings was published in the *Western Citizen* out of Chicago. The headline read "Indignation Meeting."

> On the 30th ult. the inhabitants of Somonauk met en masse — without distinction of party or sex — to give expression to their feelings of indignation against the late act of Congress — the infamous fugitive slave bill. Having gone through the preliminaries of organization and the meeting opened by prayer, the Chairman appointed a committee of five to draft resolutions.
>
> After a short absence they returned with the following — there being in them but two slight amendments from the original — all of which were most heartily responded to in the affirmative.
>
> 1. Resolved, That the law passed at the recent session of Congress for reclaiming fugitives from labor, is a base violation of the Constitution of the United States — a flagrant infringement upon the sovereignty of the States, and is deserving the execration, contempt and indignation of the friends of Human Liberty throughout the State, the country, and the world; and that we feel under no moral obligation to obey it.
>
> 2. That said law is an utter violation of those safeguards of personal liberty, the writ of habeas corpus, and the right of trial by jury; that the freedom of all persons without regard to color, circumstances, or condition, is placed in jeopardy, as they may be hurried off in a "summary manner" on the "proper affidavit" of the veriest knave in Christendom.
>
> 3. That the authors, aiders, abettors, administrators and defenders of this law — and those, also, from the Northern States, who "basely dodged the question," are traitors to Freedom, serviles of Slavery, and must stand condemned at the bar of an enlightened public sentiment.
>
> 4. That we pledge ourselves not to support for office any man who aided, in any way, directly or indirectly, the passage of this law; nor for any man that will not use his voice, vote and influence for its repeal.

5. That it is the duty of all officers, when called upon to execute the provisions of this act, to resign.

6. That a law so at variance with the laws of God, and the acknowledged principles of Holy Religion; so at war with all the sentiments of Humanity and Justice — so wanting in the true spirit of Republicanism, is unworthy even of the veriest despot of the Old World, and a foul blot upon our free institutions.

7. That when human enactments conflict with the laws of God, and the plainest dictates of humanity, we are at no loss "whom we shall serve — whether God or Bael," for "whether it be better to obey God or man, judge ye."

8. That to "feed the hungry, clothe the naked, succor the needy, and relieve the distressed," are duties from which no human laws can absolve us; and we are firmly resolved to practice those virtues, and to hold as null and void all conflicting laws, though at the peril of fine and imprisonment.

9. That, "There is a power behind the throne, higher than the throne itself"—*a correct public sentiment*— and that we will "agitate! agitate!"— back petition by petition, till this infamous law is repealed.

10. That a copy of the proceedings of this meeting, signed by the Chairman and Secretary, be forwarded to the *Chicago Democrat, Chicago Tribune, Western Citizen, National Era*, and *Western Recorder* with the request that they publish them in their respective papers, and that all papers North and South, be requested to copy same.

After the adoption of the resolutions, we had several short but spirited and stirring speeches, of which, if we could not boast of an oratorical flow of words, we could at least of a flow of soul — of expression that came from the heart. Me thinks I saw shadowed forth much of the spirit which animated our ancestors, when they set at defiance the aggressor — the mother country; a spirit strong and unshaken to battle for the Right — for Liberty — "even unto death."[18]

The recorded minutes of the meeting were signed by [Samuel] H. Lay, Chairman, and [Thomas] G. Beveridge, Secretary, at Somonauk, Illinois, and dated November 2, 1850.

(There is a correction regarding the date of this important town meeting. Both Patten in her *History of the Somonauk United Presbyterian Church* and Beveridge in the sequel *Church of the Pioneers* transcribe "30th Ult" as referring to November 30. This is incorrect. "Ult" is the Latin abbreviation for "ultimo" or "last month." The date of the newspaper in which these momentous minutes were published was December 3, 1850, and it is easy to understand that theoretically within that time frame, "ult" could have referred to November 30. However, a more detailed examination of the report as originally printed in the *Western Citizen* reveals that the minutes themselves were actually dated November 2, 1850, a month prior to their publication. The correct reference, then, to "30th Ult," and the correct date of the meeting, therefore, was October 30, not November 30, 1850.)

The Somonauk community was described as being in a "white heat of wrath and opposition."[19] James H. Beveridge, at age 33 was a leading member of the committee which drafted these resolutions. In contrast, Chairman Samuel Lay was a seasoned 55 years old and would later serve as the esteemed chairman of the DeKalb County Anti-Nebraska Convention in 1854. Thomas Beveridge, James's brother and the committee secretary, was a young 28 years old. Without a doubt, the Beveridge brothers, like all Presbyterian Scotsmen before them, were not afraid of a fight.

James Beveridge was a successful farmer with his father and brothers in Somonauk, as well as having an illustrious career in politics. He served as an associate justice, DeKalb County assessor, circuit clerk and recorder, and was a member of the Resolution Committee for the 1854 DeKalb County Anti-Nebraska (antislavery) meeting. Additionally, James was one of the Free-Soil Party delegates from the county to the 1854 convention in Aurora, Illinois, organizing the new Republican Party. Later in 1865 when his brother, John Lourie Beveridge, was governor of Illinois, James served as the state treasurer. His wife, Elizabeth, joined the Congregational

Church in Sycamore after James was elected to the various county offices requiring his proximity to the county seat. She later moved her church membership to the Second Presbyterian Church in Springfield when they lived in that city. James, however, always retained his membership in the Somonauk United Presbyterian Church.

The Somonauk resolutions drafted in part by James Hoy Beveridge at the recorded Indignation Meeting are unmistakably angry and resolute, echoing the Scot heritage of the citizenry, and perhaps reflecting James Beveridge's personality, as well.

Simultaneously, the town of Marion, Illinois, also took action regarding the Fugitive Slave Law. Their submission to the *Western Citizen* was published on the same day and included the resolution: "That the plains of the Prairie State are not the appropriate sporting grounds of southern despots, for the hunting of men whose only crime is love of life, liberty, and the pursuit of happiness." They further entered their "solemn protest against the whole nefarious scheme, as unjust and unchristian; and ask to be released from its disgrace, and discharged from its burdens."[20] By comparing the Somonauk resolutions with those of Marion, Illinois, and others, it is apparent that Somonauk's declarations are neither boilerplate language nor borrowed statements. At crucial points in a nation's history, like men have similar thoughts and sometimes express themselves in a similar fashion.

These common farmers who were struggling to forge a life on the frontier exhibited bravado in calling members of Congress traitors. They further reiterated that they would exercise their opinions at the ballot box and not vote for anyone who supported the Fugitive Slave Law. In DeKalb County, both the first and later elected representatives in the state legislature, Henry Madden of Mayfield and William Patten of Somonauk, were antislavery men and both subscribed to the *Western Citizen*.

The Somonauk resolutions called upon local government officials to resign from office if they were asked to arrest someone for an infraction of the Fugitive Slave Law.

Citing their religious principles, the citizens of Somonauk asserted that the new law was against the laws of God and the principles of "Holy Religion." They mention "Republicanism" in context as a form of government where the people are sovereign. Note that the Republican Party as a partisan organization did not exist in 1850. Adhering to the historic principles of Republicanism, the Somonauk citizenry was committed to civic virtue and felt it incumbent upon society to thwart tyranny. They truly believed that the Fugitive Law of 1850 was tyrannical. The Somonauk resolutions recognized that the laws of God and principles of religion coincided with Republicanism in their minds. They further acknowledge more than once that there is a higher law and when the laws of God and those of man conflict, it is better to obey God.

With a direct reference to assisting the fugitive slave, the resolutions assert that no human law can absolve mankind from following the Biblical admonishments to feed the hungry and clothe the naked. The end consequence was that Somonauk residents planned to continue their efforts in the Underground Railroad. They again called upon the spirit of their ancestors with echoes of the battles fought to obtain religious freedom in Scotland. A new national law in the United States was not going to dissuade them from their purpose.

Strong Abolitionists

The fervent antislavery people in the Presbyterian end of DeKalb County included William Davis, William Eddy, William Howison, William Patten, and William and Rachel Poplin. "William" was a popular name among the Scots, undoubtedly used to honor the historical Scot patriot and hero, William Wallace. Also active in the antislavery movement were Elijah Stewart,

Joseph Sly, Francis and Julia Telford plus his second wife, Ann Dobbin Telford, and John Walker. All of these people were subscribers to the *Western Citizen*, and their spouses were equally involved in both the church and in antislavery activities.

Among these strong Abolitionists was a "good pious deacon" who one day traveled east down a road towards another station on the Underground Railroad. As he drove his horse-drawn wagon, he was "overtaken by slave catchers who asked him if he had seen any runaway 'niggers.'"[21] A.C. French, Rensselaer's son, recounts the story. "At that moment he had two or three [fugitive slaves] under a load of green cut corn on his wagon. It was a case of prompt truth or falsehood and the brother did not hesitate but make unqualified denial. My opinion may not have any significance but I think the Lord would forgive him, and the Recording Angel would insert an asterisk with an explanatory footnote in the book."[22]

That fervent Abolitionist driving the wagon could easily have been Burrage Hough, who was exceptionally ardent in his antislavery ideas. It was not surprising that he named two of his 12 children after religious radical reformers. Mary and Burrage Hough's boys included John Wesley Hough and Martin Luther Hough. A simple farmer in DeKalb County prior to 1840, Hough also subscribed to and avidly read the *Western Citizen*. Additionally, he was a regular contributor to the antislavery newspaper's columns, and there was nothing simple at all about this Illinois farmer.

Hough wrote in the florid style of the day, beginning one long letter with a poem after which he referred to "slavery, that personification of all vice."[23] He then wrote about a slave auction, "related to me by an eye witness."[24]

> A few years since in the city of New Orleans, [there] was exposed for sale under the auctioneer's hammer, a yellow woman. Her only child a boy, some four or five years old was torn from her embrace, and sold to a mercenary stranger, and she was to see him no more. Her grief was too deep for utterance.... She stood before that assembled multitude in all the agony of a mother's bereavement. She was recommended as being a "good cook, a good house servant." She was bid up to eight hundred dollars and there the bidding stopped.
>
> The master anxious to obtain as high a price as possible for his property, stepped forward and whispered something in the auctioneer's ear. Turning to that company of men traffickers, he exclaimed as an additional recommendation, as in fact the highest recommendation which he could give her.
>
> "Gentlemen," says he, "she is a good Christian, says her prayers regularly, and is conscientious in the discharge of her duty." Amazing! Astonishing beyond measure! Who before ever heard of a *piece of property* being a good Christian, saying its prayers regularly, and being conscientious in the discharge of its duty! But such it seems was the case, and it appears that that company of slave-mongers who feared not God, nor yet regarded man, knew how to appreciate the recommendation. Mark [its] effect. Behold how it enhanced the value of that property!
>
> "Gentlemen, she is a good Christian, says her prayers regularly, and is conscientious in the discharge of her duty." Nine hundred dollars, ten hundred, eleven hundred, and so on up to fifteen hundred dollars!
>
> Eight hundred dollars was the price of her body, and seven hundred dollars was the price of her soul![25]

Abruptly leaving his reader with much to contemplate, Hough signed his letter "Yours for freedom, B.H., Somonauk."[26] Burrage Hough was an unreasonable man.

Political and Religious Freedom Found

During his tenure, the Rev. Rensselaer W. French saw George Beveridge build a new frame house, with a large second story left open so as to provide a more comfortable meeting space for worship services. Perhaps there was even a hidden closet, stairway or root cellar to hide the continuing stream of fugitive slaves coming through Somonauk. Maintaining stations on the Underground Railroad was as much a priority for the townspeople as providing a place to worship. The band of Scot believers finished building their first house of worship in 1853.

The very next year 26 people seceded from the Associate Church and created a new Reformed Presbyterian Church of Somonauk. This was not a new thought process; it was the Covenanters once again asserting themselves. There is no record of exactly what their complaint was with the local Associate Presbyterian Church.

Two hundred years after the original Covenanters were routed out of the Anglican Church to become the Church of Scotland, in Somonauk, Illinois, a small band of covenanters simply decided that they did not concur with the theology of the seceders and determined once again to become their own church body. This new Reformed Presbyterian Church of Somonauk had a very brief life, however, for in 1858 at the national level, the Associate Presbyterians (the seceders), and the Reformed Presbyterians (the covenanters), agreed enough on their common theology and doctrines, to merge to become the United Presbyterians. From that time forward, the Presbyterians in Somonauk were one body again and the stalwart little church became the Somonauk United Presbyterian Church, or the "UP's." It is obvious from the absence of information in local histories regarding this brief division that church members wanted to put that time of local disunion behind them.

We already know that the Congregationalists and Presbyterians upheld the religious framework for the antislavery movement, with support from the Wesleyan Methodists and Universalists. In the Eastern United States, the Unitarians were vocal on antislavery issues, but DeKalb County had no Unitarian church. Locally, any Unitarians felt comfortable with and tended to affiliate with the Universalist Church. At the national level, the Presbyterians issued a strong statement about slavery as early as 1818. They determined that "(1) it was a sin (2) it was inconsistent with the laws of God (3) it was a gross violation of the sacred rights of nature (4) it was totally irreconcilable with the spirit and principles of the Gospel and finally (5) it was the duty of all Christians ... to obtain the complete abolition of slavery."[27]

Historically, however, the slavery issue ultimately split the Presbyterians, as it did the Methodists and Lutherans nationwide. The divisions within each denomination were easily defined by the Mason-Dixon Line, dividing antislavery churches and their proslavery brethren. Each side used Biblical passages to justify their positions on the slavery issue, and each side believed in their hearts that their beliefs were correct. True to their Scot heritage, the Presbyterians in DeKalb County, Illinois, had no compunctions against their congregation being known as antislavery. An entity with such strong public convictions regarding antislavery was expected to act on those beliefs, which they did, over and over.

At the national level, the Presbyterians argued about whether or not to include slavery as an issue for discussion at the 1837 meeting of their General Assembly. For a few years, a minority of Southerners prevented the Assembly from taking an abolitionist position. Five years later, in 1842, the newly formed Associate Presbyterian Church in Somonauk, Illinois, had no trouble determining their particular position. Their opinion on slavery was not unlike that of their compatriots in northern DeKalb County, the Congregationalists. Their active support of the Underground Railroad foreshadowed the case of fellow Scotsman, John Hassock, from neighboring LaSalle County. "I have no apologies to make for being an Abolitionist,"[28] he proclaimed in 1860 before a U.S. District Court judge. His statement reverberated throughout the Northern Illinois area, echoing those who had gone before him — both the Congregationalists in Sycamore and the Presbyterians in Somonauk.

The Scotsmen who were the core members in the Somonauk Presbyterian Church knew well what they believed and what they would and would not tolerate in their new world. George and Ann Beveridge, along with their entire family and all their friends, believed in the vision borne by their parents and grandparents that somewhere in the American wilderness they "might hope to find political and religious freedom."[29] And in Somonauk, Illinois, political and religious freedom is exactly what they found.

Chapter 10

Evangelistic Lawbreakers: The Wesleyan Methodists

Actually, there are three political parties in the United States, Democrats, Republicans and Methodists.[1]— Ulysses S. Grant (1822–1885), United States president, Civil War general

"Near Centenarian: A Distinguished Pioneer"[2]

William A. Nickerson was raised as a Methodist. He believed in the traditional Christian view of the triune God: Father, Son and Holy Spirit. He also adhered to the Methodist approach that personal salvation necessitates service and mission to the world. The Methodists were more liberal in their theology, holding the view of free will rather than predestination, as the more Calvinistic Presbyterians believed. The average person could readily understand Methodist theology, and William's parents, Mulford and Eunice (Hanchett) Nickerson, respected the regimented approach to both religion and daily life. John Wesley, founder of the denomination, used a specific method to study the Bible, thus method-ism. With an emphasis on discipline, Wesley's teachings became invaluable to frontier communities on the edge of contemporary civilization. As a result, converts to Methodism increased proportionate to the growth of the Northwest Territory.

Yet William Nickerson could not remain a Methodist Episcopal. His very being demanded that he go one step further. He was always a loyal member of his church, but Nickerson was an unreasonable man. He realized that his own feelings about the slavery issue were no longer aligned with the position of the church he attended. During the previous year, before Nickerson moved to Mayfield Township, the Methodists at Brush Point determined that they would break from the Methodist Episcopal Church doctrine to become a Wesleyan Methodist Church. They followed the 1843 nationwide division, which was completely based on the slavery question.

The *Western Citizen* addressed the issue of the split in the Methodist Church succinctly. Publisher Zebina Eastman editorialized, "The ecclesiastical connections are regarded as the strongest bonds that can unite the people; these once severed, and the way is paved for sundering the political ties which bind the States together."[3]

Eastman took the reader's thought process another step further with strong declarations and questions:

> If then, the churches have such a controlling influence over the political institutions of the country ... how important that they should take a right position on the subject of slavery! If the Government is to follow the lead of the church, would not the political power abolish slavery, if the church speak out in plain terms, and bear true testimony on that subject? ... If the church can dissolve, or preserve the Union, could not the church then, dissolve the connection of slavery with the Government, and thus decree that it shall be abolished?[4]

The Wesleyan Methodists aimed to "speak out in plain terms and bear testimony" on the subject of slavery. In the new church, slaveholding and using intoxicating beverages was strictly prohibited.

Inspired by denominational activists in the East, the rank and file Methodists organized the new denomination with antislavery as a basic tenet of their philosophy. It was a perfectly logical expansion of the Methodist viewpoint of Christian mission and world service. Because Nickerson was adamantly antislavery and was impatient to end slavery, he found himself in a quandary because it was difficult to forsake the church of his parents. He still harbored a loyalty to the Methodist Episcopals.

After he moved from Kane County to DeKalb County in 1846, Nickerson recounts, "Finally, the preacher in charge made up his mind to get rid of me, and came to me with a letter saying that I was not at home with the M.E. and that the Wesleyan Methodists would welcome me." As his story continues, "Some members of the M.E. church were very much disturbed and went to the Wesleyan preacher complaining of giving me a letter that was never written."[5] An argument ensued within the Methodist Episcopal Church hierarchy and escalated to a full-blown church trial. Nickerson agreed to attend the trial to testify on behalf of the Methodist Episcopal preacher who was in danger of losing his position. Thanks to Nickerson's testimony, the minister was exonerated and did not lose his job. And thanks to a sensitive minister who knew the heart of the man, William A. Nickerson, his wife Roxana, and his parents left the Methodist Episcopal Church, joined the Wesleyan Methodists, and "worked with them and for them till the Civil War was ended."[6] Ultimately Nickerson was ordained a Wesleyan Methodist minister, becoming the first resident minister for the established group at Brush Point in Mayfield Township. He further distinguished himself by spending a great deal of time riding horseback about the countryside preaching on both temperance and slavery.

Camp Meeting at Brush Point

The Wesleyan Methodists never thought of themselves as being especially political and they never sought to craft a new political party, yet in 1843 their separation on a national level from the Methodist Episcopal Church almost created that effect. During the early 1800s, Methodism had grown to become one of the larger Christian denominations in the United States, which fact prompted President Ulysses S. Grant, himself a member of that religious persuasion, to have "a great respect for the Methodists."[7] When he jokingly referred to the denomination as a distinct political party in the United States, along with the Republicans and Democrats, Grant recognized the power of churches to rally people to a particular point of view.

And rally they did, whether for a religious cause or political motivation. Like mosquitoes ascending from a moist marsh to find their prey, the call for a Methodist camp meeting brought swarms of people to the designated forested grove. DeKalb County was not immune. These were people with a purpose. An 1845 notice in the *Western Citizen* heralded the camp meeting movement in the area:

> There will be a Wesleyan Methodist Camp Meeting held at Brush Point, four miles from Sycamore, commencing on Wednesday, the 18th of June next, and continue over the Sabbath. We earnestly

invite all of our Wesleyan brethren both in the ministry and laity to come and worship with us. It will be tolerable central for the Fox River, Rock River, Aurora and Half Day circuits. Come, dear brethren, in the spirit of Christ, and then you will be prepared to labor for the salvation of precious souls. We also earnestly invite all of our anti-slavery brethren of the sister churches to come and worship with us.

By order of the Aurora Circuit Quarterly Conference.

Milton Smith, Cor. Sec'y[8]

Anyone reading this announcement already knew to bring his own tent and food, as well as pots and pans for cooking. Attendees would set up rudimentary housekeeping in the secluded woods or exposed prairies for five days, from Wednesday through the Sunday climax.

This was actually a highly anticipated break from the routines of daily rural life on a farm. The heightened excitement in expectation of a camp meeting experience motivated people to endure the arduous travel of 30 to 50 miles to attend. It was a vacation of sorts. And camp meetings delivered on their promise. Once the masses were assembled, the preacher would step up onto an old log, or hold forth from the back of a wagon bed. He could talk for hours without notes, quoting the Bible and exhorting the hearer to bear witness to the Word of God.

But what else is implied in the published notice? While it is a direct open invitation to a religious gathering, it is combined with an obvious summons to antislavery advocates. Wesleyan Methodists who lived anywhere west of Chicago were encouraged to gather together to worship and prepare themselves to "labor for salvation." Whose salvation? They would labor for both their own spiritual salvation — and heed the subtle plea for physical salvation of the slaves.

The placement of the church camp meeting notice on the printed page of the newspaper was just above that of the announcement for the DeKalb County Antislavery Society. Either the same person submitted both announcements for publication, or the editor of the *Western Citizen* chose to group various same-county notices together, which was not always a common practice. The Wesleyan Methodists specifically invited "all of our anti-slavery brethren," not just those of their same religious denomination, but anyone professing to be antislavery. Publicizing upcoming camp meetings was a very deliberate method to attain an antislavery identity.

The Brush Point Wesleyan Methodist group was an organized entity within the Rock River Circuit. Charged with the leadership of that circuit was the circuit preacher, the Rev. Jeptha Noe. This circuit, formed in December of 1844, originally contained eight congregations. Consequently, a call for a camp meeting encompassing four circuits, the Fox River, Rock River, Aurora and Half Day, meant an invitation to approximately 32 churches. If each Wesleyan group only sent 30 people, then nearly one thousand people planned to camp out at Brush Point in Mayfield Township that June of 1845.

Attendees arrived at camp meetings with shotguns and rifles by their sides. They came by horse, by wagon and on foot, and there was always an absence of alcohol due to the prevailing temperance practices in the church. They renewed their spirits by listening to the firebrand preaching, singing inspirational hymns, praying, and visiting with their like-minded friends. It was a revival of the soul.

Among evangelical Christians, Methodists maintain they created the concept of a camp meeting. Numerous other denominations, as well as various states and geographical areas in the United States, all claim to know when and where the very first camp meeting was held. Presbyterians assert they held the first camp meetings in Kentucky, albeit with a Methodist minister. Others suggest that the Disciples of Christ or maybe even the Baptists came first. The Disciples of Christ denomination has a Methodist connection through its founder, Francis Asbury, who was originally sent by John Wesley from England to help propagate Methodism throughout the United States. Still others declare that the Spiritualists convened the first camp meeting.

Additionally, in December of the previous year, the Sycamore First Congregationalists had "Voted. That we hold a protracted meeting — as soon as practicable & that our pastor have liberty to call in such ministerial aid as he shall see fit."[9] The middle of winter was not conducive to an outdoor gathering, of course, but a "protracted meeting," lasting for several days, used an evangelical approach similar to that of camp meetings. The pastoral leaders excited participants and encouraged them to convert to Christianity. New members were enticed into the fold of Christianity through this sustained evangelical fervor. Religious historians agree that the Methodists, if not the very first, were indeed the denomination that carried the idea of an outdoor religious revival through to the present day. Methodism retains the title through the years as champion in proliferating camp meetings in our nation's religious history.

A Reformer and Performer

Many pioneer traveling preachers did not receive their education from institutions of higher learning; they were self-educated. They looked like backwoodsmen and as they traveled, their Bibles, hymnbooks and books of church discipline were their faithful companions at evening campfires in the woods. The appearance of being an uneducated frontiersman created a bond between the circuit rider preacher and the people he wanted to convert. He could talk to the western farmer in his own language. A guest preacher, usually a Methodist circuit rider, would be the invited main speaker during the protracted event, and many times that guest preacher was a major entertainment factor as well. Lorenzo Dow, one of the most famous circuit rider preachers, was entertainment personified. Eccentric and passionate, crazy or insane, unkempt and disheveled, discourteous and rude — these are all words used consistently to describe Lorenzo Dow. Dow was the "foremost itinerant preacher of his time ... the first Protestant who expounded the gospel in Alabama and Mississippi ... a reformer who at the very moment when cotton was beginning to be supreme, presumed to tell the South that slavery was wrong." Lorenzo Dow was a "gaunt, restless preacher [with] long hair, flowing beard, harsh voice, and wild gesticulation."[10]

After a series of dreams, which included a vision of John Wesley himself, and Dow's subsequent conversion to Methodism, he applied to the Methodist Church in Connecticut, requesting to be sent out into the countryside to preach the gospel as a circuit rider. Several times he was rebuffed by the church, which categorized him as unsuitable for the task. "The young preacher was not only ungraceful and ungracious in manner, but he had severe limitations in education and frequently assumed toward his elders an air needlessly arrogant and contemptuous."[11] Finally in 1798, the Methodists accepted him on a trial basis to begin his missionary form of evangelistic ministry.

Lorenzo Dow was no ordinary preacher. His lack of formal education and his unkempt appearance, combined with his emotional ranting approach to the gospel, led people to sometimes think him insane and label him "Crazy Dow." He always considered himself a Methodist in principle, even though he was never officially ordained as a Methodist minister, due to his less than humble demeanor and his inordinate preaching methods.

Dow's unorthodox preaching techniques actually prevented his ecclesiastical accreditation. Because the Methodists refused him access to pulpits in established church buildings, he sometimes preached in a schoolhouse or a barn. "In pleasant weather some grove was chosen, for thereby his hearers were saved the cost of a room or the inconvenience of a barn offered freely."[12] Increasingly, his passionate desire to evangelize led him to the open air as his preferred venue, affording him a large, free space for a religious gathering wherever he went, and thus the practice of camp meetings was born. Dow is the acknowledged originator of the idea of camp meetings both in England and in the United States. At such a gathering, the maniacal inventor of camp meetings stood atop grassy knolls, or on the back of a wagon, warning of hell and damnation and promising a heavenly paradise for those who repented of their earthly sins. Dow's brand of fire-and-brimstone sermonizing, emotional testifying and hymn-singing very often lasted for a week at a time. It is a paradox that although it was the Methodists who initially decried Dow's unorthodox method of preaching at camp meetings, it was also the Methodists who successfully perpetuated the practice of camp meetings.

The Sycamore Connection

Why be interested in an itinerant preacher who never set foot in DeKalb County, Illinois? In addition to the fact that Lorenzo Dow's influence in the creation of camp meetings is unparalleled, the remarkable truth is that he was a first cousin to Agrippa Dow of Sycamore, an avowed DeKalb County Abolitionist. He was also a first cousin once-removed to Agrippa's son, Roswell Dow, and a distant cousin to Kimball Dow, the secretary for the DeKalb County Antislavery Society. The diary of Agrippa Dow's father, Salmon Dow of New Hampshire, records several occasions when Lorenzo Dow preached near his hometown.[13]

However, the local Dow men were not Wesleyan Methodist. Agrippa had strong connections to the Congregational Church, where his son and daughter-in-law, as well as his daughter, were members. Kimball was firmly entrenched in the Universalist Church. Besides the familial relationship, all three DeKalb County Dow men followed in their famous cousin's footsteps by espousing antislavery attitudes and being vocal about their beliefs in that regard. It is most appropriate, then, that the DeKalb County Mayfield Wesleyan Methodists decided to combine their religious fervor with a strong abolitionist message. Camp meetings had arrived at Brush Point.

Local Methodists Organize

Before there were camp meetings in DeKalb County, a land company named C. Sharer and Company arrived in the area. This was the original New York land company that sent agents to Northern Illinois to survey and lay out towns. The four men who first came to Sycamore with C. Sharer and Company were Christian Sharer himself, Evans Wharry, Clark Wright and Mark Daniels. Wright and Wharry both had Congregational affiliations, but Daniels happened to be devoutly Methodist, and as early as 1836 invited the circuit minister Levi Lee to come to his home in Sycamore to preach. The Rev. Lee's very basic sermon title was "Have Faith in God,"[14] and with that strong faith in God, the Methodist Episcopal church found a place in the Northern Illinois county. One could say that the original land surveyors were truly the ones who first brought Methodism to DeKalb County.

Other followers of John Wesley's disciplined routine, or method of spiritual devotion combined with a social consciousness, soon created small congregations elsewhere throughout the county. Wesley thought he was reforming the Anglican Church in England, but when Methodism came to America, the new denomination survived on its own. Spread through the circuit rider system, which enabled fewer preachers to cover a large territory, and supported by revival meetings, Methodism advanced with the westward frontier. In DeKalb County, Methodist churches sprang up in the townships of Clinton, Franklin, Sandwich, Sycamore, Genoa, and later DeKalb. But it was the Mayfield Township religious group which soon proved to be the most progressive.

Ira Douglass, together with his first wife Cyrena Goodrich, hosted the very first Mayfield Methodist gathering about 1837 in their log cabin country home. At that time, it would most likely have been categorized as a Methodist Episcopal Bible study class. However, because Douglass soon subscribed to the *Western Citizen*, one might surmise that the evening conversations may have turned to social causes of concern and to discussion of slavery in particular. The small group continued to worship regularly at the Douglass home for a couple of years until they moved their meetings to the new Pleasant Hill School, and later to the Brush Point School.

The first minutes for the Mayfield Wesleyan Methodists, however, were not recorded until May 4, 1845, and indicate that particular meeting occurred at the Brush Point School.

The Methodist Episcopals

Sycamore Methodists never withdrew from the mother church to become a Wesleyan congregation, but retained their affiliation with the Methodist Episcopal Church. Carlos Lattin's brother, Wesley Lattin, was a minister with that denomination and served a couple of years on two separate occasions for the Sycamore congregation. Even after Wesley moved to Wisconsin to continue his liturgical career, Carlos was obligated to his brother to maintain his own membership in the Sycamore M.E. Church. Additionally, Carlos himself had donated the land upon which the first Methodist church building was constructed, further bonding him to the M.E. congregation. Carlos Lattin was one of the very first settlers in Sycamore; he subscribed to the *Western Citizen*, and was described as being "hospitable to homeless strangers."[15] This unreasonable man even named two of his sons "John Wesley Lattin" and "Charles Wesley Lattin" after the Wesley brothers who created the Methodist denomination. Although he was not an official member of the Wesleyan Methodists, he espoused an antislavery position.

Marshall Stark was another Sycamore Methodist member who subscribed to the antislavery newspaper. He was elected DeKalb County sheriff in 1849, and was one of several county sheriffs who were antislavery. Therein lies one of the primary reasons no one in DeKalb County was every arrested or charged with the crime of aiding a fugitive slave. Even the sheriffs were antislavery and considered themselves to be Abolitionists.

George Washington Gandy fit the stereotype of the antislavery man in DeKalb County. Like both Carlos Lattin and Marshall Stark, he settled in the area before 1840, owned a land patent and was a farmer. More importantly, he subscribed to the *Western Citizen*. Gandy also never joined the Wesleyan Methodists, remaining a member of the Methodist Episcopal Church. Since he lived in Pampas Township southeast of Sycamore proper, perhaps it was simply easier to ride into town to Sycamore to attend church, rather than to travel farther northwest to Mayfield Township.

The Methodist freedom fighters living in Mayfield Township originally named their corner of the county Liberty Township. It was extremely important that they express their love of free soil for everyone, not just the white man, and openly maintain their extreme opposition to slavery. Their church organization was the perfect entity to perpetuate their beliefs. Before the American Civil War, the Mayfield Wesleyan Methodists were considered to be the strongest antislavery group in the township. "It was the members of this religious organization that conducted the workings of the underground railway."[16] Aiding fugitive slaves north through Mayfield Township to Canada and freedom were the Townsend family, Joshua and his sons, Stephen and Charles; the Nickerson family, Mulford and his son, William A.; and the large Nichols family, including Peter, John and Ira Nichols. These Wesleyan Methodists were all evangelistic lawbreakers when they acted as either station agents or conductors on the local

Underground Railroad trails. Later historians wrote, "At the time these men were active in this work they were regarded by many as lawbreakers, but ... these men had the courage of their convictions and did so much for the freedom of humanity."[17]

Mayfield Underground Railroad

There are more Underground Railroad stories recorded about the residents of Mayfield Township than about any other township in DeKalb County. As Boies related in his 1868 *History of DeKalb County, Illinois*, the homes belonging to the Nickersons, Nichols and Townsends "were well known as homes & places of refuge for the fugitive Negroes." Boies continues with a comment on the social atmosphere at that time in our nation's history: "Many an interesting story of their experience in aiding and secreting these oppressed people, are now told with a freedom, that before the downfall of American Slavery would have been dangerous."[18]

In 1884 there appeared in *The Sycamore True Republican* a story reprinted from the *Polo Press*. The writer related his own experience when he accompanied Solomon Shaver,[19] a known Underground Railroad conductor from neighboring Ogle County, to transport a fugitive slave family of four, plus a mother and father-in-law. The narrative gave the background of the head of the family, indicating that he had escaped from slavery, fled to Canada and then went back to rescue his family and with the help of the antislavery sympathizers was once again headed north. "Freedom was so sweet to him that he resolved to risk liberty and perhaps life in securing his wife and children from bondage."[20]

Because they left on their journey on July 3, a prominent American flag flew attached to the wagon. The small band of travelers rode northeastward across Ogle County in Northern Illinois—from Polo to Mt. Morris to Byron—then veered slightly south. "Uncle Sol," as Solomon Shaver was familiarly called, seemed to know a lot of people as they rode through the area. In Byron a large group was celebrating in patriotic style and as they drove up to the tent, they heard the words, "We hold these truths to be self-evident, that all men are created equal; that they are endowed by their Creator with certain unalienable rights; that among these are life, liberty and the pursuit of happiness." The familiar phrases from the Declaration of Independence seemed prophetic to the family of former slaves. By evening time, the fleeing fugitives entered South Grove Township in DeKalb County.

> We had supper at the tavern, but when we offered to pay for it the woman said she "could not think of charging anything." Uncle Sol asked the Justice of the peace, Mr. Byers, to take the fugitives on, but he said, holding the office he did, he could not do it, but, he added, "I will pay you twenty-five cents a head for all you bring." Mr. Byers' daughter was going to a party that evening, and when she saw the four horse team and flag, hurried to get ready, supposing it was her company coming. Her mistake gave the old gentleman [Uncle Sol] a hearty laugh.
>
> A few miles beyond South Grove we came to a settlement of Wesleyans [at] a place called Brush Point. Here we found true anti-slavery men, loving freedom for others as well as for themselves. We spent the evening very pleasantly, the people of the settlement coming together for a general good time. The next morning we left for home, and at the same time the fugitives left for Canada.[21]

The "Mr. Byers" referred to in the story was William M. Byers, a Scotsman by descent, and like many other antislavery men in DeKalb County, he was born in New York. Byers arrived in the county in 1841 with his parents James and Jane (Scott) Byers and two younger brothers. He and his first wife, Mary Ann Adee, had two sons; when she died, he married her sister Jane, who gave birth to three daughters. The daughter referred to in the anecdote was either Adell, Mary Anna, or Jane.

A member of the Congregational church, Byers was always active in county politics, serving as a county supervisor, a school commissioner, a road commissioner and a justice of the peace. He was a Whig delegate to the 1854 convention organizing the Republican Party, and in 1876 was elected as a Republican to the Illinois state legislature. Byers knew who could be counted on to help in the Underground Railroad, and his Wesleyan Methodist neighbors to the east were highest on his list. He was an unreasonable man who aided conductors on many occasions.

At the suggestion of William Byers, Solomon Shaver from Polo, Illinois, left his tired group of freedom seekers in the hands of the Brush Point Wesleyan Methodists. One of the many Mayfield Township Underground Railroad conductors took over the reins from there, aiding the fugitives further in their trek northward to Canada.

Vivid Memories of Fugitive Slaves

The Congregationalist Deacon David West was not the only person in DeKalb County to utilize a homemade wagon with a secret compartment in the bottom used to smuggle fugitive slaves. It was a known fact in the Brush Point community that the Townsend family owned a wagon with a built-in concealed hiding place. In *The History of Five Points, 1847–1937*, Mrs. Nellie Marshal related stories of her Grandfather Townsend's home utilized as an Underground Railroad station. "The slaves were brought there from the South," apparently past the location of the Five Points Rural Training School, "and he would take them to St. Charles. As he often hauled grain east to St. Charles, his triple box going through Sycamore was a familiar sight. The slaves were always terrified when visitors happened in at the stations."[22] St. Charles is a city about 20 miles east of DeKalb County's eastern border.

She further relates that on one occasion when Townsend "had a load of negroes the postmaster at Sycamore came out and stopped him."[23] This postmaster may well have been Sycamore's own William Parker Dutton, the proslavery, anti–Abolitionist government employee who later recanted his slavery position. "The slaves in the bottom of the wagon were frightened but they never made a noise and Mr. Townsend was able to go on, without the postmaster suspecting what was in the load. Rewards were posted for the runaways."[24] Joshua Townsend and his sons, Stephen and Charles, were all known conductors on the Underground Railroad and their homes were often used as station houses.

When she was about 11 years old, little Mary Ann Rote first witnessed the Underground Railroad in Mayfield Township, an experience that she never forgot. The Rote family moved from Pennsylvania to Illinois sometime between 1855 and 1858. Her father, Henry, farmed the property adjacent to William Nickerson's farm. Her mother, the former Esther Carpenter, performed the typical duties of a frontier wife. She spent most of her time keeping house and watching over her family of seven children.

Early one morning, Mary Ann's mother asked her to run over to the neighbor's house to borrow a cup of sugar. She may have taken one of her younger brothers, William or Joseph, with her. The Nickerson family was still eating their sumptuous farm breakfast. "As she opened the door she saw several Negroes disappearing down the cellar steps."[25] Her parents may have known that the Nickersons harbored fugitive slaves, but Mary Ann Rote was completely surprised to see such strange faces in her neighbors' kitchen. She recounted the story many times over. In 1937 her daughter, Arvilla (Ramala) Nichols once again related the story for inclusion in the *The History of Five Points*.

The Presbyterian Scotsman John Dick arrived in Mayfield Township around 1844. Dick considered himself to be an Abolitionist, as his obituary proudly proclaimed, and "extended his aid and sympathy to the escaped slave fleeing to a land of safety from bondage."[26] His friends and neighbors knew that he was not an active "operator" on the Underground Railroad running through the area, but they also knew that they could drop off special baggage at Dick's home temporarily. "The closely pursued refugee was often side-tracked to [John Dick's] residence until his pursuer had passed by."[27]

Around 1850, John and Eliza Dick lived and farmed the property next door to Ira Nichols. Nichols was one of the first Wesleyan Methodist church trustees, and a "station agent" for the Underground Railroad.[28] Nichols's wife, Esther, was the daughter of John Mullen, a pioneer settler in Mayfield Township and, of course, a *Western Citizen* subscriber. At one point during the early 1840s John Dick was invited over to Ira and Esther Nichols's home "to see two fugitive slaves. When he got there he didn't want to go near because the big negroes were armed. They kept the guns leveled at him all the time, because they thought he was hunting them."[29] This was John Dick's introduction to the inner workings of the Underground Railroad.

Ira Nichols, along with his brothers Peter, John and Latin, and his brother-in-law Charles Townsend, were part of "that large settlement [in Mayfield] that gave much time and energy in the assistance of slaves on their way to Canada. These abolitionists advocated emancipation of slavery when ministers behind pulpits denounced it."[30]

On one particular occasion during the early 1850s "a slave holder appeared on the streets of Sycamore with a warrant for the arrest of an escaped slave."[31] Word reached the environs of Mayfield, where the "Negro sought was hidden somewhere about the premises of Ira Nichols."[32] Nichols solved the dilemma in typical Abolitionist fashion by filling "several grain sacks with hay and laid them upon the Negro who was in the bottom of the wagon, and on top of these sacks he placed a tier of grain sacks filled with oats and started for St. Charles."[33] He pretended to transport his crops, following the way to the Chicago grain markets east through Sycamore, then St. Charles. As the evangelistic lawbreaker Nichols drove slowly through Sycamore, he saw the owner of the slave with a U.S. marshal, "and notwithstanding the fact that a reward of $500 was offered for the return of the Negro, he passed on to St. Charles. During the night the Negro was taken to the shore of Lake Michigan, north of Chicago, where he was placed on a steamer and [ultimately] liberated in the province of Ontario."[34] Nichols was never arrested; the fugitive slave was never apprehended.

William and Agnes Deyoe were transplanted New Yorkers who farmed adjacent to Mayfield Township in South Grove Township. William also subscribed to the *Western Citizen* and was "a well-known conductor on the underground railway."[35] His hired hand was an Irish immigrant named James Purcell. Purcell was often pressed into service when needed to carry fugitives for part of their journey.

> [In the early 1850s] two Negroes appeared at the home of Mr. Deyeo [sic] ... and he thought best not to be caught in transporting slaves to Canada, so he secured the services of his hired man, Mr. James Purcell and some time during the night started him for the home of Joshua Townsend of Mayfield, with these directions. "Look neither to the right nor to the left. Do not look behind you or you will become a pillar of salt, but drive directly to Joshua Townsend's house and back up to his cellar door." Appearing there some time after midnight he found Mr. Townsend awaiting him according to the directions of Mr. Deyeo [sic], and the load was taken out and hidden in the cellar and Mr. Purcell invited to breakfast.[36]

A brief reference appears in *Past and Present of DeKalb County*, Vol. I about the time Ed Becker of South Grove Township was asked by William Deyoe to take "runaway negroes" to William Nickerson's home in neighboring Mayfield Township. The fugitives were "to be sent on to the station in St. Charles."[37] It was business as usual.

Spiritual Leaders Among the Lawbreakers

The Wesleyan Methodists actually had many "first pastors" because of the itinerant preacher circuit rider system: the circuit rider Jacob Alexander McGilvra and Mayfield resident William Nickerson; followed by circuit riders Calvin Morris Webster and Amos Richardson Brooks, then residents James Linneus Clark, and Brooks's grandson, Jonas Brooks. When the Rev. Amos Brooks resided in Ohio, he served on the Wesleyan committee that determined there should be a "station" for the Wesleyan Methodist church near Sycamore. In 1851, delegates from the Mayfield Wesleyan Methodist church were sent to a Chicago antislavery convention. Brooks could not know that ultimately both he and his grandson would end up serving as pastors at the same Mayfield location.

According to historical sources, Calvin Morris Webster approached his ministry with great energy.[38] He received his training for the ministry when he attended Ohio Wesleyan University, founded by Methodists in 1842 in Delaware, Ohio. The university's charter promised that the institution "is forever to be conducted on the most liberal principles, accessible to all religious denominations, and designed for the benefit of our citizens in general."[39] In 1850 Webster lived with 21 other male college students in the town of Delaware.

Ann Catharine Parker accepted Calvin's proposal of marriage and they were married in 1853 soon after graduation. Calvin and Ann Catharine Webster headed west to preach the gospel to the new settlers in the prairie lands, following the trail of many young missionary ministers of his time. Their first son, Parker, was born in 1855 in Chickasaw County, Iowa, followed two years later by Edward, born in Winnebago County, Illinois. By 1860 they moved to Kingston in DeKalb County, Illinois, in time for the birth of their third son, William. While in Kingston, as the minister in charge of the Methodist Kingston Circuit, Calvin personally spearheaded the construction of two Mayfield Township Wesleyan Methodist churches, one at Pleasant Hill and one at Brush Point, gladly assisting in the physical labor himself.

At some point in his career, Webster's passion for his calling grew, prompting him to change his first name to "Calvary," perhaps better reflected his spiritual life. The Rev. Calvary/Calvin Webster worked closely with William A. Nickerson, the resident minister for the young Mayfield congregation, and the Rev. Jacob Alexander McGilvra, who was the new circuit minister assigned to oversee the group. Webster announced in May, 1860 that he was going to preach a Sunday sermon based on the "devil's pre-emption,"[40] and the hundreds who came to hear his message also heard him announce plans to build a church building. By the following October the group elected their first trustees: William A. Nickerson, Stephen Townsend, Reuben Nichols, Ira Nichols, and Demmon Decker, and three days later had received donations and pledges totaling over $1,100 towards the new structure. The Wesleyan antislavery congregation established itself rapidly.

By 1906 the church membership voted to affiliate with the Congregational church, which was closely aligned with the Wesleyan Methodist philosophy, and it remains today the Mayfield Congregational Church, U.C.C.

The church came first. It was always the church. For the unreasonable men and women in DeKalb County it was the Congregational, the Universalist, the Presbyterian, and the Wesleyan Methodist churches that told them how to live their daily lives and gave all of them the moral fiber to be evangelistic lawbreakers. They truly believed in William H. Seward's pronouncement before the United States Congress that there is a "higher law than the Constitution, which regulates our authority over the domain."[41] They believed that God was on their side.

CHAPTER 11

The Western Citizen Reads the *Western Citizen*

The Supremacy of God and the Equality of Man.[1]— A motto for the *Western Citizen*, Zebina Eastman, ed. (1815–1883), abolitionist and publisher of the antislavery newspaper

---

Eastern Becomes Western

The new western citizens who established themselves in the Old Northwest Territory were all former citizens of the East. They were the early Northern Illinois settlers who were accustomed to more sophistication than what they experienced on the frontier. For the most part, they were well-read, they attended church, and they listened to lectures and participated in other cultural diversions when available. They were not ignorant. Because of necessity they needed to carry a rifle or handgun with them at all times for defense against wolves, snakes and other encroachers upon their land. The stereotype of the rough frontiersman belies the fact that they had important opinions and recognized the value of both expressing those viewpoints and using political means to achieve goals within their society for the good of their community. DeKalb County's quiet antislavery movement merged with the equally peaceful local Abolitionists and discovered a power within their means that they did not know they possessed.

Individuals supporting runaway slaves, those brave seekers of freedom, quickly learned that "but little can be done without the instrumentality of the Press, and an energetic, well-executed weekly or daily newspaper."[2] These friends of liberty readily recognized the "importance of sustaining the anti-slavery Press, and extending its influence"[3] through the publication and distribution of the *Western Citizen*. It was a widely read arm of the Liberty Party and an influential tool for the Abolitionists in Northern Illinois. According to the *Chicago Tribune*, within a few years of its initial 1842 publication, it "had the largest circulation of any paper in the West."[4] When the *Western Citizen* mailbooks, or subscription lists, are compared with named antislavery activists throughout DeKalb County communities, the parallels are apparent. The same names are evident in the church membership records and the lists of elected officials. From 1842 through 1855, the *Western Citizen*, followed by its sister publication the *Free West*, rallied antislavery forces around the abolitionist flag in the new West.

Immediately following the American Civil War, and about 30 years before the Ohio historian William Siebert gathered information for his landmark 1898 book *The Underground Railroad from Slavery to Freedom*, an avid antislavery supporter in Chicago collected stories from former Abolitionists across the Illinois plains and prairies. The letters, solicited and assembled by Zebina Eastman, editor and publisher of the *Western Citizen* and *Free Press*, gave personal accounts of the Illinois Abolitionists' activities. Eastman's strong desire and intent was to publish the firsthand stories about the Underground Railroad, especially in Illinois, but he was ultimately overcome by his failing health and was unable to complete his dream before he died in 1883. Today numerous boxes containing Eastman's never-published collection of handwritten correspondence reside in the archives of the Chicago History Museum waiting to be fully examined.

One unpublished letter in the collection, dated December 19, 1854, was written to Zebina Eastman by the Honorable Elihu B. Washburne, member of Congress, and a close political associate of Abraham Lincoln. Before he was elected president, Lincoln served in the House of Representatives for two years, from 1847 to 1849, then chose not to run again for Congress. In 1854, he had just been elected to the Illinois legislature when he promptly resigned in order to run for the U.S. Senate against Stephen A. Douglas.

In an earlier letter dated December 11, 1854, written by Abraham Lincoln to Washburne, he mentioned that he had "not ventured to write to all the members in your district.... Could you not drop some of them a line?"[5]

The subsequent December 19 letter from Elihu Washburne to Zebina Eastman honored Lincoln's request. Washburne wrote about Lincoln's virtues: "Not because he had been a Whig, but because he is a man of Splendid talents, of great probity of character, and because he threw himself into the late fight on the republican platform ... I know he is with us in sentiment."[6] He entreated Eastman to support Lincoln as the U.S. Senate candidate. As a well-known Abolitionist and publisher of a widely read newspaper, Zebina Eastman was a powerful ally in the political arena.

The Reading Public

Although the *DeKalb Republican Sentinel* had the distinction of being the first newspaper published in DeKalb County, it was by no means the first newspaper read by the citizenry living in that area. Long before resident businessmen decided to publish a local newspaper, local residents throughout the area faithfully read the *Western Citizen* each week.

The *Western Citizen* was published in Chicago, but it still had enormous relevance for the newly settled westerly rural area. Traditional reports of world and national news were combined with folksy touches, and the editor incorporated marriage and death notices for DeKalb and many other Northern Illinois counties. Since it was the only regional published newspaper being delivered to the area, county residents claimed ownership of its philosophy and ideas. And that philosophy and those ideas were decidedly antislavery.

As an antislavery publication, the *Western Citizen* had a pedigree to match its crusading editor. Zebina Eastman migrated first from his home state of Massachusetts to Connecticut, then to Vermont. Orphaned at a young age, Eastman quickly learned the printer's trade. By age 18 he was the solitary editor for the *Vermont Free Press*. While in New England, Zebina "pondered much on the question of slavery."[7] Then, after the murder of Elijah Lovejoy in 1837, he decided to "devote his life-work to the cause of human freedom."[8] His quest took him first to Michigan, then to Peoria, Illinois, working for the *Peoria Register*, and finally to work with veteran Abolitionist Benjamin Lundy, who published the antislavery *Genius of Universal Emancipation* in Hennepin, Illinois, southwest of Chicago.

When Lundy died unexpectedly, Eastman formed an alliance with the early Illinois Abolitionist Hooper Warren and soon published a very similar newspaper titled the *Genius of Liberty* in Lowell, Illinois. The LaSalle County, Illinois, Anti-Slavery Society and the Illinois Anti-Slavery Society both adopted the *Genius of Liberty* as their official publication. This, however, was the genesis of the publication arm for the Illinois Liberty Party, a branch of the national antislavery political party.

By 1842 Zebina Eastman returned to Chicago where the *Genius of Liberty* developed into the *Western Citizen* and, later, the *Free West*. From 1842 through 1855, through both newspapers, Eastman exerted untold influence throughout the Northwest in the formation of the Liberty Party and the Republican Party. One of the first mottos for the paper emphasized both its religious and political foundations: "The Supremacy of God and the Equality of Man."[9]

The existing mailbooks for the *Western Citizen* and *Free West* include subscription lists and receipts of payments for those subscriptions. According to manuscript notes in the Zebina Eastman Collection, "virtually all of the subscribers to the *Western Citizen* were abolitionists."[10] The northern one-third of the State of Illinois accounted for 80 percent of the 3,000 subscribers by 1855. DeKalb County had the highest concentration of subscriptions in the state outside of Cook County.[11] This was also the largest percentage of readers nationwide. With over 500 newspapers delivered regularly to as many households, one can multiply that number by the number of adults in a family unit (usually two or more), then add the hired hands, neighbors and friends who borrowed the newspaper to read after the subscriber was finished with it. It is easy to come up with a total far exceeding 1,000 people who regularly read about antislavery in just Sycamore, Mayfield, Genoa, and Somonauk Townships.

Over one thousand readers of an antislavery newspaper lived in DeKalb County at a time when the entire general population was still under 2,000. Two years earlier, in 1840, the total population of DeKalb County was 1,697, with only 442 adult males over the age of 20. By the Federal Census of 1850, Sycamore Township alone approached 1,000. There were no slaves; slavery never existed in DeKalb County. The total number of males in 1850 in Sycamore Township was 520 and females 434. Although substantial growth occurred during the decade between 1840 and 1850, we can assume that in 1842, when the *Western Citizen* was first published and delivered to DeKalb County, almost every adult man and woman read the articles denouncing slavery.

An important earlier Abolitionist, John Rankin, had previously published numerous letters about the evils of slavery. Rankin, an Ohio Presbyterian minister extremely active in the Underground Railroad, contended that slavery "infected society with a poisonous retinue of wretched habits that would damage the nation for generations into the future."[12] Publications of Rankin's antislavery letters were advertised in the *Western Citizen* and DeKalb County residents could easily purchase a collection of the letters offered for sale.

A typical masthead for the abolitionist newspaper *Western Citizen*, the print arm of the Liberty Party, published in Chicago. DeKalb County had the highest reader concentration.

Antislavery Advertises and Expands

Each week the newspaper printed more notices of antislavery societies meeting in various surrounding counties: Kane, Kendall, McHenry, DuPage, LaSalle, and, of course, DeKalb County. Each week there were editorials reminding the reader of the evils of slaveholding. And every week these same people attended churches where their ministers regularly reminded the congregations about the sin of slavery and encouraged citizens to help the downtrodden.

There were distinct levels of involvement in the antislavery movement. Some people were only subscribers to abolitionist newspapers and read vicariously about current antislavery issues. This involved a yearlong commitment of $2.50 per year, and subscribers were well aware that their subscription to the paper was "equivalent to financially backing the enterprise which was furthering the cause."[13] Being apprised of current events and philosophies gave the readers strong arguments in their public discourse with others about slavery. Some were outspoken in their personal opinions regarding antislavery and considered themselves to be bona fide Abolitionists, much like belonging to a political party. Some supported the idea of aiding the fugitive slaves, and were indeed active conductors in the Underground Railroad. In 1843, the *Western Citizen* proclaimed: "Illinois abolitionists made it a matter of principle to aid any passing fugitives who might need assistance."[14]

An initial working list of DeKalb County antislavery proponents and Abolitionists only included those individuals who were specifically named as such in local printed historical sources. Recent research significantly expanded that first list to include all residents of the county who subscribed to the *Western Citizen*, as well as those individuals identified through their personal actions, activities and associations.

Also added to the list of known antislavery sympathizers were people from the compiled membership rolls of the Sycamore First Congregational Church. Since belonging to that congregation required that they affirm their belief that slavery was a sin against God, we can assume that they were indeed antislavery proponents. The Congregationalists' role was important, because "Being among the most radical advocates of [the abolition of slavery], they made their weight felt in the political life of the day."[15]

Next added to the list were members of the Mayfield Wesleyan Methodist Church, the Somonauk Presbyterian Church, and the Sycamore Universalist Church. One cannot have been a member of those congregations without having strong opinions about the antislavery movement. As various lists were cross-referenced, it was evident that an extreme amount of duplication and overlap existed.

To recap, in DeKalb County, the same people were (1) *Western Citizen* subscribers, (2) active members of the same churches, (3) county officials, (4) identified with the Underground Railroad, and (5) early settlers with eastern United States antislavery philosophies and Puritan theologies. Again, they transplanted those same ideas along with their physical belongings to the Western Frontier in Northern Illinois where their religious and political beliefs blurred and merged into even stronger antislavery attitudes.

The Chicago Connection

Zebina Eastman, through his *Western Citizen*, provided the new western citizens in DeKalb County with a strong Chicago connection. Even in rural areas, still considered the "boonies" well into the end of the 20th century, the leading Abolitionists acknowledged a Chicago connection. A report appeared in a DeKalb County history: "In the city of Chicago a Dr. Dyer was a well-known conductor of the Underground Railroad and he was attacked by an assistant U.S. marshal and a bloody battle ensued on his doorstep. Dr. Dyer was wounded but he killed the officer and wounded another. Excitement ran high but the sentiment by this time had grown rapidly in favor of anti-slavery and he escaped without punishment."[16]

Dr. Charles Volney Dyer was a "fierce opponent of slavery."[17] After the murder of newspaper editor Elijah Lovejoy in 1837, Vermont-born Dyer, together with druggist Philo Carpenter, teacher Calvin De Wolf, Presbyterian minister Flavel Bascome and others, met "to condemn this assault on the constitutional right of the freedom of the press."[18] By 1840 they officially organized the Chicago Anti-Slavery Society.

Dyer, one of Chicago's first medical practitioners, personally encouraged Zebina Eastman to bring his newspaper publication to Chicago. He lauded the value and the success of such an antislavery periodical and recognized that Chicago's Anti-Slavery Society could be a leader in abolitionist activities in Illinois. In 1842 Dyer wrote to Eastman, "There is enthusiasm in the matter and I have no doubt of the success of the enterprize [sic] when once the paper is commenced."[19]

In the Underground Railroad in Chicago, Charles Dyer "was the recognized station master, or head of the city's network."[20] In 2003 a hidden cellar used in the Underground Railroad was discovered at the site of the former home of Charles Dyer's brother George.[21] Undoubtedly hundreds of fugitives passed through the city which was at the end of that imaginary funnel draining into Lake Michigan. Perhaps some runaways remained in Chicago, but "most journeyed on to Canada on foot or boarded *The Illinois* and *The Great Western*, lake steamers bound for Windsor, Canada."[22]

If Dyer was the white Abolitionist leader in Chicago, John Jones was "the black community's predominant leader."[23] In Chicago, fugitives found another new friend in Jones, a "free African-American from Tennessee.... [He] was the son of a free mulatto mother and a father of German ancestry."[24] At age 23, he quickly became friends with Charles Dyer, and the Jones home was yet another "haven for escaped slaves and a meeting place for white as well as black abolitionists."[25]

After many years of extensive religious and political antislavery activism, after the Civil War concluded and ten years after Eastman organized the 1874 Chicago Abolitionist reunion, Dr. Dyer's son, Edward Dyer, wrote from his home in Burlington, Wisconsin, to his father's longtime friend Zebina Eastman:

> You have been a true—faithful—efficient instigator and helper, in a great work which has resulted in a Revolution—a Revolution which has struck off the chains of 4,000,000 human beings. Your name is worthily connected with events that will long be perpetuated in the annals of your country. Forty years ago Abolitionists were sneered at as hair-brained [sic] fanatics, but I hold, that among the early abolitionists were some of the best minds, and profoundest thinkers, this country ever produced.[26]

Zebina Eastman and his friends, the western citizens in DeKalb County who read the *Western Citizen*, the Abolitionists who were characterized as harebrained fanatics, were first unreasonable men and women.

The Underground Railroad

It is obvious that Abolitionists were in charge of the local civic government structure. No one in DeKalb County was ever arrested, prosecuted, or convicted of aiding and abetting a fugitive slave, while in other counties surrounding DeKalb County such incidents occurred. For example, in 1845, in a smaller adjacent county to the southeast, there transpired a very real

"Negro Sale." Dubbed "the Kendall County affair," it involved a "colored man" named James Alexander Campbell, who was arrested and imprisoned because he did not have on his person the proper bond and security allowing him to be traveling "free" in Illinois. This created a situation whereby "humanity was enraged and our most precious rights trampled upon."[27]

Friends of Liberty throughout the county were encouraged to attend a public meeting at which the assemblage passed resolutions which vindicated the "universality of human rights, and strongly condemn[ed] the Black Code."[28] When Illinois was officially admitted to the Union as a free state, the Constitution of 1818 read, "Neither slavery nor involuntary servitude shall *hereafter* be *introduced* into this state."[29] However, blacks could become indentured servants of their own free will, which translated into a legal form of slavery. These social practices of the day sanctioned true slavery and were especially prevalent in the southern half of the state. Then in 1831 a new Illinois law decreed: "That no black or mulatto person shall hereafter be permitted to come and reside in this State, until such person shall have given bond and security."[30] The eager Abolitionists in the area determined that in order to bring the "odious Black Code more distinctly before the people for their detestation and abhorrence,"[31] they would leave James Campbell in jail for six weeks and then he would "be sold out according to the provisions of the statute."[32]

The antislavery supporters were afraid that the sheriff might seek to return the man to his "pretended owners" in the South prior to the appointed day of sale, and so "an eye was kept upon the Sheriff and jail in order that [Campbell] should not be smuggled away secretly."[33]

In the meantime, while the Friends of Liberty waited patiently for James Campbell's six week imprisonment to pass, they created a strategy to gain his freedom: Through various individual bidders, they planned to purchase him and then simply give Campbell a "railroad ticket out of town." The "railroad ticket" did not have a literal meaning. There were no real mechanical railroads functioning in this area until later in the early 1850s.

By offering a "nominal sum" at the auction, they complied with the letter of the law, but "disregard[ed] its spirit and intent, upon the ground that it would be morally wrong to be a party in the bargain or sale of inalienable rights."[34]

The plan needed several people to accept assigned tasks at the auction, and "if necessary, remove any bidders who should manifest that they were not friendly to the negro."[35] One member of the group was instructed to "leave under his control a corps of reserve for any emergency which might arise."[36] Were they expecting a mob action or possible violence against Campbell?

The first bid was for 25 cents. The antislavery group thought that it would end there. However, an interested spectator, who did not know of the planned strategy, started to bid. At that point "he was told by friends standing by to stop."[37] The final bid was $1.50, still an extremely nominal sum, and "as soon as the result was known, the air was rent with the shouts of the assembled throng. It was known and felt to be by all present, both friend and foe, a most single and glorious triumph of the friends of liberty."[38] Unreasonable men spirited James Alexander Campbell out of Kendall County to points unknown. His railroad ticket out of town was underground.

Overall, the proslavery forces in Illinois were undaunted by this small courageous act by a few of its citizens. In 1853 the state legislature passed the infamous "Black Laws" which were based in part on similar laws in southern states. As *Harper's Weekly* commented:

> [The new code] was much a part of the code of slavery as any slave law of Arkansas or Mississippi; for they were the work of what was called the Democratic party, and that party was the minister of slavery. In Illinois, for instance, all colored persons were presumed to be slaves unless they could prove themselves to be free; in other words, were held to be guilty until they proved their inno-

cence: thus directly reversing the first humane maxim of the common law. By another act, if any negro or mulatto came into the State and staid [sic] ten days, he was to be fined fifty dollars, and sold indefinitely to pay the fine.[39]

Antislavery Sheriffs

One reason no one was ever arrested and jailed in DeKalb County for aiding a fugitive slave during the mid–1800s was that all the succeeding elected sheriffs were antislavery sympathizers. If not active Abolitionists themselves, they never pursued anyone involved in the Underground Railroad. Whether or not they were personally involved in the county antislavery movement, their restraint resulted in no arrests of any Abolitionists in DeKalb County.

Little is known about the county's very first law and order official, Sheriff Joseph C. Lander. He was elected on the local Anti-Claimjumpers ticket in 1837, serving as sheriff from 1838 to 1839. Lander is listed in the 1840 Census with his wife and young daughter, and by the next year he owned three land patents totaling 240 acres in the county. Both Joseph and Rachel Lander died before 1850.

Morris Walrod, born in New York, was the next county sheriff, and served from 1840 to 1845. He was a lumberman by trade, and the brother-in-law to Dr. James Harrington, who was a Free-Democrat delegate to the organizing Republican convention of 1854. Walrod subsequently moved to Wisconsin by 1850.

After a brief stint as County Clerk, Ellzey P. Young followed Walrod as sheriff. Young came to DeKalb County from Ohio and soon became part of the prolific Waterman family when he married Caroline, one of Mary and John Dean Waterman's daughters. Several of the Waterman siblings were prominent in county civic affairs. After Caroline died, Young married Alida L. Ellwood, of another local entrepreneurial family, who was a sister to Isaac Ellwood, one of the inventors of barbed wire. The house which Ellzey and Caroline Young built around 1847 is still an occupied residence and contains a hidden small room or closet entered only through a visible closet door in an upstairs bedroom. If walls could speak, one wonders if they would tell of Underground Railroad activity in the household.

The man who succeeded Young in office had a lot of credits to his name. Marshall Stark was a teacher, farmer, lumber dealer, hotel owner, one of the first petit jurors for the Circuit Court, superintendent of schools, Sycamore Township supervisor, school commissioner, county assessor, as well as DeKalb County sheriff. He served from 1848 to 1849. His reading material included his subscription to the *Western Citizen*.

Stark was followed by Kimball Dow's brother-in-law, Herman Furness. Dow became the secretary of the DeKalb County Anti-Slavery Society. Furness, a farmer and grocer, was elected sheriff in 1850. Together with Morris Walrod and Marshall Stark, he had been a member of the original "Regulator" or "Lynching Clubs"[40] formed earlier in the county by citizens hoping to thwart horse thieves. By 1870 Furness moved his family from Sycamore Township to the state of Kansas.

The brother of a *Western Citizen* subscriber was next to serve. Joseph F. Glidden, older brother to Josiah "Willard" Glidden, was elected sheriff in 1852. It is noteworthy that Joseph moved back into the family home with his widowed mother and other adult siblings after he was widowed himself. Since Willard already subscribed to the *Western Citizen*, one copy was sufficient to spread the antislavery news within the household. Joseph Glidden later invented barbed wire, and in partnership with Isaac L. Ellwood, created an empire that fenced in the West.

Another *Western Citizen* subscriber, William H. Phelps, became sheriff in 1854. Phelps was also a farmer who lived in Sycamore Township, worked at a sawmill and attended the Universalist Church. It was during Phelps's tenure that the county Board of Supervisors finally decided to build a county jail. Of necessity, the previous sheriffs Lander, Walrod, Stark and Furness often allowed and encouraged prisoners to escape "if the crime of which they were guilty was not of much consequence."[41] There was a sound reason behind this seemingly lackadaisical execution of justice: "In many instances when the county had a criminal charged with murder, forgery or some other heinous crime, the sheriff or his deputy was compelled to sleep with him, having the hand of the criminal tied to that of the sheriff."[42] Allowing a criminal to escape was preferable to sleeping with one.

With a new jail ready for his use, yet another farmer, Silas W. Tappan, took over as sheriff in 1856. After serving as sheriff, in 1860 Tappan ran for county recorder. The Republican political candidates for that office that year included the incumbent James Beveridge, as well as Roswell Dow and Caleb Brown. Tappan and the others lost the election to Brown.

Congregationalist Henry Dudley Safford followed Tappan in office, becoming county sheriff in 1858. Sheriff Safford farmed in both South Grove and Sycamore townships, and like several predecessors, subscribed to the *Western Citizen*. The last pre–Civil War DeKalb County sheriff was Baldwin Woodruff. He was born in New York, farmed in Clinton township, and was elected to office in 1860. Woodruff was also the first chairman of the Clinton Township Republican Party, organized in 1856.

As a group, these men who swore to uphold law and order in DeKalb County are not known to have met together to declare a common political philosophy. They all hailed originally from different states, Maine, Pennsylvania, New Hampshire and New York. Yet, something in their backgrounds, something in their churches, something in the newspapers they read, or something in their personal environment in Northern Illinois created in all of them a sense of morality, which caused them never to arrest someone who aided a fugitive slave. Consequently, David West, Horatio Page, Jesse Kellogg, William Nickerson, George Beveridge and all of the other hundreds of western citizens in DeKalb County were free to follow the dictates of their collective conscience when they aided those liberty-seeking pilgrims traveling from the southern states to Canada.

The political and religious leaders of the 1840s and 1850s did not have the advantage of our historical hindsight to identify why they acted in a particular way at certain times. Today we can review an event or the actions of influential community leaders and recognize the causes and consequences of their actions. Were our predecessors less complex than what we now want to make them appear? Not necessarily, but their priorities were different. On the new western frontier, underneath the religious and political overtones, the western citizens' primary concern was to complete their daily routines, living from day to day, and surviving to see another.

Thanks to hundreds of known and unknown unreasonable men and women, the Underground Railroad in DeKalb County, which was so much a part of their everyday lives, was never delayed by public officials; it never had an accident and it always ran according to schedule as needed.

CHAPTER 12

God Will Thank the Republican Party

> Look at our politics... Have they ever addressed themselves to the enterprise of relieving this country of the pest of slavery? Our politics have run very low, and men of character will not willingly touch them.[1] — Ralph Waldo Emerson (1803–1882), Universalist minister, antislavery advocate and essayist

Politics and Deacon Kellogg

The Honorable Jesse Churchill Kellogg was a man of character but he did not necessarily use conventional political means to achieve his goals. However, keeping politics out of church matters or civil concerns was not a dilemma for the seasoned deacon. Even as a highly principled person, Kellogg appeared to rise above any argument of church theology vs. political philosophy. He probably intended to do what was proper in order to accomplish his objectives. His aim, of course, was always to do what was best for his church. Another parallel goal was to do what was best for his community. If what was good for his church actually turned out to be what was best for the community in his estimation, then so be it. However, for Kellogg, the opposite could also be true: If a political course of action might be best for his community, and it would also augment his church organization, then that was an added enhancement.

Jesse Kellogg was a well-read man whose trimmed beard gave him a kind and gentlemanly appearance. But behind his mild demeanor was a stern countenance supporting his determined ideas about his church, his village, and society in general. He was a keen observer of frontier life and was occasionally outspoken regarding social concerns. As president of the DeKalb County Bible Society, he was an "ardent advocate of temperance and was elected trustee of Sycamore by the anti-saloon element."[2] More importantly, this unreasonable man was a "faithful conductor on the Underground Railroad," and was considered by the citizenry as a "staunch old hero of justice and humanity."[3]

Coming from Vermont, Jesse Kellogg, like his DeKalb County compatriot David West, may also have been influenced by the crusading Vermont Congregational minister, Beriah Green. Green was an activist in national abolition politics and helped to organize the American Anti-Slavery Society, as well as the Liberty Party. Kellogg's own antislavery philosophy may even have been intensified by that of Beriah Green.

At the age of 28, Kellogg emigrated from Vermont to Illinois with his young bride, the former Phoebe Wood. Through his marriage, Jesse Kellogg was a brother-in-law to DeKalb County antislavery sympathizers Henry Wood and Thomas Wood, who were Phoebe's brothers. The newlyweds traveled via the Erie Canal and through the Great Lakes to reach Chicago, then overland westward to Will County, where they first rented a farm. They soon claimed land in what would become Sycamore Township in DeKalb County. All five of their children were born in Illinois.

As one of the original members of the First Congregational Church, Kellogg served officially as the church clerk. In 1841, about a year after the church organized, he penned a church trustees–sanctioned letter to the American Home Missionary Society (AHMS). The missive entreated the Rev. Flavel Bascome of Chicago's First Presbyterian Church, who was an antislavery organizer and agent for the American Home Missionary Society, to please send a minister immediately to the struggling Sycamore congregation. The AHMS supplied pastors to both the Congregational and Presbyterian churches across the Western Frontier. Unfortunately, at that particular time there were no missionaries, Presbyterian or Congregational, available for duty on the western frontier in Northern Illinois.

Initially, the Sycamore Congregationalists found the ministerial services of the Rev. James Mackie to be satisfactory for their spiritual purposes, but at age 73 Mackie was described by Kellogg as being "of advanced age and increase[d] infirmities."[4] Because of worsening personal health concerns, Mackie was only able to periodically lead the congregants in worship during the five-month period from April to September of 1840. Occasionally a visiting minister satisfied their religious needs for one Sunday. Quickly, led by Deacon Kellogg's determination, by March 13, 1841, the church officially formed a Congregational Church Society, which was the business arm of the organization. They could then act as a corporate body instead of a small Bible study or prayer group. And so with the elected Trustees' blessing, a week later Jesse Kellogg's letter describing the "feeble church in Sycamore"[5] thirsting for spiritual guidance went forth to the American Home Missionary Society.

Kellogg laid out the terms for a minister. He would receive $200 per year, one-half in cash and the other half "in good merchantable produce delivered in Sycamore."[6] This was expected to be matched with an additional $200 from the AHMS for a total salary package value of $400 per year. All expenditures were considered covered by this sum, including firewood, clothing, house rent, and any medicines.

Kellogg further extolled the amenities of the locale, as well as the particular advantages in placing a minister in the new village. He included the observation that "this town which now is, and in all probability, will continue to remain the permanent seat of Justice for this County, is situated nearly in the center of a small but beautiful, healthy and mostly improved prairie ... surrounded by heavy groves of excellent timber ... [and is] increasing in wealth, population and influence." He requested that the ministerial candidate have "ardent, unaffected piety, and solid literary acquirements, one who can endure with his people the privations and hardships incident to the infancy of society."[7]

A postscript to the letter contains two subtle warnings, perhaps meant to intimidate the receiver. After once again requesting that a minister be sent to Sycamore "immediately," Kellogg suggests that if the clergyman does not possess the expected "preaching talents," the congregation might withdraw their monetary support. Additionally, there is a veiled threat that unless a Congregational church is established posthaste, the area would be solely "occupied by other denominations."[8] Deacon Kellogg did not want the Methodists or any other religious group to get ahead of the Congregationalists!

Although Kellogg indicated that his own chosen community was the center of local government, the permanent seat of justice was not always in Sycamore. For a brief time after 1837 when DeKalb County organized, the focal point of government was in Coltonville. Coltonville, so named after its foremost resident, Rufus Colton, was a small village slightly southwest of Sycamore. The first court to convene in DeKalb County took place in Rufus Colton's home on the bank of the Kishwaukee River where the Potawatomie Indians frequently camped.

A general election determined, however, that Sycamore would be the county seat. By 1839 a new frame courthouse was partially completed at the chosen site, but the circuit court was still held at Coltonville. "Judge [Thomas] Ford was ordered by the county commissioners to adjourn his court to Sycamore," but the order "was opposed by [Rufus] Colton, [Henry] Madden and others, on the claim that the papers were made returnable to Coltonville and that suits could not legally be tried in Sycamore."[9] It is assumed that Colton and Madden wanted the seat of county government to remain closer to their own homes. Enter Jesse Kellogg, who was the county's first clerk and recorder, and "not withstanding the vigorous protest," personally confiscated the court docket and papers. "Then with Judge Ford, lawyers, litigants and witnesses followed Captain [Erastus H.] Barnes on his famous spotted pony to Sycamore."[10] Because Kellogg obviously thought it was in the best interests of the larger community to remove the county seat to Sycamore, rather than to maintain it in Coltonville, he took possession of the official legal documents, and along with his political friends, promptly transported them to Sycamore via horseback.

While the presiding Circuit Judge Thomas Ford was destined to become the seventh governor of Illinois, our local citizen Kellogg was quickly arrested for the deed. However, the civil court vindicated this determined county clerk and recorder and the county seat remained in Sycamore. Deacon Jesse Churchill Kellogg, the "active Abolitionist and powerful adjunct of the Underground Railroad,"[11] was in all ways a most unreasonable man.

Politics and the Church

In answer to Kellogg's prayers, in July of 1841, the Rev. David I. Perry arrived in Sycamore unsolicited and unannounced. He carried with him "letters of commendation from the Presbytery of Bath in the State of New York directed to the Presbytery of Ottawa in the State of Illinois."[12] Because Ottawa was some 30 miles south of Sycamore, First Congregational Clerk Jesse Kellogg approached the American Home Missionary Society to grant financial support for Perry to become their new missionary in DeKalb County. Perry wrote that he "landed with my family consisting of ten souls in Chicago on the 23rd of June. My first object was to seek a field for ministerial usefulness."[13] He left his wife, children, and mother-in-law in Chicago while he scouted out the Northern Illinois area. He did not previously apply for support from the AHMS, apparently not wanting a pre-determined assignment, but hoped to discern where "the leadings of providence" would bring him.

For nine months, the Perry family suffered what to him were great physical sacrifices in terms of home and comfort, against "my own inclinations and even the wishes of my family for the sake of preaching the gospel." He soon learned that the small group of Congregationalists had "overstated their ability" to build him a new house, the financial support from the AHMS was slow to arrive, and the congregants "were not only poor but seemed to know nothing of the business of taking care of a minister. In fact they all had as much as they could do to provide for their own comfort." Perry decided, "It was a gloomy business when compared with that of preaching to the congregations which I had formerly served."[14]

In his letter of April 1, 1842, to Milton Badger and Charles Hall of the AHMS, the earnest frontier minister discussed the spiritual mind of the church. The organizing body consisted of 12 souls, but according to Perry, by two years later he was preaching to about 100 people on Sunday mornings, although not all were tithing members of the church. Even so, at that point Perry was still discouraged. He "found no spirit of prayer in the church, and it was exceedingly difficult to converse with the people on the subject of their spiritual state."[15]

> But there was another discouraging circumstance which developed itself in the meantime; and which convinced me that unless the Lord should appear for us at the expiration of the present year the church would be left to support the gospel or to give it up. I became satisfied that a large proportion of the subscription [by the church members to financially support a new minister] had been made from motives that would cease to operate on some minds. There had been a long and somewhat bitter contest in regard to the location of the county seat, and when it was settled at this place the people felt that to prevent attempt to remove it everything that could be done must be done to give character and importance to Sycamore. Many who cared nothing for the gospel on its own account thought that it might be of importance in building up their favorite village.[16]

The Rev. David I. Perry realized that Congregational organizers Judge Jesse Rose, Erastus Hamlin, Horatio Page and especially Jesse Kellogg had ulterior motives underlying their intense desire to create a strong Congregational church in Sycamore. The local political aspirations of a judge, a gentleman, a doctor and a county clerk to place Sycamore as the county seat superseded any spiritual motivation. It is possible that DeKalb County Abolitionists were idealistic at first, but soon recognized a certain political expediency in supporting antislavery. The Rev. Perry was very concerned that with only political gain as their motivation, the congregation might not be willing to continue their monetary support. The line between matters of church and state was indeed blurred.

In spite of the spiritual and temporal roadblocks, Perry and his wife Mariah persevered. He encouraged weekly and monthly prayer meetings, sought to engage church members in discourse about the gospel, joined with the local Methodist congregation in a quarterly prayer meeting, and overcame the overtures of a new Universalist minister in town seeking to lure the Congregationalists away. By the end of the first year of his commission to Sycamore, the committed membership had more than doubled to 29 communicants. County and state politics, however, still dominated the activities of many of the members. "In fact the only discouraging thing in regard to the feeling and action of the church is that they have delayed to act [to subscribe to Perry's financial support] till this late hour when the whole affair should and might have been arranged two weeks ago. The excuse which I have for them in this matter is the state election which occurred on Monday last, and in which some of the church were more deeply interested than I desired to see them."[17]

The state election to which the Rev. Perry refers was that of Judge Thomas Ford to the governorship of the State of Illinois. Ford was the judge who agreed with Jesse Kellogg that Sycamore should be the DeKalb County seat a few years previous, and local politicians were anxious that he be elected. Perry served the First Congregational Church one more year until August 1843.

Morals and Politics

In an 1844 issue of the *Western Citizen*, the editor pointedly declared, "Politicians say that slavery is a moral evil, and only to be remedied by moral suasion. Church men say that it is [also] a political evil, and the only appropriate place to approach it is at the ballot box."[18] If people recognized the distinction between right and wrong, antislavery vs. proslavery, then those same people should elect a political candidate who best addressed their beliefs on the issue.

With an upcoming presidential election, the voting public was in a quandary. What was a man to do? Women did not yet have the right to vote, but they became increasingly vocal through the Female Antislavery Societies created at state and local levels. As the Universalist minister and abolition advocate Ralph Waldo Emerson observed, the citizenry listened to the "higher law" of God and to their inner voices while still faithfully following the precepts of their churches. Enlightened ministers bellowed from their pulpits about the evils of slavery and loyal members of the congregations responded to this moral suasion by enabling the liberation of slaves through the Underground Railroad. However, the issues were clarified when upon reflection they asked themselves: how could the individual conscience address a perceived corrupted Constitution except through political means?

If, according to Emerson, "conventional political means were incapable of redressing an immoral law," then unconventional means must surely be utilized. The unconventional means included first recognizing the indisputable fact that a moral and ethical matter was becoming a political issue.

Before Political Activism

Prior to acting in the political arena, DeKalb County residents needed to focus on exactly what they believed. Their heartfelt thoughts and opinions were soon clearly expressed at a Sycamore gathering.

The courthouse provided the formal setting for the "meeting of the inhabitants of DeKalb County" on March 27, 1843. A detailed account appeared on the front page of the April 13 edition of the *Western Citizen*.[19] Thomas Woolsey was the farmer turned Methodist minister who acted as chair to this particular meeting, and J.A. Bill, about whom nothing is known, was appointed secretary. The well-known Congregational minister, David I. Perry, intoned "an appropriate prayer," followed by "an able and eloquent address." Remarks by several others were given, and then a committee was appointed to "draft a constitution for an anti-slavery society."[20] Jesse Rose, Abner Jackman and Kimball Dow comprised the constitution committee.

It would appear that perhaps this committee had already worked on the proposed constitution, because "after retiring for a short time, the committee reported ... [and] the constitution was unanimously adopted and signed by thirty-nine individuals present."[21] That original DeKalb County Anti-Slavery Society constitution is reprinted here:

> Whereas the most high God "hath made of one blood all nations of men to dwell on the face of the whole earth," and has thus established the common brotherhood of all mankind;
> Our national existence is based on the above fundamental principles, which the Declaration of Independence sets forth as being self-sufficient "that all men are created equal; that they are endowed by their Creator with certain inalienable rights, among which are life, liberty, and the pursuit of happiness";
> Slavery is the antagonist of these principles and rights, and is opposed to national justice, to a republican form of government, and to the Christian religion; it violates the rights of humanity, usurps the prerogatives of God, is destructive to the prosperity of a country, and hostile to the best interests of a civil community;
> Although slavery is confined to a certain portion of our country, it extends its blighting influence over the whole body politic, corrupting the moral and social relations, endangering the peace, union and safety of these United States;

And whereas the laws of humanity and religion, as well as the interest of all concerned, require its immediate abolition:

Therefore we do hereby form ourselves into an Anti-Slavery Society, on the basis of the following constitution:

Article 1st. This society shall be called the DeKalb County Anti-Slavery Society.

Art. 2d. The objects of this society shall be to free ourselves from all participation in the sin of slavery, and to promote the cause of liberty and emancipation throughout our country and the world.

Art. 3d. This society shall aim to elevate the character and condition of the people of color, by encouraging their intellectual, moral and religious improvement, and by removing public prejudice.

Art. 4th. The measures of this society shall be free discussion, the circulation of books, tracts, papers, &c., and any other means, moral, religious, or political, that may be deemed necessary and suitable.

Art. 5th. The officers of this society shall be a president, two vice-presidents, secretary and treasurer, to be chosen annually, and they shall hold their respective offices until others are chosen. These officers shall constitute an executive committee, three of whom shall form a quorum.

Art. 6th. The executive committee shall preserve a written report of all the doings at each annual meeting of the society, and shall have power to call special meetings.

Art. 7th. This society shall meet annually for the election of officers and the transaction of business at such time and place as the executive committee may designate.

Art. 8th. This constitution may be altered or amended by the votes of two-thirds of the members present at any annual meeting.

Art. 9th. Any person may become a member of this society by adopting its principles and signing its constitution.[22]

Officers elected for the 1843-44 term were Thomas Woolsey, president; Jesse Rose and Ezra Starr Gregory as the two vice-presidents; Aaron C. West, treasurer; and Kimball Dow as secretary. The preamble invoked both God and the Founding fathers' Declaration of Independence, and announced to the world that they were a society of immediatist abolitionists who would use "any other means, moral, religious, or political, that may be deemed necessary." This included the Underground Railroad. The DeKalb County Anti-Slavery Society was official.

Antislavery Blends with the Abolitionists

If we follow succeeding notices for public meetings published in the *Western Citizen*, it was a natural, workable progression to move from local antislavery sympathizer to named Abolitionist, to politics, to the Liberty Party and finally to the Republican Party.

While the first meeting of the society was simply reported under the headline of "DeKalb County," an important "Notice" appeared on February 29, 1844: "The annual meeting of the DeKalb Anti-Slavery Society will be held at Sycamore on Saturday, the 23rd of March, commencing at 11 o'clock, A.M. Friends and enemies are invited to attend. By order of the Executive Committee, Kimball Dow, Sec'y."[23]

The words "annual meeting" suggest that this is now an established entity, which has performed important work since the last regular meeting and now wishes to update the general public. Following this gathering of antislavery "friends and enemies," Society Secretary Kimball Dow wrote a brief report in a letter to *Western Citizen* editor Zebina Eastman. This assembly also convened at the courthouse in Sycamore, with the Congregational minister as the keynote speaker. The Rev. Edwin E. Wells was the successor minister to David I. Perry. The letter is dated March 25, 1844.

> Our cause is advancing in this county. Last Saturday we held our first annual meeting in this village; and although the going was bad [due to the weather], we had a good attendance. About the time

specified for the commencement of the meeting, the friends, male and female, were seen coming in from different quarters, some on horseback, some in their double wagons, and others on foot. About an hour after the time, the Court House was filled, when, after transacting necessary business, the audience listened to an address from the Rev. Mr. Wells, pastor of the Congregational church in this place. After which we had a kind and friendly discussion of our principles. Several names, in all about 17, were added to our constitution. We hope to give a strong vote for Liberty at the next presidential election. Kimball Dow, Sec'y.[24]

In the following spring of 1845, the *Western Citizen* once again published a notice

The DeKalb county Anti-Slavery Society will hold its annual meeting at the courthouse in Sycamore, on the second Tuesday in June next. Friends will be punctual to attend at an early hour in the day, as it is suggested that it will be a good time to make our nominations for the August election. Let each precinct see that they are represented in this meeting. An address may be expected. Kimball Dow, Sec'y, Sycamore, May 7, 1845.[25]

An identical announcement appeared in the newspaper the next week. The "second Tuesday in June" in 1845 was June 10. This date created a conflict for the county organizers, as some of the participants planned to attend the meeting of the Illinois Anti-Slavery Society at Alton, Illinois, on June 4, which was the preceding Wednesday that year. Traveling by horseback to attend an assembly in Alton required adequate time to complete the round trip. Alton had been chosen specifically for the state meeting because it was considered a hallowed place in abolitionist history. This "Martyr Ground of Liberty" was the very place where the antislavery newspaper editor, the "lamented [Elijah] Lovejoy,"[26] was murdered by an anti-abolitionist mob in 1838. A large "assemblage of the friends of the slave as has never been witnessed in the State"[27] planned to gather for their eighth annual state meeting at that location, which was several hundred miles away from DeKalb County. As a result, the county Anti-Slavery Society wisely changed their meeting date to the following month.

The next notice to appear took a jump in terminology and merged the Abolitionists with the antislavery sympathizers.

ABOLITIONISTS OF DEKALB COUNTY TAKE NOTICE!
The annual meeting of the DeKalb county Anti-Slavery Society will be postponed until the 4th of July next at 10 o'clock, A.M. at the Court House, in Sycamore. The object of the postponement is to give time for the return of the delegates from Alton, and also to extend an invitation to friends from other counties. Will friend Codding, and others who have never visited this county, contrive to be present at that meeting?
By order of the President, KIMBALL DOW, Sec'y[28]

It is interesting to note that although the Sycamore First Congregational Church had been ousted from the courthouse because of their professed antislavery beliefs, the DeKalb County Anti-Slavery Society, as well as the antislavery political body known as the Liberty Party, were both allowed the use of the public building. Both the political group and the abolitionist assembly were candid about their philosophies and goals. As private civic entities, working within a freedom of speech atmosphere, they could express themselves freely. However, the church members were perceived as meddling in government business. In doing so, they placed the local perceived separation of church and state at peril. They were a threat.

One might surmise that an antislavery society discussed the pros and cons of slavery, and maybe the "hows" and "wherefores" of eliminating the practice. The original public notice of the society's meeting, however, clearly indicates that they planned to nominate antislavery candidates for public offices for an upcoming election. It further suggested that they hoped to have representation from each voting precinct in the county. Clearly, they were acting as a political group through which they hoped to bring about the downfall of slavery. The unreasonable men and women in DeKalb County were impatient to move forward.

The meeting notice that appeared in the *Western Citizen* was only one of many similar advertisements published during that time period. Other antislavery groups posted frequent announcements regarding similar gatherings in the nearby counties of Kane, Kendall, Boone, Bureau, and LaSalle, as well as DuPage and Cook.

A month later when the proceedings of the Anti-Slavery Society meeting were reported in the newspaper, the gathering was specifically acknowledged as actually having been a meeting of the DeKalb County Liberty Party. The DeKalb County Anti-Slavery Society, whose members called themselves Abolitionists, was in reality the core membership of the DeKalb County Liberty Party. For them, it was indeed a natural progression; in county history, they were one and the same. The entities merged to become an organized moral and political group.

DEKALB COUNTY LIBERTY CONVENTION

The friends of Human liberty held a Convention at Sycamore, DeKalb county, on the 4th of July. A very large assembly convened in a spacious bower, erected for the purpose, and were addressed by the Rev. Mr. Taylor, in a most able and eloquent manner. A committee of delegates from the various precincts, made the following nominations: For probate Justice, Henry Madden; for School Commissioner, Kimball Dow; for county Commissioner, Jeremiah L. Brown; for Treasurer, Curtis Smith.[29]

Also among the attendees were William Patten and James Beveridge, who traveled the thirty-plus miles on horseback from Somonauk to Sycamore. William's first wife, Elizabeth, wrote to her sister in Cossayuna, Washington County, New York, that Patten and Beveridge were delegates to an "Abolition County convention" in Sycamore on July 4.[30] Once again we see that the lines of distinction between the antislavery movement and the Abolitionists in DeKalb County were greatly blurred. Twenty-first-century authors comment, "On the frontier, religion and politics fused in such a manner as to make antislavery tenets acceptable to the masses."[31] And so the DeKalb County Anti-Slavery Society became a political party in its own right. They affiliated at the national level with the Liberty Party, whose supporters "sought the abolition of slavery and other social evils as a preliminary step to the establishment of the government of God on earth."[32] The DeKalb County Anti-Slavery Society with all its dedicated denominational church members openly labored to free the slave through political means. This very opinionated group enthusiastically nominated a slate of officers for the upcoming county elections.

After the election, the *Western Citizen* reported the results "extremely discouraging and mortifying to the friends of Liberty who did attend the polls."[33] Voter turnout was not as high as they hoped and the editorial comments reflect that.

DEKALB COUNTY ELECTION OFFICIAL

	Liberty		Democrat
Probate Justice, Madden	96	Mayo	223
Co. Commissioner, Brown	199	Hill	245
School Commissioner, Dow	111	Harrington	221
Treasurer & Assessor, Smith	107	Waterman	211

A large number of our friends thought their work of more consequence than their principles, and let the election go by default. The Whigs, with one or two exceptions, voted the Democratic ticket. Many of our friends split their ticket, alleging dissatisfaction with the nomination. On the whole, we have only to say that the result of our election is anything but gratifying to the Liberty cause in our county.[34]

In 1847 the DeKalb County Liberty Party publicly chastised George Hill for his vote at the Illinois Constitution Convention. That convention was called to overhaul the original 1818 state constitution and further address the rights of blacks within Illinois, partly by prohibiting slaveholders to transport slaves into the state specifically to free them.

> On motion, *Resolved*, That we have seen with deep regret the recent vote of George H. Hill, Esq., the delegate from this county in the State Convention to amend the Constitution of this State, by which all persons who are not WHITE are denied the [adjective illegible] privilege of voting for their rulers.
>
> *Resolved*, That we are the more grieved at this recreant vote of our delegate, from the fact that on the day of his election, the friends of the said delegate assured the voters that he was as good an anti-slavery man as there was in the county, and in consequence of said assurance, quite a number of abolitionists were induced to vote for him.
>
> *Resolved*, That we cannot but look with abhorrence on any man or set of men, who will thus invade the dearest rights of man on account of COLOR, and take from him that imprescriptible inheritance which alone is the gift of God.
>
> *Resolved*, That the proceedings of this convention be published in the Western Citizen.
> DAVID WEST, Chairman[35]

Democrat turned Liberty Party man, George H. Hill, later switched parties and again ran successfully for political office on the 1856 new Republican ticket.

DeKalb County was slower than other counties to join the Liberty Party movement, or perhaps they were not as eager or punctual in reporting their activities. The *Western Citizen*, the publishing entity of the Liberty Party, dependably printed detailed election results. DeKalb County soon became the largest block of subscribers in the entire *Western Citizen* mailed subscription list.

Politics and Religion

The *Western Citizen*, whose masthead now declared that it was "The North-Western Advocate of Universal Liberty" and proudly proclaimed "The Supremacy of God and the Equality of Man," pointed out to its readers, "There is no question that a great portion of those who are now exerting an influence for the amelioration of the condition of the slave, are professors of the Christian religion."[36] As the professors of Christian religion unified, they realized that "a moral question gives to the politician an opportunity and a power which carries a momentum which cannot be checked at will."[37]

It was increasingly evident that the devout Christians who wanted to eliminate slavery based on moral principles needed to be politically astute. They were admonished, again by the editor of the *Western Citizen*, to look at the entire slavery issue as both moral and political. And if they would do that, they would see "that we have duties to perform in [both] church and state."[38]

Following the well-honed Pilgrim model, the populace sought guidance from their church leaders to support their ethical and moral positions. Finally, they recognized that "the abolition movement in Illinois had become a political rather than a moral agitation."[39]

One man who understood the value of playing the political game was attorney John Wentworth. Wentworth, a pioneer from New Hampshire who moved to Chicago in 1836, was first elected as a Democrat to Congress in 1843, serving four consecutive terms. His congressional district included DeKalb County, and he visited there occasionally, especially during election cycles. In September 1844, Wentworth addressed an interested Democrat group in Sycamore at the DeKalb County courthouse. A "looker on," who was undoubtedly antislavery, reported to the *Western Citizen*, "[Wentworth] had no speaking talent — nothing but a sort of pump handle oratory, common among children at school when *speaking pieces*."[40]

The congressman was well aware of the undercurrents of the antislavery movement at the time and proceeded to inform the Abolitionists of his contemporary Democrat philosophy. His speech did not end "until he had given the clergy and religious people a good sound thrashing."[41] He alluded to the anti–Mason fever prevalent in recent years, remarking that "the clergy got so zealous that they would pray for the ghost of Morgan."[42] Wentworth chastised the clergy and church members because "now they were actually praying and whining over the negro!"[43] The manner in which he presented his case and the inflections in his voice carried with it his entire proslavery mentality at the time.

Later Wentworth had a change of political heart, switched parties and was elected the Republican mayor of Chicago. Following the Civil War he once again ran for Congress, this time as the Republican he had become.

The involved antislavery population in Northern Illinois discovered what sometimes takes civic leaders a long time to learn: Morality and politics ultimately go hand in hand. Without a sense of morality, a nation could eventually fail. So far, even with all their efforts in the Underground Railroad, and all their antislavery posturing on Sunday mornings, the Abolitionists in DeKalb County were only acting in a moral vacuum with no means to effect any comprehensive changes. Somehow the unreasonable men and women would have to either discover or create a political instrument to carry their high principles forward.

Friends of Liberty Rally

The lovely young Agnes Beveridge, daughter of George and Ann Beveridge, received a letter directed to her in Somonauk, Illinois, from her friend Elizabeth Miller, who lived in Washington County, New York. The letter is dated October 12, 1844. Included among her ramblings about mutual friends still living in New York was the pointed question, "Are there any Liberty party men or voting Abolitionists in your part of the world? That party is coming on with rapid strides in the East."[44] Elizabeth was certain that Agnes would be aware of what was happening in the West. A descendant of Agnes Beveridge Patten later commented on Elizabeth's query: "The question of slavery more and more assumed not only a political but a moral aspect."[45] Although women did not have the right to vote, that did not keep them from expressing their heartfelt political thoughts to their husbands and acquaintances. They were not living in exile without communication to the outside world. Most women on the western frontier enjoyed strong relationships with their contemporaries and freely discussed their ideas through their correspondence. Young women communicated daily gossip with distant friends who were cognizant of the political forces swirling around them.

Because the Liberty Party had its roots in the East, Agnes Beveridge's friend knew of its existence. The new political party was organized specifically as an antislavery political entity by evangelical abolitionists who were members of a church in Warsaw, New York. Originally Presbyterian, the Warsaw church group seceded from the organized church when they felt the Presbyterians were becoming proslavery. The parishioners were correct in their assessment at the time. A vote at their 1837 General Assembly meeting moved a discussion of slavery off the agenda, and less than 25 years later the proslavery vs. antislavery factions (South vs. North) split the denomination.

Concurrent with the DeKalb County Anti-Slavery Society, Liberty Party men were also "coming on with rapid strides" in the West. Before Elizabeth Miller's letter ever reached Agnes Beveridge, the Liberty Party convened in September 1844 at the DeKalb County Courthouse in Sycamore "for the purpose of effecting a more perfect organization prior to the Presidential election."[46] Slated to speak at the gathering were James H. Collins, a prominent Chicago attorney who would later run for Congress as a Free-Soil Party candidate, plus Underground Railroad operator Dr. Charles Volney Dyer of Chicago. More important was the opportunity to hear neighboring LaSalle County Abolitionist and antislavery lecturer, John Hope Henderson, whose home was an Underground Railroad station, and who was their chosen candidate for Congress in the Fourth Congressional District.

Earlier on the Thursday preceding the 1844 August congressional election, the *Western Citizen* was not entirely optimistic about the upcoming contest. They listed the "Liberty Ticket" candidates, which included John H. Henderson in the Fourth District, and attempted to give hope to antislavery electors:

> Next Monday ... the people of Illinois will again be called upon to choose between Liberty and Slavery. It is probable that Slavery will again, in most places, be triumphant, but we call upon all the friends of Liberty, not to be discouraged, but to vote, and in all ways act, as if success were sure ... [and] at the next trial, it will be the time for the Democrats to surrender to the all-conquering power of Truth, and the triumph of the Liberty cause.[47]

The Liberty Party did not prevail; slavery still triumphed. Undaunted by the outcome of the August elections, and ever encouraged by community leaders to "let the friends of human Liberty rally from every precinct in the county,"[48] local Abolitionists campaigned against all odds for their chosen presidential candidate, James G. Birney, in the November election. Former president Martin Van Buren, a Democrat, was initially the frontrunner, but could not garner enough votes to be nominated at the party's convention. James K. Polk received the Democrat nomination on the ninth ballot and became the first dark-horse candidate to run for president. In the national campaign which followed, Whig Henry Clay was favored, but when he said he was against the annexation of Texas, the South perceived that he was against the spread of slavery. Although both Clay and Polk were slaveholders, Clay consequently lost the Southern vote. Thrown into the political mix were the aspirations of Joseph Smith, the Mormon leader, who decided he wanted to run for president. The campaigns relied heavily on personal attacks played out in the press, and the abolitionist Liberty Party with Birney at the head of the ticket was unable to make any gains in DeKalb County. "All they could do was to stand their ground."[49]

Democrats, Free-Soilers and Whigs

The Democrat Party of the mid–1800s evolved in the U.S. political arena from the original Federalists. George Washington and John Adams, the first two presidents of the United States, were the only two men to be elected as Federalists. That party's name was taken from the *Federalist Papers*, which were a series of essays written in 1787 and 1788 to persuade New Yorkers to vote in favor of the proposed U.S. Constitution.

Thomas Jefferson was part of a faction opposed to some of the Federalist political positions in the late 18th century, and created the Democrat-Republican party. They considered themselves to be Republican in philosophy, and Jefferson and the two successive presidents Madison and Monroe were elected under the Democrat-Republican affiliation.

By 1824 politicos determined that perhaps they did not need to have political parties, and the nation's activists held regional conventions at which candidates were chosen with support from each geographic area. As a final expression of this so-called Era of Good Feelings, John Quincy Adams was consequently elected with no particular party affiliation. Within months of Adams's inauguration, the Tennessee legislature nominated Andrew Jackson for president. Calling themselves Democrats, they completed the evolution of Thomas Jefferson's brand of

Republicanism into what became the modern Democratic Party, and set the stage for Jackson's election four years later.

During Andrew Jackson's tenure as president, he acquired a reputation for being authoritarian, which reminded many of the kings of England. Because the Whig Party existed in that country as the party opposing the dictates of the then current King, the Americans borrowed the English name "Whig" for their new political party. The Whigs were united in their extreme opposition to "King Andrew I" (Jackson), but were so disorganized as a party that in 1836 they reverted to running regional candidates in opposition to the Democrat candidate, Martin Van Buren. Van Buren won and became the eighth president of the United States.

In 1840, when the Sycamore First Congregational Church organized and affirmed antislavery as a belief requirement for membership, James G. Birney was the first antislavery candidate for president under the Liberty Party banner. That same year the Whig Party initially supported Henry Clay, but anti–Masonic factors defeated Clay in the nomination process. Consequently, William Henry Harrison became the party's nominee, defeating the incumbent Democrat Van Buren. The Whigs had no platform as a party, but because the Democrats opposed federal interference with slavery, the Whigs prevailed. Third-party candidate Birney could not garner enough votes for election.

Harrison was only president for one month before he died and John Tyler became the first vice-president to accede to the presidency. The Whigs had their second president. It was during this decade that the slavery issue increased in importance with each succeeding election.

The year was 1844 when David West and his family arrived in DeKalb County and he began his work in the Illinois Underground Railroad. It was the year when the antislavery resolutions were passed at the First Congregational Church in Sycamore and both the DeKalb County Anti-Slavery Society and the new Liberty Party met at the courthouse. This was the same year that James K. Polk was nominated as the dark-horse Democrat candidate for President. Polk was lucky. Although popular Henry Clay was favored to win the general election, James Birney's candidacy for the Liberty Party's Abolitionist ticket assured that Whigs would split their votes, which is exactly what happened. James K. Polk was elected U.S. President.

Although no one was aware of it at the time, Zachary Taylor was the last Whig to be elected president. In 1848 the dominant campaign issue was the antislavery Wilmot Proviso, which was a bill to ban slavery in the territories acquired in the Mexican War. Taylor's Democrat opponent opposed the Wilmot Proviso and proposed "squatter sovereignty" to allow territories to decide the slavery issue, a thought later borrowed by Stephen A. Douglas in the Kansas-Nebraska Bill's doctrine of "popular sovereignty." This was also the year the Free-Soil Party entered the fray.

In March of 1848, First Congregational minister Oliver W. Norton left the Sycamore church because the church membership was not unanimous in their support of his antislavery views. Local conflicting attitudes in DeKalb County were indicative of what was happening nationwide. Five months later, the Free-Soil Party became a political entity created from the antislavery factions of the Democrat, Whig, and Liberty Party members. Former President Martin Van Buren, disgruntled because he was passed over in previous election cycles, was the obvious candidate for the Free-Soil Party. Free-Soilers were against the extension of slavery into the territories.

Because in 1848 Whig candidate Zachary Taylor owned over 100 slaves, he gained the Southern vote and won the election over the Free-Soil candidate Martin Van Buren. Within the next four years the Free-Soil Party would elect twelve congressmen, but never a president. They may have been a minor party, but their influence was great in the total political picture. DeKalb County Free-Soil members Pierpont Edwards, Stephen Townsend, Thurston Carr, David West, James Beveridge and Ezra "Starr" Gregory, among others, subsequently became Republicans.

Three years later President Zachary Taylor died and Vice-President Millard Fillmore, a

Whig, acceded to the presidency. Fillmore had presided over the discussion in Congress surrounding the September passage of the Compromise of 1850, which included the Fugitive Slave Law. Two weeks after it passed, and in direct response to the new law, Somonauk residents in southern DeKalb County held an "Indignation Meeting," resulting in the passage of local antislavery resolutions.

Slavery continued to be the dominant campaign issue for the 1852 presidential campaign. Democrat Franklin Pierce, a compromise candidate who was not even introduced as a nominee until the 35th ballot in convention, was finally elected as the party's standard-bearer on the 49th ballot. Both party platforms for the Democrats and the Whigs supported the Compromise of 1850, but the "cotton" Whigs (Southern) and the "conscience" Whigs (Northern) were divided in support of their candidate, Winfield Scott. This constituted the proslavery and the antislavery elements within the Party. Without strong party support, the Whigs lost the election, and the party was critically split over the slavery issue.

As a rejoinder to the highly charged political atmosphere, the Sycamore First Congregational Church passed stronger antislavery resolutions. But the timely passage of earnest resolutions by churches and communities was not enough. More was needed.

The Abolitionists Embrace Politics

A report in the August 2, 1854, issue of the DeKalb County *Republican Sentinel* heralded the recent "Anti-Nebraska Meeting." The publicity posters preceding the gathering announced it as an "Anti-Nebraska meeting," but in reality it was so much more. On the surface, the call to convention was specifically to gather local support to oppose the Kansas-Nebraska Act, as sponsored by Illinois Senator Stephen A. Douglas and recently passed by Congress in May. The bill admitted slavery in the proposed states of Kansas and Nebraska by allowing the residents to determine the issue themselves. This issue created much controversy from 1854 to 1859, and Kansas soon earned the title of "bleeding Kansas" as a result of the bloodshed in that state over the slavery question. The issue was also the focus of the renowned debates between Stephen A. Douglas and Abraham Lincoln in their pursuit of the office of senator from the state of Illinois.

In truth, the 1854 meeting's organizers intended to thoroughly discuss their very definite opinions about slavery, and then to address the need to work through political channels to alleviate the problem. James Hoy Beveridge was "one of the leading spirits in calling the Anti-Kansas-Nebraska Bill convention held in Sycamore."[50] Beveridge served on the convention's resolution committee. Remember that he had also assisted the resolution committee for the 1850 Somonauk Indignation Meeting protesting the Fugitive Slave Law. He was experienced and recognized what action to take; he understood and used the correct vocabulary to stir people to action. Beveridge was destined to become treasurer of the state of Illinois when his brother John was elected governor.

The official resolutions from the Sycamore Anti-Nebraska Meeting gave credibility to a more structured antislavery movement in the county. Held the evening of July 31, 1854, in the small frame courthouse, the meeting was attended by "citizens ... without distinction of party"[51] from all over DeKalb County. This was not a Democrat or Whig political function. This was pure antislavery. Looking to the future, "Protestant politicos ... hoped to create a coalition of Temperance men, Free-Soilers, Conscience Whigs, and Barnburner Democrats."[52] Delegates were chosen to attend an upcoming September 20 antislavery meeting in Aurora, Illinois, which in reality was an organizing convention for the Republican Party, called the Second Congressional

District's Republican Nominating Convention. Similar meetings in north-central Illinois were held earlier in Ottawa, Rockford, and Bloomington.

At 59 years old, Samuel H. Lay of Somonauk was a good choice to be appointed chairman of the Sycamore assembly. Four years earlier he had served as chairman of the 1850 Somonauk Anti-Fugitive Slave Law meeting. Lay, with his wife and seven children, moved to DeKalb County from Connecticut before 1840. Therefore, his age, his experience and his comparative longevity in the area gave his chairmanship high credibility.

William J. Hunt, 48 years old, of Sycamore, was appointed the Secretary for the meeting. Hunt was an attorney who would later be elected as one of the Whig delegates to the organizing Republican convention of 1854. Both Lay and Hunt were loyal subscribers to the *Western Citizen*, and Hunt was affiliated with the First Congregational Church. The Anti-Nebraska gathering served to exploit existing attitudes and proved to be a catalyst for the majority of the voters. A political movement could only gain strength from such conventions.

Dr. Henry Madden, age 54, was a member of the resolutions committee with James Beveridge. As a farmer turned grocer and druggist, he was not really a medical doctor; the title was perhaps self-appointed, but remained his out of respect. Madden served as the first Representative to the Illinois state legislature from DeKalb County and also served as a county supervisor and a grand juror, and was the 1845 candidate for probate justice on the Liberty Party ticket. Of course he subscribed to the *Western Citizen*. Like Jesse Kellogg, he wanted his town of Mayfield to become the county seat. As we have seen, that objective was not attained.

Three men were appointed to a subcommittee which would call for a district convention and oversee the nomination of a slate of candidates for upcoming local elections. They were J.C. Waterman, J.H. Beveridge and W. Fordham. John Calvin Waterman was one of ten children, six boys and four girls. He and his brother James were the first of the Waterman siblings to arrive in Sycamore and were soon followed by their adventurous sister, Charlotte. Waterman was no stranger to DeKalb County; he was one of the original settlers prior to 1840. He was a farmer, a merchant, and the postmaster of both Newburg (in Winnebago County) and Sycamore. He would serve as DeKalb county treasurer, and later on the staff of Illinois Governor Richard J. Oglesby. Chairman Samuel Lay picked a solid committee member in John Waterman.

A lesser-known figure was William Fordham of Sycamore. Fordham also came to Northern Illinois from New York. He was an accomplished attorney, which was undoubtedly why he was one of those asked to serve on more than one committee. Fordham, Beveridge and Madden were solicited in advance to prepare certain resolutions to be considered at the general meeting. Although the report indicates that they were appointed to form a new resolution committee at that July 31 meeting, they actually already had the appropriate resolutions written and ready for presentation. The resolution committee obviously convened prior to the publicized public event.

Opening remarks at the gathering were given by none other than Zebina Eastman of Chicago, the Abolitionist owner and editor of the publication arm of the Liberty Party, the *Western Citizen* newspaper. His comments were followed by "the eloquence of Codding."[53] The DeKalb County Anti-Slavery Society had hoped Ichabod Codding would be present at their much earlier 1845 meeting. Now, nine years later, Codding visited DeKalb County to present his passionate antislavery address. Since he was a representative of the greater American Anti-Slavery Society, antislavery political factions underwrote the trip for this fiery New Yorker. At stops in Joliet in Will County, and Geneva in neighboring Kane County, Codding gave his succinct reply to Stephen A. Douglas's proposals to extend slavery in Kansas. Codding was also a Congregational minister and his lectures were known to raise "such a storm of opposition that his life was several times in danger."[54] The DeKalb County attendees were certain to be inspired.

Following the antislavery speeches, the resolutions, as drafted by the Messrs. Beveridge,

Madden and Fordham, were adopted unanimously. The first resolution was very basic as it pertained to the foremost subject of the day, slavery: "Resolved, That we are opposed to Slavery in every form and in favor of freedom in its most comprehensive sense, wherever man exists through God's heritage."[55] The second resolution alluded to the Northwest Ordinance, passed by the Second Continental Congress, which created the great Northwest Territory. This included the future states of Ohio, Indiana, Illinois, Michigan and Wisconsin. Article VI of that federal ordinance prohibited the introduction of slaves into that territory west of the Ohio River. In the same sentence, this resolution refers to the Declaration of Independence and its author, former President Thomas Jefferson: "Resolved, That we regard the ordinance of 1787 a perfect exemplification of those self-evident truths, contained in our Declaration of Independence, and exhibiting a degree of consistency, on the part of the great Democratic prototype (T. Jefferson) worthy the imitation of his professed followers."[56]

Next was a second statement regarding slavery, which offered the thought that God has not created any laws authorizing slavery. Therefore, these unreasonable men believed that there was no need to follow any law that was in opposition to the Law of God. The Northwest Ordinance also stated: "That any person escaping into the [Northwest Territory], from whom labor or service is lawfully claimed in any one of the original States, such fugitive may be lawfully reclaimed and conveyed to the person claiming his or her labor or service as aforesaid."[57] This predated the more rigid 1850 Fugitive Slave Law by 63 years, and allowed a presumed slaveowner to reclaim his property. The assembled Sycamore group responded with: "*Resolved*, That we regard the state of Slavery a mere municipal regulation, limited to the State creating it, and that we are not bound by the Law of God, or by a just construction of the Constitution of our government to aid or assist in the capture of fugitives from Slavery."[58]

The subject of the Nebraska-Kansas Act was addressed in the fourth resolution. On the surface, it might sound like a contradiction because the convention declared that they supported "popular sovereignty," which was the principle that Stephen A. Douglas used to advance his Kansas-Nebraska bill. Following Douglas's definition, the new states could choose themselves whether or not to allow slavery. The DeKalb County Anti-Nebraska Convention announced that they also supported "popular sovereignty." However, the Abolitionist's understanding and interpretation of the definition is the opposite of what Douglas and Congress decreed. In essence, man cannot give men the power to take away someone's liberty. It was an antislavery vs. proslavery argument:

> Resolved, That we are the advocates of popular sovereignty, and the rights of men to make laws and regulate their institutions for themselves, and on that ground we are opposed to the Nebraska Kansas Bill because of its violation of this principle. And we are opposed to the extension of Slavery to those Territories, because there is no power under heaven given to man, or a combination of men, to deprive any man of his liberty, and because the Democratic principle of popular sovereignty confers no right on the majority to establish a wrong and Polygamy, Robbery, Horse stealing, or murder, may as well be established in Nebraska on the ground of popular sovereignty as Slavery.[59]

As a final and very important thought, the Anti-Nebraska Convention decided to convene a gathering for the express purpose of electing delegates "one from each political party" to attend a "district convention." The group easily moved into a political realm:

> Resolved, That the Citizens of this County and of this Congressional district, be requested to meet in convention at some suitable time and place to be appointed by a union committee selected from the several counties in this Congressional district, to unite on a platform of principles, which shall strictly conform to the true democratic doctrine of THOMAS JEFFERSON. And put in nomination suitable candidates for the respective County and District offices, and that to enable the people to carry this plan into effect we recommend the appointment of a committee of three, one from each

political party to issue a call for a district convention. And do hereby appoint J.C. Waterman, J.H. Beveridge, and W. Fordham, a committee for DeKalb County, to confer with other Committees in regard to this proposed plan of operations.

SAM'L H. LAY, Ch'n
Wm. H. Hunt, Sec.[60]

It was obvious that the great western frontier in Northern Illinois, a "frontier section made up largely of rural communities, had no difficulty in combining morality and extension of territory."[61] The antislavery issue preached by the Congregational, Presbyterian and Wesleyan Methodist ministers, in theory, merged quite seamlessly with the politics surrounding a new state's admission as a slave state. Unreasonable men and women gained political power.

Birth of the Republicans

As a direct result of the July Anti-Nebraska Convention, six weeks later on September 14, 1854, there was "held at Sycamore a political mass meeting of such a peculiar nature that a part of the record of its proceedings are worth perpetuating."[62] A later county historian commented that "in some respects it was the most notable political event of our county."[63]

Mayfield's own Dr. Henry Madden, former Illinois state representative, presided over the meeting and introduced the speaker, the Honorable Joshua Reed Giddings. Giddings had served in Congress for over 20 years and was already famous in the antislavery movement for debating slavery issues on the floor in Congress. His home in Jefferson, Ohio, was a station in the Underground Railroad, and he is considered to be one of the founders of the Republican Party. An early 20th century historian observed, "Mr. Giddings' oration was listened to with a great deal of interest. This meeting marks the organization of the Republican Party [in DeKalb County]."[64] Historians agreed that "this section of the state early became [a] political battle-ground of Illinois."[65]

And so the Republican Party of DeKalb County was born. In keeping with the dictates of the important resolutions passed at the July Anti-Nebraska convention, delegates were chosen from the existing three traditional political parties to attend the Republican convention in Aurora, Illinois.

Contemporary scholars acknowledge that "the abolitionists played a crucial part in defining the responsibilities of citizens in an era when American politics was transformed and given much of its modern, party-oriented character."[66] The Missouri Compromise of 1820 was a catalyst for the antislavery movement in eastern states, like Ohio. But for Illinois, the Kansas-Nebraska Act of 1854 motivated the Abolitionists to take political action.

Delegates to the 1854 Republican organizational assembly met at the First Congregational Church of Aurora, Illinois. Ripon, Wisconsin, claims to be the birthplace of the national Republican Party, but in Northern Illinois, Aurora was one of the sites for the state party's first assemblies. Politically, the Congregationalists in Illinois were lauded for their important role on the national scene. By advocating slavery abolition and supporting a "unified program of political action, [they were] among the most radical advocates [and] made their weight felt in the political life of the day."[67]

A later report of the Aurora political gathering indicated: "This convention was attended by many outside of the regularly appointed delegates and great enthusiasm prevailed. Opposition to the fugitive slave law was growing rapidly and during this period the operations of the underground railroad were extensive."[68]

The DeKalb County delegates to the 1854 organizational meeting of the Republican Party were as follows:[69]

Former Party	*Church affiliation*	*Residence*
Free-Democrats:		
Horace W. Fay	Unknown	Squaw Grove
Gustavus A. Colton	Unknown	Sycamore/DeKalb
Joseph Sixbury	Methodist	Sycamore
James Harrington	Congregational	Sycamore
Jacob "Royal" Crossett	Meth. Episcopal	Pampas Twp.
Free-Soilers:		
Pierpont Edwards	Presbyterian	Paw Paw
Stephen Townsend	Methodist	Sycamore
Thurston Carr	Universalist	Sycamore
David West	Congregational	Sycamore
James H. Beveridge	Presbyterian	Somonauk
Ezra Starr Gregory	Unaffiliated/Methodist	Genoa
Whigs:		
Reuben Pritchard	Unknown	Clinton
William J. Hunt	Congregational	Sycamore
Harry A. Joslyn	Universalist	Sycamore
William Byers	Congregational	Sycamore
Dr. Ellsworth Rose	Congregational	Sycamore
John N. Braddock	Unknown	Somonauk

Historian Henry Boies in the *History of DeKalb County, Illinois* only named five Democrats, and yet he listed six named delegates for each of the other political parties. However, William A. Nickerson on two separate occasions included himself and Judge George H. Hill as having been among those who helped to organize the Republican party of DeKalb County. Whether or not either Nickerson or Hill was a delegate to the Republican convention in Aurora is unknown. Nickerson was a Wesleyan Methodist from Mayfield. Hill was a Democrat who became Republican and was at the top of the list on the "Republican County Ticket" in the fall of 1857. This was at a time when some county leaders, especially the proslavery thinkers, rallied against having a partisan election. They were desperate to keep party politics out of elections and felt that criteria for candidates should include, for example, the proximity of a person's residence relative to the county seat, rather than affiliation with a particular political party. Hill was defined as being a strong Democrat supporter for years, but recently joined the "young, vigorous and promising"[70] Republican Party. The entire Republican County ticket as printed in the *True Republican* included George H. Hill, county judge; Aaron K. Stiles, county clerk; Roswell Dow, treasurer; Horace W. Fay, surveyor; and James Harrington, school commissioner.

All the Free-Soiler and Whig delegates were identified antislavery men who called themselves Abolitionists. The Liberty Party was not represented at the Republican convention because the Liberty Party was no longer viable. Most Liberty men joined the Free Soil Party.

Democrat delegates were Free-Democrats who had personal antislavery sentiments. Only one of the named Democrats subscribed to the *Western Citizen*, but the others undoubtedly read the newssheet secondhand. Out of the remaining 12 delegates, nine were loyal *Western Citizen* subscribers. These men of character were willing to touch the issue of slavery by creating an entirely new political party, with antislavery as its flagship. The Republican Party was "the first major party in America formed around a single principle — the nonextension of slavery — and the first to have no Southern wing at all."[71] It was obviously *the* antislavery party. "The politician and the moralist became necessary to each other."[72]

On October 27, 1857, a newsman asked Judge Stephen A. Douglas "how he ever expected to beat the Republicans in Northern Illinois. 'Divide them,' was the reply."[73] Ten days later, one of the headlines in *The True Republican* was "Old DeKalb All Right! The 'Dividing' Game Checked!"— followed by, "We have met the enemy and they are ours.... We are proud of [the Republicans] and with them at our back we shall feel like saying many a stout word and striking many a hard blow in the cause of Freedom. We came among them a stranger, and found a ticket just being nominated, with not a man on it we had ever seen before.... [We are] grateful to the Republicans of the county for giving us this encouraging testimonial of their fealty to the cause in which we are enlisted."[74]

The cause célèbre was antislavery. In 1857 every Republican in DeKalb County was successful in his election bid.

Politics, God and Newspapers

Later that same year, a local group calling themselves the "People's Party" convened a "mass meeting" in the City of DeKalb to nominate candidates for public offices. The People's Party was a loose local Democrat organization, yet speakers forcefully requested the assembly to keep party politics out of the coming elections.[75] Their desire was to try to maintain a non-partisan election. Keep politics out? If political beliefs could not be expressed during a nomination and election proceeding, then certainly those principles could never be used in general elections to further philosophical ideas, moral or otherwise. This was a major dilemma for the social activists who were the involved citizens in DeKalb County. The People's Party ran candidates professing to be "real Republicans" in the historical sense of citizens committed to saving the country from tyrannical political philosophies, while the new Republican Party with its antislavery platform had its own slate of candidates.

Masthead names of the local newspapers changed to reflect the changing definitions of "Republican" and "Democrat." The two predominant local purveyors of news were very combative through the printed word. Editorial columns in the *True Republican* were antislavery, while the *DeKalb County Sentinel*, formerly named the *Republican Sentinel*, was now a more "democrat" newspaper politically, and was decidedly proslavery. "During those stirring times there was no place for the neutral paper and in time all of them became identified with a [political] party."[76] It was confusing because of the changing definitions of the terminology. Most men had considered themselves to be "republican" in their political philosophies. They supported the United States of America as a group of sovereign people sworn to support the "republic" and as such, they were "republican." Suddenly, what had been "republican" was now "democrat," and the Republican Party was a new entity with a new identification and direction.

The *Republican Sentinel*, with its now Democrat leanings, accusatorily questioned another local newspaper:

What is Republicanism? A Query for the *Western World*:
The *Western World* published at DeKalb, in this County indignantly denies that it is a Republican paper, but is flaunting at its mast head, the names of the Republican, State ticket.[77]

The newspaper was king. "In contrast to the more genteel literary culture of the East, in the West ... here newspaper editors were men of influence, equal in power to politicians and ministers."[78] And the editors did not let the reader forget that fact.

The seasoned editor of the *Republican Sentinel*, a decidedly proslavery "Democrat" newspaper, was adept at using sarcasm in his published comments about the new Republican Party and its professed platform with regard to slavery. In the October 4, 1858, issue of the *Sentinel*, a small column item included a quote from a resolution recently adopted by the Republican convention held at the DeKalb County courthouse. The published resolution excerpt read: "[Republicans] will, if possible place [slavery] where the public mind shall rest in the belief that it is in course of ultimate extinction — in God's own time."[79] The cynical editor then added his own sardonic comment: "Perhaps God will thank the Republican party for placing the Slavery question in a position where He can reach it."[80]

It took many years for the DeKalb County Abolitionists to become the subject of derision in a local newspaper. Fully thirteen years before the disdainful newspaper editor berated local Republicans about being antislavery, the DeKalb County Anti-Slavery Society had already placed the issue where God could find it, which was squarely in the middle of the county political arena. The Republican Party evolved over a period of time, a time that included heated political contests at the national level. When the political opportunity presented itself, DeKalb county's unreasonable men seized it.

CHAPTER 13

Lincoln Knew the *True Republican*

The union of all for the preservation of the liberty of all; Not the union of many for the destruction of the liberty of the few.[1]—A motto of the *True Republican*, Campbell W. Waite, editor

A Young Editor Finds Sycamore

In his heart, Campbell W. Waite was a resolved Abolitionist. He came by it naturally. Campbell was born in 1832 in the center of abolitionist country in Cayuga County, New York, and was only eight years old when his father, Dr. Daniel D. Waite, moved the family to Illinois. They lived first in Chicago, relocating later to St. Charles in Kane County. Initially, Waite had to "hoe his own row to a great extent"[2] as from the age of 12 he earned his own living working for a printer. By the time he was 18 years old, he was writing for newspapers, which was his first love.

C.W., as he liked to be called, was associated for five years with Thomas J. Pickett, editor of the *Peoria Evening Republican*. Zebina Eastman, Chicago publisher of the *Western Citizen* and *Free West* abolitionist newspapers, had also worked in Peoria with the editor of the *Peoria Register*. Although Waite was too young to have worked with Eastman and only arrived in Peoria after Eastman had already left, Waite appreciated Eastman's antislavery publications. Eventually, through his position with the *Peoria Evening Republican*, he became acquainted with Peoria and Fulton County individuals who were involved in the Quincy-to-Princeton routes of the Underground Railroad. Extending that same route as it traveled northeast brought one through DeKalb County, and ultimately to the Great Lakes and Canada. When Waite's understanding of the Underground Railroad combined with his knowledge that DeKalb County had a large subscription base for the abolitionist press, he headed for Sycamore.

C.W. Waite moved to Sycamore, Illinois, just prior to 1857, perhaps too late to become an active participant in the local Underground Railroad. Because he was an outsider, as well as a single young man, he was probably not fully trusted at first by entrenched locals who knew the details of the secret road. Initially, Waite only knew a few select individuals who were considered to be Abolitionists in the area, but he would soon be involved in Sycamore with residents who professed his same antislavery viewpoints.

Very soon after his arrival, through his expressed vocal opinions and his talent for writing,

Campbell Waite endeared himself to the DeKalb County Abolitionist cause. Writing about the evils of slavery became his life's work.

Newspapers in the mid–1800s were the most powerful communication medium. Not only did they render the local and national news of the day, even if a week later, but the editors learned very early that they had a tool by which they could sway public opinion. Fifteen years before Waite's arrival, the *Western Citizen* explained to its readers that some newspapers were "too much engaged in the [political] party scramble for office to enlighten their readers much about the actual conditions and wants of the people."[3] If folks investigated, they would soon see that the country's "suffering has been produced by slaveholders and servile office-seekers — and the reformation the country needs is emancipation for the slave, and a change in the administration of our government from a partiality for slavery to the support of Liberty."[4] There was no mincing of words, just straight talk about what the editor, or the financial group supporting the paper, felt was important. They published opinions to convince the reading public of a particular point of view. Newspapers everywhere promoted causes.

Enter Campbell W. Waite on the Sycamore scene, who was a "gentleman of fine education and a practical newspaper man,"[5] "with plenty of ability to advocate the cause which he espouses."[6] Waite established the *True Republican* newspaper in 1857[7] with the financial backing of James H. Beveridge, 39, Caleb M. Brown, 41, and Daniel B. James, 37.[8] The three entrepreneurs were seasoned businessmen who were all also subscribers to the abolitionist *Western Citizen* until its demise. It was obvious to the men involved in the creation of the *True Republican* that a printed voice was needed for antislavery proponents and their message. Since 1854 the only newspaper in all of DeKalb County had been the *Republican Sentinel*, which called itself "Republican Democratic" in principle. The United States was originally considered to be a "republic" in the old-world sense, and as the form of government involved democratic elections, the differences between a "republic" and a "democracy" became blurred. Because the two terms were intermingled, becoming a "Republican Democrat" in name was an accepted transition.

In reality, the *Sentinel* was anything but "Republican" as defined in the present 21st century. The word "Republican" had changed in meaning. By 1857 "Republican" stood for the new antislavery political party and "Democrat" referred to the conservative, proslavery party. The *Republican Sentinel* endorsed and supported Stephen A. Douglas, who campaigned for the United States Senate seat on a decidedly proslavery platform. By supporting Douglas, the newspaper promoted the extension of slavery, the exact opposite of the position espoused by the radical new Republican Party. The former *Republican Sentinel* with its new name, the *DeKalb County Sentinel*, was not to be identified in any way with the new Republican Party. The publisher referred to the publication simply as the *"SENTINEL"* and always printed this name in all capital letters when used in its editorial columns.

One of the elected delegates to the organizational meeting of the new Republican Party was James Hoy Beveridge, the Free-Soil Party man who became a financial supporter and owner of the new *True Republican* broadsheet.[9] The newspaper office was first located in a small building on State Street, across the street from the courthouse After construction of the D.B. James Building at the northwest corner of State and Maple Streets, the periodical was published every Tuesday morning at No. 1 James Block, over F. Wilkins's dry goods store. From that location emanated a seven-column "handsome sheet ... large and ably edited, beautifully printed — and thanks to the liberal contributors of its friends unembarrassed for means of support."[10] With Waite at the helm ready to create his weekly editorial, the business was off to a good start. Subscriptions were $1.50 per year.

As editor of the new opposition newspaper, Waite "took up the fight against slavery through the columns of the *True Republican*. He remained the editor all through the intensive Lincoln-

Douglas political campaign until the outbreak of the Civil War,[11] when he briefly joined the 8th Illinois Cavalry Regiment with the enlisting rank of Adjutant. In February 1862, Waite was in Alexandria, Virginia, editing a newspaper, but resigned his position with the 8th Illinois Cavalry shortly thereafter so he could serve as the war correspondent for the *Chicago Tribune* and the *St. Louis Democrat*. Campbell W. Waite was later elected chief secretary of the Illinois state Senate, and by 1865 would become the private secretary to Governor Thomas C. Fletcher of Missouri. The year 1876 saw him back in Sycamore as the founder of yet another newspaper, the *DeKalb County Democrat*.[12]

Waite was initially an antislavery Democrat in his politics, and it was through C.W.'s gifted writing that the fledgling Sycamore newspaper, the *True Republican*, became known as a "red hot political paper." It carried its motto across the masthead, "The union of all for the preservation of the liberty of all; Not the union of many for the destruction of the liberty of the few."[13]

Investors in Antislavery

On March, 30, 1858, Waite sold the paper to James H. Beveridge, Caleb M. Brown, and Daniel B. James, who retained Waite as editor.[14] They provided the financial backing with J.H. Beveridge & Co. and O.P. Bassett listed as both publisher and as one of the proprietors. Eighty-three years later, Beveridge, Brown and James were still characterized as "militant abolitionists" who created the *True Republican* specifically to "champion [those] who disagreed with the policies of the Democratic, Whig and Free Soil parties, to form the Republicans."[15] They were true champions of the antislavery cause, but definitely not "militant." There is nothing in DeKalb County history to even remotely suggest that the local Abolitionists and antislavery sympathizers were ever combative in their approaches to the proslavery thinkers. In fact, just the opposite is true. If someone was considered to be an Abolitionist, it did not necessarily mean that he was militant. Certainly, they were verbally quarrelsome with those holding opposing views. J.H. Beveridge & Co. gave its financial backing to the new antislavery newspaper to support a political approach to the slavery issue through the printed expression of opinions and arguments against slavery.

The Messrs. Beveridge, Brown and James did not decide to initially finance and then ultimately purchase the paper on a whim. Their antislavery philosophy had existed for some time and the publication of print material with their message was a necessary extension of their issues and ideals.

First, all three gentlemen had associations with the First Congregational Church in Sycamore, which espoused strong antislavery views. Daniel James's wife Ann (George) James was a member at First Congregational, and Caleb Brown and his first wife, Catherine (DuPue) Brown, were also both members. James Beveridge and his wife, Elizabeth A. (Disbrow) Beveridge, were originally both members of the Somonauk Presbyterian Church, but Elizabeth moved her membership to the First Congregational Church when the couple came to live in Sycamore in 1852 after Beveridge's election to the DeKalb County office of circuit clerk.[16] In order to affiliate with either of these church bodies, one had to first affirm one's belief in the church's stated antislavery covenants.

A second shared practice was that Beveridge, Brown and James were already longtime subscribers to the Abolitionist newspaper, the *Western Citizen*.

And finally, the personal backgrounds of each of these men supported their intense antislavery feelings.

James H. Beveridge

At the time the *True Republican* was founded, James Hoy Beveridge was already serving his second term as DeKalb County circuit clerk and recorder. Like the majority of other local Abolitionists and their spouses, he was born in the state of New York. James was the fourth of George and Ann (Hoy) Beveridge's nine children, born while the family still lived in Washington County, New York. When he was 20 years old, he moved with his parents and siblings to Somonauk Township in DeKalb County. Between the years 1848 and 1850, James Beveridge set claim to over 217 acres of land.[17] The Beveridge family, including James's father George and brothers John and Thomas, owned over 657 acres in the Somonauk Township area.[18] There, set among the timber along Somonauk Creek, his family's log cabin "was long a prominent station on the Underground Railroad."[19]

Beveridge was an "inflexible temperance man" and very "outspoken in favor of the Liberty party."[20] The Liberty Party was a forerunner to the Free Soil party and was the first political party in the United States to focus on the slavery question. James G. Birney became the first antislavery candidate for president in 1840, garnering exactly one vote in DeKalb County. Ezra Starr Gregory, who would become a local agent for the western citizen, claimed that he was the person who cast the only Abolition vote that election year.[21] Many later obituaries for DeKalb County residents indicated with pride that they had voted for Birney, undoubtedly in a later election.

As a supporter of liberty, Beveridge fit right in with the practicing antislavery convictions of the Somonauk community and the Somonauk Associate Presbyterian Church. On October 30, 1850, when the mass meeting was called "without distinction of party or sex"[22] by antislavery Somonauk citizens, Beveridge served on the committee that drafted the published resolutions.

James was a family man first. He and Elizabeth had five children, three of whom died quite young. The remaining two, Gertrude and Merritt Hoy Beveridge, lived to adulthood. Throughout Beveridge's long career in civil service, he provided another example of the many citizens in DeKalb County leadership positions who were not afraid to be involved in the Underground Railroad. Beveridge and his brother-in-law, Alexander R. Patten, "both prominent among the younger members of Somonauk church,"[23] became the proprietors of the general store. It stood at the intersection of the Chicago-Galena highway and the road running north from Ottawa to Wisconsin, and the location became known as Somonauk Corners.[24] Somonauk Corners became Freeland Corners in 1853 when the post office name was changed to avoid confusion with the new C.B.& Q. Railroad establishment of a station five miles south called "Somonauk." Although a merchant at Somonauk Corners for several years, by 1849 James was elected associate justice of DeKalb County, and in 1852 was elected county assessor. Additionally, in 1852 he served the first of two terms as elected county circuit clerk and recorder, which made it necessary for him to move his family to the city of Sycamore.

But James Hoy Beveridge had an even larger political objective on his mind: the creation of a new political party — a coalition that would have the antislavery cause as its central focus. "Early in 1854 the scattered Free-soil forces, or more properly those opposed to the Anti-Nebraska Bill, and opposed to the further extension of slavery, began to crystallize."[25] "Beveridge was instrumental in calling the Anti-Nebraska Convention held at Sycamore and which developed the true sentiments in the hearts of the majority of the voters, and the movement resulted in giving strength to the Republican party."[26] On September 14, 1854, a "mass convention of those holding these views was held at Sycamore to appoint delegates to a Republican convention to be held at Aurora."[27] The delegates were representative of all three of the existing political parties in the county: Democrats, Free-Soilers and Whigs. All the delegates espoused prevailing antislavery views, and many were already avowed abolitionists who subscribed to Zebina Eastman's activist *Western Citizen* newspaper. The creation of a fresh political party named Republican, and dedicated to the idea that slavery should be abolished, was the impetus behind the formation of the innovative newspaper in Sycamore. Loyalists to the new party needed a voice, and that voice was the *True Republican*.

Daniel B. James

Of the three older business partners, Daniel B. James was the more recent resident in DeKalb County, having arrived only five years earlier in 1852. He was a practicing attorney in Sycamore, first admitted to the bar in his native state of Vermont about 1847.[28] Following the thoughts of many men during that time in our nation's history, he was smitten with the idea of hitting it rich in the gold mines in California. Consequently, in 1849 he traveled west to California, remaining there approximately two years, "engaged in mining, but with poor success." He returned to Vermont and "made arrangements to come to Illinois."[29] It was during his brief time back in Lyndon, Vermont, that he married Ann George, and together they headed for the Midwest prairie. In 1853 Ann affirmed her belief in antislavery and joined the First Congregational Church in Sycamore, remaining a member until dropped from the rolls after her death. She died in 1877 in Vermont, where she resided after the death of her husband.

Upon arriving in Sycamore, Mr. James formed a partnership with Edward L. Mayo and became an "especially active member of the Republican party."[30] He practiced law with Mayo until 1858, succeeded by several other law office partnerships in the city. Most likely, his law partnership with Mayo broke up because of their opposing views on slavery. Judge Mayo was the editor of the proslavery *Republican Sentinel* in Sycamore. Daniel James was elected as Sycamore Township supervisor during the late 1850s, following the term of his business partner, E.L. Mayo, in that same office. During the Civil War, James was appointed aide-de-camp to Governor Oglesby, with the rank of colonel, and was later elected as a DeKalb County judge in 1864.

Throughout the years leading up to and including the formation of the *True Republican*, Daniel B. James was referred to as a "Sycamore orator." He gave "expression to the deep indignation felt by the community over the border ruffian outrages in Kansas" and denounced slavery. This occurred at a "mass meeting called to assemble in Champlin's Hall in Cortland Township."[31] However, D.B. James, along with several other speakers including Dr. Daniel Dustin and Chauncey Ellwood, was outdone by a young upstart. After the Sycamore speakers had "vied with each other in denunciation" of slavery, the chairman of the meeting called upon Cortland's own Dave Champlin. *Western Citizen* subscriber Champlin was also a "freshly ordained" Freewill Baptist preacher.

> He was a man with a swinging style of gait and oratory [and] he saw his opportunity to discount the Sycamore talent and embraced it; he commenced his speech by saying in the most solemn and impressive manner: "Mr. Chairman, I feel that this is a time when every prayin' man oughter pray (then raising his arm above his head and bringing it down with all the emphasis possible), and every swearin' man oughter swear." This was a culmination that brought down the house in thunderous style, and ... was the only thing uttered at the meeting that has gone into history.[32]

Another public debate in which James participated was held in the new Dow Academy. The private schoolhouse, built on South Main Street about 1849 or 1850, was the first masonry building built in Sycamore, and fellow Abolitionists, mason George Weeden and carpenter David Farnsworth, did much of the work during construction. This particular debate centered around the question, "Should An Obnoxious Law Be Lived Up To or Repealed?"[33] One wonders if the question was actually designed to provoke discussion about the 1850 Fugitive Slave Law. Daniel James participated eagerly and enthusiastically expressed his antislavery opinions to the public. The political excitement of the liberty movement coursed through his veins, culminating in the formation of the new Republican Party in 1854 and the subsequent creation of the new Republican newspaper in DeKalb County.

Caleb M. Brown

The third partner in the newspaper venture, Caleb Marshall Brown, and his first wife, Catherine, were both born in New Jersey around 1817. They moved to Sycamore in 1841, living on the east side of North Main Street in Sycamore, adjacent to the First Congregational Church building. Their modest house was just south of the church on the adjoining lot. The couple was very active in the life of the church, with Caleb donating much time and energy in the construction of the new church edifice begun in 1846. He directly donated some money towards the construction, "giving the congregation their own time to repay him."[34] The church suffered several setbacks during the construction of the church, including the death of the contractor, and did not actually complete the building and occupy it until December 1849. Caleb suffered his own personal setbacks with the death of his beautiful Catherine in September 1849. A year later when the U.S. census was taken, the enumerator lists Brown in a household all by himself, and there is no mention of his five-year old child, David DuPue Brown.[35] We can only surmise that his young son, who was called by his middle name of DuPue, was with relatives, perhaps back in New Jersey, until Brown married a second time to Louisa A. Jackman in September 1850. As the daughter of Abner and Mary Jackman, Louisa carried her own pedigree in Abolitionist circles. Her parents were also longtime subscribers to the *Western Citizen*, and Louisa's mother maintained her subscription even after the death of her husband. Additionally, two of Louisa's sisters, Armena Jackman and Eliza Jackman, were married to Lattin Nichols and Jeremiah L. Brown, respectively, both well-known local Abolitionists. Caleb and Louisa Brown raised two more sons, Fred C. and Marshall L. Brown.

Throughout the course of his personal reverses, Caleb, or "Jersey" Brown, as he was fondly called by friends and family, privately espoused the antislavery causes. "He was conscientiously opposed to negro slavery, and was a faithful engineer on the 'Underground' railroad, that conveyed many a poor slave to Canada and to freedom."[36]

Living so close to the church probably made it easy for Brown and either of his wives to individually aid fugitive slaves. He was a "stanch abolitionist and was one of the active movers in the underground railroad, his home being a station on that famous line."[37]

In 1860, after a full eighteen years in the mercantile business, C.M. Brown decided to run for circuit clerk and recorder in DeKalb County on the Republican Party ticket. True to form, and in opposition to Brown's strong abolitionist views, the proslavery newspaper *Republican Sentinel* publicly lambasted him and the Republican Party. The *Sentinel* called them "negro thieves" and charged that the Republican policy was to "overrun the country with free negroes."[38] Not to be outdone in the editorial department, the *True Republican* countered with equally strong language: "Beelzebub and his chief lieutenant devil must yield the palm to the graceless liar, the cowardly slanderer, the low, filthy, blackguard that now conducts the *Sentinel*. His distortions of the record, and his bare-faced, utterly inexcusable lies, make him without an equal in his line."[39] Defending Caleb Brown, the editor of the *True Republican* accused the editor of the *Sentinel* of "abusing our candidate for circuit clerk.... He insists that the party in this county are in favor of giving the negro the right of voting, and that we are generally committed to a policy whereby the negro will be a principal ingredient in our population.[40]

That election year, DeKalb County gave Abraham Lincoln 3,049 votes and Stephen Douglas only 950.[41] Caleb Marshall Brown won his election, beating his good friend, incumbent Circuit Clerk James H. Beveridge, for the office. For purely partisan political reasons, the *Republican Sentinel* subsequently eliminated the word "Republican" from its masthead and changed its name to the *DeKalb County Sentinel*. The paper continued its strong proslavery position and soon went out of business. The entire company and its subscription base were absorbed by the *True Republican*, which better reflected the political viewpoint of the majority in DeKalb County.

Orlando P. Bassett

A retrospective of the first ten years of the *True Republican*'s existence appeared in 1867:

DeKalb County had always been decidedly anti-slavery in sentiment and action, and when ten years ago [1857] the *Sentinel*, the only paper published in the county, was sold, the party whose chief characteristic had come to be a devotion to the interests of slavery, the liberty-loving people of the country felt that their interests required the establishment of a journal which would counteract and expose the insidious counsels of those who would leave slaves to run and be glorified, to become the dominant power in the nation, and which would encourage our people in a love of liberty, in a hatred of slavery and in a devotion to its first great principles so nobly enunciated in the immortal Declaration of Independence from which principles, alas! the country was shamefully straying.

With this purpose they met and counseled and organized and under the especial lead of James H. Beveridge, D.B. James, C.M. Brown and other warm and devoted friends of the Republican party, they purchased the press and material for a new paper; scoured the country to secure the co-operation of and subscriptions of the people, obtained the services of an editor who, although youthful, had great experience and earnest enthusiasm for the cause and by the expenditure of a large amount of money and a great deal of labor, finally established and firmly established *The True Republican*.[42]

Under the new ownership, the fourth shareholder in the newspaper was Orlando P. Bassett, a 22-year-old printer from Pennsylvania. He was the youngest member of the publishing partnership and had previously been in charge of the "mechanical work"[43] of the *True Republican* under its former owner and editor, C.W. Waite. He was listed as part owner, but it is not clear if he invested any substantial funds. Perhaps his mechanical expertise was what was needed and for that he was given part ownership. He knew the printing business; knew how to set type; and knew how to maintain the machinery to keep the printing presses running properly. Bassett and his wife, Betsy, soon became settled in Sycamore and later even built a "large, very pleasant and thoroughly built dwelling house"[44] on Somonauk Street, where they lived with their only daughter, Kittie.[45]

A Witness to Lincoln

When Beveridge & Co. purchased Waite's interest in the newspaper, O.P. Bassett was given the title of "publisher" and was immediately elevated to a position above the common labor force. Considering his young age, one wonders if he ever received an elevated monetary compensation to go along with his new title. Apparently, though, Bassett felt that he was ready to prove himself in the publishing world. And prove himself he did! Within only a few months after Bassett became publisher, the *True Republican* created the first separate printing of Abraham Lincoln's "House Divided" speech. One of perhaps only five existing 5" × 3" original copies

> # SPEECH
>
> OF
>
> ## HON. ABRAM LINCOLN,
>
> BEFORE THE
>
> REPUBLICAN STATE CONVENTION,
>
> June 16, 1858.
>
> "The result is not doubtful. We shall not fail—if we stand firm, we shall not fail."
>
> ——◆◆——
>
> Sycamore.
> O. P. BASSETT, PR., TRUE REPUBLICAN OFFICE.
> 1858.

Cover of the first separate printing of Abraham Lincoln's renowned "House Divided" speech as first published in 1858 by the Sycamore *True Republican*.

may be found in the Illinois State Historical Library, now the Abraham Lincoln Presidential Library.

Lincoln presented his soon-to-be famous speech on the evening of June 16, 1858, at the Republican State Convention in Springfield, Illinois. He had just been selected by the Republican Party to oppose Stephen A. Douglas in the contest for the United States Senate. Douglas was running for his third term in that office. Seated in the crowd that night in the chamber of the Illinois House of Representatives was none other than Campbell W. Waite, the enthusiastic young editor of Sycamore's *True Republican*. Waite undoubtedly attended the convention as a journalist, as he was not an elected delegate from DeKalb County. This was to be Abraham Lincoln's acceptance speech and it clearly held Waite's attention.

In 1834, when Campbell Waite was only two years old, Abraham Lincoln at age 24 was elected to the Illinois General Assembly as a Whig party member. By 1836 Lincoln had his law license and was re-elected to the same position. He was a member of the legislature and continued to practice law for six years until he decided not to run for re-election. But Lincoln could not stay uninvolved in politics. He bounced back and forth several times, spending the intervening years practicing law. In 1846 he was elected to the United States House of Representatives, and then left politics again three years later. However, after being elected to the Illinois legislature in 1854, he declined the seat in order to put in a bid for the United States Senate. Senators were not elected through popular elections at this time. Instead, the state legislators voted among themselves to choose the state's two senators, and in 1854 Lincoln was not chosen. When the Republican Party was formed two years later, Abraham Lincoln was on the scene to help organize this new antislavery group. He had demonstrated through previous public speeches that he was antislavery and now, in 1858, at the Illinois Republican State Convention, he was their chosen candidate for the United States Senate once again.

C.W. Waite must have been transfixed at the politically charged event as he listened to the tall man begin to speak. Lincoln was unquestionably the candidate he supported! Waite paid attention to the opening statement, "If we could first know *where* we are, and *whither* we are tending, we could then better judge *what* to do and *how* to do it."[46]

Lincoln referred to the federal government's current policy regarding slavery and "putting an end to slavery agitation."[47] Candidate Lincoln had provided himself with visual cues in the form of italicized words so he would create the emphasis he desired as he spoke. He continued his acceptance speech, gesturing to add importance to his remarks, "Under the operation of that policy, that agitation has not only, *not ceased*, but has *constantly augmented*. In *my* opinion, it *will* not cease, until a *crisis* shall have been reached, and passed."[48]

Abraham Lincoln followed his opening remarks with the phrase, "A house divided against itself cannot stand."[49] This was a paraphrase from the King James version of the Bible, Mark 3:25, which reads, "If a house be divided against itself, that house cannot stand." Lincoln frequently interspersed Biblical paraphrases in his speeches, and this address was no exception. The "house divided" phrase gave it the name by which this presentation would always be known. Lincoln concluded with, "The result is not doubtful. We shall not fail — if we stand firm, we shall not fail."[50] This was the phrase Waite and publisher O.P. Bassett would quote on the title page of the printed speech. By the time the acceptance speech concluded, it was obvious to Waite that Abraham Lincoln's remarks portended of a Civil War to come.

After C.W. Waite's return to DeKalb County, he gave a brief account of Abraham Lincoln's speech in the subsequent weekly issue of the *True Republican* on June 22, 1858. Waite was very excited about what he had just heard. The following week, he and publisher Bassett printed the entire text of Lincoln's speech, along with this editorial endorsement: "Of course every Republican will carefully read the speech of Hon. Abram Lincoln, which we publish in another column.... As we glance over the emphasized portions, every gesture is vividly recalled to our mind, and the convincing and earnest tones again ring in our ear."[51]

Eighty-three years after the "House Divided" speech, in an account reprinted from an oral presentation to the Bibliographical Society of America, Paul M. Angle, then librarian for the Illinois State Historical Library, stated, "Perhaps the demand for copies of the paper containing Lincoln's speech outran the supply; perhaps it was simply Waite's enthusiasm that led him to lift the type from his issue of June 29 and print Lincoln's speech separately in a sextodecimo pamphlet of 16 pages. Whatever the reason, the honor of issuing the first exclusive publication of one of Lincoln's greatest speeches must go to him and to the Sycamore *True Republican*."[52]

It is interesting to note that it is not editor Campbell W. Waite's name that appears on that first separate printing of Lincoln's "House Divided" speech, even though he was the person who actually heard Lincoln speak, and even though he was the named editor for the printing house.

Neither do the names of Beveridge, Brown or James appear on the published speech, even though they were the older, more seasoned politicians and financial backers of the *True Republican.* Rather, it is the name of O.P. Bassett, in Sycamore, as "Proprietor, *True Republican* Office." His ego was young and strong. He was the person who ultimately decided to publish the separate printing of Lincoln's speech, and he took the credit. The copies of the "House Divided" speech's original separate printing which are still in existence are some "of the very rarest items in Lincolniana."[53] Orlando P. Bassett later moved to Chicago and became very wealthy after starting his own successful printing business.[54]

There were others, though, who worked on the groundbreaking newspaper in 1858. They were Angeline Harnard, 20, the only female and the only typesetter on the staff, from Ohio; Milo Thompson, 18, and Robert Williams, 17, both apprentice printers from Illinois; and Charles E. Cobb, 17, an apprentice printer from New York. They were the labor force who produced the first published copies of Lincoln's "House Divided" speech.

Little is known about these young employees. They were enumerated together in the same household in 1860 with Orlando Bassett and his wife. They lived together at No. 1 James Block, in the same building as the newspaper business and in rooms probably adjacent to the printing press operation. They worked together each day, with the eagerness of youth through the ages who find common ground in an exciting cause. Their cause was simply stated: Freedom for slaves. They, too, believed in the strong public sentiment that existed for the antislavery movement in DeKalb County. Working for the antislavery *True Republican*, this group of four employees furthered the Abolitionists' cause by giving a voice to that movement through the printed word, the product of their daily labor.

Lincoln Refers to DeKalb County

As a candidate in Illinois for the U.S. Senate, Lincoln challenged his adversary Douglas to a series of debates. Their debates drew national attention because the underlying issue in the political campaign was slavery. The incumbent Senator Douglas had been instrumental in the passage of the Fugitive Slave Act of 1850. Four years later he helped write the Kansas-Nebraska Act, which repealed the Missouri Compromise and allowed slavery the possibility of expansion into the new states of Kansas and Nebraska. The reading public awaited the printing of the debate speeches and the newspapers in DeKalb County did not disappoint their readers.

Abraham Lincoln and Stephen A. Douglas provided quite a physical contrast, between Lincoln's tall, sometimes unkempt look and Douglas's short, professional appearance. Northern Abolitionists received all the blame, in Douglas's estimation, for the entire issue of slavery. He believed in "popular sovereignty," that a state could decide its own future regarding slavery. In the mind of Stephen A. Douglas, the Abolitionists further agitated the public. Lincoln's opposing arguments included his belief that a crisis would probably have to occur to either end slavery entirely or extend it into the territories. Like many in society prior to the Civil War, even in the northern United States, Lincoln did not necessarily believe in equality of the races, but he was resolutely against slavery.

Even before the first debate against Douglas on August 21, 1858, in Ottawa, Illinois, Abraham Lincoln was informed about what was periodically printed in the DeKalb County newspapers. Lincoln certainly was aware that the *True Republican* had published the first separate printing of his "House Divided" speech. Either he read the county newspapers himself, or aides and informants filtered information to him. On July 26, 1858, Edward L. Mayo, senior editor of the proslavery *DeKalb County Sentinel*, had this to say in his newspaper:

Our education has been such, that we have ever been rather in favor of the equality of the blacks; that is, that they should enjoy all the privileges of the whites where they reside. We are aware that this is not a very popular doctrine. We have had many a confab with some who are now strong "Republicans," we taking the broad ground of equality and they the opposite ground. We were brought up in a State where blacks were voters, and we do not know of any inconvenience resulting from it though perhaps it would not work as well, where the blacks are more numerous. We have no doubt of the right of the whites to guard against such an evil if it is one. Our opinion is, that it would be best for all concerned to have the colored population in a State by themselves, but if within the jurisdiction of the U.S. we say by all means they should have the right to have their Senators and Representatives in Congress, and vote for President. With us "Worth makes the man, and want of it the fellow." We have seen many a "nigger" that we thought much more of than some white men.[55]

September 15, 1858, was the date of Lincoln's third debate against Douglas at the Union County Fairgrounds in Jonesboro, Illinois. According to one Lincoln historian, David Herbert Donald, "Lincoln knew he was at a disadvantage in the third debate."[56] Located in the extreme southern part of Illinois, Jonesboro was "an isolated town of 842 inhabitants. Rural, mostly poor, and relatively untouched by commercial ambition, voters in Union County had little use for the Republican Party and its candidate. Fewer than 2,000 listeners attended the debate."[57] Several "interrogatories" followed Lincoln's more formal speech presentation. It was during this question-and-answer period that Lincoln remarked:

> But what I was going to comment upon is an extract from a newspaper in DeKalb County; and it strikes me as being rather singular, I confess, under the circumstances. There is a Judge Mayo in that county, who is a candidate for the Legislature, for the purpose, if he secures his election, of helping to re-elect Judge Douglas. He is the editor of a newspaper [*DeKalb County Sentinel*], and in that paper I find the extract I am going to read. It is part of an editorial article in which he was electioneering as fiercely as he could for Judge Douglas and against me. It was a curious thing, I think, to be in such a paper.[58]

And then Abraham Lincoln quoted that same portion of Mayo's editorial printed here from the *DeKalb County Sentinel*, which, of course, was the newspaper politically opposed to the *True Republican*. Lincoln thought it "a curious thing" to find such a reference in a DeKalb County newspaper, although he may have been aware of the passionate antislavery movement which pervaded the area. After reading that part of the editorial verbatim, Lincoln referred to Edward L. Mayo and remarked, "That is one of Judge Douglas's friends."[59] The DeKalb County press and the general population living in the county did not know at the time that they were going down in history through a reference in the Lincoln-Douglas debates. The area received subsequent national notice, although minor, in the contemporary state political arena all because of the power of the printed word.

The *True Republican* was unfazed by Judge Mayo's rhetoric and continued to oppose the proslavery northern Democrats exemplified by Stephen A. Douglas. With the "hottest kind of editorials," as a "graceful and polished writer on any subject,"[60] Campbell W. Waite attacked the proslavery group "with vigor and marked ability. With the heavy artillery of solid argument, with the lighter musketry of wit and satire, with all manner of harassing charges and lively skirmishing it demoralized and routed the enemy...."[61]

James H. Beveridge, Caleb M. Brown and Daniel B. James, together with Campbell W. Waite and Orlando P. Bassett, shaped the thinking in DeKalb County, Illinois, via the printed word in their antislavery newspaper. Immediately preceding the Civil War, the *True Republican* was the decided voice of the majority in DeKalb County to express their antislavery views. Through the printed word in the *True Republican*, the printers, publishers and editor, all unreasonable Abolitionists of DeKalb County, created, supported and perpetuated antislavery sympathies in the surrounding geographic area.

Chapter 14

Reasons to Be Unreasonable

When you get into a tight place, and everything goes against you, 'till it seems as though you couldn't hold on a moment longer, never give up then, for that's just the place and time that the tide'll turn.[1]— Harriet Beecher Stowe (1811–1896), abolitionist, author of *Uncle Tom's Cabin*

Mr. Browning, a Black Man

Boldly written in the back of a nineteenth-century Sycamore First Congregational Church record book is the notation that $3.00 was given to "Mr. Browning, Black man."[2] The year was 1862, after the start of the Civil War, but before Lincoln's 1863 Emancipation Proclamation which ostensibly freed most of the Southern slaves. The bitter war that many thought the North would win within the first few battles still raged on interminably. The condition of war had become a way of life, and there was no sign of a quick conclusion. Sacrifices at home and on the battlefields existed on both sides of the conflict; some thought it would never end. And while the War of the Rebellion continued in the South, "Mr. Browning, Black man" somehow traveled through Sycamore, Illinois.

The belief is that Mr. Browning was a fugitive slave in the flesh. Where was he headed? Chicago? Canada?

How far had this man journeyed? In what state did he start his trek? Mississippi? Alabama? Tennessee?

Had Browning traveled the Underground Railroad route through Princeton, Illinois? What entry point did he use to enter Illinois? Did he cross the Mississippi River and gain access through a southern port? Quincy? Chester? Alton? Or did he utilize a lesser-used northern port? Rock Island? Port Byron? Albany?

Did Mr. Browning have a family? Was he traveling alone? Did he leave his family behind? Or was his family in hiding somewhere outside the church awaiting his return while he solicited the church fathers for financial aid?

Research in U.S. Census records reveals several black men named Browning, but there is no proof that any particular person was the Mr. Browning who came through Sycamore that day in 1862. Eight years later, the "Browning" surname was given to Census enumerators by 289 males living in Illinois. They were all white. We deduce, then, that our "Mr. Browning,

Black man" was just passing through. He did not remain in Illinois and we will never learn who he was.

Did Deacon David West or another antislavery member of the Congregational Church hide Browning and his family during the day until it was safer to travel at night? Because the American Civil War was underway, the Underground Railroad did not need to function as before, so perhaps security was not as much of an issue in Northern Illinois. Bounty slave hunters no longer hunted their quarry as frequently in the region.

Beginning around 1839, the Underground Railroad was a vital network in Illinois. The many unselfish people who voluntarily aided hundreds, maybe thousands, of fugitive slaves traversing the state, themselves numbered in the thousands. For years the Abolitionists and antislavery advocates in DeKalb County relentlessly aided the southern freedom seekers to achieve their goal to travel north.

Over 150 years later, in the church records of the Sycamore First Congregational Church, we discovered the handwritten notation in the weekly financial records from 1862 showing that the sum of $3.00 was given to "Mr. Browning, Black man." The script has not faded, in keeping with the import of the message it imparted. The First Congregational Church was publicly on record as a religious organization that helped a black man needing assistance. They did not assist only white destitute people in need of financial support; they lent a hand to a black man. There is a cavalier message inherent in the declaration to the world about what kind of person they assisted. By 1862, they were confident that they could record this information without repercussions. But what about all the other times since the church's founding in 1840 when similar instances were never recorded? Earlier, the church fathers kept silent and followed the Abolitionists' unwritten edict not to create a paper trail of their antislavery activities.

Jesse C. Kellogg, who maintained the church record books, accounted for every penny received and spent on behalf of the church. The $3.00 was not a capricious donation given without the church society's consent. In the Congregational Church any financial decision was decided by the church body as a whole. They voted upon an annual budget; they reviewed the various church board expenditures at monthly meetings. If the money given to Mr. Browning had been part of a ministerial discretionary fund, then it probably would not have been itemized, but rather would have been included within a total sum expended for that particular month. This was not an anonymous donation. "Mr. Browning, Black man" was the specific recipient.

To give perspective to the dollar amount given to this stranger passing through Sycamore, note that the average DeKalb County wage paid to a day laborer, not including room and board, was 75 cents per day. On top of that base pay, room and board averaged $1.50 per week, or the equivalent of two day's wages.[3] The needs of a family would be greater than those of a single man, which could explain the gift of $3.00, rather than a lesser amount. A three-dollar gift addressed an exceptionally strong need on the part of the recipient and was an exceedingly generous gift! The parishioners in the First Congregational Church did not save up their stores in heaven; they gave to their fellow man, not regardless of color, but especially *because* of his color.

Mary and Her Child

Mayfield Township Abolitionist William Nickerson always loved a good story. Born in Connecticut in 1811, during his 98 years, he had ample opportunities to witness the DeKalb County Underground Railroad in action and eagerly related his experiences:

> I was home one cold wintry night when the prairie winds were howling. I was reading and heard a timid knock at the door. I went and opened it, and there stood a woman — a mulatto with a little

girl. As she stood there she asked: "Do Mr. Nickerson live here?" I said, "Yes." She said: "I was told that you were a friend of the colored people." I answered, "Yes, walk in." It was very cold, but the man who brought her, had driven off immediately.[4]

This was not an unusual occurrence; it happened frequently in Mayfield Township. The person who brought the freedom seeker to Nickerson's home had completed his portion of the job. Now it was someone else's turn to aid the downtrodden. Nickerson quickly informed his fellow Abolitionists, Mayfield residents Joshua Townsend and his sons, Stephen and Charles. Transporting a fugitive on to the next station in the Underground Railroad network was always a priority for the Townsend men and Nickerson knew he could count on them to help.

The young woman carried with her a certificate indicating that she was "an excellent cook," which helped in their decision where to send her. After a brief discussion, Nickerson and the Townsends determined that the middle of winter was too cold for a young mother and child to travel. It was "a hard time to send that woman on to Canada and [we] thought to try and find a home for her. We went to Sycamore and found a home for her in Dr. Page's cellar kitchen. She remained there four months and then we sent her on her way to Canada."[5]

Consequently, in the June 1860 Census enumeration we see listed in the home of Dr. Horatio F. Page and his wife Eliza, a young woman listed as Mary A. Wadgen and her two-year-old daughter, also named Mary. On the surface there is nothing unusual about the woman, except that she and her little girl are distinctly designated as being mulatto. The fact that she is living with the Page couple is quite understandable. They are identified antislavery activists who several times over in historical records are mentioned as aiding fugitive slaves in their quest for freedom. Wadgen was only 28 years old — if she was a fugitive, certainly old enough to know that she no longer wanted to be enslaved by an unkind master. The record further states that she was born in Virginia, while her daughter was born in Iowa. There is no husband listed. The mystery deepens.

Her surname was Wadgen, or a variation thereof. It could have been correctly spelled differently, such as Widgen or Widgeon. Or, if sounded out loud, it could have actually been Watkin or Watkins. Either way, there are a few theories that might fit her particular situation.

In the first scenario, we note in the 1850 Census for Norfolk, Virginia, there are enumerated an Able Widgen and his wife, Elizabeth. Widgen or Widgeon was a common surname in the Portsmouth and Norfolk area at that time. Able Widgen was a 52-year-old tailor born in Virginia. His wife, Elizabeth, 44, was also born in Virginia, with no occupation given. It appears that they lived within the seaport town, not out in the country, as their neighbors on the same street are a sailor, a stevedore, a blacksmith, an auctioneer, a clerk, and a merchant.

Three doors down from Able and Elizabeth Widgen lived the Miller family. Robert Miller is a 51-year-old laborer living with his 40-year-old wife Cynthia. Their daughter, Mary, is 18 years old, which coincidentally is just the right age for a girl born in Virginia to be if 10 years later she is 28 and lives in Illinois.

Able and Elizabeth Widgen are white. Robert and Cynthia Miller are black, and it appears that they are free blacks. However, their daughter, Mary, is mulatto. The deduction in this scenario is that Mary is most likely Cynthia Miller's child born of a white father. Did Mary suddenly learn that Able Widgen was actually her birth father? Was that part of her reason to leave her family in Norfolk? Is her last name really Widgen and not Miller?

Although Mary Miller in Virginia in 1850 is not listed as a slave belonging to Able Widgen, she very likely could have been a freed slave previously belonging to Widgen. Widgen, in turn, could have felt he still had some control over her.

By 1860 Able and Elizabeth Widgen still lived in Norfolk, although it is not clear if they resided in the same neighborhood. Robert and Cynthia Miller were apparently gone from that area. And a young mulatto girl named Mary Wadgen, who was the same age as Mary Miller would be, showed up in Sycamore, Illinois. Did Mary take the name of the man she now knew to be her natural father? It could be a coincidence or she could be the same person. In the meantime, she gave birth to a daughter, whom she also named Mary, and gave her the same surname of Widgen or Wadgen. The Illinois census enumerator wrote down "Wadgen." Curiously, a search of two separately compiled census indices shows no other person in the entire United States with the last name of "Wadgen" in either 1850 or 1860. It would appear that the spelling of her surname as "Wadgen" may not be accurate.

The journey from Virginia to Iowa to Illinois, though, is a logistical dilemma. If she was free and not a slave, why did she go to Iowa before the birth of her daughter? If she was not free and was a fugitive from slavery, even given the physical and emotional reasons for wanting to escape slavery, again why would a young mulatto woman travel from Virginia to Iowa? It was the wrong way to go for freedom. If she was a fugitive headed to Canada when she left Norfolk, on the eastern coast of Virginia, geographically she overshot the acknowledged path to freedom. Again, we ask why did she travel overland westward to Iowa? If one's origins are in Iowa, then the route from Iowa to Illinois is a more logical, understandable progression. But the route from Virginia to points west of Illinois seems out of the way. If she was indeed from Norfolk, Virginia, and if she was in truth the Mary Miller who lived there in 1850, then the logical escape route was by sea and northward up the eastern coast of the northern states.

However, the answer to the dilemma may lie in the very obvious fact that she was mulatto. Perhaps she thought she could pass for white in 1858 and thereby be safe. As she traveled north, though, she may have learned that she was not as safe and secure as she anticipated. In 1858, before the Civil War, there were still bounty slave hunters roaming the Northern states, eager to capture any black or mulatto person to sell back to someone, to anyone, in the South. When she became pregnant with her baby girl, she may have set upon her course immediately, but then "laid low" in Iowa until she felt the baby was old enough to travel. By 1860, the child was two years old, and, whatever her reasons, Mary decided to be on the move again. The state of Iowa had an active Underground Railroad network. In fact, John Brown himself was in West Liberty, Iowa, near Muscatine when he was training men prior to his standoff at Harpers Ferry, Virginia. Muscatine is just over the Iowa border from Rock Island, Illinois, and Rock Island was one of the northern entrance points sometimes used by the Abolitionists in their mission to aid fugitives. Escape routes easily headed towards the town of Princeton and on to DeKalb County.

A second hypothesis could be that the same girl, the 18-year-old freed slave Mary Miller, was impregnated by her older, white neighbor, Able Widgen. Shamed, she left town in her maternal state and subsequently gave birth to the little girl to whom she gave the last name of the known father. However, the questions surrounding her travel from Virginia to Iowa and then to Illinois remain the same.

A third scenario is simply a general theory that a girl named Mary (last name unknown) escaped the travails that fell upon her somewhere in Virginia (fugitive slave or not) and made her way to Iowa (for whatever reasons), where she there married (or not) a man whose last name was Wadgen/Widgen/Watkin/Watkins or some variation thereof. Whichever story may be correct, the truth is that according to the 1860 Census records, which are only as accurate as the local enumerator's personal comprehension, spelling and handwriting, a mulatto woman named Mary Wadgen lived in DeKalb County and was indeed born in Virginia, while her daughter was born in Iowa.

The final hypothesis regarding Mary Wadgen and her young daughter could well be the true story. In the 1850 U.S. Census Slave Schedule for Wilkinson County, Mississippi, we see enumerated a young female slave owned by a woman named Mary Watkins. Ditto marks on the page indicate that perhaps the slave was also named Mary Watkins, or she could have simply taken on the name later as a convenience. The slave Mary Watkins is a female, 17 years old, and is mulatto. This fits precisely with the description of gender, race and approximate age for the Mary A. Wadgen who showed up later in Sycamore, Illinois. The theory that Mary Wadgen/Watkins was actually a fugitive slave who escaped the horrors of slavery in the South fits all the circumstantial evidence garnered from William Nickerson's story. Although born in Virginia, she probably was sold at a slave auction at a very young age to a plantation owner in Mississippi. Once old enough to determine a way out of her enslavement, Mary Wadgen/Watkins bravely accepted the help offered through the Underground Railroad network.

Additionally, with this postulation, the questions regarding the route used to travel to Iowa are laid to rest. For a slave fleeing from the state of Mississippi, it was geographically logical to follow the Mississippi River northward and remain in Iowa long enough to become pregnant (perhaps not willingly) and give birth to a baby. A year and a half to two years later, Mary determined to continue her final quest for freedom, which brought her and her little girl to DeKalb County. As Harriet Beecher Stowe wrote, Mary had been in a "tight place," but she held on for a moment longer knowing that "the tide will turn."[6]

The competent conductors in the Northern Illinois Underground Railroad knew what to do. Passed from station to station, Mary ultimately arrived at the home of William Nickerson, where he or the Townsends promptly transported her to the home of Dr. Horatio Page. That much we know for certain. And there she lived for several months for the entire population of Sycamore to see. Page deliberately told anyone who asked that she was a servant, even though he had never had a servant before. In Sycamore, DeKalb County, Illinois, Mary Wadgen/Watkins found safety.

John Shepherd

Previously, in 1850 Horatio Page courageously declared to the government census taker that the young black 17-year-old John Shepherd who lived in his home was a student. Page even told the census enumerator that Shepherd was born in Massachusetts, and whether Shepherd was from that eastern state or not, that piece of information lent credibility to the story of why he was living with Page, since Horatio Page himself came from Massachusetts. Shepherd was therefore considered by the government to be a "northern Black." The esteemed doctor unabashedly and perhaps frequently made such declarations to friends and neighbors. John Shepherd was listed as a student, and not as a servant. Later, Shepherd is not enumerated in the 1860 DeKalb County census. Since the census records are only taken every ten years, we know exactly what his assertions were in those particular decades. There is no written record of the many fugitives Horatio and Eliza Page may have harbored in the interim. Remember, Horatio Franklin Page was an unreasonable man.

A Free Man Named Edward

The 1860 Census only lists one other young black girl, one black man, plus two separate mulatto men living in DeKalb County. By virtue of his surname, we may assume that the black man enumerated was a former slave. That man was Edward Freeman. Freeman was born in Kentucky about 1800 and prior to moving to DeKalb County, he lived slightly northwest in Jo

Davies County. While near the town of Elizabeth in Jo Davies County, Freeman worked as a miner, ostensibly in one of the numerous lead mines in the area close to the Mississippi River. When he moved to Kingston Township in DeKalb County sometime between 1850 and 1860, he no longer mined, but probably became a farm laborer. No occupation is given for him in the 1860 Census, when he lives next door to the Butterfield families.

George W. and Matilda Butterfield resided immediately adjacent to Edward Freeman. George was the son of Benjamin and Nancy (Harper) Butterfield, who were loyal antislavery advocates and who, of course, subscribed to the antislavery newspaper, the *Western Citizen*. Freeman was one of the first black men to actually settle in DeKalb County and chose a place to live where he knew he would be welcome. Having freedom lovers as one's neighbors was a good choice. The Butterfields may even have loaned or rented him the hired hand's house in which to live.

By 1870 Edward Freeman is no longer living in DeKalb County. The U.S. Census indices for that year list seven men named Edward Freeman who were all born in Kentucky. Not one is listed as a black man. There is one listed as mulatto, but with a birth date of 1854, he is much too young to be the Edward Freeman who previously lived in DeKalb County. However, a closer examination of the original census records reveals that one of the Kentuckians named Edward Freeman is not white, as first indicated in the index, but is actually enumerated as mulatto. The 21st century census transcriber apparently mistook the cursive "M" for a "W" and listed him as white instead of mulatto. This Edward Freeman, whose occupation is given as farm laborer, lives in Kalamazoo, Michigan, is married to a white woman named Elizabeth who is 21 years or more his junior, and has two mulatto children. Clues point to the possibility that this is the same Edward Freeman, the black man who first settled in DeKalb County. One of those clues is that his oldest child is only eight years old and was born in Illinois. Without the benefit of original vital records, we cannot prove that this is the same person, but the preponderance of evidence indicates that it is. Edward Freeman was perhaps one of the first black persons who visited Illinois as a freed slave and then felt safe enough to settle there even before the Civil War concluded.

Matilda

The only black female listed in the DeKalb County 1860 Census was 14-year-old Matilda Dublin, who was born in New York. Matilda most likely accompanied the family of Abraham and Sarah "Sally" Ellwood when they moved to Sycamore in 1856. The Ellwoods emigrated from Herkimer County, New York, and ten of their twelve grown children also came to the Midwest with their parents. Two sons, Reuben and Chauncey, had emigrated from New York about ten years before their parents. Reuben was elected the first mayor of Sycamore.

The Abraham Ellwood family belonged to the Sycamore Universalist Church, which was antislavery in philosophy. However, the Matilda Dublin who lived with them was probably not a fugitive slave. Dublin's occupation is not given, but because she was only 14 in 1860 and because she was black, it is safe to suggest that she was a live-in domestic servant at that time. She did not stay in DeKalb County long enough to see Abraham and Sally's son, Isaac Leonard Ellwood, become famous as part owner of the patent for the invention of barbed wire. By 1870, census records show that Dublin was no longer living in the Ellwood household in Illinois. It is possible that she married and had a different surname. However, there are no black females named "Matilda" living in DeKalb County at that time. Yet, we see a Matilda "Doublin" listed back in Herkimer County, New York, still working as a domestic servant. This is most likely the same person. After the Civil War, the non-slave Matilda Dublin went back to her home and family on the East Coast.

Joseph

Another person who listed his occupation as servant in 1860 was Joseph Roe. Sometime between 1850 and 1860, Joseph moved in with John Calvin Waterman and his first wife, Caroline (Hoyt) Waterman and their five children. Joseph Roe was mulatto, and in his particular case, it is quite possible that he was a fugitive slave who found a safe haven with the "zealous Republican"[7] Waterman. Waterman was a member of the appointed political subcommittee at the well-advertised 1854 DeKalb County Anti-Nebraska (antislavery) Meeting. However, according to census records, Joseph Roe, like Matilda Dublin, was born in New York and not in a Southern state. The moneyed Waterman family, like the Ellwood family group, all emigrated from New York together. Consequently, a more likely theory is that Roe was a domestic servant brought from the East with another family member. Roe was probably not a freedom seeker fleeing from slavery.

John Wilson

John W. Wilson is the last of six non-white people to be enumerated in the 1860 pre–Civil War Census period in DeKalb County. Wilson was born in Virginia and is listed as mulatto. John Wilson was most likely a freed slave who, like Edward Freeman, settled in DeKalb County for a short time. John even decided to become an entrepreneur when he became a Sycamore barber. As a businessman in the downtown area of Sycamore, Wilson resided above his barbershop.

This was a man who quietly lived his life in relative safety in Northern Illinois, yet who, because his skin color, became the subject of a local newspaper editor's column. Edward L. Mayo was the senior editor of the proslavery *DeKalb County Sentinel* and he publicly argued each week with Campbell Waite, editor at the antislavery *True Republican*. On one such occasion, Mayo reflected that he had recently examined his beliefs "upon the subject of the natural rights of our colored brethren" and drew a comparison between the antislavery editor Campbell Waite and local barber John Wilson.

> Neighbor Waite is a white man, and by the laws of Illinois is entitled to the right of suffrage. Neighbor Wilson is a colored gentleman; that is no fault of his, if it be a fault, for he was born so. Now we consider Mr. Wilson a man of more ability than Mr. Waite, more the gentleman and less the blackguard; but his skin is colored and by the laws of this State he cannot vote to help make the laws by which he must be governed.[8]

To compare a white man to a black man was considered an insult. It was socially outrageous for the white man to be publicly called less of a man than the black man, yet the manner in which it was done was an acceptable form of journalistic writing for the times.

Editor Mayo apologized to his readers (assumedly all white) by writing: "To our readers we say that we sincerely regret the necessity for the use of any language that might appear to any wise personal to any one. We heartily [*sic*] deprecate personalities ever, and will never indulge in them, except in self-defense — and not often then."[9] Edward L. Mayo needed to justify his action; he explained it was purely self-defense in retaliation for pointed questions posed to him by the *True Republican* editor Campbell Waite. In Mayo's mind it was appropriate to use an innocent man in the example in order to further his own personal agenda. As a result, John Wilson attained brief notoriety simply by being a quiet businessman, who happened to be "colored."

If John Wilson was a freed slave, then like Edward Freeman, he undoubtedly carried with him at all times his own certificate of freedom in order to be able to prove he was a free slave to anyone who questioned him. Wilson apparently either died or moved elsewhere as he is not listed in the 1870 Census for DeKalb County. One of the published indices for the entire 1870 Census lists 1048 men in the United States named John Wilson. To follow where the Sycamore John Wilson went or who he might have married and to prove that a person is the same person who was the barber in Sycamore, is fairly impossible. Fugitive or freed slave, for a few years John W. Wilson found a safe haven in DeKalb County.

The First Henry

By the year 1870, after the Civil War, the U.S. Census for DeKalb County listed 45 black men and women, plus three persons designated as mulattos living in the area. We do not know all the personal stories of each of these individuals and whether or not they were former slaves. However, two people are noteworthy of mention.

William and Rose Beard's son, Henry Beard, was born into slavery in Tennessee on January 1, 1841. Henry was never sold while a slave, but remained with the same owner for about 21 years. While either a runaway slave or a freed black, during the summer of 1863 he encountered the 105th Illinois Infantry after they moved their position from Kentucky into Tennessee. It was there that Elias West, son of Deacon David West of Sycamore, befriended Henry, who was a big, strong man "of good disposition."[10] Elias was but a private in Company A of the 105th, serving alongside Henry and Herman Kellogg, who were brothers to his good friend Hiram Kellogg and sons of Jesse C. Kellogg. Elias and his friend Hiram had helped their fathers conduct fugitive slaves on to the next safe house ten years earlier.

Elias was always a friend of the black man; he was raised to be so. Henry Beard needed a friend. If he was a fugitive, he was considered to be "contraband" by the Union Army, and could be enlisted into the military on the spot to serve the Union cause. If he was already freed, he still required the security afforded by the army to pass through the southern states at that time. Enlisting fulfilled that need as well. Beard's Civil War pension records show that he was mustered into the 105th Regiment of the Illinois Infantry at Lavergne, Tennessee, on August 6, 1863. Henry served as an undercook for Company A until he was discharged on June 19, 1865. In the published lists of Illinois military units in the Civil War, Henry is duly recognized as one of the 2,391 soldiers who served from DeKalb County, Illinois.

Beard's activities between his discharge from the Union Army and his appearance in Sycamore, Illinois, five years later are vague. He accompanied the 105th Regiment back to Illinois and at some point he visited Ft. Scott, Kansas, where he met his future wife, Julia "Judy" Jones. Judy was also a former slave whose parents were each owned by separate plantation owners. She recounted that when the slaves were freed her family was reunited, but "our family had to go out and make a living."[11] She was hired out to work at a salary of $35.00 per year plowing fields — very hard work for a 12-year-old girl. The Jones family finally determined to move to a Northern state, and along with her family she walked barefoot from Texas to Kansas in search of jobs. It was there that she met Henry Beard. Henry and Judy traveled back to Illinois and were married in 1871 in Geneva, Kane County, which was about the same time Henry purchased five acres of land in Sycamore from Elias West's father, David.

Elias West is credited with inviting Henry Beard to come back to DeKalb County after the Civil War. The Beard family ultimately became one of the first black families to permanently live in Sycamore. They gave birth to 14 children and "for many years the family occupied a small tract of land in the Big Woods north of Sycamore where their children were born."[12] Several of the Beard children worked for Elias West on the West family farm. When Henry died in 1924, he was lauded as the "only colored man in [the] county who served in the Civil War."[13]

The Second Henry

Henry Donald may have been a freed slave, or he may have been a fugitive when he first met *Western Citizen* subscriber Timothy Wells. At the time they met, Wells was the quartermaster for the 105th Illinois Infantry. Wells was an adventurous young man who came to DeKalb County from Ohio when he was only about 19 years old. He was one of thousands who headed to the new western frontier to seek his fortune. In 1839, along with a few other Sycamore businessmen, he purchased lots at auction in Sycamore, the proceeds from which were designated to build a courthouse and jail. By 1840, in partnership with Charles Waterman, he was co-owner of the state route for the stagecoach line running between St. Charles and Sycamore. According to historical reports, the business "had an elegant four horse coach."[14] Wells married Mary Waterman, sister to his business partner, and also sibling of both Charlotte and John Waterman, who were both vocal antislavery advocates.

After enlisting in the military during the Civil War, Timothy Wells met Henry Donald purely by chance. His story is similar to Henry Beard's, as Henry Donald encountered his northern benefactor around 1863 when the 105th moved from Kentucky to Tennessee. After the war was over, Henry married his wife, Josephine, who was also from Tennessee. They accepted Timothy Wells's invitation to come to Northern Illinois, and the couple is enumerated in the 1870 U.S. Census living in Sycamore.

Here the story takes a different direction from Henry Beard's tale. Itching to further his fortune, Henry Donald's friend, Timothy Wells, moved westward to Kansas just prior to 1870. Donald continued to work as a laborer in DeKalb County.

One early fall morning in 1876, a young boy walked into Lund's jewelry store in the city of DeKalb to leave some jewelry for repairs. Although it was early morning, he noticed a light on in the store even though the jeweler was not present. Following his boyhood curiosity, the boy continued through the retail section of the store into a rear room where he discovered "the body of the proprietor lying on the floor and indicating he had been killed with an ax."[15] Henry Donald was the suspected murderer. There is no explanation as to why the law enforcement officials thought that Donald was the perpetrator. Unfortunately, it may have been because he was one of only a few black men living in the DeKalb area.

Apparently a Pinkerton detective assisted DeKalb County Sheriff Reuben Holcomb in tracing the assailant and they promptly arrested Donald. The suspected criminal was transported to the Sycamore jail, where he spent the night. All was not calm, however, as the next day Sheriff Holcomb received word through a telegram from DeKalb indicating that a lynch mob of 150 or more men "planned to move on to the jail that same night to lynch the prisoner."[16] The sheriff immediately "swore in fifty special deputies, had them armed, and also arranged to have the armory of the Sycamore guards kept open in case the situation reached a desperate stage."[17] Luckily for Henry Donald, the mob of lynchers never appeared.

It is not clear if Henry Donald was convicted of murder, or a lesser charge of robbery. He does not appear in the DeKalb County 1880 Census, but reappears in 1900 residing as a servant in the home of Jonas Kepple in Kingston. Donald was widowed by this time.

The tale of two Henrys: Both were born in Tennessee; both were former slaves who may have been "contraband," fugitives who found safety with the Union troops. They were both befriended by two soldiers who were friends in the 105th Illinois Infantry, and were both invited to come back to Sycamore in DeKalb County by those same men. And there the similarities end. One chose to stay in the area, work and raise a family, while the other Henry's life fell apart. Like millions of men through history, whether slave or free men, who had gone before them, and the many millions who would come after them, their lives took diverse routes, partly of their own choosing. Henry Beard and Henry Donald each pursued a different course in their newfound freedom and ended up at dissimilar destinations. Safety and freedom are not guarantees for happiness.

Stephen Depp

Stephen Depp was a prominent former slave who, though he never lived in the area, visited in DeKalb County. He was called "Judge Depp," a title that may have been one of respect rather than one denoting educational or judicial achievement. Depp was born a slave about 1794 in Virginia and remained a slave until the death of his owner in 1830. At that point, Depp was liberated and was the beneficiary of 143 acres of land from his master's estate. He and his wife, Lydia, had at least six children, all whom survived him after his death in 1861.

Following Stephen Depp's emancipation from slavery, he was very successful as an anti-slavery speaker, much like the more famous Frederick Douglass. According to the *Republican Sentinel*, around 1854 Depp delivered a lecture in DeKalb County, most likely in Sycamore, "which created considerable excitement. Judge Depp had been a slave and had become free, and was well educated and a speaker of considerable force and his story gave quite an impetus to the anti-slavery cause in this locality. It was thought by many that he was the equal of Fred Douglas[s]."[18] To attract a speaker of national renown to a small rural town on the western frontier speaks volumes about the unreasonable antislavery proponents in DeKalb County.

African Americans in DeKalb County

The citizens of DeKalb County did not own slaves. We cannot know for certain that no one who lived in this area of Northern Illinois ever owned a slave, but coming as they did from New York and New England, and understanding their strong religious ties, the postulation is that slaveholding was either not a part of their heritage, or they had abandoned any thought of owning slaves in deference to their religious beliefs. No slaves were ever enumerated in the United States Census records for DeKalb County, Illinois.

The region also never had a settled free black population. Even in 1840, there were no designated "free persons of color." Census records support the fact that only a few blacks were listed in DeKalb County prior to 1870. Those few who were counted provide a human face for the reasons to be unreasonable. The men and women in DeKalb County knew well who they helped.

Chapter 15

Hail and Farewell!

"I would like ... to thank [the Abolitionists] for all they have done...."[1]— Frederick Douglass (1818–1895), freed slave and Abolitionist activist

Indebted to Abolitionists

There is no argument with the historians who through their research have given us the many stories of the brave African Americans who provided leadership and encouragement, gave directions and passed on meaningful songs. The enormous contributions of people like Frederick Douglass, the freed slave turned Abolitionist activist, and Harriet Tubman, who returned to the South to personally escort runaway slaves to the North, are still lauded today.

In all of DeKalb County, Illinois, however, no free black population existed. The 1850 Census lists only one black in DeKalb County. John Shepherd was that 17-year-old black man, enumerated as a student living in Dr. Horatio Page's household in Sycamore. The Abolitionist Page and his wife, Eliza, helped several known liberty-seeking pilgrims to travel beyond the reach of the overseer's whip. They undoubtedly aided numerous unidentified fugitives. In spite of the strong antislavery sentiment in DeKalb County, local political pressures and the prevailing law of the land through the 1850 Fugitive Slave Law caused any Underground Railroad activities to remain secret. As in other resolute antislavery areas in the northern United States, there is no precise written record of its active presence in the area. Strong oral tradition, when combined with recorded anecdotes in historical tomes, continue to be the greatest indicators of the quiet, yet powerful activity of the local Abolitionists.

In more recent studies of the Underground Railroad in the northern U.S., emphasis is given to the importance of the African American community and the assistance they rendered to the clandestine system. The experience in Floyd County, Indiana, for example, was the exact opposite of DeKalb County, Illinois. In that area, the African American community of free blacks aided runaways. Author Pamela R. Peters correctly asserts that for that region it was a myth that only white citizens operated the system called the Underground Railroad.[2] However, DeKalb County, Illinois, did not have an African American community; there were no free blacks. There were no fugitive slaves who settled out of the mainstream of Southern escapes. Indeed, in all the towns with active known Abolitionists—Sycamore, Somonauk, Genoa, Paw Paw, and Mayfield—it was always the white evangelical citizens who were the

Underground Railroad activists. They not only provided the sole means of transportation, shelter and support, they were the entire backbone of the known Underground Railroad operation in DeKalb County.

When studying Abolitionists and the antislavery movement, it becomes evident that the real war began many years before the actual Civil War. The first shot fired at Ft. Sumter was only an announcement to the world that the fight was in earnest. If the Abolitionists who were subscribers to the *Western Citizen* ranged in age from 30 to 49 years, then by 1861, with the commencement of the Civil War, these men would have been 50–69, most of them far too old to serve in the military. Their war was already fought; they had openly expressed their concerns for the antislavery cause over the previous twenty years. Their sons and grandsons would risk their youthful lives in a far more dangerous physical war to eliminate slavery. Young boys carried the antislavery flag forward in the American Civil War. As one historian observed, "No words can describe the horror the Civil War visited upon the people of the sundered nation. It began, as most wars begin, with bursts of patriotism and pride and optimism on both sides. Young men rushed to sign up to fight — amateur soldiers led by amateur commanders, joining the militias that cities, towns, and villages cobbled together in every state, North and South."[3]

New DeKalb County recruits by the thousands in their unsullied blue uniforms became members of the 105th Illinois Volunteer Infantry, the 8th, 10th, 14th, and 17th Illinois Cavalry, the 13th, 42nd, 52nd, and 58th Illinois Infantry, as well as a few in the 102nd and 156th IVI.[4] Regiments waved goodbye to the towns of Sycamore, DeKalb, Genoa, Somonauk, Sandwich, Mayfield, and the other small rural villages nestled in the prairie grasses. They marched off to war behind the drummer's cadence as friends and family both cheered and cried. Mothers knew their sons were leaving to fight for a cause that had fermented for decades. Four years later, "when the fighting finally shuddered to a close,"[5] over 600,000 were dead and more than a million more were maimed and wounded.

All the retrospective discussion by history researchers over the years about economics being the root cause of the Civil War means nothing if we do not acknowledge that it was slave labor that undergirded the entire economic system of the South.

People like Deacon David West understood that. West's name never became a household word anywhere outside of DeKalb County, Illinois. He was never touted in national history books, or in literature written for children about America's early heroes. Yet, in DeKalb County, the stories about David West are still told today. His outspoken, succinct comments about the horrors of slavery; his admonitions about what would happen to you in hell if you supported slavery; his open example of how, through small acts of kindness, sometimes taken at risk, one person could accomplish great feats — these stories are all a part of local folklore. By helping fugitives travel to freedom using his familiar handcrafted wagon, David West gave his best portion of a good man's life. In 1877 the Sycamore *True Republican* commented on "That venerable carriage used by Deacon David West ... it was one of the passenger coaches on the underground railroad which ran through this place."[6]

The simple farm cart which locally advanced the liberty of an entire people gives credence and authority to the stories. Now we know the stories were all true. In DeKalb County, Illinois, and in the history of the United States of America, David West was a hero.

For the Abolitionists and antislavery sympathizers who facilitated the Underground Railroad, it was the very basic thought of man's inhumanity to man that motivated them. They were the conscience of a nation who understood that in order to be true to America's own Declaration of Independence, they needed to first rid the country of the institution of slavery. The well-known phrase from that long-famous Declaration, "We hold these truths to be self-evident, that all men are created equal, that they are endowed by their Creator with certain inalienable rights, that among these are life, liberty, and the pursuit of happiness," became their credo for action.

Frederick Douglass was a nationally well-known freed slave. He escaped from a plantation near Baltimore, Maryland, and soon became a fiery, eloquent antislavery speaker, who traveled incessantly to spread his Abolitionist message. It was Frederick Douglass, "not Washington or Lincoln, who fully perceived the Constitution as including all Americans, regardless of skin."[7] Speaking at a meeting of the American Abolition Society in 1857, Douglass reminded the attendees, "We, the people — not we, the white people — not we, the citizens, or the legal voters — not we, the privileged class, and excluding all other classes — but we, the people, not we, the horses and cattle, but we the people — the men and women, the human inhabitants of the United States, do ordain and establish this Constitution."[8]

The charitable contribution from the Sycamore First Congregational Church for temporary aid to the black man who passed through town publicly documented the fact that area antislavery advocates were willing to openly help a fugitive slave. It was a courageous act, given that the Federal Fugitive Slave Law was still in effect. Three dollars was a substantial amount of money to give away when we consider that their entire regular collection "for the poor" usually only amounted to a total of $2.30. "To balance the sharp truth of slavers and bounty hunters and betrayals, one finds accounts of people who did what was right, choosing conscience over safety, and human dignity over personal reputation."[9]

There is reason to agree with historian Wilbur H. Siebert that alongside the Abolitionists, "the Underground Railroad was one of the greatest forces which brought on the Civil War, and thus destroyed slavery."[10] DeKalb County was sometimes forgotten in the annals of history when the Underground Railroad was discussed. It was forgotten, but not deprived. It was not deprived of the presence of unknown, unpresuming individuals who courageously acted in a calm manner in order to support a cause which they knew in their hearts to be right. The dramatic, violent encounters experienced by other Abolitionists and antislavery groups throughout the United States did not occur in DeKalb County, Illinois.

William A. Nickerson of Mayfield Township commented that "the anti-slavery men in the state of Illinois ... were conscientious Christians, and the noblest men that I ever met."[11] Stalwart in their Christian beliefs, resolute in their attitudes towards slavery, the citizens in this rural Midwest frontier locale performed their quiet drama without pretense, and ultimately contributed towards changing the course of history. These heroes and heroines were unreasonable men and women.

Contemporary African American history scholar Lerone Bennett echoes Nickerson's comments about DeKalb County: "I pay the highest tribute to these people. It is not only just the Abolitionists and Underground Railroad in Illinois. I think it's one of the greatest movements in the history of this country. It's just unfortunate we know so little about it that we never honor the people who were involved in that whole process and what they did for America."[12]

Finally, we honor those courageous men and women, the *Unreasonable* Abolitionists.

Zebina Eastman, former owner and editor of the antislavery newspaper the *Western Citizen*, conceived a reunion plan and organized the 1874 Chicago gathering of Abolitionists. Known Abolitionists throughout the United States received invitations. Former DeKalb County *Western Citizen* agent Ezra Starr Gregory was among the invitees on Eastman's handwritten "Special Invitation" list,[13] along with John Hossack of Ottawa, Mrs. Owen Lovejoy from Princeton, as well as Mrs. Elijah Lovejoy, widow of the assassinated Abolitionist. United States Vice-President Henry Wilson was unable to attend and sent his regards, which were printed in the *Chicago Tribune*. This historic reunion was originally planned for 1872, but the massive Chicago Fire prevented that earlier gathering. The former Abolitionists looked forward to the assembly. William Nickerson recalled that previously, "the incidents connected with the underground railway were never written, for we were under the ban. We had to do our work in the night."[14] Finally they could converse, reminisce and write about their experiences. Between speeches from well-known antislavery people, those "stanch old heroes of justice and humanity"[15] visited extensively with one another, recounted their escapades and remembered the many fugitive slaves they had aided to freedom.

DeKalb County's own John Lourie Beveridge, a former Abolitionist and sitting governor of the state of Illinois, issued a warm welcome to the former Abolitionists. Zebina Eastman had invited the renowned black Abolitionist and former slave Frederick Douglass to address the assembly. Douglass was unable to attend at the last moment and sent a letter to be read to the gathering. Those assembled could envision his formidable figure with his graying beard and full head of hair as the letter was read. The esteemed Douglass spoke emotionally to the gathered fellow antislavery proponents, all unreasonable men and women. Frederick Douglass closed a chapter in our nation's history when he aptly commented, "I would like to meet the Abolitionists of the great Northwest, and thank them for all they have done and suffered in the cause of my recently enslaved people and to say hail and farewell!"[16]

Hail and farewell to Dr. Horatio Franklin Page and wife, Eliza, Elmwood Cemetery, Sycamore, Illinois.

Antislavery Advocates: A Biographical Dictionary

> The value of history lies, in a great degree, in the biography of the personages concerned therein.... Only biography can fitly portray with perfect justice the precise attitudes and relation of men to events and conditions.[1] — Chapman Brothers (editors)

When the government said it was against the law to help a fugitive slave, when some churches elsewhere in the United States were preaching tolerance for the institution of slavery and patience with regard to its elimination, the unreasonable men and women in DeKalb County, Illinois, were people who quietly persisted in changing the world.

What follows is a list of over 600 progressive men and women and their families who lived in this Northern Illinois county during the mid–1800s. Brief information indicates their state of origin, their immediate families plus extended relationships, occupation, church or political affiliation if known, and specific historical references to the antislavery movement. The township of residence is according to the 1840, 1850 or 1860 U.S. Census enumerations for DeKalb County, Illinois, and was compared with the records of subscription lists for the *Western Citizen* antislavery newspaper. An absence of census records showing DeKalb County as the place of residence suggests that the person most likely lived in the county between census enumerations. The *Western Citizen* mailbooks specified in what post office mail was received by the subscriber and so identified the correct person in the census if there were duplicate names. Including spouses and family members, a total of over 3,800 names are cited.

Are there other individuals who could have been named? Of course. For example, many children of those identified could be listed in a paragraph of their own. Not included in the compiled list of antislavery advocates are those who, 20 years after the Civil War, proclaimed that they were Republican. After the close of the war, a majority of people sought to be identified with the Republican Party because of its antislavery platform. From 1861 to 1885, from the time Abraham Lincoln was sworn into office, each succeeding elected president was Republican. It is evident why, in Chapman's 1885 *Portrait and Biographical Album of DeKalb County*, we find more people who profess to be Republican than Democrat. The focus for this book, however, is on those who overtly supported the antislavery cause prior to the War Between the States. Being Republican after the war was not enough.

Sources for biographical information are Federal Census records, church membership records, obituaries, cemetery records, local newspapers, printed county and family histories, plus records of the Bureau of Land Management General Land Office to determine land ownership. It was not a goal to compile primary vital statistics from original birth, death and marriage records for each individual. Extensive genealogical research of secondary sources is included and may be considered as clue material for aspiring family genealogists.

Many of the identified antislavery advocates served in the military during the Civil War. However, because the majority of Abolitionist leaders in the county were thought to be too old to serve, military pension records were not a major research resource. People who moved into DeKalb County after 1860 are not included. Spouses are listed separately if they had a subscription to the *Western Citizen* in their own name. Children are mentioned with the family unit unless an historical reference warrants a separate listing, and familial relationships with other antislavery people are given when known. Intermarriages between the antislavery-minded people were not surprising; they comprised the majority in the population from which to choose a spouse. Names in quotes indicate a nickname by which the person was known.

Membership in one of the four overtly antislavery churches in DeKalb County is very significant. Admission to the Sycamore First Congregational Church required affirmation of a person's antislavery beliefs prior to confirmation as a member. The Sycamore Universalist Church ministers and congregation expressed strong antislavery ideas. Members of the Somonauk Presbyterian Church boldly supported a public resolution against slavery, and the antislavery Wesleyan Methodists openly split from the Methodist Episcopal Church. Consequently, individuals and families are named if they retained membership in these churches between 1840 and 1860.

Although many of the rank and file Abolitionists in DeKalb County lived in the young cities and villages, like their Western New York mentors before them "the social composition of the movement itself was distinctly rural."[2] It is evident that DeKalb County Abolitionists followed the precise pattern of their New York predecessors. "Educated, moderately prosperous, pursuing the most influential occupations in their communities and actively engaged in public service, [they were] the secure and substantial citizens of their towns and counties — men who were not being elbowed aside or losing status."[3]

The following abbreviations are used in the biographies:

af	after	D	Democrat	R	Republican
bc	born circa	d	died	sis	sister
bf	before	dau	daughter	Twp	township
bro	brother	farm	farmer	UGRR	Underground Railroad
ch	church	m	married		
Co	county	mbr	member	Univ	Universalist
Cong	Congregational	Meth	Methodist	West Cit	*Western citizen* subscriber
CW	Civil War	Presby	Presbyterian		

ABBOTT, Abiel Boynton, bc1809 Canada, son of John and Lydia (BOYNTON) ABBOTT; d1885 CA; m Sabrie YOUNG, issue Edwin Kirke, Osman/Othman, Marcus Riley, Louella Almena, Martha Jane, Aai/Abiel H., Edgar A./Perley; Kingston Twp; farm; West Cit; moved to CA bf1880.

ABBOTT, Bryant C. bc1826 NY; m Sylary, issue, David, Luaba/Luciba; Paw Paw Twp; land patent; farm; West Cit.

ADAMS, Asher, bc1825 NY, son of Amos and Pamelia (BARBER) ADAMS, bro to Calvin H. ADAMS; d1865 MN; m Jane Eliza WHITE, issue Ellen Jane, Joseph Asher, Etta P., Charles T/S.; Pampas/Cortland Twp; farm; West Cit; Cong affiliation; moved to MN by 1855.

ADAMS, Calvin Henry, b1820 NY; son of Amos and Pamelia (BARBER) ADAMS, bro. to Asher ADAMS; d1907 OR; m Catharine Julia BARTLETT, issue Sophia, Joseph Spencer, Amos C., Marion C., Flora A., William C.; Pampas/Cortland Twp; farm; both Calvin and Catharine were Cong; moved to OR 1852.

ADAMS, Pamelia (BARBER), bc1787 CT, dau Oliver and Sarah (MUNROE) BARBER; d1860 NY; m Amos ADAMS, issue Amos Barber, Joseph Herrick, Calvin Henry,

William, Asher; Pampas/Cortland Twp; lived with son, farm; Cong; moved to MN 1852.

ALEXANDER, Elizabeth Ann (WATERMAN), b1816 NY; d1873 MN; m George William ALEXANDER, issue Nancy J., Mary E., John W., George Waterman, Ellen J.; Pampas/Cortland Twp; husband farm; West Cit.

ALEXANDER, James M., bc1837 NY, son of Henry and Betsy (GALLUP) ALEXANDER; Shabbona Twp; farm; West Cit.

AMSDEN, Noah Cummings, b1820 NY, son of Benjamin Cummings and Achsah/Anna H. (NICHOLS) AMSDEN; d1891 MN; m Sarah HUBBERT (HULBURT/HOLBROT), issue Charles M., Monroe R. (twins), William S., Ellen; Boone Co., P.O. in Genoa, DeKalb Co, IL; merchant; West Cit; moved to IA bf1860, to MN aft1880.

ANDERSON, David P., bc1821 NY; d1883 IL; m Laura Ann BROOKS, issue Jenny B., Carolyn "Carrie," Juniata "Junie," Cora, Nellie, John G. "Johnnie"; Sycamore Twp; carriage maker; Univ.

ARBUCKLE, Joseph T., b1805 PA; d1897 IL; m Amanda, issue Eliza Ann, Benson Baldwin, David B., William H., Charles J.; Kingston Twp; land patent; farm; West Cit; lived in DeKalb Co. bf1840.

ARMSTRONG, David, b1770 Scotland/Ireland; d1866 IL; m (1) Elizabeth CREIGHTON, issue Robert C., William, Thomas, David, John, Jane; m (2) Jane ARMSTRONG, no issue; Somonauk Twp; farm; charter mbrs Somonauk Presby Ch.

ATTIX/ATTICKS, Sophronia BOWKER, b1833 NY; m James DeMott ATTIX/ATTICKS, issue Frank, Herbert/Henry, Orville O.; Sycamore Twp; husband carpenter; Cong; moved to Kane Co, IL, 1859.

AUSTIN, Charles, bc1822 NY; d1904 IA; m Amanda Roxanna DENNIS, issue Louisa, Martha, Mary Jane, Marilla/Miraett, Lenora/Milly, Charles, George M.; Mayfield Twp; farm; Wesleyan Meth; moved to IA bf1870.

BAILEY/BAYLEY, William, bc1788 England; m Mary, issue Fredrick, Ann; Pampas/Cortland Twp; West Cit.

BAKER, Joseph L., bc1816 NY; dc1874 IA; m Sarah "Elizabeth" DENNIS, issue Mary E., Albert, Grant Joseph; Clinton Twp; farm; West Cit; moved to IA bf1860.

BALLARD, Esther M. (CALL), b1824 OH, dau Hannah (PARKER) CALL; d1907 IL; m James S. BALLARD, issue Esther Holt Call; Sycamore Twp.; husband brick and stone mason; Univ.

BANNISTER, Daniel P., bc1828 NY, son of Norton W. and Martha P. BANNISTER; d af1900; m Mary "Elizabeth," issue Mary E., Josephine P., Ida L., Martha "Mattie" S., Cora B., Nettie L., Daniel M. "Montie"; Pampas/Cortland Twp; farm, produce merchant; West Cit; Cong affiliation; R; lived in DeKalb Co. bf1840; moved to SD bf1900.

BARBER, Henry Harrison, bc1819 NY, son of Benjamin and Elizabeth "Betsy" (MARVIN) BARBER; d1898 IL; m Lucy HATCH, issue Albert, Hiram, Miles, Alice, Charles W., Eva, Loretta, Lucy Melvinia; South Grove, Franklin Twps; land patent; farm; West Cit; lived in DeKalb Co bf1840; moved to Boone Co, IL bf1870.

BARBER, Levi Clark, b1789 VT, son of Gideon and Mary (CLARK) BARBER; d1859 IL; m (1) Sally ROOD, issue Henry/Harry, Lyman, Clark L., Amelia, Adelia; m (2) Hannah BROWNELL, issue Wanton Brownell, Mary Polly, Laura E.; DeKalb Twp; land patent; farm; West Cit; lived in DeKalb Co. bf1840.

BARBER, Wanton Brownell, bc1829 NY, son of Levi Clark and Hannah (BROWNELL) BARBER; d1900 IL; m Maranda/Myranda SHELBURN/SHERBURN, issue Jennie, Manley, Arthur, Charles; DeKalb Twp; farm; West Cit; lived in DeKalb Co. bf1840; moved to KS bf1860, back to DeKalb Co bf1870.

BARNES, Erastus H., bc1815 VT son of Eli and Almira (HURLBUTT) BARNES; d1878 IL; m Elizabeth, issue Henry W., Helen A.; Sycamore Twp; shoemaker, Co Surveyor, Co Coroner; West Cit; Cong; lived in DeKalb Co bf1840.

BARRINGER, John H., bc1826 NY, son of William and Catherine (SMITH) BARRINGER; d bf1860; m Gertrude Delia MULFORD, issue William H.; Clinton Twp; farm; West Cit.

BARRINGER, William, bc1787 NY, son of Hans Georg and Elizabeth (BEEM) BARRINGER; d bf1870; m Catherine SMITH, issue John H.; Paw Paw Twp; farm; West Cit.

BARTHOLOMEW, George bc1811 PA, son of Philip and Elizabeth (HESS) BARTHOLOMEW; d af1880; m Peninnah M/W., issue Sarah C., Philip, Elizabeth, Henry D., Hannah Wood, Daniel, George, Andrew; Genoa Twp; farm; West Cit; moved to IA bf1880.

BARTLETT, Joseph Jr., b1790 MA, son of Joseph and Lucy (POST) BARTLETT; d1869 IL; m Temperance POMEROY, issue Wealthy, Sally(1), Sally (2), Marcus A., Roxana, Lucy, Moses, Joseph, Lester A., Eli O.; Paw Paw Twp; farm; West Cit; Presby/Cong; "antislavery man" and "harbored and assisted many a fugitive slave"[4]; lived in Illinois bf1840.

BARTLETT, Joseph Pulsifer, b1810 NH, son of Tristam B. and Hannah (PULSIFER) BARTLETT; d1893 IL; m Julia Ann Elliott McQUESTIN, issue Julia F., Alice Elizabeth, Sarah Adelaid, Lowell Edwin, John Edgar, Henry W.B.; Campton Twp, Kane Co, IL; land patent; teacher, farm, Kane County Justice of the Peace, Associate Justice, Coroner and Supervisor; Cong; R; "wished to form an anti-slavery society" and "conductor on the underground railway"[5]; lived in IL bf1840.

BARTLETT, Marcus Augusta, b1816 OH; son of Joseph and Temperance (POMEROY) BARTLETT; d1906 IA; m (1) Mary Ann FOWLER, issue Caroline Cora, Louisa, Alice, Emma/Anna J., Albert Fowler; m (2) Elizabeth ARLAND, no issue; Paw Paw Twp; land patent; farm; Meth; R; West Cit; lived in IL bf1840; moved to IA bf1900.

BARTLETT, Moses, b1825 OH, son of Joseph and Temperance (POMEROY) BARTLETT; d1908 IL; m (1) Martha R. HARPER, issue Lester Alonzo; m (2) Mary (McALLISTER) CHRISTY, issue Eva (adopted) and step-children James B., Martha J., Alpha, Alice and Charles W. CHRISTY; Paw Paw Twp; land patent; farm, Ross Grove Postmaster; Elder at Ross Grove Presby Ch, then joined Somonauk Presby Ch; R; lived in Illinois bf1840.

BARTLETT, Theodore, b1805 MA, son of Joseph and Lucy (POST) BARTLETT, bro to Joseph BARTLETT, Jr.; d1887 IL; m Sarah TRASK, issue Louisa, Jane, Lydia Alvira, Samuel, Mary, Minerva; Paw Paw Twp; farm; West Cit.

BASSETT, Orlando P., b1826 PA; d1921 CA; Betsy M. SHELDON, issue Kittie; Sycamore Twp; printer; part owner and publisher of the *True Republican*[6]; published the first separate printing of Abraham Lincoln's "House Divided" speech.[7]

BATIE, John, bc1815, NY; d af1880 NE; m Frances/

Francena, issue Matilda, Caroline, Elizabeth, Ellen, Francis, Mary, John; Paw Paw Twp; farm; West Cit; moved to Nebraska Territory bf1860.

BEAVERS, Mary A., bc1822 NJ; m Theodore H. BEAVERS, issue William H., Anna, Caroline; Sycamore Twp; husband was cabinet maker; Cong; moved to MI bf1880.

BECKER, Edward L., b1837 NY, son of Richard and Hannah (CRONK) BECKER; d1920 IL; m1863 Mary S. IRVIN, issue infant d; Franklin Twp; farm; Meth; R; conductor in UGRR.[8]

BEITEL, Julius T., b1825 PA, son of George Leibert and Anna (STOTZ) BEITEL; d1892 IL; m Emma L. TROEGER, issue Eugene Fredrick, Milton Henry, Julius Howard, Agnes Emma, Arvid George, Clement Theodore, Bertha Louisa, Rhoda Elizabeth, Esther Augusta, Herman Lucius, Rachel Anna, Jesse Cornelius; Somonauk, Squaw Grove Twps; West Cit.

BELLES, Margaret, bc1815 NJ; m Mathius BELLES, issue Edward, Mathius, Jr., Charles W., Ervin; Sycamore Twp; husband mason; Univ.

BELLES, Mary "Mollie" Eliza (HOUGHLAND), b1837 OH, dau-in-law of Mathius and Margaret BELLES; d1920 IL; m Charles Wesley BELLES, issue Lou A.; husband plasterer, CW 132nd IL Inf; Sycamore Twp; Univ; moved to IA af1880.

BENEDICT, James Nathaniel, bc1820 NY, son of Andrew and Sarah (STANCLIFT) BENEDICT ; d 1864 MD; m Betsey Ann INGERSOLL, issue Ezra B., Homer, Sarah Kathinda/Rothilde, Lucy Altina/Altana, James Laran/Lorrin; Pampas/Cortland Twp; farm, CW 72nd IL Infantry; West Cit; moved to IA bf1856.

BENTON, John F., bc1824 MA; m Julia A.; Sycamore Twp; farm; Cong; moved to Winnebago Co, IL bf1860.

BEVERIDGE, Andrew, b1802 NY, son of Andrew and Isabella (CUMMINGS) BEVERIDGE, bro to George BEVERIDGE; d1883 IL; m Jane MARTIN, issue Isabella, Margaret, Andrew, Sarah Isabella; Somonauk Twp; farm; West Cit; Elder in Presby Ch; R.

BEVERIDGE, George, b1785 NY, son of Andrew and Isabella (CUMMINGS) BEVERIDGE; d1870 IL; m1788 Ann HOY, issue Jeannette, Isabella (1), Isabella (2), James Hoy, Andrew M., Thomas George, John Lourie, Agnes, Mary; Somonauk Twp; land patent; farm; West Cit; George and Ann charter mbrs. Somonauk Presby Ch, their home was the first building used for worship services; conductor and home a station for UGRR,[9] "a man of radical views and an active Abolitionist"[10]; lived in DeKalb Co bf1840.

BEVERIDGE, James Hoy, b1817 NY, son of George and Ann (HOY) BEVERIDGE, bro of John Lourie and Thomas George, bro-in-law to Alexander R. PATTEN and Charles H. MERRITT; d1896 IL; m Elizabeth A. DISBROW, issue Gertrude, Lewis, James Henry, Lois Annie, Merrit Hoy; Somonauk Twp; land patent; farm, merchant, Associate Justice 1849, Co Assessor 1852, Circuit Clerk and Recorder, owned the *True Republican* newspaper with Daniel B. James and Caleb M. Brown; West Cit; Presby, wife Cong; Free Soil delegate to organizing Republican convention 1854,[11] Treasurer of State of Illinois 1865–67, Mbr of Resolution Committee for 1854 DeKalb Co Anti-Nebraska (antislavery) Meeting.[12]

BEVERIDGE, John Lourie, b1824 NY, son of George and Ann (HOY) BEVERIDGE, bro to James Hoy and Thomas George; d1910 CA; m1848 Helen M. JUDSON, issue Alla May/Ella A., Philo Judson; Somonauk Twp; land patent; teacher, lawyer, engineer, surveyor, Major in IL 8th Cavalry, Brig. Gen. 17th IL Cavalry, Sheriff of Cook Co, IL 1866, IL State Senator 1870, mbr of Congress 1871, Lt. Gov.1872, Governor of IL 1873, assistant U.S. Treasurer 1881; West Cit; Presby, later Episcopal; R; "did not love the institution of slavery,"[13] conductor on UGRR.[14]

BEVERIDGE, Thomas George, b1822 NY, son of George and Ann (HOY) BEVERIDGE, bro to James Hoy and John Lourie; d1859 IL; m Elizabeth IRWIN, issue William G., Ann M.; Somonauk Twp; farm; Presby; Secretary for 1850 Somonauk anti–Fugitive Slave Law meeting.[15]

BILLINGTON, Thomas W., bc1820 NY; m Emiline, issue Adela; Sycamore Twp; carpenter; Cong; moved to Kane Co. bf1860.

BIRDSALL, Sarah (HAGAMAN), bc1780 NY, mother-in-law to David J/I. PERRY; d af1870; m George A. BIRDSALL, issue Mariah/Maria, Charlotte, James Edwin; Sycamore Twp; Cong; moved to McLean Co, IL bf1850.

BLACKMAN, Seth Beal, b1831 NY, son of David and Deborah L. (BEAL) BLACKMAN; m (1) Nancy E. PERRY; m (2) Delilah/Della PERRY; Pampas/Cortland Twp; land patent; farm, butcher, clothier; West Cit; moved to Kane Co, IL bf1870, to IA bf1880.

BOARDMAN, Cyrus, bc1833 NY, son of Benjamin and Mary (PRESCOTT) BOARDMAN; d1924 IL; m Harriet E.KING, issue Alice A., Sherwin W., Mary A., Grace Ella, Edwin Arthur, Willard B., Ernest L., Cassius Martin; DeKalb Twp; carpenter; West Cit.

BOSTON, Thomas, b1795 Scotland; d1866 IL; m Mary Ann JONES, issue Robert, Anne, Catharine, Thomas, Isabella, Mary, William, J. Nimrod, plus Solomon ROSS/BOSTON adopted; Paw Paw Twp; farm; West Cit.

BOYD, Daniel Nelson, b1823 NY, son of George and Elizabeth NELSON) BOYD; d1906 IA; m (1) Nancy SCHROUDY, issue W.J., m (2) Margaret (DARLING) WALLACE, issue Nancy Ann, Thomas N., Jennette "Nettie"; Somonauk Twp; farm; first chorister for Somonauk Presby Ch; moved to IA bf1880.

BOYD, John, b1825 NY, son of George and Elizabeth (NELSON) BOYD, son-in-law of Elijah STEWART; d1905 IL; m Mary STEWART, issue Effie Elizabeth; Somonauk, Squaw Grove Twps; land patent; carpenter, farm; West Cit; Presby.

BRADDOCK, John Norman, b1809 CT, dau of Henry and Eunice (TOOKER) BRADDOCK; d1874; m Sarah J. FULLER, issue Sarah J., Mary, Alabel/Arabell, Oscar; Somonauk Twp; merchant; Baptist; Whig delegate to organizing Republican convention 1854[16]; moved to Putnam Co, IL bf1870.

BRANCH, Charles W., b1812 VT, son of Freelove BRANCH; d1879 IL; m Esther HAIT, issue William Henry, Olive Irene, Hiram E., Edwin H., Mary, Charles, Esther A., Jonas H.; widowed 1854, sister Mary Ann BRANCH raised children; Kingston Twp; land patent; blacksmith, farm, first Kingston Postmaster, Twp Supervisor; West Cit; lived in DeKalb Co bf1840.

BRAYTON, Horatio S., bc1822 NY; m Janette/Jeanette Francis LAY, issue Eugene L., Flora J., Althea, Ward M., Clifford S.; Squaw Grove Twp, farm; West Cit.

BROOK, Clement H., bc1824 OH; d af1870 IA; m (1) Charlotte A.BLISS, issue Rebecca, Emily Fredelia, Cyrus Edwin, Lurania/Mary, Matilda; m (2) Martha, issue Charles,

John, Ellen, Mahala; Somonauk Twp; land patent; farm, teamster; West Cit; moved to IA bf1857.

BROOKS, Amos Richardson, bc1822 OH, son of Jonas and Rachel (RICHARDSON) BROOKS; d1898 KS; m Mary Elizabeth GARDNER, issue Armenta, Ida May, Sarah Belle, Leroy Baium, Charles Hiram, Jonas Gardner, Mary Hattie; Mayfield Twp; farm, minister at Mayfield Wesleyan Meth; 1851 delegate to antislavery convention[17]; son Jonas later minister at same church; grandson was C. Wayland Brooks U.S. Senator.

BROOK(S), Thomas, bc1793 VA; d1870 IL; m (1) Unknown, issue George, Mary; m (2) Charlotte A. DENNIS, issue Hannah W., Jacob D., Lucia O., Lucius E.; Somonauk Twp; carpenter, farm; West Cit; lived in DeKalb Co bf1840.

BROUGHTON, Chauncey Washington, bc1817 MA son of William and Ruth (WINTERS) BROUGHTON; d1893 IL; m (1) Mary CHURCHILL, issue Charles Preston, Joseph; m (2) Caroline Cook CHURCHILL, issue Ellen, William A., May, Judson K., Benjamin; m (3) Isabella BEERS, issue Charles B., Chauncey Washington Jr.; Afton Twp; farm; West Cit.

BROWN, Arnold, bc1803 VT; d bf1880; m Thankful H. FOSTER, issue Hannah, Agnes Julia and Abner Allen (twins), Lucia Marsha/Marea; Sycamore Twp; farm; Univ; lived in DeKalb Co bf1840.

BROWN, Benjamin Putney, "Uncle Put," bc1810 ME, son of Jeremiah and Ruth (LIBBY) BROWN, bro to Jeremiah L. BROWN; d1885 IL; m Charlotte R. GRIGGS, issue Anna M., Benjamin, George, Charlotte R., John, Henrietta, Henry P.; Genoa Twp; land patent; farm; West Cit; Meth; voted with DeKalb Co. Abolitionists af1840 election,[18] "full of zeal for his political opinions,"[19] R; lived in DeKalb Co bf1840.

BROWN, Caleb Marshall "Jersey," bc1818 NJ; son-in-law of Abner JACKMAN, bro-in-law to Jeremiah L. BROWN and Latin NICHOLS; d1874 IL; m (1) Catherine A. DEPUE, issue David Depue; m (2) Louise/Louisa A. JACKMAN, issue Fred C., Marshall L.; Sycamore Twp; merchant, Co Circuit Clerk and Recorder, Co Supervisor; West Cit; Cong, one of 11 men consenting to 1848 tax assessment on personal property to construct new house of worship; Liberty Party political candidate; R; owned the *True Republican* newspaper with James H. Beveridge and Daniel B. James; conductor and home a station for UGRR.[20]

BROWN, Eben, b1801 NH, son of Ebenezer and Susanna BROWN; d1879 IL; m Lepha NICHOLS, issue Sarah Jane; Pampas/Cortland Twp; land patent; West Cit; Baptist, R.

BROWN, Jeremiah Libby, b1805 ME, son of Benjamin and Ann Ruth (LIBBY) BROWN, bro to Benjamin P. BROWN, son-in-law of Abner JACKMAN, bro-in-law to Ezra S. GREGORY, Caleb M. BROWN and Latin NICHOLS; d1882 IL; m (1) Judith RICHARDSON, issue Julia Ann, James Putney, Judith Ann, Esther E/F, Abigail J., Ruth Sina, Jeremiah William; m (2) Eliza A. JACKMAN, issue Emma R., Dillon "Sidney," Charles Abner, Elizabeth "Lizzie" M.; Genoa Twp; land patent; farm, largest antislavery landowner, Twp Supervisor, Justice of the Peace; Meth; R; voted with DeKalb Co. Abolitionists after 1840 election,[21] Liberty Party political candidate; West Cit; lived in DeKalb Co bf1840.

BROWN, Morris, bc1827 NY, son of James and Fanny BROWN; Clinton Twp; farm; West Cit.

BROWN, William W., bc1824 NY, son of William Avery and Matilda (HATCH) BROWN; d1900 MI; m Lydia Louise/A. RHERMANN, issue Harriet A., Mary, Emma, Eunice E., Franklin, Ella Elizabeth; Twp; farm; West Cit; lived in DeKalb Co bf1840; moved to MI bf1860.

BRYAN, Jane Leslie (VAN VOORHEES), b1824 NY, dau James Leslie and Martha (NORTHRUP) VOORHEES; d1889 IL; m Orlando M. BRYAN, issue Evania/Maria/Urania, Florence, Martha, Jane "Jennie," Martin Laurence, James "Leslie"; Sycamore Twp; husband physician; Cong.

BUCKINGHAM, Nathan, b1799 CT, son Nathan and Rhoda (TUCKER) BUCKINGHAM; d 1859 IL; m (1) Mary/Margaret E. PRATT, issue Frederick E. and William Francis (twins), Almus Woolcott, Mary Jane, Joseph M.; m (2) Ann W. STEVENS; Somonauk Twp; farm; West Cit.

BURCHIM, Joshua, b1792 NY, son of Henry BURCHAM, d1867 IL; m Mary TYRELL/TYRREL, issue Mary Malinda, Simon, Phedelia, Edwin, Addison, Alexander Vincent, Jennett, Charles Wesley, Martha Ann, William Henry; Somonauk Twp; land patent; farm; West Cit.

BUTTERFIELD, Benjamin, bc1800 VT; d af1870 IL; m Nancy HARPER, issue George W., Juliet, Clarissa E.; Kingston Twp; farm; West Cit.

BUTTERFIELD, George W., bc1830 OH, son of Benjamin and Nancy (HARPER) BUTTERFIELD; d1892 IA; m Matilda RAYMOND, issue Edwin, Sylvester, Hiram and William (twins); Kingston Twp; farm; West Cit.

BUTTERFIELD, William S., bc1806 NY; d1863 IL; m Elena/Ellen/Eleanor SHELEY, issue Lucy M., William "Andrew," Betsey C., Marsh K., Ellen; Kingston Twp; farm; West Cit.

BYERS, William M. b1821 NY, son of James and Jane (SCOTT) BYERS; d1908 IL; m (1) Mary Ann ADEE, issue John T., Augustus; m (2) Jane E. ADEE (Mary Ann's sister), issue Adell/Della, Mary Anna, Jane/Jenny; South Grove Twp; land patent; farm; Cong; DeKalb Co Supervisor, School Commissioner, Road Commissioner, Justice of the Peace, mbr IL State Legislature 1876; Cong; R; aided conductors for UGRR, offered to pay 25 cents a head for fugitive slaves brought through South Grove Twp[22]; Whig delegate to convention organizing Republican Party 1854.[23]

CALKINS, Asa Matthew, b1796 NY, son of Matthew and Lois (SMITH) CALKINS; d1872 NY; m (1) Ruth AMBLER, issue Maria A., Lois A., Melissa J., Caroline M., Mary E., Matthew B.; m (2) Mary HOVEY, step-children Salla A., William and Albert Hovey; Sycamore Twp; farm; West Cit; Meth Episcopal.

CALL, Alfred Brunson, bc1825 OH, son of Ezra Dudley and Amanda (HOAG) CALL; d1879 KS; m Sabrina DURHAM, issue Edmund Dudley, Amanda C., Catharine, Mary S., Homer A., Howard A.; Sycamore Twp; Meth Minister; West Cit; attended Sycamore Univ Ch; moved to Kane Co., IL, bf1860.

CAMERON, Alexander R., bc1815 New Brunswick; d1886 IL; m Lucy C. PERDY, issue Mary "Adelia," Samuel, Sarah, Woodford, Lucy C., Alexander J., Albert J., Edwin C.; Sycamore Twp; harness maker, carriage trimmer; Cong.

CAMP, Franklin, b1824 NH, son of David and Theoda Elvira (BRIDGMAN) CAMP, son-in-law of Agrippa DOW; d1905 IL; m (1) Eliza/Elizabeth B. DOW, issue Laura "Esther," Charles Franklin, Lucy Maria, Lida Elvira, Cora Elizabeth; m (2) unknown TROOP; Mayfield Twp; farm; West Cit; Baptist; R.

CAMPBELL, Daniel/Donald, bc1788, son of Neil and Mary (McKELLAR) CAMPBELL; d1861 KS; m Barbara McKECHNIE/McGEACHIE, issue Catherine, Neil, Malcolm, Archibald, Mary Ann, Janet C., Ellen/Helen, Barbara Jean; Sycamore Twp; Cong; moved to Kansas af1860.

CAMPBELL, Hugh George, bc1835 Scotland, son of Mary CAMPBELL; d1906 IL; m Amanda J. KNIGHT, issue Mary Ellen, George Argyle, William Hugh; Mayfield Twp; farm; Wesleyan Meth.

CAMPBELL, John, b1814 MA; d1888 NE; m (1) Hannah BREWER, issue Mariah/Mary Louisa, Emily Jane, Mary Janette, John Henry, Martha Clarinda, Margaret/Elizabeth Ann, Albert Elias, James William, Clara Isabelle, Hannah A.; m (2) Sarah Anne JOHNSON, issue unknown; Shabbona Twp; farm; West Cit; Presby.

CARD, Orson, bc1818 NY, son of Richard and Anna (PALMER) CARD; d1857 IL; m (1) Amanda Malvina REDFIELD, issue Henry Truman; m (2) Louisa, issue Cashus/Cassius, Allen, Frances Cordelia; Squaw Grove Twp; farm; West Cit.

CARNEY, Thomas Johnson, b1818 ME, son of James CARNEY; d1871 IL; m Julia Abigail FLETCHER, issue Amanda JoAnna, William Thomas, Julian "Fletcher," Illinois and Maine (twins), Julia Louisa, Charles Henry, James Weston, Eugene Francis; Sycamore Twp; first resident minister Univ Ch, Sycamore.

CARPENTER, Laura Ann, b1843 NY, dau Orange and Rebecca (HURD) ROSE, orphaned at age nine, niece of Elsworth, Jesse and Chauncey ROSE, niece of David and Lucinda (ROSE) WEST; d1915 IL; m William Edwin CARPENTER, issue Harlen Edward, Nellie Rose; Sycamore Twp; Cong; moved to Bureau Co, IL bf1870; Cong.

CARPENTER, William, b1813 NY, son of John and Joanna CARPENTER; d1893 IL; m (1) Clarissa C. WHITELY; m (2) Mary S. FROST, issue Mary C., William Dwight; m (3) Laura Salina FROST; Mayfield Twp; farm, blacksmith; School Director, Highway Commissioner; West Cit; Wesleyan Meth; R.

CARR, Elizabeth (ARMSTRONG), bc1828 NY, dau Robert C. and Rebecca (HALL) ARMSTRONG; d1880 IL; m William Henry CARR, issue Sarah Lucretia, George A., Robert A., Mary R.; Squaw Grove Twp; husband farm; Presby.

CARR, Thurston, bc1810 NY, son of Thurston and Bethany (BAILEY) CARR; d1878 IL; m Nancy LACKEY, issue Alonzo E., Patrick, Jane, Spencer/Samuel T., George M., Mariah, Byron T. Robert E., Pearl; Genoa, Sycamore Twps; land patent; carpenter; West Cit; Univ; R; Free Soil delegate to organizing Republican convention 1854.[24]

CARTER, Jared, b1801 VT, son of Gideon and Johanna (SIMS) CARTER; d1849; m Lydia AMES, issue Evaline, Ellen, Orlando, Clark, Lydia, Jared W., David, Rosabella, Joseph; DeKalb Twp; farm; West Cit.

CARTWRIGHT, James, bc1790 England, father-in-law to Carlos LATTIN; m (1) Ruth (PIERCE) POWELL, issue Nancy, step dau Melintha; m (2) Elizabeth, issue Sarah, Caroline; DeKalb Twp; land patent; farm; West Cit; lived in DeKalb Co bf1840.

CASE, Charles, bc1835 PA, son of Jonathan and Maria (COX) CASE; d1913 OR; m Martha M. GRASON, issue Clinton Almeron, Arthur, May, Clinton, Venus; DeKalb Twp; printer; West Cit; moved bf1860.

CHAMPLIN, David E., bc1826 OH, son of Jesse and Martha CHAMPLIN, bro to Hiram; d bf1880; m Lorinda JOSLYN, issue Martha, Emma, Elena/Elinor; Pampas/Cortland Twp; land patent; farm; Freewill Baptist Clergyman; West Cit; moved to IA bf1860.

CHAMPLIN, Hiram bc1821 OH, son of Jesse and Martha CHAMPLIN, bro to David CHAMPLIN; d af1910 IA; m (1) Lucy J. FRANCES, issue Edward, Raymond, William, Cecelia, Ida M., Francis, Jesse I./J.; m (2) Fanny C., issue Edwin J., Ranso M.; m (3) Lovinia OWEN, no issue; Pampas/Cortland Twp; land patent; farm; West Cit; moved to Iowa bf1860.

CHAMPLIN, Horace S., bc1825 NY son of John and Mary (BROOKS) CHAMPLIN; m Abigail M. WATTERMANS, issue Mary A., Abigail M., Clara, Lizzie, Carrie M., Grant, Sherman, Kate; Pampas/Cortland Twp; farm, produce dealer; Twp. Supervisor; Univ; lived in DeKalb Co. bf1840; moved to LA bf1870.

CHAPMAN, Julius, bc1813 OH; m Sarah/Sally DURHAM, issue unknown; Kingston Twp; land patent; farm; West Cit.

CHATFIELD, John, b1802 England, d1888 IL; m Julia Ann HOLMES, issue Susan S., John R. Holmes; Sycamore Twp; land patent; farm, merchant; West Cit; Univ; R.

CHEASBRO, Enos Larkin Jr., bc1824 NY, son of Enos Larkin and Sally (BURDICK) CHEASBRO, cousin to John Larkin CHEASBRO and Joseph CHEASBRO, son-in-law of Rufus and Caroline COLTON; d af1880; m Abigail Ann COLTON, issue Gustavus/Gustave A., Francis H., Evangeline R., Herman F., Carrie Larkin, Arthur "Mont"/"Mat" Fremont, John Romaine, Edward E., Adella Ann, Mabel E.; Pampas/Cortland Twp; farm; West Cit; Cong; moved to KS bf1870.

CHEASBRO, John Larkin Jr., bc1817, son of John Larkin and Orilla (FAIRBANKS) CHEASBRO, bro to Joseph CHEASBRO, cousin to Enos CHEASBRO, Jr.; m Patience Penelope WHEELER; issue Omar Delos, Amelia Addleide; Pampas/Cortland Twp; farm; West Cit.

CHEASBRO, Joseph, bc1820 NY, son of John Larkin and Orilla (FAIRBANKS) CHEASBRO, bro to John Larkin CHEASBRO, Jr., cousin to Enos CHEASBRO, Jr.; d af1900; m Antoinette JOSLYN, issue Orphenia, Lorinda, Lorenzo D.; Sycamore, Pampas/Cortland Twps; miner, farm, CW 52nd IL Inf.; West Cit.

CHEEVER, Mary B., bc1808 CT; m Ezra CHEEVER, issue Mary E.; Shabbona, Somonauk Twps; land patent; husband farm; West Cit.

CHURCH, Charles, b1799 VT, son of Nathan and Susanna (CHASE) CHURCH; d1882 IA; m (1) Sally DUTTON, issue Reuben, Polly; m (2) Calista SMITH, issue Charles Mann, Susan Minerva, Maranda E., Cyrus A., Carryl, Caroline, Eva A., Henry Nelson, Edna/Edda A.; Kingston Twp; land patent; farm; West Cit; moved to IA bf1860.

CHURCHILL, Castle, b1813 NY, son of Zenas and Almira (CASTLE) CHURCHILL, bro to David CHURCHILL; bro-in-law to Marcenus HALL and Elias HARTMAN; d1885 CA; m (1) Patty M. CROSSETT, no issue; m (2) Caroline F. (HATHAWAY) SMITH, issue Almira B, plus stepsons Ralph and Thomas Carl SMITH; Pampas/Cortland Twp; land patent; laborer, Co Surveyor, first teacher in Ohio Grove, minister; West Cit; lived in DeKalb Co bf1840; moved to Kane Co. bf1850, to IA bf1860, to CA bf1880.

CHURCHILL, David, bc1808, NY, son of Zenas and Almira (CASTLE) CHURCHILL, bro to CASTLE CHURCHILL; bro-in-law to Marcenus HALL and Elias HARTMAN; father-in-law to George KINYON; d1860 IL; m Maria PARKER, issue Marilla (whose body was later stolen by grave robbers[25]), Alfie, Hanmer/Harrison D., Caroline, Cyrus

Jasper; Pampas/Cortland Twp; land patent; farm; West Cit; lived in DeKalb Co bf1840.

CHURCHILL, Zenas, bc1784 VT, son of Samuel and Anna (CAMP) CHURCHILL; m Almira CASTLE, issue David, Ann, Sally, Castle, Daniel, Angeline, Zenas, Almira, Malinda M., Enos; one of first settlers in Pampas/Cortland Twp; land patent; farm; West Cit; lived in DeKalb Co bf1840; moved to IA bf1870.

CLARK, George, b1823 England; d1902 IL; m Amelia Louisa/Lucy MUNT, issue Lucy L., William R/E, Alpha/Alfred/Albert L., George E., Alice B.; Mayfield Twp; land patent; farm, minister; Wesleyan Meth; R; West Cit.

CLARK, James Linneus/Limon, b1837 Ireland, son of Nathaniel and Mary Ann (FLEMING) CLARK, son-in-law of James HENDERSON; d1912 IL; m Martha Harriet HENDERSON, issue Victor Irving, Maybell Eva, James Manly, John Henderson, Mary Elizabeth, Arthur Joseph Fleming; Victor, Mayfield Twps; farm, minister at Mayfield Wesleyan Meth; West Cit.

COBB, Charles E., bc1843 NY; m unknown; Sycamore Twp; apprentice printer *True Republican* newspaper.

COBB, Eliza A. (RICHMOND), b1813 VT; d1887 IL; m Charles COBB, issue Mary Wilmouth, Charles E., Henry; Sycamore Twp; housekeeper, husband blacksmith; Cong.

COLE, Tobias Britt, b1821 NY; d1883 KS; m (1) Anna COWDEN, issue Orrin, Isaac Newton, George E./Clark Graham, Laura A., Marcus D., Elliot L.; m (2) Elizabeth (SELDERS) WOOD McMILLAN, issue Anna, Ruth, Chase, Hugh Moffett, Ralph E., Abner; Somonauk Twp; farm; Presby.

COLTON, Gustavus A., b1830 VT; d1894 OH; m Phoebe BEESON, issue Alice Maud, Phoebe, Gertrude, Gustavus A., Jr., Reubie; Sycamore or DeKalb Twp; attorney, farm; Democrat delegate to organizing Republican convention 1854[26]; "one of framers of Leavenworth Constitution and noted freesoiler"[27]; moved to Paola, Lykens Co, Kansas 1858.

COLTON, Harriet HATCH, bc1806 NY/OH, sister-in-law to Rufus COLTON; m Calvin Swan COLTON, issue Amanda/Amandell, William H., Calvin Swan Jr., Julia A., Rufus, Josiah Burton, George A., Charles H.; DeKalb Twp; land patent; husband farm; Cong; lived in DeKalb Co bf1840.

COLTON, Rufus, b1802 VT, son of Abishai and Abigail Ann (DENISON) COLTON, bro to Calvin S. COLTON; father-in-law to Enos CHEESBRO; d1850 IL; m Caroline ROBINSON, issue Abishai, Abigail Ann, Job Lyman, Gustavus Adolphus, Josephine Benoise, Caroline Robinson, Clarissa Gertrude, Betsy Maria, Amra/Arunah Clark; Sycamore Twp; farm, Justice of the Peace, first Probate Justice, Co Recorder, one of first Co Commissioner, Coltonville Postmaster; West Cit; both Rufus and Caroline Cong (his father also Cong. minister); R; sympathized deeply with the "down trodden and oppressed"[28]; lived in DeKalb Co bf1840.

COOK, Randolph, bc1828 PA; son of Orin and Barbara Anne COOK; no spouse; DeKalb Twp; farm; West Cit.

COONFARE/COONFAIR, Daniel, bc1801 PA, father-in-law to Philip KING; d1878 IL; m Elizabeth DAWALT, issue John, Elizabeth, Daniel Jr., Mary A., Margaret, Phillip Byron; Mayfield Twp; farm; Wesleyan Meth; R.

COOPER, George C., b1808 NY, son of William and Sarah (CRAGE) COOPER; d1862 IL; m Elizabeth H. MOORE, issue James C., Mary C.; Paw Paw Twp; land patent; farm; West Cit; R; "Abolition sympathies."[29]

CORSER, Hiram, bc1809 NY, son of Nathan and Ann (FREEMAN) CORSER; d1871 KS; m Roxana BLACK, issue Ann Eliza, Michael Rose, Myron Merrill, Milton Lemond, Ida; Sycamore Twp; farm; West Cit; moved to KS bf1870.

CORY, Jesse, b1818 NJ, son of David and Susan (OWENS) CORY; d1881 IL; m Catharine NICHOLSON, issue Susan Rebecca, Christina "Elizabeth," Jonathan "Edgar," Andrew Agnew, William Henry, David Nicholson, Jesse/Jessie Ella, Charles Clinton; Paw Paw Twp; farm, mbr Union League; West Cit.

COSTER, Joseph C., b1815 NY, son of Richard and Rachel (COOK) COSTER; d1907 IL; m (1) W. Maria WEEKS, issue Harriet "Hattie" P., Melvin; m (2) Sophronia (REDFIELD) BATHWICK, issue Joseph Arthur, Harriet M., Susan R., Mary C., Alfred J., plus stepson Daniel BATHWICK; m (3) Mary E. EVANS; m (4) Keziah E. (OWENS) SCOTT, step-children George R., Louis K., Hugh W., Lillie F., Walter W. and Clara M. SCOTT; Squaw Grove Twp; farm, Justice of the Peace, School Director; West Cit; R; Meth.

COWEN, Marilla, bc1822 NY; d1892 WI; m Theodore Smith COWEN, issue Helen S., Sarah/Mary A., Frank Edward; Sycamore Twp; husband farm; Cong; moved to WI bf1880.

CRANDLE, Phineas, bc1822 NY, son of John and Ruth (CROSS) CRANDALL; d1913 SD; m Betsy M./Enrilla/Urilla HOOVER, issue Wesley and Leslie (twins), Ruth, Ellis, Amy M./Urilla; South Grove Twp; carpenter, farm; West Cit; moved to IA bf1870, to SD bf1900.

CRAWFORD, Alexander Jr., b1822 PA, son of Alexander and Rachel (KIDD) CRAWFORD, son-in-law of David SHURTLEFF; d af1880 IL; m Laura SHURTLEFF, issue Theresa, William "Henry," Milton "Howard," Clark "Everard," Carl "Burton"; Genoa Twp; farm, merchant, Justice of the Peace, Assessor, Genoa Village Pres.; West Cit; Cong, R; lived in DeKalb Co bf1840.

CRAWFORD, Alexander Sr., bc1800 PA, son of David and Unknown (WICKHAM) CRAWFORD; d1866 IA; m (1) Rachel KIDD, issue John, Alexander Jr., Elizabeth, Woods, Henrietta; m (2) Sarah P. REED, no issue; Sycamore Twp.; land patent; farm; Cong, one of 11 men consenting to 1848 tax assessment on personal property to construct new house of worship; West Cit; lived in DeKalb Co bf1840; moved to IA 1856.

CROSSETT, Jacob "Royal," b1812 VT, son of Jacob and Sarah (DUNNING) CROSSETT; d1885 IA; m Abigail PERKINS, issue Ellen Ruth, Martial Edson, Elza "Elzie" Augustus; Pampas/Cortland Twp; farm, Co Supt. of Schools, Co Coroner; Democrat delegate to organizing Republican convention 1854[30]; Meth Episcopal; moved to IA bf1870.

CUTLER, Silas M., b1813 NY; d1900 IL; m Jane SUTTEN; Sycamore Twp; laborer, carpenter; Univ.

DAVIS, Albert bc1819 Canada; d bf1870; m Martha ROBINSON, issue Jordon, Levi, Nelson, Lucy, Mary Clara, Jason, Allie Emily; Clinton, Victor Twps; land patent; farm; West Cit.

DAVIS, Ruel Stephen, b1816 MA, son of Stephen and Anna (WADSWORTH) DAVIS; d1887 IL; m Ellen WYMAN, issue Orvil D., Gustavus Vasa, Cazneau W., Ella A., Edna Julia; Sycamore Twp; clergyman, shoemaker; Univ; wife Cong.

DAVIS, William, b1802 MA son of Joseph and Judith (BRIGHTMAN) DAVIS; d1890 IL, bro-in-law to Major

DENNIS; m (1) Mary "Polly" WILSON, issue Clemmy, Willie, Lou; m (2) Eliza DENNIS, issue William, Eliza, Mary Ann, George W., Amy; Somonauk Twp; land patent; whaler, farm, one of first Co Grand Jurors; West Cit; Presby; lived in DeKalb Co bf1840.

DECKER, Demmon, bc1827 NY, son of William H. and Esther DECKER, son-in-law of Peter and Lucretia (CARPENTER) NICHOLS; d af1880; m Hannah NICHOLS, issue Ida Louisa, Eva G./Genie E., Elizabeth/Edith A., Lorenzo D., Juliette, Leona B.; Mayfield Twp; farm; one of first Trustees for Mayfield Wesleyan Meth Ch.

DEITZ/DEETS, David, bc1813 NY; m Gertrude, issue John, Albert; Paw Paw Twp; farm; West Cit.

DENNIS, Major, bc1813 RI, son of Major and Eunice (KING) DENNIS, bro-in-law to William DAVIS and to Jacob M. HALL; d1856 IL; m Mary A. HARMON, issue Weighstel O./Waite A., Shepherd, Rebecca, William A.; Somonauk Twp; land patent; farm; West Cit; lived in DeKalb Co bf1840.

DEYOE, Peter M., bc1827 NY, son of William P. and Agnes DEYOE; dc1895 MI; m Emeline MACK, issue Duane, Agnes C., Walter; South Grove Twp; farm; West Cit; moved to IA bf1880.

DEYOE, William P., bc1801 NY; d1889 MI; m (1) Elizabeth HOGEBOOM, issue seven children including Peter M., Sophroma Jane; m (2) Agnes S. BECKER, issue six children including Polly A., Eliza Caroline, Elizabeth, Sarah Marie (unclear which children belong to whom); m (3) Hannah LANCEY, adopted Henry NORTON; South Grove Twp; land patent; farm; West Cit; "well-known conductor on underground railway"[31]; moved to MI c1863.

DICK, John H., b1810 Scotland; d1894 IL; m Eliza Meriam CARD, issue Eliza, Jane, Ann, John, Andrew Kenneth, Joseph, Mary; Mayfield Twp; land patent; farm; West Cit; Presby, then Wesleyan Meth; R; home a station for UGRR.[32]

DICKSON, John, bc1820 Scotland; Paw Paw Twp; farm, laborer; West Cit.

DOBBIN, David Miller, b1813 Ireland, son of William and Margaret (ANDREW) DOBBIN, bro-in-law to Robert GRAHAM, James W. McALLISTER and Nancy A. (GRAHAM) FERGUSON; also son-in-law to Jonathan and Ann (EDGAR) FRENCH, bro-in-law to William and James W. FRENCH; d1898 KS; m (1) Charity Irvine GRAHAM, issue William John, Mary Jane; m (2) Mary Jane FRENCH, issue Margaret Ann, James Blair, m (3) Eliza STOTT, issue Sarah Mary, Eliza Jane, Agnes Isabella, Emma; Somonauk, Squaw Grove Twps; land patent; cooper, farm; West Cit, Somonauk; David one of first Elders and both David and Mary Jane charter mbrs Somonauk Presby Ch.

DOUGLASS, Ira, b1814 NY, son of Joseph and Hannah (SYMONDS) DOUGLASS; d1888 IL; m (1) Cyrena GOODRICH, issue Sarah, Ariadna C., Dilana L., Caroline "Carrie"; m (2) Hannah J. POWELL, issue Cyrus A., Ella V., William H., Ira W.; Mayfield Twp; farm; West Cit; Meth, first meeting of Mayfield Meth. held in his home; R; lived in DeKalb Co bf1840.

DOW, Agrippa, b1794 NH, son of Salmon and Luna (BENTON) DOW, father-in-law to Franklin CAMP; d1888 IL; m Polly STORRS, issue Roswell, Eliza B., Augustus Storrs, Julia Augusta, Mary Frances, Lewis, Laura Ann, Clara Benton; Mayfield Twp; land patent; farm, twp. supervisor; Univ and Cong affiliation; R; one of "aging Abolitionists" who attended David West's 80th birthday party.[33]

DOW, Kimball, b1813 VT, son of Jonathan and Polly (WOLCOTT) DOW, cousin to Agrippa DOW; d1897 KS; m1837 Euphrasia HISCOX, issue Polly E., Harriett E., Clement Kimball; Sycamore Twp; land patent; merchant, Co Justice, mbr 1849 committee to confront grave robbers, built Sons of Temperance Hall; charter mbr Sycamore Univ Church; first Secretary of DeKalb Co Anti-slavery Society;[34] political candidate for Liberty Party; West Cit; moved to KS c1864.

DOW, Levias/Lavius T., bc1817 VT, son of Jonathan and Polly (WOLCOTT) DOW; bro to Kimball DOW, cousin to Agrippa DOW, bro-in-law to Harry A. JOSLYN; d bf1860; m Aristeen JOSLYN, issue Mary, Augusta, Fillmore L.; Pampas/Cortland Twp; land patent; farm; charter mbr in Sycamore Univ Ch; lived in DeKalb Co bf1840.

DOW, Roswell, b1824 NH, son of Agrippa and Polly (STORRS) DOW; d1901 IL; m Theresa Emilia RICHARDS (step-dau of Ellsworth P. ROSE), issue Thirza, Flora Jeannette "Nettie," Edmund Terry, Mary E., Elsie A., Ray Storrs; Sycamore Twp; teacher, Co Treasurer 1855, farm; Cong; R; aided the UGRR.[35]

DRAKE, Hiram, bc1820 VT, son of Abijah and Abigail C. (SMITH) DRAKE; d1899 IL; m Maria WALROD, issue Sarah Ann, Helen Jane, Marshall Orlando, Hiram Augustus, John Franklin, James Edward, Elva A., Milla A.; Mayfield Twp; land patent; farm; West Cit; Wesleyan Meth.

DUFFEY, James, bc1808 PA, son of James DUFFEY; d1872 IL; m (1) Lydia BELL, issue John, Robert, Elizabeth A., MacKintire, Sylvanus, Nancy J., Mary E.; m (2) Martha Maria JORDAN, issue Eliza E., May, Merritt, Charles, Otis, Susan, Marjorie, plus stepson George; DeKalb Twp; farm; West Cit.

DURHAM, Henry, b1798 NY son of Michael and Sarah (CHAMPION) DURHAM; d1855 IL; m Losina "Jane" WAGER, issue Norman, Sarah, Sabrina, William Rochester, Ersala/Ursala M., Rachel, Ethan A., Caroline, Alexander Henry, Milton, Sarah; Genoa Twp; land patent; farm, one of first Co Supervisors; West Cit; lived in DeKalb Co bf1840.

DUSTIN, Daniel, b1820 VT, son of John Knight and Sallie (THOMPSON) DUSTIN; d1892 MO; m (1) Isabelle TAPLIN, issue Emma A., Electa J., William G.; m (2) Elmira E. PAULY, issue Zada Belle; Sycamore Twp; teacher, Physician, Pharmacist; Mbr of California State legislature before moving to Sycamore; DeKalb Co Clerk, Treasurer, Circuit Clerk and Recorder; 1890 U.S. Assistant Treasurer under President Harrison; Major 8th IL Cavalry, Brigadier General 105th IL Inf; Cong; R; "thorough antislavery man."[36]

DUTTON, Everell Fletcher, b1838 NH, son of William Parker and Lucinda Jane (BLOOD) DUTTON; d1900 IL; m Rosina Adelpha PAINE, issue George Everell, William Paine; Sycamore Twp; Deputy Co Clerk, Co Circuit Clerk and Recorder, CW Brig. General 105th IL Inf; Univ; R; received reports from his father about Kansas and Nebraska issue, and "resolved that if an attempt was made to overthrow the Union he would stand loyally for its support."[37]

DUTTON, Henry Turner, b1826 NH, son of William P. and Mary (TURNER) DUTTON, bro to William Parker DUTTON; d1909 IL; m Elizabeth Zilpha BLOOD, issue Ella M., Ernest S., Florence M.; Sycamore Twp; husband laborer; both Henry and Elizabeth Cong.

DUTTON, Rosina Adelpha (PAINE), b1844 NY, dau Harmon and Clarinda (VAN HORN) PAINE, dau-in-law of William Parker DUTTON; d1915 IL; m Everell Fletcher

DUTTON, issue George Everell, William Paine; Sycamore Twp; husband Circuit Clerk, Brig. General 105th IL Inf; Univ.

DUTTON, William Parker, b1817 NH, son of William P. and Mary (TURNER) DUTTON, bro to Henry T. DUTTON; d1888 KS; m (1) Lucinda Jane BLOOD, issue Emily, Everell Fletcher, Willard Joel, Charles Edward; m (2) Sarah BANNITER, no issue; Sycamore Twp; farm, merchant, Sycamore Postmaster, Sheriff, Treasurer of Lykens/Miami Co, KS, mbr of Kansas state constitutional convention; returned to Illinois after the Civil War; Son Everell was General in 105th IL Inf; Univ; D turned R; antislavery[38]; lived in KS 1857–1871.

EARL, Rhoda (BARBER), bc1796 VT; d1882; m Lawson EARL, issue Eveline M., Harriet M., Susan L., Lawson E., William D., John B., Silas Newton, Joel T., Daniel W.; DeKalb Twp; farm; West Cit.

EASTABROOKS, Decatur Moses, bc1824 PA, son of John and Elizabeth (HOWARD) EASTABROOKS, bro of John Theophilus Bradbury and James Lawrence EASTABROOKS; d1890 IL; m (1) Mary WOOD, issue Carlos, Sarah; m (2) Elvira CALL, issue Selden, Mary; m (3) Mary Ann DAY; land patent; Sycamore Twp; farm; West Cit; lived in DeKalb Co bf1840.

EASTABROOKS, James Lawrence, b1818 NY, son of John and Elizabeth (HOWARD) EASTABROOKS, bro of John Theophilus Bradbury and Decatur EASTABROOKS; d1902 IL; m Elizabeth C. CONE, issue Mary E., John H., Archibald C., Julia A., Delia E., James A.; Squaw Grove Twp; farm; West Cit; Meth and Presby; lived in DeKalb Co bf1840.

EASTABROOKS, John Theophilus "Bradbury" Chandler, b1808 CT/RI, son of John and Elizabeth (HOWARD) EASTABROOKS, bro of James Lawrence and Decatur Moses EASTABROOKS; d1884 OR; m (1) Clarinda Adeline BROWNING, issue Alfred, Adeline, Eliza Emaline, Franklin, John, Charles Lee, Lucy, William John, Howard, Emily Irene; m (2) Elizabeth OLDS; Somonauk Twp; farm, Somonauk Postmaster; West Cit; lived in DeKalb Co bf1840; moved to Kane Co, IL bf1850, to OR bf1860.

EASTON, Henry/Harvey, bc1824 NY; m Agnes J./L. (THOMPSON?), issue Ida R.; Somonauk Twp; farm, grocer; Presby; moved to MO bf1880.

EATON, John, bc1823 OH, son of Isaac and Philinda (ROOT) EATON; m Susan Samantha CRANDALL, issue Arline "Arlie" F., John F.; Pampas/Cortland Twp; farm; West Cit; moved to KS bf1870, to CO bf1880.

EDDY, William Henry, b1802 NY, son of John and Mary (AIKEN) EDDY; d1868 IL; m Eunice B. METCALF, issue Sarah Ann, Henry William, Oscar Singleton, Agnes C./Caroline Ann; Somonauk Twp; land patent; farm, insurance agent; West Cit; Presby; home a station on UGRR.[39]

EDWARDS, Pierpont, bc1807 NY, son of Ogden and Harriet (PENFIELD) EDWARDS; d1881 IL; m Miranda/Myranda M. WHEELER, issue Orin D., E.H., William F.; Paw Paw Twp; land patent; builder and contractor, farm, one of first Co Supervisors; West Cit; Presby; R; Free Soil delegate to organizing Republican convention 1854,[40] Abolitionist,[41] home a station on UGRR.[42]

ELLIOTT, Minerva (LEONARD), bc1831 OH, dau Isaac and Jane (FINLEY) LEONARD; d c1862, IL; m Joshua ELLIOTT, issue Sarah Jane, Mary; Pampas/Cortland Twp; husband carpenter; West Cit.

ELLIS, John, bc1812 England; m Betsey, issue unknown; Paw Paw Twp; farm; West Cit.

ELLWOOD, Abraham, b1792 NY, son of Isaac and Magdalena (SNYDER/SCHNEIDER) ELLWOOD; d1872 IL; m Sarah "Sally" DE LONG, issue Nancy, Malinda, Chauncey, Eliza, Reuben, Alonzo, Livingston, Hiram, James Edmund, Alida L., Isaac Leonard (one of the inventors of barbed wire); Sycamore Twp; cooper; Univ.

ELLWOOD, Alonzo, b1823 NY, son of Abraham and Sarah (DE LONG) ELLWOOD; d1872 IL; m (1) Angeline, no issue; m (2) Mary Maud BAKER, issue Leana Maud, Glen Baker, Ella Baker; Sycamore Twp; hardware, drugs, grocery merchant, Assessor United States Revenue; Univ.

ELLWOOD, James "Edmund," b1831 NY, son of Abraham and Sarah (DE LONG) ELLWOOD; d1907 IL; m Lodeski H. FELLOWS, issue Sarah "Sadie" A., James B., Dustin Daniel; Sycamore Twp; grocer, druggist; Univ.

ELMER, Nathan, b1795 VT, son of Benjamin and Sarah (GOSS) ELMER; d1864 IL; m (1) Tamar HINDS, issue Phoebe H., William, Levi, Asahel, Harriet, Celestia, Phebe H, Lavinia, Minerva, Nathan, Lorinda; m (2) Lucinda; Clinton Twp; farm; West Cit.

EMERICK, Marcella Mariah (WARNER), b1835 NY; d1873, IL; m Warren EMERICK, issue step-children George William and Edward John, children Perna Maria, Warren Marcellus, Irving Grant, Benton Elsworth, Linden Ray; Sycamore Twp; husband farm; Cong; moved to WI bf1860, back to IL bf1870.

ERWIN/IRWIN, Samuel, bc1832 NY, son of James and Maria (GOTT) ERWIN; d af1870; no spouse; Clinton Twp; farm; West Cit; moved to Lee Co, IL bf1860, back to DeKalb Co bf1870.

FAIRBANK(S), Joseph, bc1766 MA; m Mary Ann, issue Polly; Pampas/Cortland Twp; West Cit.

FAREWELL/FARWELL, George G., bc1826 VT; m Alice, issue Laura E., George S., Ira S.; Mayfield Twp; farm; West Cit.

FARNSWORTH, David, b c1813 MA, son of David and Sophia (HOWE) FARNSWORTH; d bf1876 IL; m Hannah BROWN, issue William H., Ada F., Flora L., David "DeMay"; Sycamore Twp.; carpenter, farm; West Cit; Univ.

FAY, Horace Wright, b1801 NY, son of Jonathan and Rhoda (WHITE) FAY, bro to Wells FAY; d1864 MS; buried at Vicksburg, MS; m (1) Roxanna EATON, issue Edwin Horace, Mahala P., Mary Juliet, Rhoda L./S., Frances Cordelia; m (2) Alida ADAMS, issue Julia Cordelia; m (3) Margaret A. STIPP, issue Alice, Charles "Walter," Frank Leslie, Perley S., plus step-children William "Herman" STIPP and Georgetta STIPP; Squaw Grove Twp; land patent, farm, Co Surveyor, second IL State Representative from DeKalb Co, itinerant minister; musician in CW 8th IL Inf (at age 60), later chaplain 1st Mississippi Heavy Artillery; Democrat delegate to organizing Republican convention 1854;[43] lived in DeKalb Co bf1840.

FAY, Wells Alvirus, bc1814 NY, son of Jonathan and Rhoda (WHITE) FAY, bro to Horace Wright FAY; d1897 IL; m Harriet Emilet LAY, issue Emily/Emma F., Jane/Jennie L., Alcott W./N., Ida Cordelia, Ashley H.; Squaw Grove Twp; land patent; farm, Justice of the Peace; West Cit; Meth; R; lived in DeKalb Co bf1840.

FENTON, Merritt, bc1809 NY; m Eliza TURNER, issue Harriet Anna "Ann"; Shabbona Twp; farm; West Cit; moved to Kane Co, IL, bf1860.

FERGUSON, James, b1798 NY, son-in-law of John W. and Margaret (IRVINE) GRAHAM; d1872 IL; m Nancy A. GRAHAM, issue Robert, Nancy Maxwell, Margaret, William Connell; Somonauk Twp; Presby.

FERGUSON, Robert, bc1829 Scotland son of Sherman FERGUSON; d1911 IL; m Elizabeth GIBSON, issue Mary Ann, Janette, Eliza J., David, Robert, Elizabeth, Hattie, Eva Mawde; Squaw Grove, Cortland Twps; farm; West Cit; Presby.

FINLEY, David F., bc1798 VA, son of John and Sarah (MOORE) FINLEY; d1872 IL; m Mary LOWRIE, issue Sallie Ann, Mary J., John C., Elizabeth/Margaret; Pampas/Cortland Twp; land patent; farm, one of first Co Supervisors; West Cit.

FIRKINS, Asahel, b1819 NY, son of George and Lydia (CHAPPEL) FIRKINS; d1856 IL; m Harriet MILLER, issue Marietta, William, John, Harriet A., Emma F., Josephine, George A.; Paw Paw Twp; land patent; farm; Meth; "avowed Abolitionist."[44]

FLINT, Mary, bc1814 PA; d af1900; m John FLINT, issue Lewis, John H., James C., William G., Charles V., Chauncey D., Elizabeth J., Emma J., Frank; Sycamore, Genoa Twps; husband farm; Cong.

FORDHAM, Melissa (FAIRCLO), bc1827 NJ, dau Isaiah and Sophia Munday (HUGG) FAIRCLO; d1860 IL; m Fitz Henry FORDHAM, issue Melissa C.; Sycamore Twp; Cong.

FORDHAM, William, bc1816 NY; m Caroline A./E., issue Josephine, Florence, John Denniston, William L.; Sycamore Twp; land patent; attorney; Co Recorder, mbr of 1854 Resolution Committee for DeKalb Co Anti-Nebraska (antislavery) Meeting[45]; moved to MI bf1860, to TN bf1880.

FOSTER, Moses Cleveland, bc1805 OH, son of Nathaniel Watson and Esther (SMITH/CLEVELAND) FOSTER; dc1890 CO; m Anna Burns ROBB, issue Joseph Watson, Thomas Polk, Robert R., Rebecca, James Robb, Esther Elizabeth, Harriet Ann, Mary C.; Kingston Twp; farm; West Cit; lived in DeKalb Co bf1840; moved to CO 1882.

FRENCH, Alexander bc1823 NY, son of Jonathan and Ann (EDGAR) FRENCH, bro to William, Mary Jane and James, bro-in-law to David Miller DOBBIN, second cousin to Rensselaer W. FRENCH; m Eliza Jane THOMPSON, issue William "Martin," Joseph Alexander, Jane Anna, James H., Mary Alice; Somonauk Twp; land patent; farm; charter mbr Somonauk Presby Ch; moved to OR bf1860, to CA bf1870.

FRENCH, Avery, bc1790 NY, son of William and Elizabeth (AVERY) FRENCH; d1866 OH; m Betsey MARTIN, issue Catherine J., Ersula, Louisa, Lucinda, Mary, Prudence, William Martin, Avery Martin, Cornelia Elizabeth, James Marcus, Sluman Morgan, Charlotte, Abiel/Abel Marlow; Shabbona Twp; farm; West Cit; moved to OH bf1866.

FRENCH, James W., b1826 NY, son of Jonathan and Ann (EDGAR) FRENCH, bro to Alexander, William and Mary Jane, bro-in-law to David Miller DOBBIN, second cousin to Rensselaer W. FRENCH; d1890 IA; m Mary Ann SKINNER, issue Susan, Alexander Skinner, Anna Elizabeth, William J.; Somonauk, South Grove Twps; land patent; farm; West Cit; Presby.

FRENCH, Jonathan, b1781 NY, son of David and Susanna (BLAIR) FRENCH; d1849 IL; father-in-law to Isabel (BEVERIDGE) FRENCH and to David Miller DOBBIN; d1848 IL; m Ann EDGAR, issue Elizabeth, Ann, William, Jonathan B., Alexander, Susanna, Mary Jane, Sarah, James W.; Somonauk Twp; farm; Jonathan, Ann, plus Alexander and Sara all charter mbrs Somonauk Presby Ch.

FRENCH, Rensselaer W., b1814 NY, son of John Blair and Robena (McMICKEN) FRENCH; d1902 IL; m Nancy POLLOCK, issue John Pollock, Robena Jane, Mary Anne and Albert Collins; Clinton Twp; land patent; farm, minister; organized Somonauk Presby Ch 1846,[46] served as their minister 1848–1860; West Cit.

FRENCH, William, b1811 NY, son of Jonathan and Ann (EDGAR) FRENCH, bro to Alexander, James and Mary Jane, son-in-law of George BEVERIDGE, bro-in-law to David Miller DOBBIN; second cousin to Rensselaer W. FRENCH; d1880 IL; m Isabel BEVERIDGE, issue Ellen Ann, Mary Elizabeth, Sarah Agnes, John Blair, George Beveridge, Andrew L., Jeannette; Somonauk Twp; land patent; farm; wife Isabel charter mbr. Somonauk Presby Ch.

FURMAN/FIRMAN/FREEMAN, John, bc1796 NY, son of Aaron and Phebe (COE) FURMAN; d af1860; m Mary E., issue Jane E., Coe, Emma, Juliet; Somonauk Twp; land patent; farm, Twp. Supervisor; West Cit; lived in DeKalb Co bf1840.

FURNESS, Herman, bc1804 MA, son of Benjamin and Rosannah (ROGERS) FURNESS, bro-in-law to Kimball and Levias DOW; d af1870 KS; m Sophronia DOW, issue Orlando, Margaret, Jane, George, Lavinia, Herman, Harriet; Sycamore Twp; farm, grocer, Co Sheriff 1850, CW Co. C, 105th IL Inf; never arrested UGRR activists; moved to KS bf1870.

GALLAHER, Benjamin, bc1808 PA, son of James and Margaret (RAMSEY) GALLAHER; d1895 IA; m Jane Boyd FULLERTON, issue William Fullerton, Eli, Mary Elizabeth, John Adam, James Monroe, Richard Isaiah, Hugh C., Caroline Viola, Mary, David Wilmont, Sarah A.; Monroe Twp, Ogle Co, IL; land patent; farm; West Cit; moved to Ogle Co, IL bf1850.

GAMBLE, Alexander, bc1815 Ireland; d1863 TN; m Henrietta/Euretta, issue Harriet E., Martha A., James A., Charles E., Samuel, George W., Nathaniel K., Adoniram C.; Afton Twp; farm, minister, CW 105th IL Inf, Co. K; West Cit.

GAMMON, Ansel Elder, bc1824 ME, son of Samuel and Malinda GAMMON; d1916 CA; m (1) Sophia Henrietta WILBUR, issue, John Preston, Malinda, Marinda Mary, Jennie; m (2) Maria B. WISE; lived in LaSalle Co, IL, P.O. at Shabbbona Grove, DeKalb Co; land patent; farm, hardware merchant, laborer, CW 52nd IL Vols.; West Cit; moved to Livingston Co, IL bf1870, to ME bf1880, to CA bf1900.

GANDY, George Washington, b1804 NJ, son of Henry Harris and Tamson (GARRISON) GANDY, half-bro to Henry Harrison GANDY; d1854 IL; m Mary MEACHAM, issue Emeline, Lydia D., Sophronia, Elias, Diana, Mary Jane, Cecilia; one of first settlers in Pampas/Cortland Twp; land patent; farm; West Cit; Meth Episcopal; lived in DeKalb Co bf1840.

GANDY, Henry Harrison, bc1810 OH, son of Henry Harris and Sarah "Sally" (HARRIS) GANDY, half-bro to George Washington GANDY; d1891 IL; m Lucinda MEACHAM, issue Joseph, Julia A., Marcus, Jerusha L., Matilda Jane, Francis Marion, Andrew J.; Pampas/Cortland Twp; farm; charter mbr Sycamore Univ Ch; lived in DeKalb Co bf1840.

GARDNER, George, bc1795 CT, son of Jabez and Katharine GARDNER; d1857 IL; m Harriet AVERY, issue David M., George "Nelson," Mary A., Henry; Mayfield Twp; land patent; farm; West Cit.

GARDNER, Ira, bc1811 PA; d af1870; m Catharine; issue Charles, Frederick, Maria, Herman, Ira G., Eugene; Somonauk Twp; farm; West Cit; moved to Cook Co, IL bf1870.

GILBERT, Eli B., b1822 NY, son of Abner and Betsey (BALCOM) GILBERT; d1895 IL; m Lois Anna/Louisiana NEEDHAM, issue, Josephine L., Betsey Viola M., Jessie Luella E.; DeKalb Twp; carpenter, attorney, Justice of the Peace; R; "advocated the election of the celebrated Mr. Lincoln."[47]

GLIDDEN, Joseph Farwell, b1813 NH, son of David and Polly (HURD) GLIDDEN, bro to Josiah "Williard" GLIDDEN; d1906 IL; m (1) Clarissa FOSTER, issue Virgil, Homer, Clarissa; m (2) Lucinda WARNE, issue Elva/Elvira Frances; DeKalb Twp; farm, inventor of barbed wire, Co Supervisor, Co Sheriff 1852; never arrested UGRR activists.

GLIDDEN, Josiah "Willard," b1822 NY, son of David and Polly (HURD) GLIDDEN, bro to Joseph Farwell GLIDDEN an inventor of barbed wire; dc1876 IL; m Mary Powell McCONNELL, issue Lizzie Mary, Clara/Cora Louisa, Annie Laurie, Bertha McConnell, John Willard; DeKalb Twp; land patent; farm; West Cit; Univ.

GOBLE, Lucy Ann (SEAVY/SEAVEY) PARTRIDGE, bc1818 NH, dau William and Samantha SEAVY/SEAVEY; m (1) Charles Paine PARTRIDGE, issue Lucy A., Charles S., William Seavy, Zelotes Bingham, Augusta W./Arista M.; m (2) Jonathan Pollard GOBLE, no issue; Sycamore Twp; Cong.

GOOD, William, bc1835 England, son of Titus and Elizabeth GOOD; Squaw Grove Twp; farm laborer; West Cit; moved bf1870.

GORE, Chester, bc1816 MA; d bf1870; m Cynthia M. GLEASON, issue Julia Ann, Henry H.; Mayfield Twp; farm; Cong.

GORE, Darius, b1814 MA, son of John and Anna (CARPENTER) GORE; d1873 IL; m (1) Charlotte Holbrook BRUCE; m (2) Lucretia (MASON) DEAN, issue Mary C., Carrie D., Anna L., Lucy Jane; m (3) Caroline J. MCARTHUR; Sycamore Twp; minister First Cong Ch, Sycamore, 1853–1860; "We hold that this sin [slaveholding] is the sin of our nation & the sooner individuals as Christians & the sooner churches as bodies get wholly clear of it the better."[48]

GRAHAM, Houten, bc1812 OH; d IL; m Mary McDONNAL, issue William, Columbus, Mary, Eliza, Ellen, Sarah, Martha, Harriet, Augusta, Margaret; Mayfield Twp; land patent; farm; Wesleyan Meth; lived in DeKalb Co bf1840.

GRAHAM, Isaac, b1817 NY, son of George & Anna (COWDEN) GRAHAM; d1893 IL; m Nancy LIVINGSTON, issue Edward, Alexander, William John, Mary Jane, Anna; Somonauk Twp; farm; West Cit; Presby, Elder in Somonauk Presby Ch.

GRAHAM, James, b1836 OH, son of George D. and Amelia Dean (SEELY) GRAHAM, nephew of Robert GRAHAM; d1870 IL; m Sarah McALLISTER, dau James and Jane (DOBBIN) McALLISTER, issue Jennie Millie, George Dean; Squaw Grove Twp; farm; Presby.

GRAHAM, Robert B., b1805 NY, son of John and Margaret (IRVINE) GRAHAM, father-in-law of James W. McALLISTER Jr.; d1891 IL; m Sarah WILLIAMSON, issue Margaret, Mary Ann, Andrew, Russell, James; Somonauk, Victor Twps; land patent; farm; West Cit; Presby; lived in DeKalb Co bf1840.

GRAHAM, Thomas, b1828 OH, son of William GRAHAM, grandson of George & Anna (COWDEN) GRAHAM, nephew of Isaac GRAHAM; d1902 KS; m Margaret Jane TAYLOR, issue William Marshall, Martha Eliza, David Wilson, Andrew Harper, May, Albert; Victor Twp; farm; Elder in Somonauk Presby Ch.

GREEN, Alanson B., bc1809 NY or PA, son of Benjamin and Joanna (REYNOLDS) GREEN; d af1880 IL; m Sybil DEAN, issue Sally, Dewitt Clinton, Benjamin F., Jane Elizabeth, Nancy; Kingston, Genoa Twps; lawyer, farm; West Cit.

GREGORY, Ezra "Starr," b1803 CT, son of Joseph and Sarah (COZIER) GREGORY, bro-in-law to Jeremiah L. and Benjamin BROWN; d1887 IL; m Jane BROWN, issue William James, Ann Mariah, Mary Jane, Judith, Phebe Ruth, Starr Cozier, William Green; Genoa Twp; land patent; farm, Twp Treasurer; West Cit; no official church affiliation, Meth tendency; home a station for UGRR,[49] only Abolitionist vote cast for James G. Birney for President 1840,[50] 1843 elected one of two Vice-Presidents of DeKalb County Anti-slavery Society,[51] Free-soil delegate to convention organizing Republican Party 1854;[52] lived in DeKalb Co bf1840.

HALL, Amasa, b1818 NY, son of William Clark and Dorcas (THURSTON) HALL, bro to Jacob M. HALL; d af1880 IL; m Mercy MEAD, issue, Louisa, Lucinda, Jacob Myron, Lurana Melissa, Henry A. Charles Wesley, Melvina Annette, Ida Eva; Somonauk Twp; farm; West Cit.

HALL, Ephraim, b1808 CT, son of David Moss and Mindwell (BEECH) HALL, bro-in-law to Justus PRESTON; d1896 IL; m Caroline HALL, issue Cornelia, Ruth, Franklin, Eunice, Henry; Sycamore Twp; land patent; farm, Justice of the Peace, Road Commissioner, 1837 hosted first July 4th celebration in DeKalb Co., one of financial subscribers for first courthouse; West Cit; "stalwart supporter of the Republican party"[53]; lived in DeKalb Co bf1840.

HALL, Jacob M., b1815 NY son of William Clark and Dorcas (THURSTON) HALL, bro to Amasa HALL, bro-in-law to Major DENNIS and William DAVIS; d1890 IL; m Lurena/Lurana DENNIS, issue Dorcas, Elvina/Alvira, Sarah Ann, Myron Clark, John W. H.; Somonauk Twp; farm; West Cit; Meth; lived in DeKalb Co bf1840.

HALL, Marcenus, bc1811 NY, son of Elihu and Nancy (MAXON) HALL, son-in-law of Zenas CHURCHILL, bro-in-law of David and Castle CHURCHILL; d 1906 OK; m Angeline CHURCHILL, issue Emery Esmond, Alta Malinda, Florina/Philina, Florilla Roseanne, Marcenus Jr., Guy Benson, Alonzo E/A.; Pampas/Cortland Twp; land patent; farm; West Cit; lived in DeKalb Co bf1840; moved to IA bf1870.

HAMLIN, Erastus, bc1779 CT, son of Jabez and Dorcas (BARANES) HAMLIN; d1863 IL; m Harriett TOBY, issue Milton Pratt, John Randolph, Adoline, Orville, Julia, Sophronia, Jane Aderline, Sophronia "Harriet," Mary Ann, Caroline, Edward Stowe, Eveline; Sycamore Twp; founding mbrs of First Cong Ch, with wife and dau Mary Ann, Caroline and Harriet, one of first ch Trustees; moved to Byron, IL, returned to Sycamore and reaffirmed antislavery belief for re-admission to First Cong Ch; lived in DeKalb Co bf1840.

HAMLIN, Joseph J., bc1810 CT, son of David and Hannah (VEELER) HAMLIN; d1899 IL; m Mercia "Mercy" TYRRELL, issue Almond, Horace, Hannah, Ira Wood, Charles, Elizabeth, Benjamin, Mary E., Sarah J.; Somonauk Twp; land patent; farm, blacksmith; West Cit; Meth.

HAMMOND, Elias Mathewson, b1817 NY, son of Lebbeus and Cynthia P. (MATHEWSON) HAMMOND, bro of James "Monroe" and Jacob Miller HAMMOND; m Adelia, issue Charles, William; Sycamore Twp; land patent; farm; West Cit; Cong.

HAMMOND, Jacob Miller, b1819 NY, son of Lebbeus and Cynthia P. (MATHEWSON) HAMMOND, bro to Elias Mathewson and James "Monroe" HAMMOND; d1883 IL; m Melissa Jane CALKINS, issue Adelbert C., Frank A., Fred; Kingston Twp; farm; West Cit.

HAMMOND, James "Monroe," b1820 NY, son of Lebbeus and Cynthia P. (MATHEWSON) HAMMOND, bro to Elias Mathewson and Jacob Miller HAMMOND; d1900 MI; m Rebecca L. STOWE, issue Edward "DeWitt," Frank, Park; Sycamore Twp; land patent; farm; West Cit; Cong, one of 11 men consenting to 1848 tax assessment on personal property to construct new house of worship; moved to NY bf1860.

HARNARD, Angeline, bc1840, OH; m unknown; Sycamore Twp; typesetter *True Republican* newspaper.

HARNED, Edmund B., b1829 OH son of Hosea and Rosetta (BROWN) HARNED; d1897 IL; m Susan H. SIVWRIGHT, issue Eugene A., Rosetta, Merton R., Armanella P. "Nellie," James E., Susan A.; Mayfield, Sycamore Twps; farm; Wesleyan Meth.

HARPER, James B., b1819 NY, son of James and Elizabeth (BLACK) HARPER, bro to Thomas, Robert and William HARPER; d af1880; m (1) Elizabeth SMILEY, issue Mary E., Dewitt C., Andrew G., Thomas A., Alanson C.; m (2) Elizabeth COMINS, issue James H., Alice E., William, Robert, Mary J., Margaret A., Charles; Paw Paw Twp; farm; Ross Grove Presby Ch, then Somonauk Presby Ch.

HARPER, Robert b1813 NY, son of James and Elizabeth HARPER, bro to Thomas, William and James HARPER; d1882; m (1) Ann OSWALD, issue James, George, Malcolm; m (2) Ann Anderson, issue Malcolm C., Anne Mary, Alice M., Robert B.; Paw Paw Twp; farm; Elder at Ross Grove Presby Ch, then Somonauk Presby Ch.

HARPER, Thomas, b1811 Ireland, son of James and Elizabeth HARPER, bro to Robert, William and James HARPER; d1897 KS, buried IL; m (1) Sarah HOLT, issue Norman; m (2) Harriet "Hattie" BECKER; Paw Paw Twp; land patent; farm; Ross Grove Presby Ch, then Somonauk Presby Ch; moved to KS bf1880.

HARPER, William, b1815 NY, son of James and Elizabeth HARPER, bro to Thomas, Robert and James HARPER; d1881 IL; m Sarah IRWIN, issue Mary J., William, Thomas, James, John K.; Paw Paw Twp; farm; Ross Grove Presby Ch, then Somonauk Presby Ch.

HARRINGTON, Caroline, b1816 MA; d1879 IL; m (1) Ruffus HARRINGTON, issue Mary E., Jane C., Julia Ann, Laura Elizabeth; m (2) Harrison H. ROWE; Sycamore Twp; housekeeper, Rufus farmed, Harrison was store clerk; Cong.

HARRINGTON, Dr. James Franklin, b1807 NY or Canada son of Lot and Sarah (SAGE) HARRINGTON, bro-in-law to Morris WALROD; d1893 IL; m (1) Charlotte WALROD, issue Diana, William, Joseph, George L., James F., Susan E., Nelson R., Mark Walrod, Mary S., Franklin; m (2) Susan (DAYTON) WYMAN, widow of Ralph WYMAN; Sycamore Twp; physician, farm, chairman first Co Board of Supervisors, 1846-47 mbr of IL Legislature, Co Supt. of Schools, Democrat delegate to organizing Republican convention 1854[54]; Meth.

HARRISON, George, bc1810 England son of James and Ann HARRISON; d1867 IL; m Elizabeth MASSINGHAM, issue Uriah Samuel, Sargeant Edmund, Walter Stephen, Morrison, Russell James, George Franklin, Henry Pliny, Charles Morrison, Mary Emily; DeKalb, Pampas/Cortland Twps; farm; West Cit.

HARRISON, John L., bc1808 NY; d af1885 IA; m Abagail/Abagale STANLEY, issue Harriet Lavinia, Mary, Theodore I., William H.; DeKalb Twp; farm; West Cit.

HARSH, Levi, bc1817 PA, son of Philip and Christina (STRIKER) HARSH; d bf1870; m Mary COOK, issue Josiah, George A., Nancy J., James, Lucinda E., Mary M., Douglass, Aldora; Sycamore Twp; laborer; Cong; moved to WI.

HARTMAN, Elias, b1810 PA, son of John and Regina (BEAR) HARTMAN, bro-in-law to David and Castle CHURCHILL; d1887 IL; m Almira CHURCHILL, issue Hiram Delos, Philo DeWitt, Carrie D., Mary A/O., Rosetta M., David Wallace; Pampas/Cortland, Sycamore Twps; land patent; mercantile, farm, hotel-keeper; West Cit; lived in DeKalb Co bf1840.

HATFIELD, Albert, b1820 NY; d1911 IL; m (1) Margaret JONES, issue Theodore W., Clarence, Mary A.; m (2) Amelia, no issue; DeKalb Twp; West Cit; moved to Kankakee Co, IL, bf1910.

HATHAWAY, John, bc1799 NY; m Maria, issue William, Huldah, Mary, Charles; Pampas/Cortland Twp; farm, CW Co C 105th IL Inf[55]; West Cit.

HECKMAN, Philip, bc1823 OH; d1893 Cook Co, IL, buried DeKalb Co; m Sarah A. FARLEY, issue Catharine E., William Wallace, Ann Eliza, Jesse F., Alfred R., Irvin Jacob, James F., Frank L.; Kingston Twp; farm, Twp Supervisor; West Cit.

HEDGES, Thomas P., bc1832, NY, son of Wheeler and Nancy HEDGES; d1855 IL; m unknown; Paw Paw Twp; farm; West Cit.

HENDERSON, John Hope, b1807 KY, son of John and Nancy (SINGLETON) HENDERSON, father-in-law to James CLARK; d1848 IL; m Elizabeth E. POWELL, issue Mary, George Washington, Amanda Frances, Erastus Franklin, Martha Harriet, Sarah Marie, Annetta Powell; Freedom Twp, LaSalle Co, IL; land patent; farm, candidate for Congress 1844; West Cit.; "advocate and lecturer on antislavery,"[56] "strong abolitionist," worked with DeKalb Co UGRR conductors, home a station for UGRR.[57]

HENRY, Chester, b1829 NH, son of John Vetch and Parmelia (JOHNSON) HENRY, bro to James HENRY, son-in-law of William and Isabella (BEVERIDGE) FRENCH; d1915 IA; m Ellen Ann FRENCH, issue Gilbert, Anna Bell, Sarah Elizabeth, John Blair, Mary Ellen, Frank R; Somonauk Twp; farm; Presby.

HENRY, James, b1812 NY, son of John Vetch and Parmelia (JOHNSON) HENRY, bro to Chester HENRY, son-in-law of George and Ann BEVERIDGE, bro-in-law to James H. and John L. BEVERIDGE; d1899 IL; m Jennette/Sarah BEVERIDGE, issue Anna Mary, Parmelia, Isabella Beveridge, John Vetch, George B., William A., Sarah T.L., Philomelia J./Lillie J./Lillian J., Agnes R., Margaret Elizabeth/Bertie E., Minnie J.; Somonauk Twp; farm; Presby.

HILAND/HYLAND/HIGHLAND, Joseph L., bc1793 PA, son of Thomas and Mary (BARKLEY) HIGHLAND; d1861 IL; m Hannah MCKILLUP/ MCKELLUP, issue David, Jane Eliza, Isabell, James, John C., Jackson, Charles Wallace, Joseph Vanderman; Sycamore Twp; land patent; farm; West Cit; Cong, left First Cong Ch in Sycamore 1854 to form Cong Ch in DeKalb.

HILL, George H., b1810 NY son of Joseph and Mercy (MORTIMER) HILL; d1890 IL; m Sarah B. WALLACE, issue Ophelia, William W., Anna E., Mary A., Sarah J., James J., George H.; Kingston Twp; land patent; farm, Kingston Postmaster, first Treasurer of DeKalb Co, 1845 elected Democrat DeKalb Co Commissioner; 1857 elected Republican Judge of Circuit Court; member of the "young, vigorous and promising" Republican Party[58]; came to DeKalb Co bf1840.

HILLS, Steven G., b1812 NY; d1895 IL; m Mary SMITH, issue Mary S., Harriet S.; Paw Paw, Shabbona Twps; land patent; farm; West Cit.

HIX, Seymour, bc1831 NY, son of Ephraim and Laura W. (WILLIAMS) HIX; d1908 IA; m Louisa MUMFORD, issue William P., Walter D., Amy S., Albert D., Charles E., Harry J., Susan "Susie" Isabel, Sarah; Kingston, Sycamore Twps; farm; Univ; D; moved to IA by 1880.

HOAG, Augustus, bc1831 NY, son of Stephen and Sally HOAG; Clinton Twp; farm; West Cit.

HOLCOMB, Corena/Corrinna E. "Cora" (BOARDMAN), b1839 IL, dau Daniel and Tryphena (MASON) BOARDMAN; d1894 IL; m Reuben J. HOLCOMB, nephew of Sylvanus HOLCOMB, issue Charles C., Jessie M., Minerva E., Zada R., Burt F.; Sycamore Twp; husband Sgt. CW 105th IL Inf, Co Deputy and Sheriff; Univ; R.

HOLCOMB, Sylvanus, b1803 NY son of Orator and Hannah (PERRY/TERRY) HOLCOMB; d1896 IL; m (1) Julia B. JOSLYN, issue Mary, Albert, Milo, Cordelia, Laura, Martha C., Oscar, Flora; m (2) Betsy (CHITTENDEN) WOODROUGH ADAMS; Sycamore Twp; land patent; farm; Township Clerk, Co Commissioner, Justice of the Peace, mbr committee to confront grave robbers, Deacon and Trustee in Univ Church; Univ; R; assisted David West as conductor for UGRR[59]; lived in DeKalb Co bf1840.

HOLDERNESS, William James, b1829 Canada, son of Joseph and Elizabeth (DREW) HOLDERNESS; d1906 WI; m Philena BLACKMAN, issue Philo Blackman, Edith, Ethel, Letta, Lemuel, Walter, Minnie; Mayfield Twp; farm, carpenter; West Cit.

HOLDREDGE/HOLDRIDGE, Gershom, bc1820 NY, son of Daniel and Eleanor (TEACHOUT) HOLDREDGE, cousin to Wayne HOLDREDGE; d af1880; m Susan Matilda MEEKER, issue William "Eugene," Theron; Pampas/Cortland Twp; farm; West Cit.

HOLDREDGE/HOLDRIDGE, Wayne/Duane, bc1827 NY, son of Ira C. and Ann (HOWE/HOWELL) HOLDREDGE, cousin to Gershom HOLDREDGE; d af1880 IL; m Clarissa L. DENSMORE, issue Ethelbert; Pampas/Cortland Twp; farm; West Cit.

HOLLEMBEAK/HOLLENBECK, Aramont Noble, b1816 NY, son of Ruluff White and Electa (AMES) HOLLENBECK/HOLLEMBEAK; d c1908; m Pamelia DECKER, issue Delia Ann, Alfred Stone, Henry, Emily, Ruloff Wesley, Ralph D.; Genoa Twp; farm; West Cit; R; lived in DeKalb Co bf1840.

HOLLISTER, Hugh S., b1808 NY, son of Ezra and Lydia (SEARS) HOLLISTER; d af1885; m (1) Maria CADY, issue Worden Cady, Lydia Maria, Mortimer Davis; m (2) Phoebe HANCHETT, issue Elysmer M., Amos C, Nancy Viola, Martin M., Cator H., Ida J.; DeKalb Twp; land patent; farm; West Cit; moved to Knox Co, IL bf1860.

HOLROYD, James, bc1823 Canada, son of William and Mary (HANSON) HOLROYD, bro to William; d1881 IL; m (1) Mary CARDINAL; m (2) Adelia "Delia" A. THURSTON, issue Margaret "Maggie" D., Grace Blanche, Martin, Henry Herbert, James A., William G.; Kingston Twp; farm; West Cit.

HOLROYD, William, b1819 England, son of William and Mary (HANSON) HOLROYD, bro to James; d1901 IL; m Augusta Ann HANNAH, no issue; Kingston Twp; farm; West Cit.

HORTON, Dexter, b1825 NY, son of Darius and Hannah (OLMSTEAD) HORTON, bro to Miles and Julius HORTON; d1904 WA; m (1) Hannah Eliza SHOUDY, issue Rebecca, Alfred, Nettie Hannah; m (2) Caroline E. PARSONS, issue Caroline E.; m (3) Arabella C. AGARD; Shabbona Twp; land patent; farm, merchant; West Cit.

HORTON, Julius, b1834 NY, son of Darius and Hannah (OLMSTEAD) HORTON, bro to Dexter and Miles HORTON; d1904 WA; m Annie E. BIGELOW, issue George M., Dora E., Mabel Maude, Howard Dexter; Shabbona Twp; land patent; farm, merchant; West Cit; R; moved to WA 1869.

HORTON, Miles, b1819, son of Darius and Hannah (OLMSTEAD) HORTON, bro to Dexter and Julius HORTON; d1848 IL; m Phebe WHITE, issue Darius J., William, Rozetta, Louisa; Shabbona Twp; land patent; farm; West Cit.

HOUGH, Burage/Burrage, b1790 CT, son of Matthew and Martha (COWLES) HOUGH, half-bro to Matthew HOUGH Jr.; d1854 IL; m Mary Polly ALEXANDER, issue Alzina Marilla, George Washington, Malona Elizabeth, Emily, Jane, Lois, Gilbert Lafayette, John Wesley, Martha, Harriet, W. Delos Fletcher, Martin Luther; Somonauk Twp; land patent; farm, Co commissioner; West Cit; lived in DeKalb Co bf1840; prolific antislavery letter writer to the *Western Citizen*.

HOUGH, George Washington, b1815 NY, son of Burage and Mary (ALEXANDER) HOUGH, bro to John Wesley HOUGH; d af1880 IL; m (1) Hester A. TIFFANY, issue, Calvin, Ellen, Mary, Daniel, Albert, Clinton, William, Henry, John; m (2) Margaret BLEE, no issue; Somonauk Twp; land patent; farm; West Cit; moved to LaSalle Co. IL bf1870.

HOUGH, John Wesley "J.W.," b1827 NY, son of Burage and Mary (ALEXANDER) HOUGH, bro to George HOUGH; d1889 NY; m (1)Elizabeth MOORE, issue Eugenia, Flora Belle, Charles; m (2) Mary G. SMITH, no known issue; Somonauk Twp; farm, drayman; West Cit; moved to Kane County, IL bf1870.

HOUGH, Matthew Jr., b1795 CT, son of Matthew and Obedience (BARNES WOODRUFF) HOUGH, half-bro to Burage HOUGH; d1883 MN; m Nancy, issue Clinton, Seth, John, Helen; Somonauk Twp; farm; West Cit; moved to LaSalle Co, IL bf1860, to MN bf1880.

HOWISON, Alexander, b1826 Scotland, son of George and Margaret (BROWN) HOWISON; d1907 IL; m Margaret McCLEERY, issue George Andrew, Margaret Jean, Ann Elizabeth, Archie H., Mary Jeannette, Ralph James, Isabella Catherine; Somonauk Twp; land patent; Presby.

HOWISON, James, b1818 Scotland, son of George and Margaret (BROWN) HOWISON, son-in-law of Richard and Julia KIRKPATRICK; d1901 IL; m Mary Jane KIRKPATRICK, issue Charles; Somonauk Twp; land patent; Presby.

HOWISON, Margaret (BROWN), b1789 Scotland, mother-in-law to Alexander WHITE; d1874 IL; m George HOWISON, issue James, Isobel, William, Eliza, Alexander,

Robert; Somonauk Twp; husband farm; charter mbr Somonauk Presby Ch.

HOWISON, Robert, b1830 Scotland, son of George and Margaret (BROWN) HOWISON, son-in-law of Richard and Julia KIRKPATRICK; d1912 IL; m Hannah Ellen KIRKPATRICK, issue George Bert, Margaret, Mabel, Fred; Clinton Twp; Presby.

HOWISON, William, b1821 Scotland, son of George and Margaret (BROWN) HOWISON; d1904 IL; m Catharine WALLS, issue James A., William J., Robert W., George W., Albert, Mary M.; Somonauk, Clinton Twps; land patent; farm; West Cit; Presby.

HOYT, Benjamin F., b1791 CT, son of Silas and Sarah (LOCKWOOD) HOYT, father-in-law to John C. WATERMAN and George W. KRETSINGER; d1861 CA; m Catherine "Arna" SMITH, issue Benjamin Franklin, Caroline Elizabeth, Sarah S., Mary J., Silas A., Nancy D., Charles Hawley; Sycamore Twp; farm; West Cit; Cong.

HUBBARD, John, bc1803 NY, son of John HUBBARD; d1875 IL; m Rachel KINNEY, issue George B. and adopted niece Freelove KINNEY; Freedom Twp, LaSalle Co, IL; land patent; farm; worked with DeKalb Co UGRR conductors and home a station for UGRR.[60]

HUBBARD, Nelson T., bc1809 VT; d1881 IL; m Livona/Livonia, issue Marcia/Maria, Lucina E., Ella, Ida Jane; Sycamore Twp; farm, brick mason; Univ.

HUDSON, Charles Frederick, b1821 OH, son of Timothy and Catherine (BROWN) HUDSON; d1867 NY; no spouse; Sycamore Twp; minister 1848–1853 First Cong Ch, Sycamore, teacher at Dow Academy, Sycamore.

HUNT, John M., bc1830 NJ; Sycamore Twp; farm; West Cit.

HUNT, William J., bc1806 NJ; d1867 IL; m Caroline M. BEAVERS; issue Edwin T., John Stafford; Sycamore Twp; land patent; attorney, banker; West Cit; wife Cong; secretary Anti-Nebraska meeting 1854,[61] Whig delegate to organizing Republican convention 1854.[62]

HUNTLEY, Luman, bc1815 NY, son of Elisha and Hannah (GLIDDEN) HUNTLEY, son-in-law of Levi C. BARBER; d af1880 IL; m Amelia A. BARBER, issue Myra A., Adelia R., Converse O.; DeKalb Twp; farm, hotel keeper, Co Supervisor; West Cit; lived in DeKalb Co bf1840; moved to Lee Co. bf1860.

HYATT, Alvin J., b1800 NY, son of Minnah and Regina/Rachel (ERSBERGER) HYATT; d1881 NE; m (1) Katherine PUGSLEY, issue unknown; m (2) Jerusha Ann SKINNER, issue Jerusha Ann, Alvin Jackson; Somonauk Twp; land patent; farm laborer; West Cit; lived in DeKalb Co bf1840; moved to Warren Co, IL bf1860, to NE bf1870.

HYDE, Jonathan W., b1789 VT, son of Elijah and Elizabeth (EDGERTON) HYDE; d1864 IL; m (1) Phoebe FILLMORE, issue Septa, Simeon, Nancy, Albert, Cleora, Benjamin F., Harriet, Lycurgus, Elliott, Eliza, H. Herbert; m (2) Eunice FLETCHER; Paw Paw Twp; land patent; farm; West Cit.

HYDE, Simeon E., b1821 VT, son of Jonathan W. and Phoebe (FILLMORE) HYDE; d1895 IL; m Marion L. THOMAS, issue Charles S., Harvey E., George, Janice; Paw Paw Twp; farm, financier; West Cit.

IDE, Harvey, bc1804 VT; d1863 IL; m Sarah Marilla DELAND, issue Elijah D., George H., Caroline F., Carlos William "Willie," Dewit Clinton; Genoa Twp; land patent; farm; West Cit; lived in DeKalb Co bf1840.

IRWIN, William W., b1800 Ireland, son of James and Jane (WINSLOW) IRWIN; d1866 IL; m Margaret HARPER, issue Elizabeth, Margaret Jane, William M., Mary, Jane, Eleanor, Thomas, Martha Ann, Sarah Ann; Somonauk Twp; farm; Elder at Ross Grove Presby Ch, then joined Somonauk Presby Ch.

IRWIN, William W., b1822 NY, son of James and Mary/Maria IRWIN; d1897 IL; m Elizabeth COLBY, issue 11 children, including John, Lewis, Lottie, Willie/Wyllie W., Charles A., Frank D., Mary C., Eucinia E.; Clinton, Shabbona Twps; farm; "ardent Abolitionist."[63]

ISMON, George L., bc1822 NY; d1907 IL; m (1) Mary D. ARNOLD, issue M. Medora, Mary L.; m (2) Harriet "Hattie" Lavina SHERIDAN, issue George William; Somonauk Twp; farm, merchant; West Cit.

JACKMAN, Abner, bc1794 VT, son of Abner and Rebecca (FRENCH) JACKMAN, father-in-law to Caleb M. BROWN, Jeremiah L BROWN and Latin NICHOLS; d1851 IL; m Louisa "Mary" KENDALL, issue Kendall, Eliza A., Martin Luther, Armenia/Armena, Louisa A., Charles D., Harriet "Hattie," Mary A.; Sycamore Twp; land patent; farm, lumber and coal dealer, one of first Petit jurors for DeKalb Co, Justice of the Peace; West Cit., wife continued her own subscription after his death; Meth Episcopal; strong Abolitionist,[64] voted with DeKalb Co. Abolitionists af1840 election[65]; lived in DeKalb Co bf1840.

JACKMAN, Louisa "Mary," bc1803; dau Thomas and Betsy (REED) KENDALL, mother-in-law to Caleb M. BROWN, Jeremiah L BROWN, Latin NICHOLS and Charles TOWNSEND; dc1872 IL; m Abner JACKMAN, issue Kendall, Eliza A., Luther, Armenia/Armena, Louisa A., Charles D., Harriet "Hattie," Mary A.; Sycamore Twp; husband farm; West Cit., continued her own subscription after death of husband; Meth Episcopal; lived in DeKalb Co bf1840.

JAMES, Daniel B., bc1817 VT, son of Levi and Rhuamah (BATCHELDER) JAMES; d1877 IL; m Ann GEORGE; Sycamore Twp; Attorney, Aide-de-Camp to Gov. Oglesby, Republican delegate to National Convention 1864, DeKalb Co Judge, Sycamore postmaster; West Cit; Meth (wife Cong); R; owned the *True Republican* newspaper with James H. Beveridge and Caleb M. Brown; outspoken orator on behalf of antislavery.[66]

JENNESS, Richard, bc1807 NH, son of Richard and Hannah (EMERSON) JENNESS; d1874 KS; m Sybil BUELL, issue Josiah Butler, Sarah Frances, Richard Emerson, Dewitt Clinton, Horace Wells, George Benning; Sycamore Twp; land patent; hotel keeper; West Cit; moved to Ogle Co., IL by 1860.

JOHNSON, Isaac bc1792 CT, son of Isaac and Elizabeth JOHNSON; d1881 IL; m (1) Nancy DOW, issue Mary Caroline, Isaac W., Nancy Elizabeth, William Lucas, Lucius, James D.; m (2) Mary KELSEY, issue Vestilina Miranda, Alfred L.; Pampas/Cortland Twp; farm; West Cit.

JOINER, Beulah (SMITH), b1786 VT, dau Nathaniel and Abigail (STEVENS) SMITH; d1863 IL; m Sylvanus JOINER, issue Alta, Andrew, Cyrus Sylvanus, Osgood C., Corinna, Henry J., Hudson H., Daniel Perry, Floretta Ann; Mayfield Twp; husband farm; Cong.

JOINER, Henry J., b1822 NY, son of Sylvanus and Beulah (SMITH) JOINER; d1869 IL; m Charlotte EATON, issue Adelburt, Mary J.; Sycamore Twp; land patent; farm; West Cit; Cong affiliation.

JONES, Harvey B., bc1828 NY; d1914 IL; m Mary, issue unknown; Sycamore Twp; carpenter; Univ; moved bf1870.

JONES, Henry R., bc1820 NY, son of Robert and Elizabeth (BAUM) JONES; d1909 IL; m Lucinda Baker KELLY, issue Preston King, Estella "Stell" Jane; Sycamore Twp; clerk, druggist, grocer; Univ.

JONES, Malden, bc1817 NY; d bf1860; m Diana HANCHETT, issue Albert, Ranson/Ransom, Evanda, Electa, Adaline; DeKalb Twp; farm; land patent; West Cit.

JONES, Owen T/S., bc1809 Wales; d af1880 IL; m Elizabeth, issue Daniel, Albert, William, Groden/Clayton, John; Sandwich, Somonauk Twp; land patent; farm; West Cit; moved to Kane Co. bf1870.

JORDAN, Moses W., b1819 NY, son of Rufus and Rebecca (BACON) JORDAN; d1891 IL; m Betsy PERKINS, issue Edward Franklin, Mary A.; Pampas/Cortland Twp; farm, physician, ordained preacher; Meth Episcopal; "earnest and decided antislavery."[67]

JOSLYN, Albert S., bc1823 NY, son of Phineas and Lorinda (WOODWORTH) JOSLYN, bro to Harry, bro-in-law to Levias DOW, Joseph CHEASBRO and David CHAMPLIN; d1892 IL; m Mabellia/Marilla BURR, issue Ellen C., Adelbert, Phineas; Pampas/Cortland Twp; land patent; farm; Univ.

JOSLYN, Harry A., b1816 NY son of Phineas and Lorinda (WORDWORTH) JOSLYN, bro to Albert JOSLYN, bro-in-law to Levias DOW, Joseph CHEASBRO and David CHAMPLIN, son-in-law of John WATERMAN; d1906 IL; m1841 Lucy Ann WATERMAN, issue Louisa A., Franklin M., James C., John Phineas, William L.; Sycamore Twp; land patent; farm, merchant, teacher, Co Sheriff 1864; West Cit; charter mbr Sycamore Univ Ch; Whig delegate to convention organizing Republican Party 1854[68]; "One of the fifteen who voted the old Abolition ticket"[69]; lived in DeKalb Co bf1840.

JOSLYN, Phineas Vison, b1792 NY, father-in-law Levias DOW, Joseph CHEASBRO and David CHAMPLIN; d1868 IL; m Lorinda WOODWORTH, issue Harry A., Phineas V., Alsirus, John, Emily, Mariah; Sycamore Twp; land patent; farm; West Cit; charter mbr Sycamore Univ Ch; lived in DeKalb Co bf1840.

JUDD, John, bc1797 NY, son of John and Hannah (LYMAN) JUDD; d1872 IL; m Mary "Ariel" PHILLIPS, issue Martha Harriett, Elizabeth E., John, Sylvester; Kingston Twp; land patent; farm; West Cit; Wesleyan Meth; voted with DeKalb Co. Abolitionists af1840 election[70]; lived in DeKalb Co bf1840.

KELLOGG, Hiram Jesse, bc1839 IL, son of Jesse Churchill and Phoebe (WOOD) KELLOGG; d1903 IA; no spouse; Sycamore Twp; merchant, Deputy Sycamore Postmaster, Deputy Sheriff, Tax Collector; Father subscribed to West Cit; Cong; R; one of first white children born in DeKalb Co; youngest identified DeKalb Co UGRR conductor at age 11[71]; "his patriotism and loyalty to principle were deep-rooted."[72]

KELLOGG, Jesse Churchill, b1806 VT, son of Aaron and Phoebe (BUTTS) KELLOGG, bro-in-law to Henry WOOD, father-in-law to Charles T. PIERCE; d1874 IL; m Phoebe WOOD, issue Emily Jane, Hiram Jesse, Henry Warner, Herman Allan, Homer William; Sycamore Twp; land patent; teacher, Justice of the Peace, first DeKalb Co Clerk and Recorder, first Sycamore Postmaster (home used as post office), involved in decision to name Sycamore county seat; Co Circuit Clerk and Recorder; entered county lands in own name, with Carlos Lattin and Curtis Smith, when county could not afford to purchase land; West Cit; founding mbr of Sycamore First Cong Ch, one of first Trustees, Clerk of the Church 1840–1873, one of 11 men consenting to 1848 tax assessment on personal property to construct new house of worship; "active Abolitionist and powerful adjunct of the Underground Railroad,"[73] conductor on UGRR[74]; lived in DeKalb Co bf1840.

KELLOGG, Mary Ann (PLACE), bc1807 VT; d1889 IL; m Orlando KELLOGG, issue Leander Post, Jerusha, Lusius, Harlow, Mabel Maria, Nancy "Electa," John Wesley, Lucy Whitney, Mary Ann; Sycamore Twp; husband farm; Cong; moved to IA bf1870; moved to LaSalle Co, IL, bf1889.

KEMP, James G., bc1828 NY, son of Samuel W. and Jeanette (GILLIES) KEMP; d1864 MO; m Sarah J. NIND, issue Sarah Maria, Herbert Clarence, Lawrence Hubert, Clarence Herbert, Flora Janette; Sycamore Twp; farmer, blacksmith, CW Co M, 9th Cavalry Reg., IA; West Cit; Cong; moved to DuPage Co bf1860.

KERNS, S.H., bc1818 Ireland; m Mary; Squaw Grove Twp; farm; West Cit.

KING, Gideon F., bc1810 NY, son of Reuben and Roxanna (DEWOLF) KING; m Lydia BROWN, issue Benjamin, Ann, Huldah, William, Thomas, Jane; Genoa Twp; land patent; carpenter, Twp. Supervisor; West Cit; voted with Co. Abolitionists af1840 election[75]; lived in DeKalb Co bf1840.

KING, Lyman Bristol, b1809 NY, son of John Sherwin and Anna (BRISTOL) KING; d1882 IL; m Almina JACKSON, issue Harriet Emily, Sherwin Warren, Lyman Bristol, Willard Belknap, Elsie Anna, Julia Mary, Charles Henry; DeKalb Twp; Baptist Minister, farm; West Cit; Baptist.

KING, Philip, b1826 Germany, son of William and Mary Louise (FEY) KING/KONIG; d1903 IL; m (1) Elizabeth COONFAIR/COONFARE, issue William, Mary E.; m (2) Maria SCOTT, issue Rosa Anna, Henry Douglas, Margaret Jane, Frank Preston, Orilla Louise, Laura Dell, Amelia Bell; Mayfield Twp; farm; Wesleyan Meth.

KINGSLEY, Eben/Elon Galusha, b1826 NY, son of Alvah Crary and Chloe B. (LEONARD) KINGSLEY, bro to Mason KINGSLEY; d1900 MI; m Elizabeth Ann DEMOREST, issue Chloe J., David A., Delos A/C., Sardine M., Cassy/Carry/Cory, Effie; Mayfield Twp; farm; Wesleyan Meth.

KINGSLEY, Mason Boardman, bc1835 NY, son Alvah Crary and Chloe B. (LEONARD) KINGSLEY, bro to Eben KINGSLEY; d1891 IA; m Margaret H. LLOYD, issue Clarissa E., Alida A., Flora May, Jay B.; Mayfield Twp; farm; Wesleyan Meth; moved to IA bf1880.

KINYON, George Merritt, b1827 NY, son of John and Lydia (POST) KINYON, son-in-law of David CHURCHILL; d1896 IL; m (1) Marilla CHURCHILL (whose body was stolen by grave robbers[76]); m (2) Nancy Peace (WHITNEY) ATKINSON, issue John William, Dexter Delos, Lydia G., step-daughter Vesta ATKINSON; Pampas/Cortland Twp, one of first settlers; land patent; farm; West Cit; R; Meth Episcopal and Baptist.

KIRKPATRICK, Hezekiah, b1813 PA, son of Moses and Margaret Jane (GARRETT) KIRKPATRICK, bro of Isaac; d1883 IL; m Nancy ELLIOTT, issue Nancy Jane, Moses Calvin, John Simpson, Eliza, Margaretta; Clinton Twp; farm; Presby; lived in DeKalb Co bf1840.

KIRKPATRICK, Isaac, b1817 PA, son of Moses and Margaret Jane (GARRETT) KIRKPATRICK, bro of Hezekiah; d1898 IL; m Sarah ELLIOTT, issue James Elliott, Robert D., Ann Eliza, John Easton, Emma Jane, Agnes May, Clara

Maria., Sarah Ellen, Flora M., Norah; Squaw Grove Twp; farm; CW Sgt. In 8th IL Cavalry; Presby; lived in DeKalb Co bf1840.

KIRKPATRICK, Jesse, b1791 PA, son of Isaac and Nancy (GRAHAM) KIRKPATRICK, bro to Richard; d1857 IL; m Ruth SMILEY, issue Ann, Isaac, Smiley, Hiram, Margaret, Eleanor/Ellen; Clinton Twp; farm, sawyer; Presby.

KIRKPATRICK, Richard, b1797 PA, son of Isaac and Nancy (GRAHAM) KIRKPATRICK, bro to Jesse, father-in-law to Robert and James HOWISON and William, Robert and John WALKER; d1871 IL; m Julia Ann KIRKPATRICK (a relative), issue Isabella, Hannah Eleanor, Matilda, Albina, Mary Jane, Julia Ann, Rebecca, Jesse Patterson, Isaac Finley; farm; Clinton Twp.

KNIGHT, Samuel, bc1815 MD, son of Peter and Anna (DELL) KNIGHT; d1900 IL; m Mary TOWER, issue Anna Dell, Harriet M., Mary E., Amanda J., George W., John H., (twins) Laura E., Lydia Augusta, Sarah Ann, Charles M., Alice A., Elijah Marvin; Mayfield Twp; land patent; farm; Wesleyan Meth.

KRETSINGER, Mary Jane, (HOYT), b1829 NJ dau Benjamin and Catherine "Arna" (SMITH) HOYT, sis-in-law to John C. WATERMAN; d1903 CA; m (1) George Washington KRETSINGER, issue Catherine, George William; m (2) Horace CLARK, issue Ella Jane; Sycamore Twp; husband lawyer and served in IL legislature one term; Cong; moved to CA bf1859.

LAMB, Curtis Armsbury, bc1804 VT, son of Isaac and Hannah (WILLIAMS) LAMB; d1886 KS; m (1) Hester WILLIAMS, issue Elizabeth "Betsy" A., Morris, Alzada; m (2) Fanny, issue Charles, Edward, Curtis Armsbury, Herman/Hiram, Charles Henry, Jerome; Victor Twp; farm, CW 105th IL Inf, 16th IL Inf; West Cit; moved to KS bf1870.

LANDER, Joseph Cogswell, b1816, son of John and Sophia Western (COGSWELL) LANDER; d1850 IL; m Rachel STRONG, issue Cyrus, Mary Sophia, Josephine E.J., Marshall Strong; Sycamore Twp; land patent; first DeKalb Co Sheriff 1838; never arrested UGRR activists; lived in DeKalb Co bf1840; moved to Champaign Co, IL bf1850.

LANGDON, Henry S., bc1822 MA; m Mary A., issue Eugene, Henrietta J., Ellen C., Emeline, Albert H.; Somonauk Twp; farm, druggist; West Cit; moved to MN bf1870.

LATHAM, Benjamin Fish bc1836 NY, son of Joseph and Mary Ann (FISH) LATHAM, bro to Hubbard LATHAM; d1930 IL; m Anna, issue Charles, Gilbert P.; Somonauk Twp; farm, produce merchant; West Cit.

LATHAM, Hubbard, b1821 CT, son of Joseph and Mary Ann (FISH) LATHAM, bro to Benjamin F. LATHAM; d1900 IL; m Ann "Lucy" BARNES, issue Anna Leonora, Hattie Belle, Harry Hubbard, Ellis Clifford, Fannie Luella, Carl Ray; Somonauk Twp; land patent; farm, Twp Supervisor; West Cit; moved to Cook Co, IL af1872.

LATHROP, Lucy E., bc1815 NY; m (1) Unknown CHAPMAN; m (2) Chandler LATHROP, issue step-dau Mary; Sycamore, Pampas/Cortland Twps; seamstress; husband blacksmith; Cong.

LATTEMORE, William, b1805 NY; d af1880; m1831 Lydia COOK, issue one child; Sycamore Twp; farm; West Cit; R; Meth; lived in DeKalb Co bf1840.

LATTIN, Carlos, b1813 CT, son of Abner and Sarah (BENNETT) LATTIN, son-in-law of James CARTWRIGHT; d1876 IL; m 1839 Nancy CARTWRIGHT, issue Jesse Leande, Ellen Dellora, John Wesley, Carlos Orlando, Marion Ella, Charles Wesley, Sadie Adella; Sycamore Twp; land patent; farm, merchant, Co Treasurer; entered county lands in own name, with Jesse Kellogg and Curtis Smith, when county could not afford to purchase land; one of committee to confront grave robbers[77]; West Cit; R; Meth; "hospitable to homeless strangers"[78]; one of first settlers in Sycamore, lived in DeKalb Co bf1840.

LAVERTY, Hamilton, b1813 OH; d1881 IL; m (1) Selennia, issue Malissa, Lemuel; m (2) Caroline, issue unknown; m (3) Nancy DAVIS, issue Frank, plus step-children John, Margaret, Cornelius and Hannah DAVIS; m (4) Almeda, no issue; Genoa Twp; farm; West Cit.

LAWRENCE, William Carlton, b1822 NY, son of Carlton William and Mary Polly (MILLET) LAWRENCE; d1866 IL; m Mary L. SELTS, issue Caroline/Cornelia/Cordelia, Diana Estella, Annetta "Nettie" Amelia, Charlotte "Lottie" Edna, Melvin William, Edith May; Sycamore Twp; land patent; farm; West Cit.

LAWYER, Maria (SETTLE), bc1810 NY; d af1880; m David S. LAWYER, issue John S., and step-children Peter H., Jacob A., Margaret, Christina, Ezra and William Minor LAWYER; Pampas/Cortland Twp; husband farm; Cong.

LAY, Samuel H., b1795 CT, father-in-law of Wells A. FAY; d1861 IL; m Emily PRATT, issue Harriett Emilet, Samuel Mills, Jeanette Frances, James Harvey, Lucy "Josepha," Amelia Chapman, Julia A.; Somonauk Twp; land patent; farm; West Cit; Chairman, 1850 Somonauk anti-Fugitive Slave Law meeting,[79] Chairman, 1854 DeKalb Co Anti-Nebraska (antislavery) Meeting[80]; lived in DeKalb Co bf1840.

LEE, Charles, b1816 England; d1893 IL; m Catharine Kate BLANCHARD, issue Harriet Adelaid, Mary M., Charles L., Edward Clayton, William McGregor, Ira/Harry Boies, Francis "Frank" E., Wilbert H./Burton W.; Mayfield, Sycamore Twps; farm, machinist; Cong.

LEE, Cyrus Beeman, bc1830 OH, son of Jacob and Rachel Jane (BEEMAN) LEE; d1903 CA; m Alma H. HOWARD, issue Willard Howard, Eugene Watson; Squaw Grove Twp; farm; West Cit; moved to NE bf1870, to CA bf1900.

LEMOIN/LAMOIN, Lucius E., bc1832 OH, son of Reuben Eldred and Prudence B. (FRENCH) LEMOIN; d1875 CA; m Anna M. FLICK, issue William H., Reuben Eldred, George, Dorah; Shabbona Twp; farm; West Cit; moved to CA bf1870.

LEYSON, John L., b1831 Wales, son of Rees and Mary (LEWIS) LEYSON; m Mary Jane McNEAL, issue Fanny R., Edgar, Eva R., John Franklin; Shabbona Twp; farm, grocer, coal miner; West Cit; moved to LaSalle Co. IL bf1870, to Grundy Co. IL bf1880.

LITTLE, Abijah, b1809 Canada, son of Abijah and Elizabeth (BEAN) LITTLE; d af1882; m (1) Eleanor McNORTON, issue William, John, Elizabeth, Edwin D., Janette/Jeannette, Ellen and Edgar (twins); m (2) Lucy A. (EASTMAN) FEARON, step-children Ida A., Alfred J.; Clinton, Shabbona Twps; farm, carpenter, joiner, first mayor of Waterman, IL; West Cit.

LITTLE, Henry H., b1824 NY, son of Henry and Amy E. (BINGHAM) LITTLE; d1889 IL; m (1) Alvira, no issue; m (2) Esther HECKMAN, issue James, Erastus B.; Kingston Twp; farm; West Cit.

LLOYD, Parthenia (HASKELL), b1799 MA, dau Roger and Mary (WEBSTER) HASKELL; d1867 IL; m Artemas William LLOYD, issue Paulina Dorr, William, Mary Webster, Sergius, Lewis, Alice Eliza, Eli W.; South Grove Twp; husband farm; Cong.

LORD, Samuel, b1828 CT, son of Joseph and Chloe (MOULTON) LORD; d1911 IL; m Frances E. TAYLOR, issue Frank Howard, Cora/Carrie, Sarah Frances, Eddy; Victor, Somonauk Twps; farm, painter, Victor Twp Supervisor; West Cit.

LOVE, Alice Chapin (WEST), b1833 NY, dau of David and Sarah (CHAPIN) WEST, sis of Elias, Orrin, Asa "Porter," Sarah Louise and Minerva M; d c1903 IL; m Frederick Dreater LOVE, Jr., issue Sarah J., Lewis David, Mary Emma, Carrie Elizabeth, Alice Minerva, Frederick C.; Sycamore, DeKalb Twps; housekeeper, husband farm; Cong.

LOVE, Frederick Decatur, b1793 NY, son of John and Sally (ROSE) LOVE, bro-in-law to Mary LOVE; dc1874 IL; m Jane DEMOTT, issue Lewis, Melinda, Frederick Decatur, Tracy; DeKalb Twp; farm; first DeKalb Co Supt. of Schools; mbr and one of first Trustees of Sycamore First Cong Ch and of DeKalb First Cong Ch; lived in DeKalb Co bf1840.

LOVE, Mary Maria (SCHOFIELD), bc1811 NY, dau Lawrence and Mary SCHOFIELD, sis-in-law to Frederick D. LOVE; d1879 IL; m Christopher LOVE, issue Wilson, Elizabeth Melvina; DeKalb Twp; husband farm; West Cit.

LYON, George W., b1819 NY, son of Jonathan and Lois (BATTLES) LYON; d af1870 IL; m (1) Fanny R. CLARK, no issue; m (2) Sophia RICHARDSON, issue Francis William, Estella, Ella, Emma, Emmett, Elva, Cecelia; DeKalb Twp; land patent; farm; West Cit.

MACKEY/MACKIE, William Henry "Harrison," b1813 NY, son of Levi and Rebecca (SCOTT) MACKEY; d1890 IL; m (1) Mary HALL, issue Mary Rebekah, Eliza Jane, Julia Anne; m (2) Eliza (BOND) WESTLAKE, step-children Charlotte, David B., Milton G., Hannah E., Mary A., John O., Morris H. WESTLAKE; Mayfield Twp; blacksmith, farm, Postmaster at Brush Point; Wesleyan Meth; lived in DeKalb Co bf1840, moved to NY bf1860, back to IL bf1870.

MACKIE, James, bc1768, father-in-law to John THOM; d1845 IL; m Susan, issue Margaret; Sycamore, Mayfield Twps; Cong minister, organizing minister for Sycamore First Congregation Ch; lived in DeKalb Co bf1840.

MADDEN, "Dr." Henry, bc1800 PA; d1867 IL; m Eliza, no known issue; Mayfield, Malta Twps; land patent; farm, grocer, druggist, first Representative from DeKalb Co to IL State Legislature 1836–40, Malta Twp Supervisor, Co Supervisor, one of first Grand Jurors for DeKalb Co.; Wesleyan Meth; R, 1845 candidate for Probate Justice, Liberty Party ticket; Mbr of Resolution Committee for 1854 DeKalb Co Anti-Nebraska (antislavery) Meeting[81]; West Cit; lived in DeKalb Co bf1840.

MALLOWS, Abigail, bc1820 Canada; m George MALLOWS, issue Maria Antoinette, Henrietta, Charles, William, Mary A., Harriet, Caroline; Sycamore Twp; husband shoemaker; Cong.

MALTBY, Joseph Hosford, b1809 VT, son of Jonathan and Susannah (HOSFORD) MALTBY; d1852; m (1) Sarah COOPER, issue Rollin Cornelius, Harriet E., John Jay; m (2) Eliza, issue Sarah A., Alice; Genoa Twp; land patent; blacksmith; West Cit; lived in DeKalb Co c1840.

MARTIN, Harry, b1807 VT, son of John and Rachel D. (BLISS) MARTIN, bro to John MARTIN; d1897 IL; m Jane Ann SLACK, issue Harry, Charles Franklin (1), Amelia Eloise, Charles Franklin (2), Marietta Frances; Sycamore Twp; farm, tanner; West Cit; R; Cong, one of 11 men consenting to 1848 tax assessment on personal property to construct new house of worship; lived in DeKalb Co bf1840.

MARTIN, John, bc1805 VT, son of John and Rachel D. (BLISS) MARTIN, bro to Harry MARTIN; d1880 IL; m Sarah PERCIVAL, issue Angelina, Harry, John A., Sarah M., Henry; Sycamore Twp; land patent; laborer; Cong.

MASON, Henry B., bc1830 NY, son of Jarvis and Experience MASON; m (1) Lucy ORPUT, issue Ida, Rosa, Anna, William H., James L.; South Grove, Mayfield Twps; farm, hotel innkeeper, CW Co C, 105th IL Inf.; West Cit; moved to KS bf1870.

MASON, Jarvis, bc1801 NY, son of Malachi and Elizabeth (HALL) MASON; d1879 IL; m Experience Achsah SQUIRES, issue Olive, James W., Henry B., Adeline M.; South Grove, Sycamore Twps; land patent; farm, became Meth preacher; West Cit; Univ; moved to Shelby Co, IL bf1876.

MATTESON, Benjamin Jr., b1799 VT, son of Benjamin and Lois (RANDALL) MATTESON Sr., bro to Joel MATTESON; d1873 IL; m (1) Miriam OLMSTEAD, issue Martin, Mary, Miranda, Lorenzo, Oscar Fitzallen, Lois S., Albert O., Eliza/Elizabeth C., Mary/Miriam, Helen Jane.; m (2) Christina TEETER, issue Helen/Hannah Julia; Clinton Twp; land patent; farm; West Cit.

MATTESON, Oscar Fitzallen, b1825 VT, son of Benjamin and Miriam (OLMSTEAD) MATTESON, nephew of Joel Pratt MATTESON; d1917 IL; m Marion Abigail HALL, issue Florence Cellestine, Eva Alfreta, Lorenzo Alvero, Eliza Jane/Jennie, Ida May, Isabelle K. "Belle," Nellie A., Sarah F., Minnie; Clinton Twp; farm; West Cit.

MAXFIELD, John, b1791 VT, son of William and Abigail (BELCHER) MAXFIELD; d1875 IL; m JoAnna "Anna" POND, issue William Munson, James Monroe, John "Nelson," Gilbert Allen, Carlos Keith; Sycamore Twp; land patent; farm, one of first Grand Jurors for DeKalb Co.; West Cit; Meth Episcopal; R; first Abolition meeting in DeKalb Co. held in his home[82]; lived in DeKalb Co bf1840.

MAXFIELD, John "Nelson," b1824 OH, son of John and JoAnna (POND) MAXFIELD, bro to William Munson MAXFIELD; d1873 IL; m (1) Mary CROCKER, issue Carlos M., Frank A., Mary V.; m (2) Rebecca HOSFORD, issue Flora Belle; Sycamore Twp; land patent; farm; West Cit; Meth Episcopal; "a staunch and true friend of the black man"[83]; lived in DeKalb Co bf1840.

MAXFIELD, William Munson, b1817 OH, son of John and JoAnna (POND) MAXFIELD, bro to John "Nelson"; d1872 IL; m Caroline PLUMMER, issue Lyman O., Forrest, Floyd; Sycamore Twp; land patent; farm, DeKalb Co Collector; West Cit; family was Meth Episcopal; lived in DeKalb Co bf1840; moved to Ogle Co, IL bf1860, to Marion Co, IL bf1870.

McALLISTER, James W., b1798 Ireland or Scotland, son of Dexter McAllister, bro-in-law to David Miller DOBBIN; d1867 IL; m Jane "Jennie" DOBBIN, issue Margaret, Mary, Eliza, Martha, William J., James W., Sarah, Ellen, Esther, Ann, Isabella, Samuel; Somonauk, Clinton Twps; farm; West Cit; Presby.

McALLISTER, James W. Jr., b1834 NY, son of James W. and Jane (DOBBIN) McALLISTER, bro to William J. McALLISTER, son-in-law of Robert GRAHAM; d1921 IL; m Mary Ann GRAHAM, issue Ward, Helen M., Robert James, Margaret, Russell, Mary Belle, Sarah Jane, William John; Somonauk, Clinton Twps; farm; Presby.

McALLISTER, William J., b1832 NY, son of James and

Jane (DOBBIN) McALLISTER, bro to James W. McALLISTER Jr.; d1879 IL; m Sarah Addie FAVOR, issue unknown; Somonauk and Clinton Twp; farm, laborer and minister; CW 105th IL Inf.; Presby.

McBRIDE, Samuel, b1825 OH, son of Samuel and Mary (BUCHANAN) McBRIDE; d1896 KS; m Rebecca STEWART, issue Alvius/Alvan Stewart, Agnes Mary; Victor, Somonauk Twps; farm; West Cit; Presby; moved to KS bf1895.

McCLEERY/McCLEARY/McLEARY, Edward Cook, b1811 NY, son of John and Margaret (COOK) McCLEERY, bro to James and John McCLEERY, bro-in-law to David ORR; d1889 IA; m Jane BELL, issue Margaret Ann, Isabel Jane, John William, Eliza Ellen, Robert James, Samuel, Mary, Isabella, Edward, David, Catherine Bell; Somonauk Twp; farm; West Cit; Presby.

McCLEERY/McCLEARY/McCLARY, James, b1803 NY, son of John and Margaret (COOK) McCLEERY, bro to Edward and John McCLEERY, bro-in-law to David ORR; d1882 IA; m Jean THOMSON, issue Jean C., John, James, Hugh, Robert, Mary Ann, Margaret, Elizabeth, William Doig; Victor Twp; farm; Presby.

McCLEERY/McCLEARY/McCLARY, John, b1813 NY, son of John and Margaret (COOK) McCLEERY, bro to James and Edward McCLEERY, bro-in-law to David ORR; d1887 IA; m Adeline COLEMAN, issue James Martin, Marie/Maria, Thomas C., Edward, John W., Elizabeth, Margaret, Andrew; Clinton Twp; farm; West Cit; Presby.

McCLELLAN, James, b1830 NY, son of James and Hannah (NELSON) McCLELLAN, bro of Samuel McCLELLAN, son-in-law of Elijah STEWART; m Emeline "Emma" Amanda STEWART, issue Theresa Agnes, William Stewart, Ernest Stewart, Mary Boyd, George, Grace Annette, Harry Vincent; Squaw Grove Twp; farm, teacher; Presby; moved to Warren Co., IL af1880.

McCLELLAN, Samuel Nelson, b1826 NY, son of James and Hannah (NELSON) McCLELLAN, bro of James McCLELLAN; d1898 IL; m Margaret MACKLIN, issue James C., Margaret, Elizabeth, Mima C., Jennie, John R., Alfred Nelson, Mattie May, William Ralph; Squaw Grove Twp; farm; Presby.

McCLELLAND, Mason, b1825 PA, son of John and Mary "Ann" (MAY) McCLELLAND; d1902 IL; m Mary OSTERHOUT/OSTERHOUD, issue Elizabeth Ann, Byron, Ellzey, Alice, James Theron, Mina; Mayfield Twp; farm; Wesleyan Meth.

McCORMICK, Charles "Wesley," bc1817 PA; d af1865; m (1) Clarissa MAXFIELD, issue Enos, Harvey; m (2) Lucinda BANNISTER, issue Martha J., Mathew, Mary, Charles, Emily, Eva, William; Sycamore Twp; land patent; farm; West Cit; mbr Nominating Committee for 1847 DeKalb Co Liberty Party Convention[84]; moved to WI bf1860, to KS bf1865.

McCOY, Addison, bc1814 VA; m Sarah; Somonauk Twp; farm; West Cit.

McDONALD, Wallace "William," b1820 OH, son of Daniel and Catherine (PENNY) McDONALD; d1903 IL; m (1) Susan HECKMAN, issue George, John, Daniel; m (2) Sarah E. BLACKLIDGE, issue Susannah A., Henry Edwin, Maria E.; Kingston Twp; farm; West Cit.

McFARLAND, James, b1797 NY, son of John and Janet McFARLAND; d1876 IL; m Mary HARPER, issue Elizabeth, Janet, Thomas; Paw Paw Twp; West Cit; Ross Grove Presby Ch, then Somonauk Presby Ch.

McFARLAND, Robert C., bc1827 NY, son of William and Sarah McFARLAND; Paw Paw Twp; farm; West Cit.

McFARLAND, William, bc1792 NY; m Sarah, issue Polly, Martha, Walter, Robert C.; Paw Paw Twp; farm; West Cit.

McGILVRA, Jacob Alexander, b1819 NY, son of John F. and Margaret Mary (GRANT) McGILVRA; d1890 KS; m (1) Mary GRAY, no known issue; m (2) Francis Ann ROSE, issue Emily H., Rosetta Ann, Leroy Emmet, Lucius M., Marilla M., Carrie Adella, Olive May, Luella S.; Kane, Lake Cos, IL; farm; circuit minister at Mayfield Wesleyan Meth Ch.

McKEE, William, b1806 PA/OH, bro-in-law to Elijah STEWART; d1883 IL; m (1) Sarah, issue Maria, Joseph, George B., William, Sarah "Sallie," Pulila E., Samuel, John; m (2) Mary STEWART, no issue; Victor Twp; farm; Presby.

McQUARIE/ MCCUIRY, John, bc1793 NY, son of Donald and Elizabeth (McINTYRE) McQUARIE; d bf1880; m Diana JACOCKS, issue Mary Ann, Daniel, Sarah, Elizabeth, Margaret, Jane Shankland, Catherine, William H., Franklin; Genoa, Kingston Twps; shoemaker; West Cit.

MENDENHALL, James, b1826 OH, son of Thomas Griswold and Elizabeth/Ellen Susan (HOLLENBECK) MENDENHALL; d1905 MT; m Geraldine PARSONS, issue Alice G., Thomas B., James William, Charles W., Stephen Hess, Susan B., Grace M., Mary E.; Somonauk Twp; farm; West Cit; moved to IA bf1860, to MT bf1900.

MERCER, David "Smith," b1827 PA, son of Robert and Elizabeth Boyd (SMITH) MERCER; d1903 IL; m Margaret THORNBERG/THORNBURG, issue Robert James, Joseph, Thomas/Elijah, John, Alvin, William Moffett, Samuel Wallace, Ida Belle, Jennie; Clinton Twp; farm, Twp official; Elder in Somonauk Presby Ch.

MERRIMAN, Peter, bc1815 PA; d af1870; m (1) Mary FRENCH, issue Milton, Orlina/Arlina "Lucy," Sidney, Abby, Richard, Marcus, William Henry, Arthur; m (2) Almira; Wyoming Twp, Lee Co, IL; received mail at Shabbona Grove, DeKalb Co, IL; carpenter; West Cit.

MERRITT, Charles H., b1818 NY, son of Joseph and Mary (DEAN) MERRITT, bro-in-law to James Hoy BEVERIDGE; d1868 IL; m Flora L. DISBROW, issue H.L., Mary E.; Sycamore Twp; clerk; Cong.

MILLER, Daniel O., bc1830 PA, son of Asa and Mary Ann (COON) MILLER; d af1880; m Jane IRWIN, issue Maggie, Lizzie B., Thomas B., Mary E.; Paw Paw Twp; farm, post office clerk; West Cit; moved to Cook Co, IL, bf1870, to LaSalle Co, IL bf1880.

MILLER, Margaret "Caroline" (SHARP), b1822 NY, dau Jacob and Nancy (WINDFALL) SHARP; d1902 IL; m Andrew MILLER, issue Nancy, Hannah, Sarah A., Adeline, Nettie M.; Somonauk Twp; husband farm; West Cit; moved to Kendall Co, IL bf1870.

MILLER, Peter, b1816 NY, son of Simeon and Betsey (BEDELL) MILLER; d1908 IL; m Elizabeth QUILHOT, issue Cornelia Elizabeth, Cornelius P., Hannah, Isaac P., Peter V., Mary Elizabeth, Minard/Myndert Sylvanus, Catherine J.; Shabbona Twp; land patent; farm; West Cit.

MILLER, Samuel G., bc1810 IN; d1880 IL; m (1) Gilley Marshall SEBREE, issue Marshall, John, William, Charles, Melissa, Augusta; m (2) Jane, issue Samuel, Archibald; Squaw Grove Twp; land patent; farm; West Cit; lived in DeKalb Co bf1840.

MILLER, William A., bc1825 IN; d1901 IL; m Jeannette PHEBUS, issue Mary E., Melinda J., Nancy E., Augusta Ann, Frances, William, Ellen; Squaw Grove Twp; farm; West Cit.

MILNE, Allen, bc1820 Scotland; d bf1870; m Laurinda, issue Ella, Byron; Clinton, Shabbona Twps; land patent; farm; West Cit.

MOORE, James, b1815 NY, son-in-law of Joseph A. THOMPSON; d1858 IL; m Mariah/Maria P. THOMPSON, issue Myron Wallace, Margaret Jane, Joseph H., Sara Elizabeth, James Irwin/Erwin; Somonauk Twp; farm; West Cit.

MOORE, Voranus "Emory," b1811 MA, son of Royal Gideon MOORE; d bf1880 IL; m (1) Silvia MATTESON, issue Clarissa Matilda, James Harrington, Charles Henry, Jonathan Fairbanks, Sarah Emeline, Voranus Emory; m (2) Phebe Anne COFFIN, issue, Cylus, Marcellus, Cynthia, William Paul, Julia Lilia, Jane Ann, Royal Robert Gideon, Mary Rosetta, Martian, Guy Emory; Genoa Twp; farm; West Cit; lived in DeKalb Co bf1840; moved to McLean Co, IL, bf1880.

MORELAND, Hugh, bc1822 Ireland, son of William And Sarah (THOMPSON) MORELAND; d1922 CA; m Prudence JENNINGS, issue John J., Hugh, Elizabeth, William H., Alfretta Evilina, Clara W., George F., Ida S., Cassifreane; Mayfield Twp; land patent; farm; West Cit; moved to LaSalle Co, IL bf1870.

MORRISON, John, b1819 Scotland, son of William and Margaret (COVENTRY) MORRISON; d1906 IL; m Jane McGUE, issue Agnes Mary, William John; Victor Twp; farm.

MORSE, Isaac Finn, b1819 OH, son of William Amos and Hannah (FINN) MORSE; d1906 IL; m Sophia Aurella/Aurellia PARK, issue Mary A., Sylvia L., Olive J., William S., Frank F., Ida Cornelia, Willis P., Llewellyn H., Althea E., Clara A., Clyde S.; Shabbona Twp; farm; West Cit.

MULFORD, Jeremiah, bc1794 NY, son of Edward and Fanny (RISAM/RYSAM) MULFORD; d1880 NY; m Mary LEE, issue, George L, Julietta G., Caroline L., Chauncey W., Edward C., Gertrude D., Ursula P., Mary L.; Clinton, Victor Twps; land patent; farm, Postmaster Van Buren, Victor Twps; West Cit.

MULLEN, John Ousterhout, b1797 NY; father-in-law to Ira NICHOLS and Ephraim P. NICHOLS; d1881 IL; m (1) Phebe BROWN, issue Esther, Elizabeth, Johnathan, Sarah Ann, Phillip, Harker; m (2) Mary, no issue; m (3) Rachel DEYO[E], no issue; Mayfield Twp; land patent; farm; West Cit; R; Wesleyan Meth; "pioneer of the town of Mayfield"[85]; lived in DeKalb Co bf1840.

MUMFORD, Thomas, bc1794 England, father-in-law to Seymour HIX; m Sarah SHILLIBEER/SILLIBEER, issue, Sarah, Louisa, Eliza; Mayfield Twp; land patent; farm; West Cit.

MURRAY, John, bc1825 Ireland; d af1900 IL; m Elizabeth "Betsey" SMITH, issue William, Mary, Hugh E., Catherine E. and Ellis/Alice E. (twins), Annie J., Margaret, Elizabeth; Franklin Twp; farm; Wesleyan Meth; moved to Boone Co, IL, bf1900.

NEEDHAM, Benjamin Cooley III, b1814 NY, son of Benjamin Cooley and Achsah (THAYER) NEEDHAM II; d1885 IA; m (1) Charlotte BOWERS, issue Achsah; Perrin O., Irvin, Alice, Charles W.; m (2) Harriet (JAMES) BARRETT, issue Emma Alice; DeKalb Twp; land patent; farm; West Cit; moved to IA bf1860.

NEWTON, Adeline S./E., bc1835 ME; d af1880; m David B. NEWTON, issue Lillian B., Sarah A., Henry C.; Sycamore Twp; husband tombstone maker, marble worker; Cong; moved to ME bf1870.

NEWTON, Clarissa Cordelia "Clara," bc1820 VT, m Liberty J. NEWTON, issue Julia C., Alexander B., Clarissa A., Elihu B.; Campton Twp, Kane Co, IL; husband blacksmith; Cong; moved to IA bf1860, then to WI bf1870.

NICHOLS, Ephraim P., b1829 NY, son of Peter and Lucretia (CARPENTER) NICHOLS, grandson of Reuben and Mercy (CAVERLY) NICHOLS, nephew of John, Ira and Latin NICHOLS, son-in-law of John MULLEN; d1914 IL; m Sarah "Ann" MULLEN, issue Voorhees Wiley, Willard G., Elmer C., Millie J., Maggie A., Lena A., David L., Peter Ford., George L., Lillian V.; Mayfield Twp; farm; West Cit; Wesleyan Meth, Cong; "earnest Republican."[86]

NICHOLS, Ira, bc1817 NY, son of Reuben and Mercy (CAVERLY) NICHOLS, bro to Peter, John, Latin, bro-in-law to Charles TOWNSEND, son-in-law of John MULLEN, uncle to Ephraim P. NICHOLS; d1892 IL; m Esther MULLEN, issue Adeline, Adelia, John N., Milton, Orin, Charles H., Eliza J.; Mayfield Twp; land patent; farm, first settler in Mayfield Twp, one of people who selected first name "Liberty" for the Twp; West Cit; Wesleyan Meth, chairman of organizing meeting and one of first Trustees for Mayfield Wesleyan Meth Ch; "station-agent" for UGRR.[87]

NICHOLS, John, bc1814 NY, son of Reuben and Mercy (CAVERLY) NICHOLS, bro to Peter, Ira and Latin NICHOLS, bro-in-law to Charles TOWNSEND, uncle to Ephraim; d bf1880; m (1) Mary Ann TOWNSEND, issue Ira, Zelpha; m (2) Charlotte MOSES, issue Lucy, Louisa, Phebe; Mayfield Twp; land patent; farm; West Cit; Wesleyan Meth; Conductor on UGRR[88]; lived in DeKalb Co bf1840.

NICHOLS, Latin, b1820 NY, son of Reuben and Mercy (CAVERLY) NICHOLS, bro of Peter, Ira and John NICHOLS, bro-in-law to Charles TOWNSEND, Jeremiah L. BROWN and Caleb M. BROWN, uncle to Ephraim NICHOLS, son-in-law of Abner JACKMAN; d1906 IL; m Armena JACKMAN, issue Mary E., Martha L., Clara E.; Mayfield and Malta Twps.; land patent; farm and Innkeeper; West Cit; Wesleyan Meth; "a man of strong convictions"[89]; lived in DeKalb Co bf1840.

NICHOLS, Peter, b1803 NY, son of Reuben and Mercy (CAVERLY) NICHOLS, bro to John, Ira, and Latin NICHOLS, bro-in-law to Charles TOWNSEND, father-in-law to Demmon DECKER and William READ; d1865 IL; m Lucretia CARPENTER, issue Benjamin, Reuben, Ephraim, Abigail, Amos, Stephen, Hannah, John, Joshua, Cirenice, William; Mayfield Twp; land patent; farm; West Cit; Wesleyan Meth; "stanch advocate of abolition principles"[90] and conductor on UGRR[91]; lived in DeKalb Co bf1840.

NICHOLS, Reuben, b1770 NY, son of Ephraim and Ester (PEET) NICHOLS; d1844 IL; m Mercy CAVERLY, issue Benjamin, Esther, Amy, Peter, Ephraim, Abigail, Phebe, John, Ira, Amos, Latin; Mayfield Twp; land patent; harness, boot and shoemaker, farm, one of first Trustees for Mayfield Wesleyan Meth Church, one of first Grand Jurors for DeKalb Co; Wesleyan Meth; lived in DeKalb Co bf1840.

NICHOLS, Stephen Luther, bc1837 IL, son of Peter and Lucretia (CARPENTER) NICHOLS; d1923; m Helen/Ellen Jane DRAKE, issue James Byron, Mina V., Verna V.; Mayfield Twp; farm; Wesleyan Meth; moved to IA bf1920.

NICHOLSON, Eunice (CLARK), b1812, dau Abram CLARK; d1879 IL; m Thomas NICHOLSON, issue Joshua, David H., John W., Charles W., Lydia A., Susan R., William L., Catharine J., Edward J., George M., Thomas C., Fremont; Paw Paw Twp; husband farm; West Cit.

NICKERSON, Mulford, b1789 CT, son of Archelaus and Dorothy (HOLCOMB) NICKERSON; d1877 IL; m Eunice HANCHETT, issue William A., Eunice Ette, Dean G.; Mayfield Twp; land patent; farm, minister, one of first Twp Supervisors, one of first Co Supervisors; West Cit; Wesleyan Meth; Liberty Party, R; "station-agent" for UGRR.[92]

NICKERSON, William A., bc1811 CT, son of Mulford and Eunice (HANCHETT) NICKERSON; d1909 MI; m Roxana, issue George, Mulford, Albert, Dewey/Dana; Mayfield Twp; land patent; farm, minister, Twp. Supervisor; West Cit; Wesleyan Meth, first minister and one of first Trustees for Mayfield Wesleyan Meth Church; R, one of DeKalb Co Republican Party organizers; conductor on UGRR.[93]

NISBET, Matthew, b1819 Scotland, son of William and Isabella (DREW) NISBIT; d1874 IL; m Nancy/Agnes HARPER, issue Elizabeth, Isabella, William, James, Mary, Lawrence; Paw Paw Twp; farm; West Cit.

NORCUTT, Norman Newell, b1814 NY, son of Winslow and Anna NORCUTT; d1887 MN; m Sarah Rose MCKINLEY, issue George Washington, Rachel Anna, Julietta, Sallie, Eliza Jane "Jennie," Nixon Hartman, Mary Annette "Nettie," Mable, Robert Newell, Georgianna, Minnie Bell, William Cyrus; Sycamore Twp; land patent; farm; West Cit; lived in DeKalb Co bf1840; moved to WI by 1860.

NORTON, Henry/Harvey, bc1812 NY, son of William and Abigail NORTON; d af1860; m Mary A. FORD, issue Sidney, Mary E., Francis E.; Shabbona Twp; farm; West Cit.

NORTON, Oliver William, b1811 NY, son of Sereno and Harriet (MORSE) NORTON; d1873 MI; m (1) Henrietta M. WILLCOX, issue Albert, Oliver Willcox, Elizabeth Lane, Edwin, Harriet Morse, Sereno, Chauncey Louis; m (2) Sarah "Sally" SWEZEY, issue Helen, Henry, Harlan Page, Horatio Nelson, Lawrence Adelbert, Grant; Sycamore Twp; minister, First Cong Ch, Sycamore, 1847; declined to remain in Sycamore when the vote to retain him as minister was not unanimous because of his antislavery views; moved to WI 1848, to NY bf1850.

OBERTON/OVERTON, Isabella C., bc1837 NY; m unknown OBERTON; Sycamore Twp; milliner; Cong; moved to Cook Co, IL by 1861.

OLMSTEAD, Isaac "Lewis," b1802 CT, son of David and Rebecca (JACKSON) OLMSTEAD, bro to Mathew William and Nathan OLMSTEAD; d1892 IL; m (1) Eleanor OWEN(S), issue Elizabeth, Aaron, Silas, Harman and Hector (twins), Lewis, John C.; m (2) Marietta (HEATH) WITHERSPOON, issue Mary E., Lewis Minard, Frederick J.; Shabbona Twp; land patent; farm, Shabbona Twp. Supervisor; West Cit; lived in DeKalb Co bf1840.

OLMSTEAD, Mathew "William" b1804 CT, son of David and Rebecca (JACKSON) OLMSTEAD, bro to Isaac Lewis and Nathan OLMSTEAD; d1887 IL; m (1) Catharine Ann LOCKERBY, issue Robert L., Hannah, Amenia/Araminta, Rebecca, William W.; m (2) Mary WALKER, stepdaughters, Wealthy, Rosetta; m (3) Armina LOCKERBY; Shabbona, Clinton Twps; land patent; farm, school treasurer; West Cit; R; lived in DeKalb Co bf1840.

OLMSTEAD, Nathan, b1809 CT, son of David and Rebecca (JACKSON) OLMSTEAD, bro to Isaac Lewis and Mathew William OLMSTEAD; d1889 IA; m Julia Ann KNAPP, issue Louisa Melissa, Alonzo L., Edwin F., Oscar, Orrin P., Theodore G., Julius, Julia Ann, Lydia, Silas; Shabbona Twp; land patent; farm, minister; West Cit; lived in DeKalb Co bf1840, moved to IA bf1860.

OLMSTEAD, William Wallace, bc1838 IL, son of Mathew "William" and Catherine (LOCKERBY) OLMSTEAD, son-in-law of John WALKER, nephew of Isaac "Lewis" and Nathan OLMSTEAD; d1876 IL; m Helen WALKER, issue John M., Minnie; Shabbona, Clinton Twps; CW 32nd IA Regt; West Cit; lived in DeKalb Co bf1840.

ORMSBY, John, bc1813 NY; m (1) Hannah, issue Jesse H., Monroe Madison, Betsy Harriet, Eleanor Josephine, Sarah Bowen, Gusta/Christopher C., Ida A., Casius M., Eva R.; m (2) Betsy KINCADE, no issue; Pampas/Cortland Twp; farm, carpenter and joiner; West Cit; moved to Kane Co, IL bf1860.

ORPUT, James M., b1824 OH, son of Richard and Relephe ORPUT, bro to John ORPUT; d1906 IL; m (1) Almina/Elmira CRILL, issue, Charlie, Frankey; m (2) Maria ROGERS, issue James M. "Jay," Amanda "Kittie," Grace; South Grove, Malta Twps; land patent; farm, machinist, wagon maker; West Cit.

ORPUT, John Buchnell, bc1821 OH, son of Richard and Relephe ORPUT, bro to James ORPUT; d1884 IL; m Sarah A. CRILL, issue Amanda Melvina, John Manfred, Eugene Lay, George D., Lefi, Cora "Carrie" L., Mabel C.; South Grove Twp; land patent; farm; West Cit; lived in DeKalb Co bf1840; moved to Winnebago Co, IL bf1870.

ORR, David, b1818 OH, son of Samuel and Mary Jane (BURNETT) ORR, bro-in-law to James, Edward and John McCLEERY; d1893 IA; m (1) Elizabeth McCLEERY, issue Mary Ann, James Doig, Margaret "Ellen," John S., William T., Edward "Smith"; m (2) Martha Jane McAFFEE, issue Levi Ray, Sarah Jane, David E.; Clinton Twp; farm, carpenter, hardware merchant; West Cit; R; Presby.

PAGE, Austin, b1809 MA, son of Phineas/Phinehas and Lynthia/Cynthia (MACOMBER) PAGE, bro to Horatio Franklin PAGE; d1884; m Sarah A. MILES, issue Elizabeth/Eliza A., Horatio F; Sycamore, Pampas/Cortland Twps; teacher, farm; R; Cong, Meth.

PAGE, Dr. Horatio Franklin, b1811 MA, son of Phineas/Phinehas and Lynthia/Cynthia (MACOMBER) PAGE; d1873 IL; m Elizabeth PRATT, issue Horatio; Sycamore Twp; land patent; physician, first doctor in Sycamore; West Cit; one of founding mbrs of Sycamore First Cong Ch, one of first Trustees, later became Episcopal; R; home a station for UGRR[94]; lived in DeKalb Co bf1840.

PAINE, Clarinda (VAN HORNE), b1824 NY, dau Philip and Margaret (ECKLER) VAN HORNE, dau-in-law of Eliza PAINE; mother-in-law to Everell F. DUTTON; d1898 IL; m Harmon PAINE, issue Julia Ann, Rosina Adelpha, William Burtis, Ida DeEtte; Sycamore Twp; husband innkeeper, farm; Univ.

PAINE, Eliza, b1799 NY, dau Garret and Elizabeth (VAN HORNE) WYCKOFF, step-mother-in-law to Clarinda PAINE; d1800 IL; m Chester PAINE, issue Seth B., Cornelius B., Harmon, Alfred, Daniel B., Brewster C., Angeline Eliza, Sarah Ann, Harrison, Grant; Sycamore Twp; housekeeper; Univ.

PARKER, Silas "Smith," bc1825 NY, son-in-law of Enos and Sally (BURDICK) CHEASBRO, bro-in-law of Enos Larkin CHEASBRO, Jr. ; d1908 CA; m Mary Ann CHEASBRO, adopted Harriet; Pampas/Cortland Twp; land patent; farm; West Cit; Freewill Baptist; R.

PATTEN, Alexander Robertson, b1823 NY, son of James and Mary (ROBERTSON) PATTEN, bro of Robert and William PATTEN, son-in-law of George BEVERIDGE; d1864 IL; m Agnes BEVERIDGE, issue James A., George

W., William Livingston, Thomas Beveridge, Henry J.; Sandwich, Somonauk Twps; land patent; farm, merchant, Justice of the Peace, Somonauk Postmaster; Presby, one of first mbrs Somonauk Presby Ch.

PATTEN, James, bc1810/1814 PA; m Elizabeth, issue Mary, James M., George; Kingston Twp; farm; West Cit.

PATTEN, Mary (ROBERTSON), b1793 NY, dau William and Mary (LIVINGSTON) ROBERTSON; d1890 IL; m James PATTEN, issue William, Eleanor Livingston, Robert, Alexander Robertson, Martha Nesbit; Sandwich, Somonauk Twps; land patent; husband farm; charter mbr Somonauk Presby Ch.

PATTEN, Robert, b1820 NY, son of James and Mary (ROBERTSON) PATTEN, bro of Alexander and William PATTEN; d1876 KS; m Catherine M. SIBLEY, issue Mary Catherine, Helen Martha, Alice Lovica, Gilbert Robertson, Julia Frances; Somonauk Twp; land patent; farm, harness maker, postmaster Sandwich; one of first mbrs Somonauk Presby Ch.

PATTEN, William, b1817 NY, son of James and Mary (ROBERTSON) PATTEN, bro of Alexander and Robert PATTEN; d1897 CO; m (1) Elizabeth Nelson PRATT, issue James Miller, Simon Newcomb, Edward Moses, Simon Nelson, Jennie M.; m (2) Jane SOMES, issue Charles J., Anna Mary, Alexander Robertson, William Somes, Frederick Livingston; Somonauk Twp; land patent; farm, CW Capt. 156th IL Inf, Twp. Supervisor, Representative in IL State Legislature 1854–1862, IL State Senator 1866–1870; West Cit; one of first Elders in Somonauk Presby Ch, William and Elizabeth both charter mbrs.

PATTERSON, John, b1821 PA, son of Joseph and Eleanor (COMPTON) PATTERSON; d1899 IL; m Mary Jane GREGORY, issue Eleanor Jane, John Robert, James Cozier, Lyman Lee, Caroline, Joseph, Fred Gregory, Lew Ezra; Genoa Twp; farm; West Cit.

PEAVY, Nehemiah Potter, b1796 NY/ME, son of Ichabod and Marjorie (POTTER) PEAVY; d1873 IL; m Selinda Jane WOOD, issue Electa, Noah Wood, Malissa Jane, Ichabod Wood, Erastus W., Julia, Samantha, William B., Joshua I., Lucy T., Selinda, Sabrina, Nehemiah Lewis, Horatio Nelson, William B., Selinda Jane, Isaac, Ira; Sycamore Twp; farm, War of 1812 Pvt. in Sprague's 55th Regt.; West Cit.

PECK, Harriet C., bc1823 CT; d bf1880; m Timothy T. PECK, issue Timothy S.; Sycamore, Cortland Twps; husband merchant, Twp Supervisor; Univ.

PECK, Nathan H., bc1816 CT; d1893 IL; m (1) Margaret ELLIOTT, issue Charles V., Mary J., Harriet; m (2) Lydia K. CALL, issue Frank; Cortland Twp; merchant, brick mason, Twp Supervisor; both Nathan and Lydia charter mbrs Sycamore Univ Ch, Ch trustee; supported doctrine of universal salvation[95]; moved to Lee Co. IL bf1860, back to DeKalb Co. IL bf1870.

PERKINS, Moses Smith, b1818 NY, son of Sylvester and Ruth (HOOKER) PERKINS; d1896 KS; m (1) Sarah Byam SHAW, issue Daniel F., Adelia M., Sylvester L., Corydon Eudelmer, Eliza R. Viola, Carlos Licineas, Sarah L., Casalia H./Moses DeCasaili, Vilettie Belle; m (2) Martha Jane RIXON; m (3) Susan M.; m (4) Lizzie HOUSTON; Pampas/Cortland Twp; farm; West Cit; moved to KS bf1880.

PERRY, David I., bc1798 NY, son-in-law of Sarah BIRDSALL; d bf1880; m Mariah/Maria BIRDSALL, issue Sarah W., Amos, Adelade, John B.; Sycamore Twp; first resident minister for Sycamore First Cong Ch 1841–1843, farm; moved to McLean Co. IL bf1850.

PETERS, Luard, bc1807 VT, son of Jesse and Elizabeth (BURNS) PETERS; d1851 IA; m Merinda/Melinda COCHRAN, issue Anson Maxwell, Edwin D., Myran, Horace and Sarah Evelyn (Twins); Genoa Twp; farm; West Cit; moved to IA bf1851.

PETERS, Minerva M. (WEST), b1845 IL, dau of David and Sarah (CHAPIN) WEST, sis of Alice, Elias, Orrin, Asa "Porter," Sarah "Louise"; d af1900 IL; m Warren Francis PETERS, issue Harry W., David West; Sycamore Twp; keeping house, husband grocery store clerk; Cong.

PHELPS, William H., bc1812 NJ/NY, son of William and Cynthia (MARSTON) PHELPS; d1889 IL; m Elizabeth H. HOLLENBACK, issue Oscar W., Edgar M., Margaret, Elizabeth E., Ella Maria, George Franklin; Sycamore Twp; farm, sawyer, inventor, Co Sheriff 1854; West Cit; R; Univ; never arrested UGRR activists; lived in DeKalb Co bf1840.

PIERCE, Charles T., b1837 MA, son of Jonas and Fanny (EARLL/EARLE) PIERCE, son-in-law of Jesse C. KELLOGG; d1905 IL; m Emily Jane "Jennie" KELLOGG, issue Jennie, Fannie, Mary E., Susan R., Catharine E.; Sycamore Twp; miller; Cong; moved to Whiteside Co, IL bf1880.

PIERSON, Timothy Freeman, b1816 NY, son of Isaac and Pluma PIERSON; d af1860; m Elizabeth B. COOPER, issue Jane M., Jacob "Isaac" Freeman, Mary E., Sophronia Sizer, Harriet E., Selina/Celina D., Euphemia "Pluma" Lucinda; Afton, Pampas/Cortland, Pierce Twps; farm, Afton Twp. Supervisor, CW Co. U, 92nd IL Inf.; West Cit.

PIKE, Silas Othello, bc1817 NJ; d1887 IL; m Elizabeth E.H., issue Silas Othello, Jr., Emma Elizabeth; Sycamore Twp; wagon/coach maker; West Cit.

PIPER, David, bc1803 PA; d bf1860; m Margaret TAYLOR, issue Samuel, Issac, William, Joseph, James, David; Mayfield Twp; farm; West Cit.

POPLIN, Rachel (HARMON), b1811 NC, dau of Amos and Rebecca (SHEPPARD)HARMON; d af1880; m William B. POPLIN, issue Sarah J., Harriet L., Mary A., Rebecca C./Caroline Rachel, Fannie E./A., Jesse F.; Somonauk Twp; land patent; husband farm; West Cit; Presby; R; "latchstring was always out [for] runaway slaves"[96]; lived in DeKalb Co bf1840.

PORTER, Jedediah, bc1813 NY; d af1870; m Mary Ann/Marian, issue Amos, George, Emily, Riley, Ellen/Elden; Mayfield Twp; farm; West Cit, Wesleyan Meth; moved to MI bf1870.

POTTER, Chester, b1796 CT, son of Daniel and Naomi (CRISSEY) POTTER; d1855 IL; m Dinah MILLER, issue Cornelia E., Henry, Daniel, William, Harvey, Mary, Joseph S., T.H. "Benton"; Somonauk Twp; land patent; stone mason, farm, DeKalb Co Coroner; West Cit; lived in DeKalb Co bf1840.

POTTER, Henry, bc1822 NY, son of Chester and Dinah (MILLER) POTTER; m Ann/Anna Maria, issue unknown; Somonauk Twp; land patent; farm; West Cit.

POTTER, John, b1802 NY, son of Capt. Jeremiah II and Polly (BARNES) POTTER; d1867 IL; m Delilah CROSBY, issue Jeremiah C., Henry L.; Kingston Twp; farm; West Cit.

POWERS, Asa F., bc1822 PA, son of David and Hannah Mary (LITTLE) POWERS; d af1893; m (1) Amanda LITTLE, issue Clarinda M., Clinton H.; m (2) Rebecca HUNTLY, issue Catharine, step-dau Elizabeth HUNTLY; m (3) Mary "Polly" ROWDEN, issue Andres Jackson and Ulysses "Grant"; m (4) Lucinda JANKINS, issue Mary A.,

Charles Francis, Lora Mabel, Jesse Austin, Katie C.; Kingston Twp; land patent; farm; West Cit; moved to Boone Co IL bf1860; to MO bf1869.

PRATT, Almus, bc1807 CT, son of Wolcott and Mary (LAY) PRATT; d af1876; m (1) Sarah "Sally" A. COLLINS, issue Sibert, Collins Lewis, Catharine, Joanna "Jenny," Phebe, Mary; m (2) Elizabeth J. BARTLETT, issue Theda M., Frederick A.; Somonauk Twp; land patent; farm; West Cit; Baptist; lived in DeKalb Co bf1840.

PRESCOTT, William Reid, bc1824 VT, son of Daniel Moulton and Henrietta (HARRINGTON) PRESCOTT; d1904 KS; m Almira/Almina Mary WILLMARTH, issue Eliza Almira/Almina, Sarah/Lavilla, Asa William, Daniel Webster, Alice A. and Agnes A. (twins), Franklin F., Mary Ellen; Clinton, Victor Twps; farm; West Cit.

PRESTON, Justus, b1793 CT, bro-in-law to Ephraim HALL; d1847 IL; m Sina HALL, issue Jared (?), Henry, Augustus, Charles, George L., Norman, Julia Elizabeth; Genoa Twp; land patent; West Cit; lived in DeKalb Co bf1840; voted with DeKalb Co. Abolitionists af1840 election,[97] "a warm friend of the slave."[98]

PRESTON, Sina (HALL), b1802 CT, dau of David Moss and Mindwell (BEECH) HALL, sis of Ephraim HALL; d1869 IL; m Justus PRESTON, issue Jared (?), Henry, Augustus, Charles, George L., Norman, Julia Elizabeth; Genoa Twp; husband land patent; West Cit, continued subscription in her own name after death of husband; lived in DeKalb Co bf1840.

PRICE, Mathias, bc1798 Nova Scotia, son of Richard and Anastasia (CODY) PRICE; d1878 WI; m Mary WATKINS, issue unknown; Shabbona Twp; laborer; West Cit.

PRITCHARD, Reuben, bc1798 VT, son of Thomas Gains and Lovina (COREY) PRITCHARD; d1856 IL; m Elotia/Maria MASON, issue Reuben Mason, Ethan A.; Clinton Twp; land patent; farm, mbr first Co Board of Supervisors, Twp. Supervisor; Whig delegate to organizing Republican convention 1854,[99] hosted c1840 Abolitionist meeting at his home.[100]

PURCELL, James, b1830 Ireland, son of James and Ann PURCELL; d1907 IL; m Lucy KEEFE, issue John L., George H., Mary C., Charles R., Valentine; Mayfield, South Grove Twps; land patent, may have belonged to his father; farm, hired hand for William DEYOE; Catholic; conductor on UGRR.[101]

PURDUN/PURDAM, John M., b1827 OH, son of David and Hannah (BLUE) PURDUN; d1882 OH; m Amanda C. STARKEY, issue Emma Jane, Allie/Olive H., Charles Franklin, John Holland, Oscar M., Albert A.; Sycamore Twp; blacksmith, farmer; West Cit; moved to IA bf1860.

RALPH, Justin, bc1814 NY; m unknown; DeKalb Twp; farm; West Cit.

RAND, Aaron, bc1793 MA, son of Daniel and Judith (ROBINSON) RAND; d1887 IA; m (1) Pamelia/Permelia AINSWORTH, issue Daniel, Aaron Jr., William O./Willard Pritchard, Henry Laben, Electa, Lucetta/Judith P., Silas; m (2) Elizabeth CRONKHITE, issue unknown; Franklin Twp; farm; West Cit; moved to IA bf1860.

RANSOM, Thomas Lord, b1820 OH, son of Truman and Temperance Colt (LORD) RANSOM; m (1) Ann PIERSON, issue Temperance Lord, Truman, Adolphus, Lorenzo; m (2) Elizabeth (PUTNAM)/MAXFIELD, issue Ellen, Mary, Clara Belle, William L., Truman Arthur; Sycamore Twp; mill wright; Cong; moved to OH bf1857, to IN bf1870.

RATHBUN/RATHBONE, Edwin Jay, b1820 NY, son of Damarcus and Amanda Emily (HILL) RATHBUN; d1894 MO; m Laura A. MUNSELL/MUNSALL, issue Cyrenus E., Frances M., Millard F., Daniel W., Alfretta, Florence; Pampas/Cortland Twp; farm; West Cit; moved to MO bf1880.

RAYMOND, Nichodemus L., bc1808 VT, son of Nichodemus and Marthy (LINCOLN) RAYMOND; d1885 IL; m Eveline M. MARSHALL, issue Harriett M., Emily, Matilda, Sarah, Ann, Ellen, Eveline, Mary/Maryette/Margaret, Sophronia, Andrew Marshall, Zeruah "Mariah," Henry "Foster" J., Flora/Laura "Jennie"; Kingston Twp; farm; West Cit.

READ, William, b1822 New Brunswick, son-in-law of Peter NICHOLS; d1899 IL; m Abigail NICHOLS, issue Ann R., Matilda J., Peter N., William Benjamin., Eva L., Eugene, Cora/Carrie W.; Mayfield Twp; farm; Wesleyan Meth.

REEVES, Michael Dean, b1816 IN/KY, son of John and Thurisa (DEAN) REEVES; m (1) Martha Patty HARRINGTON, issue Cinderella, John, Joseph Harrington, George W., Mary, Julia Phoebe, Sarah Elizabeth, Idella Elvira, James Dean, Martha, Harriet Irene, Michael, Charles; m (2) Huldah M. NEWMAN, issue Hariet, Al, Chas, Charles; Genoa Twp; land patent; farm; West Cit; moved to MN bf1860.

RENWICK, Herbert, bc1825 Scotland, son of Walter and Mary (WEIL) RENWICK; d1876 IL; m Eliza Ann BURNETT, issue John, Jannette, William; Pierce, Pampas/Cortland Twps; farm; West Cit.

RICHARDS, Nathaniel F., bc1828 NY; d1920 IL; m Ruth BAXTER, issue Mary "Ella," Charles R., Lydia; Sycamore Twp; blacksmith; Univ.

RICHARDSON, Asa, bc1797 MA, son of Daniel RICHARDSON; d1869 IL; m Betsey MERRICK, issue James Asa, Daniel Somers, Nathan, Merrick, William Lysander; Virgil, Kane Co, IL; farm; Cong.

RICHARDSON, George Washington, b1825 NY, son of Benjamin and Judith (MASON) RICHARDSON; d1887 IL; m Maria/Mariah E. HAZLETT, issue Ella P., Florence A., Clarence, Alida/Lyda B., Edgar H., George W.; Genoa Twp; farm; West Cit.

RICHARDSON, Joseph A., bc1820 VT; m Ann; DeKalb Twp; land patent; farm; West Cit.

RICHARDSON, Peter, bc1822 VT; d af1870; m Lucinda WYMAN, issue Lena, Eva/Mary, Livingston, Peter, Bessie; Sycamore Twp; farm; Cong; moved to IA bf1860.

RICHMOND, Elisha, b1817 NY, son of Elijah and Sally (STEVENS) RICHMOND; d1901 MI; m Lucina STEVENS, issue Ruth Altha, Nelson Ellis, Orange, Tyler Webster, Elisha J., Lucius Adelbert, Squire Alfred, Emily L.; Paw Paw Twp; farm; West Cit; moved to IA bf1860.

RIDDLE, Enoch, b1799 NH, son of James and Sally (CARR) RIDDELL; d1865 IL; m Mary "Polly" PRESCOTT, issue Reuben Prescott, Adoniram, James Lyman, Betsey Arozina, George W., Robert S., Cyrus S., Charles B.; Victor Twp; farm; West Cit.

ROBERTS, Robert H., b1836 NY, son of William T. and Mary (WILLIAMS) ROBERTS; m Susan Emma SMITH, issue A. Wallace; Sycamore, DeKalb Twps; clerk, grocer, County Treasurer; R; moved to KS 1857 where he was "disturbed by the strife engendered by the slave element ... espoused the Free-Soil cause,"[102] worked with Kansan James H. Lane who supplied guns to antislavery men in KS; returned to DeKalb Co 1858.

ROBERTSON, William, b1805 NY, son of John and

Christie (McLAUGHLIN) ROBERTSON); d1885 IL; m (1) Isabella WILLIAMSON, issue Mathew, John, Daniel, Charles, Alexander, Henry, William Russell, Robert Andrew, Margaret Isabel; m (2) Margaret GRAHAM, issue Angeletta "Nettie," Christie, Robert, Anna; Clinton Twp; farm; William and Isabella charter mbrs Somonauk Presby Ch.

ROBINSON, Charles Jones, bc1822 NY, son of Almon/Almond and Mercy ROBINSON, bro to Ezra W. ROBINSON; d1908 MN; m (1) Clarinda ROSE, issue Mary, Chester, Ruth; m (2) Elizabeth RAND, issue Mary E., Charles; Sycamore Twp; teacher, carpenter, joiner; West Cit; Cong; one of 11 men consenting to 1848 tax assessment on personal property to construct new house of worship; moved to DeKalb Co bf1840; moved to MN bf1854.

ROBINSON, Ezra W., bc1830 NY, son of Almon/Almond and Mercy ROBINSON, bro to Charles J. ROBINSON, son-in-law to Rufus COLTON; d1922 KS; m Clarissa Gertrude COLTON, issue Arthur, Hemte R., John; Sycamore Twp; teacher, farm, carpenter, Deputy Clerk of Circuit Court DeKalb Co., 1857 Register of Deeds and Clerk of District Court in Lykens/Miami Co, KS, Probate Judge of Miami Co. KS; West Cit; R; Cong affiliation; "enthusiastic Free-state man"[103]; moved to DeKalb Co bf1840; moved to KS bf1857.

ROBINSON, Mercy, bc1799 MA; m Almon ROBINSON, issue Almon, Amos, Ezra W., Charles Jones, Samuel, Albert, Bathena/Bethany R.; Sycamore Twp; nurse; both Mercy and Almon mbrs Sycamore First Cong; lived in DeKalb Co bf1840; moved to KS 1867.

ROGERS, Amos Jr., b1823 NY, son of Amos and Mary (CHAPIN) ROGERS; d1917 IL; m Louisa Jane CHAPPELL, issue Rhoda S./Louisa R., Clarence D., Estella "Stella" J.; Pampas/Cortland Twp; farm; Cong; told UGRR stories to granddaughter.[104]

ROGERS, Jacob Drake, b1803 PA, son of Elihu and Rhoda (DRAKE) ROGERS; d1882 MN; m Elizabeth GOBLE, issue Phebe, Ezekiel Goble, Rhoda, Margaret, Jane, Jacob, Eugene, Rosilla; Wyoming Twp, Lee Co, IL; land patent; carpenter, joiner; conductor and home a station for UGRR.[105]

ROSE, Chauncey Delos, b1800 NY, son of Joseph and Ruth (WHITNEY) ROSE, bro to Jesse and Ellsworth ROSE, bro-in-law to David WEST; d1846 IL; m Selina Emma PORTER, issue Edwin P., Louisa, Delos; Sycamore Twp; land patent; farm; West Cit; Cong.

ROSE, Dr. Ellsworth P., b1811 NY, son of Joseph and Ruth (WHITNEY) ROSE, bro to Jesse and Chauncey, bro-in-law to David WEST, stepfather-in-law to Henry WOOD; d1892 IL; m Emily (CARRIER) RICHARDS BUNDY, no issue; stepdaughters Theresa Emilia RICHARDS, Rhoda "Elizabeth" RICHARDS; Sycamore Twp; physician, one of first doctors in Sycamore; West Cit; Cong; R; Whig delegate to convention organizing Republican Party 1854,[106] one of "aging Abolitionists" attending David West's 80th birthday party.[107]

ROSE, Jesse, b1809 NY, son of Joseph and Ruth (WHITNEY) ROSE, bro to Ellsworth and Chauncey, bro-in-law to David West, son-in-law to Asahel STOWE; d1899 MN; m Louisa Jane STOWE, issue Joseph M., Henry, William H., Lydia Lucinda, Mary; Sycamore Twp; land patent; farm, shingle maker, lumberman, DeKalb Co. Judge, Mower Co, MN, Judge Probate; West Cit; both Jesse and wife founding mbrs Sycamore First Cong Ch; "in charge of a certain section of the underground railroad,"[108] "prominent abolitionist,"[109] 1843 elected one of two Vice-Presidents of DeKalb County Anti-slavery Society,[110] 1847 Liberty Party candidate for County Probate Justice; lived in DeKalb Co. bf1840; moved to MN 1862.

ROSE, John Glencairn, bc1813 RI, son of Joshua and Lydia R. (MILLIKEN) ROSE; d1897 IL; m Abigail Smith GORTON, issue John Marcelis, Sereda/Ida Abigail Z., Mary Louisa, Caroline Amelia, Ernest Gorton, Jane Lydia/Lydia Jane, Harriet Etta, Lillian Maria; Somonauk Twp; farm; West Cit.

ROSE, Ruth (WHITNEY), b1772 MA; d1849 IL, mother-in-law to David WEST; m Joseph ROSE, issue Chester, Chauncey Delos, File, Lucinda, Joseph Jr., Jesse, Ellsworth, Orange; Sycamore Twp; Cong.

ROSEBROOK, William, bc1828 NY, son of Esdras and Abagail (CRAM) ROSEBROOK; d bf1870 IL; m Lois, issue William J; DeKalb Twp; farm; West Cit.

ROUNDSVILLE, William, bc1812 NY; d1878 IL; m Elvira RANDALL, issue William, Roxana E. Felicia/Fedelia F., Letitia L.; St. Charles, Kane Co, IL; first itinerant Univ minister in Sycamore; lived in Kane Co bf1840.

ROWLEY, Louisa F/B, b1824 NY; d1913 IL; m John W. ROWLEY, issue Frank, Edgar/Edward J., Emerson, Ida May, Lily S.; Sycamore Twp; carpenter and joiner; Univ.

RUGGLES, Stanley, bc1802 NY, son of John and Aphia (WARNER) RUGGLES; d1870 OR; m (1) Mabel COOPER, issue Lawrence Nelson, Ellen Elizabeth; m (2) Martha P. BARTLETT, issue, Emily R., Delia A., Mary A/Z, Luthena/Louisa A., Samuel; (2) Lavinia, issue Daniel L., Flora, Lucy; Paw Paw Twp; land patent; farm; West Cit; moved to OR bf1860.

SAFFORD, Edward Payson, b1837 NH, son of Charles Gilman and Mary Lancaster (BRIGHAM) SAFFORD, nephew of Henry Dudley SAFFORD; d1919 IL; m Sarah Frances SAFFORD (first cousin), issue Mary E., Henry, Charles H.E., Edward Brigham; Sycamore, Mayfield Twps; teacher, farm, DeKalb Co. Deputy Sheriff and Sheriff 1868, Twp Supervisor, CW Co A, 105th IL Inf.; R; Cong.

SAFFORD, Henry Dudley, b1819 NH, son of Dudley and Elizabeth Ann "Betsey" (GILMAN) SAFFORD; d1910 IL; m Sarah LITTLEFIELD, issue Ann E., Sarah Frances, Henry Frank, Marshal Dudley, Benjamin Gilman, Charles A., Richard B., Edward Baxter; South Grove, Sycamore Twps; land patent; farm, South Grove Postmaster, Co Sheriff 1858 and 1862; West Cit; Cong; never arrested UGRR activists.

SANBORN, Rufus Slocum, b1819 NH, son of Reuben and Pamelia (BOWEN) SANBORN; d1877 IL; m Emily Fay HOWARD, issue Susan A., Albert A., Clarence A., Rufus H., Frank Leroy; Sycamore Twp.; minister at Sycamore Univ Ch 1857–1862, inventor of the Sanborn Fireproof Safe patented 1866; moved to Rockford, Winnebago Co, IL bf1870.

SANSWORTH, David, b1818 VT, son of David and Lucinda SANSWORTH; d1871 IL; m Mary D., no known issue; Mayfield Twp; Wesleyan Meth.

SCHRYVER/SCHRIVER, Hannah Jane (MARTIN), bc1826 NY; d1901 IL; m Albert SCHRYVER/SCHRIVER, issue James Martin, George Gibson, Albert Cornelius, Clinton Eugene, Talmadge, Charles M., Frank; DeKalb Twp; husband farm; West Cit.

SEARS, Andrew B., bc1819 PA; d af1860; m. Mary Elizabeth VAN DEVENTER, issue Celestia Ann, Isaac, Albert, Franklin, Willis, Andrew; Shabbona Twp; land patent; farm, mechanic; West Cit; moved to TX bf1860.

SEAVY/SEAVEY, Samantha, bc1792 MA; d1872 IL; m

William SEAVY/SEAVEY, issue Lucy A.; Sycamore Twp; husband blacksmith; Cong.

SEELEY, John L., bc1832 NY, son of Sheldon and Lola (LEWIS) SEELEY; d af1880; m Charlotte B/R. WALLACE, issue Frances F./Lola Frances, Benjamin L., Leroy L., Frederick E.; Milan Twp; land patent; farm; West Cit; moved to IA bf1874, moved to NE bf1880.

SHANKLAND, Dr. John, bc1813 NY; m M.Ellen Ann, issue Perry, Alice, Nettie; Sandwich, Somonauk Twps; physician; charter mbr Somonauk Presby Ch; moved to MI bf1860, to WI bf1870.

SHAW, William Benjamin, bc1789 NY, son of Comfort, Jr. and Elizabeth (CARY) SHAW; d af1880; m Sarah "Sally" DIXON, issue Amaza, Betsey, Sarah; Sycamore, DeKalb, Milan Twps; farm, laborer; West Cit.

SHEFFIELD, Joseph, b1817 NY, son of Joseph and Polly (BOWERS) SHEFFIELD; d1880 KS; m Sarah Mariah/Maria JACKSON, issue Albert/Alpheus Jackson, Jennet "Nettie," Mary Jane; Shabbona, DeKalb Twps; farm; West Cit; moved to KS bf1870.

SHELDON, Abigail Brewer SMITH, b1812 MA, dau John and Abigail (BREWER) SMITH; d1876 IL; m Silas SHELDON Jr., issue Newton Brewer, Mariette Eliza, Calista Angeline, Oscar E./P., Henry S.; Pampas/Cortland Twp; land patent; husband farm; West Cit.

SHELEY, John b1804 NY, son of Matthew and Catrina (VAN BENSCHOTEN) SHELEY; d1868 IL; m (1) Elizabeth Bodley OUSTERHOUT, issue Obadiah "Dier"/"Dyer," Sylvester, Alva; m (2) Elizabeth "Betsy" Aikens WASHBURN, issue Sally Ann; m (3) Amela, issue Charles, Catherine A.; Kingston Twp; land patent; farm, first Twp Supervisor; West Cit.

SHEPARD/SHEPHARD, Dr. Andrew, b1803 NY; d bf1850 IL; m Eliza (NORTON) PROCTOR, issue Emily, Andrew, Martin, Eliza B., David, step-children Mary A. PROCTOR, Richard B. PROCTOR; Franklin Twp; land patent; physician, farm; West Cit; lived in DeKalb Co bf1840.

SHEPHARD, Elizabeth (DOTY), b1819 NY, dau Lebbeus E. and Electra (CHILDS) DOTY; d1880 MO; m Alvin Bradley SHEPHARD, issue Emma B., Myrtle Emma, James William; DeKalb Twp; Cong; moved to MO bf1870.

SHEPHERD/SHEPARD, Russell Chapel, b1826 NY, son of Thomas and Phebe (LEWIS) SHEPARD; d1917 KS; m Pluma Ann HITCHCOCK, issue Arabel, Eugene, Florence, Frank A. Sera E., Juliana, Don Carlos, William; DeKalb, Pierce Twps; farm; West Cit; moved to IA bf1868.

SHERBURNE, Hezekiah Calkins, b1795 NY; d1875 NE; m Mary Elizabeth HERRICK, issue Wiley, Martha Maria, Sarah, Rachel, James H., Eliza Jane, Minerva, William Herrick/Henry, Benjamin Franklin, John "Albert," Lucinda, Marietta, Emeline; DeKalb Twp; farm; West Cit; moved to Kane Co, IL bf1860, to NE bf1875.

SHURTLEFF, Albert, b1824 Canada, son of David and Ruth (KNAPP) SHURTLEFF; d af1910; m Clarissa "Clara" Abigail RICH, issue Ann G.; Genoa Twp; farm; West Cit; Meth Episcopal, then Cong; Abolitionist, cast his first presidential vote for James A. BIRNEY.[111]

SHURTLEFF, Alfred James, b1827 Canada, son of David and Ruth (KNAPP) SHURTLEFF; d1895 IL; m (1) Lyndia MILLER, issue unknown; m (2) Mary Fairchild HIGBY, issue Mary Eva, Carleton H., Kate, Edward, Frederick; Genoa Twp.; farm, cattle dealer; West Cit; moved to McHenry Co, IL bf1870.

SHURTLEFF, David, b1790 MA, son of Ichabod and Betty (PETTENGILL) SHURTLEFF Jr., bro to Ichabod SHURTLEFF III, father-in-law to Alexander CRAWFORD Jr.; d1866 IL; m Ruth KNAPP, issue Orilla, Jerusha, Mary, David, Albert, Laura, Alfred James, Giles Waldo "G.W.," Ephraim Blake; Genoa Twp; land patent; farm; West Cit; Meth, then Cong; R; "strong abolitionist being firmly opposed to the system of slavery as it existed in the south"[112]; lived in DeKalb Co bf1840.

SHURTLEFF, Ichabod III, b1797 MA, son of Ichabod and Betty (PETTENGILL) SHURTLEFF Jr., bro to David SHURTLEFF; d1870 IL; m Mahala KEMPTON, issue George, Elizabeth, Charles, Hannah, Calvin, Willard, Hiram, Caroline, Eliza; Genoa Twp; farm; West Cit.

SIGLIN, Jacob, b1810 PA, son of Johann Jacob and Susannah (SINGER) SEIGLIN; d1902 IL; m Hannah Jane SETZER, issue Rachel, Mary, Jacob, Susan E., Joshua, Isaiah "Ise," Zachary Taylor, Michael Wesley, Hannah "Jane/Jennie," Ellen F. "Ella"; Sycamore Twp; farm, School Director; West Cit; Meth; R.

SIMONS, Jabez Hopkins, b1802 NY, son of James and Mary SIMONS; d1860 IL; m Thirza VAN TUYL, issue Jacob Anderson, James, Miles "Gaylord," Malvinia/Malvina, Walter Van Tuyl, Margaret "Catherine"; Sycamore, Paw Paw Twps; farm; Cong; moved to Lee County, IL bf1850.

SIMONS, Laura Adelia, b1832 NY, dau of Aaron Chapin and Emily Victoria (ADAMS) WEST, niece of David WEST; d1909 SD; m Jacob Anderson SIMONS, issue Cyrus Ferdinand, Inez Viola, Edward Monroe, Grace Emma, Harry Leroy; Sycamore Twp; keeping house; Cong; moved to IA bf1870.

SIVWRIGHT, Alexander, b1800 Nova Scotia, son of James and Susan (DALRYMPLE) SIVWRIGHT, bro to James SIVWRIGHT, uncle to George M. SIVWRIGHT; d1886 IL; m Mary KILCUP, issue Elizabeth, Joseph, James, Nelson; Mayfield Twp; farm; West Cit; Wesleyan Meth.

SIVWRIGHT, George M., b1837 Nova Scotia; son of James M. and Prudence (EATON) SIVWRIGHT; d1913 IL; m Maria Louisa FAIRCLO, issue Guy T.; Mayfield, Sycamore Twps; farm, conductor on Sycamore Cortland RR; Wesleyan Meth.

SIVWRIGHT, James M., b1804 Nova Scotia, son of James and Susan (DALRYMPLE) SIVWRIGHT, bro to Alexander SIVWRIGHT, father-in-law to Edmund B. HARNED; d1878 IL; m Prudence EATON, issue David S., George M., Eunice Ann, Susan H., Alexander C., Wentworth E., James L., William W.; Mayfield Twp; farm, DeKalb Co Coroner; Wesleyan Meth.

SIVWRIGHT, Nelson, b1840 Nova Scotia, son of Alexander and Mary (KILCUP) SIVWRIGHT; d1901 IL; m Lucinda J. LUCAS, issue Alice B., Nelson, John; Mayfield Twp; Wesleyan Meth.

SIXBURY, Joseph, b1810 NY, son of Manasse Mans and Mary SIXBERRY; d1879 IL; m Melinda ELLWOOD, issue Chauncey E., Mary Elizabeth, John; Sycamore Twp; farm, Twp Assessor, Co Treasurer; West Cit; Meth; Democrat delegate to organizing Republican convention 1854[113]; lived in DeKalb Co bf1840.

SLY, Joseph, bc1801 Ireland; m Joanna; Somonauk Twp; farm; West Cit; Presby; lived in DeKalb Co bf1840.

SMITH, Albert V.L., bc1821 NY; m Lucy C., issue unknown; Pampas/Cortland Twp; farm; West Cit; Baptist affiliation.

SMITH, Charles, b1817 NY; d1894 IL; m1844 Harriet Newel GUILD; issue Emma L., adopted Clarence H.; Sycamore Twp; teacher, farm, businessman; West Cit; Cong; R; lived in Kane and DuPage Counties preceding CW, moved to Sycamore, DeKalb Co, afl871; worked with David West in UGRR; one of "aging Abolitionists" attending West's 80th birthday party,[114] "uncompromising Abolitionist."[115]

SMITH, Curtis, b1811 VT, son of Asahel and Elizabeth (KENDALL) SMITH, son-in-law to Oliver WILLARD, bro to Spafford SMITH; d1881 IL; m Lucy M. WILLARD, issue Asahel Curtis, Oliver Willard, Marvin Ammi, Charles "Herbert," Hosea "Eugene," Darwin Story, Lucy Amelia, Albert F.; Mayfield, Sycamore Twps; land patent; farm, teacher, Twp. Supervisor; charter mbr and Trustee Sycamore Univ Ch; entered county lands in own name, with Jesse Kellogg and Carlos Lattin, when county could not afford to purchase land; "prominent leader in Whig politics,"[116] 1845 Liberty Party candidate for Co Treasurer and Assessor; West Cit; "conscientiously opposed to the institution of negro slavery"[117]; lived in DeKalb Co bfl840.

SMITH, David A., b1820 Canada, son of James and Sarah "Sally" (STRAW) SMITH, step-father Edmund TOWN; d1892 IL; m (1) Elizabeth J. CARR, issue, Leander, Mary, Rebekah J. "Becky," Israel, Henry, Warren, Eliza A.; m (2) Annie SEYLER, issue unknown; Shabbona Twp; land patent; farm; West Cit; R; lived in DeKalb Co bfl840.

SMITH, Lawrence, bc1795 NY; d1860 IL; m Anna/Emma, issue Charlotte, Sanford Wilson, Olive, Ann, Adelia; Shabbona Twp; farm; West Cit.

SMITH, Oliver Willard, bc1839 VT, son of Curtis and Lucy M. (WILLARD) SMITH; d1881 IA; m Esther J. STILLWELL, issue Hattie M., Leroy A., Addie F., Olive W.; Mayfield, Sycamore Twps; farm; Cong.

SMITH, Rachel (MARTIN), b1803 VT, dau John and Rachel (BLISS) MARTIN; d1882 IL; m Chester SMITH, issue John Bliss; Sycamore Twp; housekeeper; Cong.

SMITH, Spafford, b1809 VT, son of Asahel and Elizabeth (KENDALL) SMITH, bro to Curtis SMITH, son-in-law of Oliver WILLARD, bro-in-law to Hosea WILLARD; d1895 IL; m (1) Eliza SHOLES, issue Louisa, Eliza Ann, Edwin P., Jennie C. (adopted); m (2) Marcia A. (WILLARD) VAN HORN; Mayfield, Sycamore Twps; land patent; farm, one of the first settlers in Coltonville; West Cit; Univ, later became Baptist; R; lived in DeKalb Co bfl840.

SMITH, William E., bc1813 Nova Scotia; m Maria, issue William S., James M., George B., Louisa R., Harriet C.; Sycamore Twp; painter; West Cit; moved to MO bfl870.

SNOW, Benjamin, bc1832 VT; d afl900 IL; m Abigail R., issue Frederick G; Sycamore Twp; farm laborer, teamster, CW 52nd IL Inf; Univ affiliation; moved to NY afl865, back to IL bfl880.

SNOW, Frederick Jeremiah, bc1826 NY, son of John Frederick and Margaret SNOW; d1915 IL; m (1) Elizabeth (2) Mary Minerva DIXON, issue Milo C., Emma R., Mary A., Fred W., Byron J.; Pampas/Cortland Twp; farm; West Cit; Cong.

SNOW, John Frederick, bc1799 MA; d afl860; m Margaret, issue Frederick Jeremiah, William M., Charles S., Mary B., Isaac R.; Pampas/Cortland Twp; land patent; blacksmith, Postmaster of Williamsburg 1851; Cong, one of 11 men consenting to 1848 tax assessment on personal property to construct new Sycamore house of worship, later mbr DeKalb First Cong Ch.

SOWERS, William, b1799 PA, son of John and Margaret SOWERS; d1876 IL; m Mary STROUSE, issue Sarah Ann, Andrew J., Mary, James, Rebecca, Melissa; Genoa, Sycamore Twps; carpenter, farm; West Cit.

SPENCER, Henry Martin, bc1822 NY; m Elizabeth "Ann" WILTBERGER, issue Asa, Julia A., Elizabeth "Lizzie" M., Jessie May, Helen; Clinton Twp; farm; West Cit; moved to Champaign Co. IL bfl870.

SPRING, George G., bc1821 NY, son of Samuel and Lament (STRATTON) SPRING; d1895 CA; m Alpona/Aluna C., issue Lucius G., Uri O., Cora E., William O.; Pampas/Cortland Twp; land patent; farm, charter mbr and Trustee in Univ Church; moved to CA bfl880.

STAFFORD, Moses, bc1785 NH, son of Abel and Rebecca (SHORT) STAFFORD; d1862 IA; m Sarah, issue Mehitable Isabel, John G., M.George Washington; Kingston Twp; land patent; farm; West Cit; lived in DeKalb Co bfl840; moved to Winnebago Co. IL bfl860, to IA bfl862.

STARK, David "Webster," b1826 PA, son of William and Ruth (McCLEARY) STARK, cousin to Marshall STARK; d afl880; m Amanda JUDD, issue William A., Janette Elizabeth "Lizzie," Frank W., Ephraim, Clara C., Perry J.; Sycamore, Mayfield Twps; farm, Co Deputy Sheriff; never arrested UGRR activists.

STARK, Marshall, b1813 PA, son of Oliver and Elizabeth "Betsey" (DIXON) STARK, cousin to David Webster STARK; d1882 IL; m Louisa Southwick TYLER, issue Harmon Marshall, Martha Samanthe, Mary Elizabeth, Jefferson O., Henry Jerome, Theron Monroe, Ada Louise, Ella Amanda, Frank, Emma J, Hattie Marinda; Sycamore Twp; land patent; teacher, farm, lumber dealer, hotel owner, one of first Petit Jurors for DeKalb Co. Circuit Court, Co Supt. of Schools, Twp. Supervisor, School Commissioner, Co Assessor, Co Sheriff 1848; West Cit; Meth; R; never arrested UGRR activists; lived in DeKalb Co bfl840.

STEVENS/STEPHENS, Asa Jr., d1849 IL; m unknown; Sycamore Twp; land patent; farm; West Cit; Cong.

STEVENS, John, b1799 NY; d1883 IL; m Marian/Mary/Marion, issue Lydia A., Harriet E., William Riley, Emma J., Silas R., Mariette, Edgar, Laura A.; Paw Paw Twp; farm; West Cit.

STEVENS, Samuel, bc1819 PA; m (1) Rebuk, issue Joseph B.; (2) Irene; (3) Philena; Genoa Twp; land patent; farm; West Cit; lived in DeKalb Co bfl840.

STEVENS, William R., bc1834 NY, son of John and Marian STEVENS; d afl880; m Sarah "Eliza" HYDE, issue Orlinda, Norman Y. (adopted), Ida; Paw Paw Twp; farm; West Cit.

STEWART, Elijah T., b1803 PA, son of William and Mary STEWART, father-in-law to James McCLELLAN; d1881 IL; m (1) Nancy "Agnes" McGAUGHEY, issue Alexander McGaughey, William, Rebecca, Mary, Sarah Ann, Annette P., Emeline Amanda, Samuel James; m (2) Julia A. (TRUESDALE) BIGHAM/BRIGHAM; Somonauk Twp; land patent; farm; West Cit, Presby, first Clerk of the Session, Elder in Somonauk Presby Ch.

STOWE/STOW, Asahel, bc1796 NY; d1859 IL; father-in-law to Jesse ROSE and James M. HAMMOND; m, issue Louisa Jane, Rebecca, Martha; Sycamore Twp; farm; West Cit; Cong, one of 11 men consenting to 1848 tax assessment on personal property to construct new house of worship.

SUMNER, Ebenezer Quincy, b1816 VT, son of Ebenezer and Abigail (ADAMS) SUMNER; m Ada Adelia/Amelia

PLYMAT, issue Ebenezer Quincy Jr., Harriet Lodoiska, Caroline Fidelia, Laura Annette, Henry Alphonso; Genoa Twp; farm, Genoa Village Trustee; West Cit.

SWARTWOOD, James, b1822 NY, son of Daniel Baker and Jane Kirk (McMILLIAM) SWARTWOOD; d1906 IA; m Paulina E. ADAMS, issue Miradell C., William Daniel., Isabella, Anna C., Myra C.; Mayfield Twp; farm, hotel keeper; Wesleyan Meth; moved to IA bf1870.

TALBOT, Charles Albert, bc1834 England, son of Charles Henry and Susan/Susannah (KEY) TALBOT; d1888 IL; m Harriet NEWELL, issue Arthur Newell, Florence M., George S., Lillian Maud; Pampas/Cortland Twp; harness maker; Cong.

TAPPAN, Silas W., bc1817 NY; d1874 IL; m Harriet B., issue Nancy, Hattie A.; Afton, DeKalb Twps; farm, Co Sheriff 1856, County Recorder candidate; R; never arrested UGRR activists.

TAPPAN, William C., bc1806 NY; d bf1870 IL; m Harriet, issue Louisa H.; Squaw Grove Twp; farm, Twp Supervisor, Squaw Grove Postmaster; West Cit.

TAYLOR, Hugh, b1815 DE; d1876; m Harriet A. HISCOCK, issue William, Montross, Harriet H.; Pampas/Cortland Twp; clerk, well digger; Univ; moved to KS bf1870.

TELFORD, Ann (DOBBIN), b1807, dau John and Jane (McKILLIP) DOBBIN, cousin to David Miller DOBBIN; d1847 IL; m Francis "Frankie" Robert TELFORD (his 2nd wife), no issue, step-children Elizabeth, William, Robert, James M., Eliza from TELFORD's first wife; Clinton Twp; husband land patent; husband farm; Presby.

TELFORD, Julia Ann, bc1821 NY; d af1880; m Francis "Frankie" Robert TELFORD (his 3rd wife), issue Mary J., Daniel, Amelia A., Henry, Frankie, and step-children Elizabeth, William, Robert, James M., Eliza from TELFORD's first wife; Clinton Twp; husband land patent; husband farm; West Cit; Presby; moved to IA bf1887.

THOM, John, b1808 Scotland, son of Hugh THOM, son-in-law of James MACKIE; d1892 IL; m Margaret MACKIE, issue unknown; Mayfield Twp; land patent; one of first white men in DeKalb Co[118]; West Cit; Cong affiliation.

THOMAS, Ellen Louisa, bc1843 IL, dau Timothy and Mary (WATERMAN) WELLS; d1919 CA; m William Robert THOMAS, issue, Jessie Louise, Jeanie, Henry, Mary; Sycamore Twp; Cong.

THOMAS, R.B., b1799 NY, d1874 IL; m Eliza C. TUTTLE, issue three children, including Henry M.; Kingston Twp; farm, physician; West Cit; son Henry became an "uncompromising Republican"[119]; moved to Boone Co., IL bf1870.

THOMPSON, Joseph A., b1818 NY; d1856 IL; m (1) unknown, issue Marie P., Eliza; m (2) Margaret (THOMPSON DOBBIN) STOTT; Somonauk Twp; Presby, Elder in Somonauk Presby Ch.

THOMPSON, Mathew, b1802 Ireland; d1870 IL; m Rebecca O. SCHRYVER, issue Edward, Augustus, Henry, William, Harry, Lucy, Joseph, Julius, Solomon, Hannah, John A.; South Grove Twp; land patent; farm; both Mathew and Rebecca subscribed to the West Cit.

THOMPSON, Milo, bc1842 IL, m unknown; Sycamore Twp; apprentice printer *True Republican* newspaper.

THOMPSON, William R., b1818 OH, son of Samuel and Hannah (ROBERTS) THOMPSON; d bf1907; m 1843 Eliza A. PARKER, issue Elvira/Alvira, Hannah Elizabeth, William W., George L., Orson M., Ira Andrew, James S, Ida M., Emma/Emily L.; DeKalb Twp; land patent; farm, veterinary surgeon; West Cit; lived in DeKalb Co bf1840.

THRALL, Charles I/J., bc1824 OH; m Loretta "Lettie" LYMAN, issue May, Jessy, Frank, Burdetta; Pampas/Cortland Twp; farm; West Cit; moved to Kane Co, IL bf1860.

TIBBETS, William, bc1808 NH; m Delila, issue Ira, Ellen, William, Mary, Elizabeth, Laura, Mariah, Carlos, Cephas/Sephes, Ernest Adelbert; Genoa Twp; farm; West Cit.

TIMMERMAN, Marvin S., b1841 NY, son of David Thomas and Charlotte (ELWOOD) TIMMERMAN; d1888 IL; m Ione L. BOWEN, issue Charlotte L., William E., Maimie, Belle; Sycamore Twp; farm; Univ.

TINDALL, Benjamin, b1815 NJ, son of Thomas and Elizabeth (HOWELL) TINDALL, bro to Jesse TINDALL; d1848 IL; m Sarah, issue Frances, James B.; Sycamore, South Grove Twps; land patent; farm; Cong.

TINDALL, Jesse, b1812 NJ, son of Thomas and Elizabeth (HOWELL) TINDALL, bro to Benjamin TINDALL; d1880 IL; m Mary A. BARBER, issue Laura, Elizabeth "Betsey" Mahala, Thomas/Dallas, Harriet, Adelbert "Dell," Orlando "Lon" L., George Monroe, Carrie M.; South Grove, Sycamore Twps; land patent; farm, Twp Supervisor; West Cit.

TOWER, David, b1818 VT, son of Abel and Mary (MOORE) TOWER; d1906 IL; m Mary A. DAILY, issue George W., Harriet B., David J.; Mayfield, Sycamore Twps; farm; Wesleyan Meth; donated timber for Mayfield Wesleyan Meth church building; lived in DeKalb Co bf1840.

TOWNSEND, Charles, b1808 NY, son of Joshua and Phebe (PORTER) TOWNSEND, son-in-law of Reuben and Mercy NICHOLS; d1880 IL; m Phebe NICHOLS, issue Mary Ann, Edwin, Francis, Marinda, Erastus, Harrison, Clarissa, Caroline, Orisa, Charles N.; Mayfield Twp; land patent; farm, Twp. Road Commissioner; West Cit; Wesleyan Meth; R; conductor on UGRR[120] and home was a station[121]; lived in DeKalb Co bf1840.

TOWNSEND, George W., bc1822 NY; m Rachel, no issue; Mayfield, Somonauk Twps; land patent; farm; West Cit; moved to LaSalle Co, IL bf1860, back to DeKalb Co bf1870.

TOWNSEND, Joshua, b1787 NJ, son of Charles and Hannah (HALL) TOWNSEND; d1861 IL; m Phebe PORTER, issue Stephen, Charles; Mayfield Twp; land patent; farm; West Cit; Wesleyan Meth; conductor on UGRR[122] and home was a station[123]; lived in DeKalb Co bf1840.

TOWNSEND, Stephen, b1807 NY, son of Joshua and Phebe (PORTER) TOWNSEND, father-in-law to Orrin WEST; d1883 IL; m Ann DENMAN, issue Amos W., William H., Nancy Denman, Eleanor "Ellen" J/L., Francis, Louisa, Kate Ann, Jane, William Henry, Harriet "Hattie" Elizabeth; Mayfield Twp; land patent; farm; West Cit; R, Free-Soil delegate to organizing Republican convention 1854[124]; one of first Trustees for Mayfield Wesleyan Meth Ch; R; conductor on UGRR[125] and home was a station[126]; "one of the early Abolitionists, he stood firm for liberty of blacks."[127]

TRIMBLE, Job, b1791 MA, son of James R. and Sarah (JOB) TRIMBLE; d1866 IL; m Margaret FURREY, issue James R., Mary; Franklin Twp; land patent; farm; West Cit.

TUTTLE, Philo Perkins, b1807 VT, son of Joseph V. and Anna (PERKINS) TUTTLE; d1890 IA; m Phebe "Ann" SMITH, issue Smith P., George "Albert," Henry P., Wells H., William N., Anna; Somonauk Twp; land patent; farm, carpenter; West Cit; moved to IA bf1860.

VANDEBURG, Abram, b1816 NY, son of Cornelius and

Mary (STARTWOOD/SWARTWOOD) VANDEBURG; d1885 NE; m Louisa WEBSTER, issue Cornelius "Jefferson," Celestia, Addison H., Ellen, Mary, William Wilson; Kingston Twp; farm; West Cit; Wesleyan Meth; moved to NE bf1880.

WAGER, Reuben, b1819 NY, son of Frederick and Anna (PIERCE) WAGER; d1892 IL; m Philinda/Philana "Polly" ROSS, issue Frank, Caroline, Lydia, Allen; Genoa Twp; land patent; farm; West Cit; moved to McHenry Co, IL bf1860, DeKalb Co bf1870, back to McHenry Co, IL bf1880.

WAITE, Campbell W., b1832 NY son of Daniel Dyer and Lucy (CLAPP) WAITE; d1904 IL; no spouse; Sycamore Twp; printer, Secretary to IL State Senate, CW Adjutant, Co S 8th IL Cav., Secretary to MO Gov. Fletcher; 1857 established Sycamore *True Republican* newspaper with James H. BEVERIDGE, Caleb M. BROWN and Daniel B. JAMES; Episcopal; 1858 witnessed and transcribed Abraham Lincoln's "House Divided" speech as first published by the *True Republican*.[128]

WALKER, James, b1778 Scotland, son of James and Margaret (WILSON) WALKER; d1856 IL; m Helen OLIVER, issue Mary, Janet, Helen, Thomas, Euphemia, James, George, John S., Robert, William; Clinton Twp; land patent; tailor; Presby, both James and Helen charter mbrs Somonauk Presby Ch.

WALKER, John S., b1818 NY, son of James and Helen (OLIVER) WALKER; d1910 IL; m (1) Nancy WALLS, issue William James, Helen/Ellen/Elvira, Robert, John, Henry, Oliver, Roseanna, Mary, Janet; m (2) Margaret DOBBIN, issue Elizabeth "Lizzie," Edward; Clinton Twp; land patent; farm; West Cit; both John and Nancy charter mbrs Somonauk Presby Ch.

WALROD, Jonas, b1826 NY, son of Peter A. and Hannah (HARPER) WALROD; d1894 IA; m Elizabeth "Eliza" Campbell EATON, issue Ellen Charlotte, Elsie, George Myron, Benjamin Franklin, William "Harrison," Willard, Fredrick O.; Mayfield Twp; farm; West Cit.

WALROD, Morris, b1805 NY, son of Peter W. and Mary (HOYT) WALROD, bro-in-law to Dr. James Franklin HARRINGTON; d1880 CA; m Anna HORNING, issue Robert Horning, Mary Elizabeth, Davison; Sycamore Twp; land patent; lumberman, Co Sheriff 1840; never arrested UGRR activists; lived in DeKalb Co bf1840; moved to WI bf1850.

WARD, Jacob, bc1833 OH, son of William and Phoebe (BEEM) WARD; m Margaret Jane PERRY, issue Rosetta/Rosalie J., Ambrose P.; Squaw Grove Twp; farm; West Cit; lived in DeKalb Co by 1840; moved to IA bf1870.

WARREN, Anson/Ahneson, bc1826 NY; Sycamore Twp; West Cit.

WATERMAN, Charlotte Frances/Judith, b1812 NY, dau of John Dean and Mary Graves (WALDO) WATERMAN, sis to John C. WATERMAN, bro James WATERMAN was benefactor to Sycamore St. Peter's Episcopal Ch, bro Robert WATERMAN was Governor of CA, sis-in-law to Timothy WELLS and Elzey P. YOUNG; d1891 CA; no spouse; Sycamore Twp; occupation "lady"; Cong; lived in DeKalb Co bf1840.

WATERMAN, Eliza Jane (CHURCHILL), b1822 NY, dau-in-law to John and Deborah WATERMAN; d1883 IL; m John Aldrich/Aldridge WATERMAN, issue Walter, Electa, Fred W., Daniel Aldrich, John Roy; Sycamore Twp; housekeeper, husband grocer; charter mbr in Sycamore Univ Ch.

WATERMAN, John, b1794 RI, son of Richard and Elizabeth (SMITH) WATERMAN; father-in-law to Harry A. JOSLYN; d1879 IL; m Deborah ALDRICH/ALDRIDGE, issue Lucy Ann, John Aldrich/Aldridge, Henry, Lyman, Mary Ann, William, Joseph; Pampas/Cortland Twp; farm; Univ.

WATERMAN, John Calvin, b1814 NY son of John Dean and Mary Graves (WALDO) WATERMAN, bro to Charlotte WATERMAN, bro James WATERMAN was benefactor to Sycamore St. Peter's Episcopal Ch, bro Robert WATERMAN became Governor of CA, bro-in-law to Timothy Wells, son-in-law to Benjamin HOYT; d1883 IL; m (1) Caroline Elizabeth HOYT, issue Catherine "Kate" Douglas, Sarah J., Albert Hoyt, Caroline Waldo, James D.; m (2) Caroline Matilda ROGERS, issue Mary W., Emily A., John Clayton; Sycamore Twp; land patent; farm, merchant, Co Treasurer, Postmaster Newburg, Winnebago Co., and Sycamore, IL,; one of committee to confront grave robbers; Cong; "zealous Republican"[129]; mbr of appointed political committee at 1854 DeKalb Co Anti-Nebraska (antislavery) Meeting[130]; served on staff of Gov. Oglesby of Illinois, attended Pres. Lincoln's funeral; lived in DeKalb Co bf1840.

WATERMAN, Maria J., bc1822 NY, dau-in-law of John and Deborah (ALDRICH/ALDRIDGE) WATERMAN; m Lyman WATERMAN, issue Clarence, Jane/Jennie M.; Sycamore Twp; housekeeper, husband farm, gunsmith, jeweler; Univ.

WATERMAN, Mary Graves (WALDO), b1787 MA, dau Calvin and Judith (GRAVES) WALDO, mother-in-law to Elzey P. YOUNG; d1853 IL; m John Dean WATERMAN, issue Henry Franklin, Charlotte Francis/Judith, John Calvin, Mary, Charles, Hannah, James Sears, Caroline Waldo, Robert Whitney, Theodore Francis; Sycamore Twp; husband businessman; Cong.

WATERMAN, Philander, b1813 NY, son of Timothy and Lucy (TANNER) WATERMAN; d1883 IL; m (1)Emily Jane THOMPSON, issue Alice E.; (2) m Judith C., issue Arabell "Bell," George H., Lizzie/Emma, Edwin "Douglas"; South Grove Twp; farm, Postmaster in Deerfield Prairie 1857; West Cit.

WEBER, Philip, bc1831 Luxemburg; m Catharine, issue Elizabeth, Mathew, William; Mayfield Twp; blacksmith; Wesleyan Meth; moved to Cook Co, IL bf1870.

WEBSTER, Calvin/Calvary Morris, b1832 OH, son of Daniel Bromley and Lois Fulford (STEWART) WEBSTER; d1867 IL; m Ann Catherine PARKER, issue parker Steward, Edward Thomson, William Grant, Nelson Parley, Flora Belle; Kingston Twp; minister; both Mayfield Twp Pleasant Hill and Bethel Wesleyan Methodist churches built under his leadership.

WEEDEN, George W., b1807 VT, son of Samuel and M. WEEDEN; d1870 IL; m Sarah PEARSONS, issue Alvin G., Albina Stanhope, Albert, Almer; Mayfield, Sycamore Twps; land patent; mason, helped build Dow Academy, charter mbr and Trustee in Sycamore Univ Church; West Cit.

WEEDEN, Lucius, bc1825 VT, son of Samuel and Martha A. (CADY) WEEDEN, Sr., bro to Warren WEEDEN; d1898 VT; m Lorena THOMPSON, issue Mary, Samuel, Almon, Stillman, Charles, Eva; Sycamore Twp; Mason; West Cit; moved back to VT bf1870.

WEEDEN, Warren, b1829 VT, son of Samuel & Martha A. (CADY) WEEDEN, bro to Lucious WEEDEN; d1924 IL; m Frances Sally WOOD, issue Angelina C., Otis N.; Sycamore, Mayfield Twps; teacher, Assessor and Trustee Mayfield Twp; West Cit; Univ; R; Abolitionist, "cast his first presidential ballot for John P. Hale" (first Abolitionist U.S. Senator).[131]

WELLINGTON, Sparock/Sparoc, b1803 VT, son of Quincy and Betsey (COBB) WELLINGTON; d1878 IL; m Joannah SILVERTHORN, issue John Quincy, Joanna Wellington, Thomas Silverthorn, William Makinge, Jane C., Samuel B., Augusta Frances, Jepis/Luiscia/Quincy J., Sparock Jr.; Sycamore Twp; farm; West Cit; moved to Boone Co bf1860.

WELLS, Edwin Erastus, b1813 NY, d1855 IL; son of Harvey Van Rensselaer and Martha (DOTY) WELLS; m Agnes Julia SOUTER/SUITER, issue Mary J., Adeline "Ada" P., John Souter, William Cowper, Edward P., Charles H., Caroline; Sycamore Twp; minister at Sycamore First Cong Ch 1843-1846; West Cit; 1844 antislavery resolutions introduced at First Cong. during his tenure[132]; keynote speaker at 1844 DeKalb Co antislavery meeting; moved to Kane Co bf1848.[133]

WELLS, Solomon P., b1809 NY, son of Timothy and Elizabeth (HATCH) WELLS; d1883 IA; m Caroline ROSS, issue Elizabeth, Abigail, Sarah, Francis Marion, Mary Caroline, Reliatha/Lefa/Lephe, Martha Francina, William Blatchley, Louisa J., Charles E., Louis Henry, Emma, Etta; Sycamore Twp; land patent; farm; one of first Petit Jurors for DeKalb Co. Circuit Court; West Cit; lived in DeKalb Co bf1840; moved to WI bf1848, to IA bf1860.

WELLS, Timothy, bc1820 OH, bro-in-law to John Calvin WATERMAN and Charlotte Francis WATERMAN; d1902 IL; m Mary H. WATERMAN, issue Ellen Louisa, M. Elizabeth, A. Jane, Benjamin/John Frank; Sycamore Twp; clerk, merchant, first postmaster for South Grove, co-proprietor of state coach line from St. Charles to Oregon, IL, CW Quartermaster for 105th IL Inf; West Cit; Cong; lived in DeKalb Co bf1840; moved to KS bf1870, to MO bf1880; 1847 Liberty Party candidate for County Recorder; invited former slave Henry DONALD to live in DeKalb Co after CW.

WELLS, William Pride, bc1803 NY, son of William and Wealthy Ann (GILBERT) WELLS; d1887 IL; m Mary RANDALL, issue Leonard J., Matilda A., Mary E., Robert R.; Somonauk Twp; farm; West Cit; moved to Will Co, IL bf1870.

WEST, Aaron Chapman, b1809 NY son of Asa and Sarah "Sally" (PARKER) WEST, bro of David WEST; d1878 OH or CO; m Emily Victoria ADAMS, issue Laura Adelia, Nelson Adams, David Newton, Emily Victoria, Emma Vienna, Sarah, Francis Pamelia, Agnes Julia, Cyrus Aaron; Sycamore Twp; land patent; merchant; West Cit; Cong, one of 11 men consenting to 1848 tax assessment on personal property to construct new house of worship; elected first Treasurer of DeKalb Co Anti-slavery Society,[134] introduced 1844 antislavery resolution at Sycamore First Cong Ch.[135]

WEST, Asa "Porter," b1836 NY, son of David and Sarah (CHAPIN) WEST, bro of Alice, Elias, Orrin, Sarah and Minerva; d1911 IL; m Maria M., no issue; Sycamore Twp; moved to Kane Co, IL, bf1880; Cong.

WEST, David, b1806 NY, son of Asa and Sarah "Sally" (PARKER) WEST, bro of Aaron WEST, bro-in-law to Jesse ROSE and Ellsworth ROSE, father-in-law to Frederick D. LOVE; d1890 IL; m (1) Sarah CHAPIN, issue Alice Chapin, Orrin, Asa Porter 1st, Ana, Asa "Porter" 2nd, Elias Collins, Sarah Louise, Minerva M.; m (2) Lucinda (ROSE) WELLS, step-children George "Milo" WELLS, Ruth D. WELLS; Sycamore Twp; land patent; farm, Tax Assessor, Twp Treasurer and Trustee, Twp Board of Commissioners; Road Commissioner; West Cit; David and both wives mbrs of Sycamore First Cong Ch, Ch Deacon, one of 11 men consenting to 1848 tax assessment on personal property to construct new house of worship; pre-eminent Abolitionist in DeKalb Co, more stories recorded about West than any other person in DeKalb Co; conductor and home a station on UGRR; 1847 Liberty Party candidate for County Commissioner; Free-soil Party delegate to convention organizing Republican Party 1854.[136]

WEST, Elias Collins, b1839 NY, son of David and Sarah (CHAPIN) WEST, bro of Alice, Orrin, Asa "Porter," Sarah and Minerva WEST; d1932 IL; m Ella A. REESE, issue May B., Roy C., Gertrude May, Herbert; Sycamore Twp; farm; CW Co. A 105th IL Inf, School Director; Deacon Sycamore First Cong Ch; R; one of the youngest conductors in UGRR in DeKalb Co,[137] photo of Elias with the West family wagon used to transport fugitive slaves,[138] invited former slave Henry BEARD to live in DeKalb Co after CW.

WEST, Orrin, bc1832 NY, son of David and Sarah (CHAPIN) WEST, bro Alice, Elias, Asa "Porter," Sarah and Minerva WEST, son-in-law of Stephen and Ann TOWNSEND; d1919 IA; m Nancy Denman TOWNSEND, issue Harriet L. "Hattie," Anna Elizabeth, Amos P.; Sycamore Twp; land patent in IA; farmer; Cong; moved to IA bf1860.

WEST, Sarah Louise, b1842 NY, dau of David and Sarah (CHAPIN) WEST, sis of Alice, Elias, Orrin, Asa "Porter," and Minerva WEST; d afl900 IL; Sycamore Twp; Cong; moved to Kane Co, IL, bf1900.

WHARRY, Martha M. (SMITH) PERCE/PERSE, bc1820 NY, dau of Garrit SMITH; d1878 IL; m (1) Unknown PERCE, m (2) Major Evans WHARRY, issue Ossala M., Walter Ward, Parmelia J.; Sycamore Twp; husband farm, and mbr of NY land company that laid out tract of land for Sycamore; husband R; Cong; lived in DeKalb Co bf1840.

WHEELER, William P., b1810 VT son of Nathan and Abigail (KING) WHEELER; d c1896 IL; m Mary Ann AMBLER, issue Lucy, William, Wallace, Julia F., Henry K.; Clinton, Shabbona Twps; sawyer, farm, Justice of the Peace, Twp Clerk; West Cit.

WHITE, Alexander G., b1817 NY, son of Robert and Elizabeth (HUNG) WHITE, son-in-law of George and Margaret HOWISON; bro to Thomas WHITE; d1889 IL; m (1) Mary Jane ROBERTSON, issue John Robertson; m (2) Eliza HOWISON; Somonauk Twp; farm; West Cit;

WHITE, Joseph, bc1832 NY, son of William A. and Lavina (SLOSSON) WHITE; d1895 IL; m Mary ALLEN, issue Josephine A., Charles S., Edgar H., Linda; Sycamore Twp; farm; West Cit; moved to Winnebago Co IL bf1895.

WHITE, Thomas, b1815 NY, son of Robert and Elizabeth (HUNG) WHITE, bro to Alexander G. WHITE; d1882 IL; m Ann Eliza TUCKER, issue Elizabeth, William, Puella/Priscilla, Robert, Emily A., Julia, Martha and Mary (twins), Hampton E., Charles H.; Somonauk Twp; farm; Presby.

WHITE, William, bc1791 NY, son of Joshua and Rhoda (DEUEL) WHITE; d1864 IL; m Elizabeth, issue Daniel, Rachel, Theodore, Allen, Benjamin S.; Shabbona Twp; farm; West Cit.

WHITFORD, Cyrus Beaman, b1812 VT, son of William and Elizabeth (LUTHER) WHITFORD; d afl880 KS/IL; m Laura A. CARPENTER, issue Carlos C., Charlotte, Burton C., Sarah M., Susan O., Nina/Mina E.; Clinton Twp; farm, insurance agent, Twp Supervisor; West Cit; lived in DeKalb Co bf1840; moved to Kane Co bf1860, back to DeKalb Co bf1870; to KS bf1880.

WHITING, Hiram E., bc1831 ME, son of William and

Nancy J. WHITING; m unknown; Pampas/Cortland Twp; farm; West Cit.

WHITMAN, John, b1819 Germany, son of Johann Fredrich and Katharina Anastine (WEYD) WHITTMANN; d1878 IA; m (1) Sarah "Sally" Ann Estella WAGER, issue Ira W., Elizabeth; m (2) Mary MARSHALL, issue Florence, Mary, Charles L., Margaret Mattie, John, Peter, George W., Anna A.; Genoa, DeKalb Twps; farm; West Cit; moved to IA bf1857.

WHITMORE, Benjamin, b1803 NY, bro to James WHITMORE; d1880 IL; m Susan EMERSON, issue William H.H., Susan J., Albert; Somonauk Twp; land patent; farm; West Cit; Meth; lived in DeKalb Co bf1840.

WHITMORE, Enos, b1805 VT, son of Jehiel and Molly (Higgins) WHITMORE; d1877 IL; m (1) Celina REED, issue Louisa, Howard, Harrison, Henry O., Lavina; m (2) Lavina/Lavonia SKEELS, no issue; Mayfield Twp; land patent; farm; West Cit; Meth; "first a Whig, then an Abolitionist and later a Republican."[139]

WHITMORE, James, bc1811 NY, bro to Benjamin WHITMORE; d1886 IL; m Anna M. BRIGHAM, issue Emily, James, Willet and Willis (twins), Martha; Somonauk Twp; farm, CW Co C, 57th IL Inf; West Cit; lived in LaSalle Co, IL; moved to DeKalb Co bf1860.

WHITNEY, James Watkins, bc1804 NY, son of Fisher and Patty (WATKINS) WHITNEY; d1881 IL; m Betsey HARPER, issue Martha, Lorenzo, Samuel D., Eliza, Harrison, Nancy, Mary; Kingston Twp; farm; West Cit.

WHITTEMORE, Lorenzo, b1807 MA, son of Samuel and Catherine (RINGER/RANGER) WHITTEMORE; d1887 IL; m Hannah KELSEY, issue Henry Clay, Floyd K; Sycamore Twp; land patent; shoemaker, carpenter, mechanic, Co Coroner, one of committee to confront grave robbers; West Cit; Cong; R.

WHITTEMORE, Samuel, b1769 MA, son of James and Dorothy (GREEN) WHITTEMORE; d bf1870 NY; m Catherine/Katherine RINGER/RANGER, issue Lorenzo; Sycamore Twp; Cong.

WILCOX, William Charles, bc1832 NY, son of William Billings and Polly (DAN) WILCOX; d1912 OK; m Catharine "Kate" MEYERS, issue Francis "Frank" D., Mary A., Charles E., Albert L., William D., Elmer E., George W., Arthur U.; Pierce Twp; farm; West Cit; moved to NE bf1880, to OK bf1900.

WILLARD, Hosea W., b1826 VT, son of Oliver and Lucy (WEEDEN) WILLARD; d1922 IL; m Martha Ann WEEDEN, issue Clarence Hosea, Oliver Thomas; Sycamore Twp; carpenter, joiner, Constable; charter mbr Sycamore Univ Ch.

WILLARD, Oliver, b1789 VT, son of Oliver and Abigail (KEITH) WILLARD, Jr., father-in-law to Spafford SMITH; d1854 IL; m Lucy WEEDEN, issue Lucy, Oliver, Abigail, Sophronia, Hosea W., Charles O., Marcia A., George W., Helen M., Curtis A., Albert B.; Sycamore Twp; mason; West Cit.

WILLIAMS, Robert, bc1843 IL; m unknown; Sycamore Twp; apprentice printer *True Republican* newspaper.

WILLSON, George F., bc1803 PA; m (1) unknown, issue Elizabeth, Benjamin, John; m (2) Sarah, issue Thomas, George, Sarah, Edward; Sycamore Twp; blacksmith; West Cit; lived in DeKalb Co bf1840; moved to TX bf1860.

WOOD, Henry, b1824 VT, son of Zechariah and Sarah (BACON) WOOD, bro of Thomas H. WOOD, bro-in-law to Jesse C. KELLOGG; d1904 IN; m Rhoda "Elizabeth" RICHARDS, step-daughter of Ellsworth ROSE, issue Charles N., Leroy B., Shepard H., Emily S., William H., Albert Carrier; Sycamore Twp; farm, Twp Supervisor, Trustee, School Director; IL State Representative 1880–1884; Cong; R; "Abolitionist [and] became a Republican for organization of the party."[140]

WOOD, Joseph, b1803 NJ; d1880 IL; m Elizabeth GALLANO, issue Louisa, Mary, Sarah, Olive, Charlotte, Ede, Margaret E., Elizabeth, Bridget Emma, Joseph, Cecelia; Franklin Twp; farm; West Cit.

WOOD, Thomas b1822 VT, son of Zechariah and Sarah (BACON) WOOD, bro of Henry WOOD, bro-in-law to Jesse C. KELLOGG; d1896 IL; m Catherine Hannah (ALLEN) SLADE, issue Thomas Dennison, Arthur B., Glenn, and stepson Byron Allen SLADE; Sycamore Twp; farm, one of financial subscribers for courthouse; West Cit; Cong; R.

WOODLEY, Selina, bc1800 Canada; d af1880; m Thomas T. WOODLEY, issue Mary J., Cetican, John T.; Pampas/Cortland Twp; husband boot and shoemaker; Cong.

WOODRUFF, Baldwin, b1805 NY, son of Simeon and Rosanna (ADAMS) WOODRUFF; d1870 IL; m Sophrona PLUMB, issue Richard R., John J.; Clinton Twp; farm, Co Sheriff 1860; never arrested UGRR activists.

WOODRUFF, Felix, b1801 NY, son of Simeon and Rosanna (ADAMS) WOODRUFF, bro to Baldwin WOODRUFF; d1848 IL; m Pamelia BAILEY, issue Simeon, William Bailey, Pamilia Roseanna, Amelia Charlotte, Mary Adelaide, Adelia Althea, Felix Isaiah, Emma E.; Clinton Twp; Land patent; farm, 1847 Liberty Party candidate for County Surveyor.

WOODWARD, Laura L., bc1829 NY; m Charles WOODWARD, issue William M.; Sycamore Twp; she and husband teachers); Cong; moved back to NY 1864.

WOOLSEY, Thomas, bc1800 NY, son of John and Deborah Ann (WRIGHT) WOOLSEY II; d1865 IL; m Parthenia OLMSTEAD, issue Russell, John, Almira, Jonathan D., Mary A., Meridan, William B., Minerva; Sycamore Twp; farm, minister; West Cit; Meth; organizing Chairman and first President of the DeKalb County Anti-slavery Society;[141] 1847 Liberty Party candidate for Co School Commissioner; lived in DeKalb Co bf1840.

WORDEN, Benjamin Kellogg, b1812 NY, son of Amariah and Rebecca (CORBIN) WORDEN; d1884 IL; m Martha Jane FERGUSON, issue, Ephraim, George W., Mary Asenath, Francis Marion, Amariah H., Eleanor Rebecca, Martin, Stephen Henry, Benjamin J., Martha Jane, Eda; South Grove Twp; farm; West Cit; lived in DeKalb Co bf1840.

WORF, Charles "Henry," b1837 England, son of William and Mary (COCKELL) WORF; d1913 IL; m Susanna ZUBLER, issue Bessie, Charles Henry, Alta; Franklin Twp; farm, CW 105th IL Inf; R; "sympathies with the down-trodden and oppressed."[142]

WRIGHT, Clark, bc1806 NY; d1877 OK; m (1) Polly M., issue Joseph C., Henry, George, John; m (2) Eunice, issue, William A., Flora; Sycamore Twp; farm; mbr NY land company that laid out tract of land for Sycamore, one of first Petit Jurors; West Cit; Cong, one of 11 men consenting to 1848 tax assessment on personal property to construct new house of worship; lived in DeKalb Co bf1840; moved to KS bf1870.

WYMAN, James bc1823 MA, son of Asa and Sarah "Sally" (SEARLE) WYMAN, bro of Ralph WYMAN; d1893 IL; m Eliza D. ROOT, issue Cornelia A., Jane "Jennie" S., Fernando

E., Adelbert/Albert O.; Sycamore Twp; land patent; farm; West Cit.

WYMAN, Ralph, b1813 VT, son of Asa and Sarah "Sally" (SEARLE) WYMAN, bro of James WYMAN; d1864 IL; m Susan DAYTON, issue Henry D., Byron F., Helen G., Merritt, Cecelia, Frank W., Ida, Eva, Susie; Sycamore Twp; land patent; farm, one of first Grand Jurors in DeKalb Co., one of financial subscribers for brick courthouse; West Cit; Meth; "warm friend of the slave and his hospitable home was for a long time a refuge" in UGRR[143]; lived in DeKalb Co bf1840.

YOUNG, Ellzey/Elsey Pierson, b1819 OH, son of John and Elizabeth (LOGAN) YOUNG, son-in-law of Mary Graves (WALDO) WATERMAN, son-in-law to Abraham ELLWOOD, bro-in-law to Charlotte WATERMAN, John Calvin WATERMAN, bro-in-law to James "Edmund" ELLWOOD; d1874 IL; m (1) Caroline Waldo WATERMAN, issue a son and Mary Elizabeth; m (2) Alida L. ELLWOOD, issue Abbie, Kate "Kittie"; Sycamore, DeKalb Twps; merchant, banker, County Clerk 1843, Co Sheriff 1846; never arrested UGRR activists; lived in DeKalb Co bf1840.

YOUNG, Simon/Simeon, b1818 NY, son of Simon and Betsey (MEYERS/MYERS) YOUNG; d bf1880 IA; m Mary WOODRUFF, issue Elizabeth A., David L., Martin, Emma/Ellen Maria, Delos/Deloss, Cornelia, John, George, Idena/Idona, Loren, Lorena; Pampas Twp; farmer; mbr DeKalb Co. Liberty Party 1847; to Kane Co, IL bf1860.

A List of Other Individuals (No Biographical Information Found)

Western Citizen Subscribers

During the early settlement of the Northwest Territory, many people were transient, remaining only briefly in a locale and then moving on. They wanted more land, or better land, or perhaps they followed their dreams of quick riches farther west. Some succeeded and put down their roots to settle elsewhere, never to return to DeKalb County. Consequently, there are many subscribers to the *Western Citizen* about whom little information could be found. When only initials are given on their subscriptions, it is impossible to discern the sex of the subscriber. In some instances, it is likely that the head of the household purposely requested the subscription using the initials of his child's name in order to avoid being labeled publicly as antislavery. When duplicate or identical names appear on the subscription list, the names cannot be matched to those enumerated in a census and it is not known who actually held the subscription. The following list indicates the *Western Citizen* subscribers for whom no definitive contemporary information was found. Also listed is the post office where they received their mail.

Alexander, S.W., Lost Grove
Andrews, Dr. H, South Grove
Bartlett, Jesse, Somonauk
Bassett, Alanson J., New Lebanon, land patent
Baxter, Julius, Shabbona Grove
Beecher, J.E., Hicks Mills
Beigh, A.V.D., Sycamore
Bescott, D.M., Somonauk
Black, E.G., Sycamore
Black, J., Somonauk
Boon/Boone, Mrs. Rhoda, Ohio Grove; Cong
Bovee, Robert, DeKalb Center
Boybey, David, Somonauk
Bradley, N., Genoa
Brown, Jacob, Shabbona Grove
Bullard, J.H., Sycamore
Bullock, The Rev. L.F., Ohio Grove
Bush/Bark, George, Genoa
Cadwell, E., Ohio Grove
Carpenter, Adi S., Sycamore
Carpenter, B., Sycamore
Clark, E., DeKalb Center
Clark, G.W., Genoa
Cleveland, T., Ohio Grove
Coats, C.W., Somonauk
Coe, Noble, Coltonville
Colton, Timothy, Shabbona Grove
Cooper, B., Ross Grove
Cooper, H., Somonauk
Copeland, John H., Courtland Station
Countryman, Conrad, Hicks Mills, land patent
Crills, Henry, Hicks Mills
Darland, Benjamin, Van Buren
Dennis, J., Paw Paw
Dewell, D., New Lebanon
Dick, A., Brush Point
Dickinson, C.M., LeClair
Downs, E.C., Hicks Mills
Dribblelis, John, Hicks Mills
Eastabrooks, B., Somonauk
Field, A., Hicks Mills
Francis, J., Sycamore
French, B., Sandwich
Geoman, Mark, Ohio Grove
Golden, R., New Lebanon
Graham, David, Genoa, land patent
Graves, Z., Ross Grove
Greer, Genoa
Grinwold, Mrs. So, Sandwich
Guild, J.W., DeKalb Center

Haines, J., Line
Hall, Charles, Somonauk
Hall, F.F., Line
Hammond, F., Sycamore
Harrington, Joseph, Genoa
Harris, William R., Squaw Grove
Harrison, Josh, Coltonville
Haskell, E., New Lebanon
Heall, M., Lost Grove
Heaper, R., Ross Grove
Heath, John, Genoa
Highland, T.J., DeKalb (John or Jackson Highland/ Hiland)
Hillary, James, Shabbona Grove
Hills, A., Coltonville
Holroy, James, Genoa
James, P., Somonauk Depot
Johnston, J.W., Sycamore
Joies, H., Sandwich
Kelsey, D.M., South Grove
Kittle, N.J., Shabbona Grove
Latham, Mrs. James, Sandwich
Livingston, A., Somonauk
Loby, H.D., Sycamore
Loper, E.H., Van Buren
Loverage, John, Genoa
Lyons, Alexander, Ross Grove
Madison, J.W., North Pierce
Malay, James, Ross Grove
Maltby, Isaac, Genoa
Mansford, S., Genoa
Marsh, M.L., Genoa
Massary, WM., Sycamore
Masske, W., Shabbona Grove
Mattison, The Rev. I, Sandwich
McAuley, L., Sycamore
McGary, Thomas, Shabbona
McIlvanie, J.M., Sycamore
McKinley, R., Line
Merritt, Mrs. L., Somonauk
Micham, A., Ross Grove
Middleton, Edward, North Kingston, land patent
Mills, Abel, Sycamore
Murrey, John, Sycamore
Nicholson, Mrs. L., Paw Paw
Nish, J.M., Sycamore
Noble, W.J., Shabbona Grove
Noe, The Rev. J., Shabbona Grove
Palmer, P.B., New Lebanon
Pierce, Mrs. F., Van Buren
Pierson, The Rev. J.L., Somonauk
Posley, J., Coltonville
Price, George, Van Buren
Purdam, Josh, Sycamore
Rames, E., Sandwich
Reed, C.M., South Grove
Reynolds, C.N., Line Station
Rickard, Jacob, South Grove, land patent
Riddle, E., Somonauk
Ring, J.W., Genoa
Robers, William H., Sycamore
Robinson, Thomas, Somonauk
Roost, George, Dorsett

Rose, J.M., Dorsett, Clinton
Rowen, John B., Lacey
Ryan, M., Sycamore
Sanders, J.L., Genoa
Schryver, Mrs. Re., South Grove
Smith, J., Line
Smith, S.W., Shabbona Grove
Smith, Sycamore
Smith, Univ. J., DeKalb Center
Stacy, W.H., Sycamore
State, J.P., Shabbona Grove
Sterns, Newton, Van Buren
Stockhaim, Hiram or Joseph, Somonauk
Stough, George T., Sycamore, land patent
Stow, C., Sycamore
Sweeney, Neil, Sycamore; land patent; lived in DeKalb Co bf1840.
Sweet, J.B., Somonauk
Takley, James, Dorsett
Thurston, D., Genoa
Towbling, E.S., LeClair
Tuttle, J.E., Somonauk
VanDurgen/VanDurgan, William, Sycamore
Vanfelt, V., Somonauk
Walker, I., Dorsett
Walker, S.W., Genoa
Ward, Charles, DeKalb Center
Waters/Wiaters, H., Genoa
Way, E., LeClair
Wayes, John, Dorsett
Whitford, W.C., Shabbona Grove
Whitney, J.R., Genoa
Wilcox, Eld. A., Sycamore
Wilkie, C., Shabbona Grove
Wilkley, C., Dorsett
Willard, Wardness, Sycamore
Wilson, Eld. A., Sycamore
Witmore, John, Sycamore
Woolroy, J., Genoa

MEMBERS OF THE FIRST CONGREGATIONAL CHURCH IN SYCAMORE, 1840–1860

Barnard, Mrs. Alice, from MA
Barnard, Mrs. Elizabeth, from Chicago
Beavers, Elizabeth, d1845
Bowman, Mary J., (Mrs. Norman Bowman),
Bowman, Norman
Colton, Betsey M., m Robinson; moved to Clarksville, IA c1858
Colton, Catharine R., moved to Paola, KS
Cook, J.T., Minister at First Cong Church 1863–1865
Cook, Mrs. J.T.
Cook, Mrs. Mary W. (possibly J.T. Cook's mother)
Doolittle, Mrs. Louisa A.
Fox, Thomas
Furness, Sarah, m George M. Wells, moved to Chicago, IL
Halsey, Mrs. Gilbert, from NY
Hunt, Stephen, from NJ
Jennings, Isabella Jane
Maxfield, Almira W.

McCaleb, Jane
McCollum, Mrs. Rebecca, charter mbr of First Cong Church
Mix, Caroline
Murray, Mrs. Mary, m to William Murray, from Scotland
Murray, William, m to Mary, from Scotland
Putnam, Fanny
Richards, Mrs. K.
Richards, Mrs. R.F.
Sherburn, Mrs. Elizabeth, moved to Grandville, Kent Co., MI
Smith, Daniel A.
Thomas, William R.
Tower, J.B., m to Lavinia J., moved to Chicago, IL
Tower, Lavinia J., m to J.B. Tower, moved to Chicago, IL
Wells, George M, moved to Chicago 1871
Wells, Mrs. Ruth A.
Wharry, Maria E., m Theodore Hunt
Williams, Carrie, moved to Byron, IL by 1860
Williams, Mrs. Harriet S., d OH
Wood, Abby, m Mr. Dyer, moved to Chicago, IL by 1869
Wood, Mrs. Margaret, mother of Abby Wood, d1880
Wraley, Mrs. Selina

Sycamore Universalist Church Members

Barrows, Mrs. Annie S.
Foster, Mrs.
Gardner, Mrs. Jinny
Hibbard, Mrs. George H./K.
Hiles, Mrs. Jane
Huckins, Mrs. Mary
Johnson, Mrs. E.R.

Jones, Mrs. Ione
Jones, Mrs. Sarah
Mason, Mrs. Eliza
Peck, Alice
Schram, Mrs.
Simmons, Dr.
Spring, Orrison
Timmerman, Emma
Walker, Mrs. G.
Weeden, Albina
Whitcomb, Anna
Wilde, Sarah P.
Wilsey, Tillie

Contributors to the Mayfield Wesleyan Methodist Church Building Fund, 1860

Hayes, Thomas
Nichols, A.C.
Nichols, Benjamin
Ottman, J.

Somonauk Presbyterian Church Members

Easton, Mrs. James
Moffet, William T.—minister who succeeded Rensselaer W. French

Miscellaneous Person Mentioned in Historical Sources

Bill, J.A.—secretary at organizing meeting of DeKalb County Anti-slavery Society[144]

Notes

Preface

1. Gara, *The Liberty Line: The Legend of the Underground Railroad*, 191–194.
2. National Park Service, *Exploring a Common Past: Researching and Interpreting the Underground Railroad*, 28–30.
3. Kraut, "The Forgotten Reformers, A Profile of Third Party Abolitionists in Antebellum New York," Perry and Fellman, eds., *Antislavery Reconsidered: New Perspectives on the Abolitionists*, 119–145.

Introduction

1. Boies, *History of DeKalb County*, 36.
2. Siebert, *The Underground Railroad from Slavery to Freedom*, 2.
3. Ibid., Preface, xxiii.
4. Wisconsin Historical Society, microfilm P01-848, Ohio Historical Society, *Underground Railroad in Illinois*, Vols. I and II.
5. Boies, 23.
6. Ibid.
7. Ibid., 24.

Chapter 1

1. *Sycamore True Republican*, September 19, 1877.
2. Ibid., July 21, 1886.
3. Ibid.
4. Clark, *The Liberty Minstrel*, Preface, iv.
5. Ibid.
6. Ibid., 54.
7. Ibid.
8. Ibid.
9. *Sycamore True Republican*, July 21, 1886.
10. Clark, *The Liberty Minstrel*, 56.
11. Ibid., 58.
12. *Sycamore True Republican*, July 21, 1886.
13. Hossack, "Speech of John Hossack, Convicted of Violation of the Fugitive Slave Law; before Judge Drummond, of the U.S. District Court of Chicago."
14. Boies, *History of DeKalb County*, 109.
15. Gross, *Past and Present of DeKalb County*, Vol. I, 101.
16. *Sycamore True Republican*, September 19, 1877.
17. *The Republican North Western*, Belvidere, Illinois, June 28, 1910, excerpt from the *Ottawa Republic*, Ottawa, Kansas.
18. *Sycamore True Republican*, July 21, 1886.

Chapter 2

1. Douglass, "Letter to the Abolitionist Reunion, June 9–13, 1874."
2. Gara, *The Liberty Line: The Legend of the Underground Railroad*, 17.
3. National Park Service, *Underground Railroad*, Preface.
4. Patten and Graham, *History of the Somonauk United Presbyterian Church*, 58.
5. National Park Service, *Exploring a Common Past: Researching and Interpreting the Underground Railroad*, 17.
6. Dumond, *Antislavery: The Crusade for Freedom in America*, 46.
7. Ordinance of 1787, adopted by Congress August 7, 1789; Lowance, *Against Slavery: An Abolitionist Reader*, 332.
8. Second Congress, Statute 2, Chap. VII, February 12, 1793; Lowance, *Against Slavery*, 321.
9. Switala, *Underground Railroad in Pennsylvania*, 7.
10. Ibid.
11. Boies, *History of DeKalb County, Illinois*, 46.
12. Mayer, *All on Fire: William Lloyd Garrison and the Abolition of Slavery*, Preface.
13. National Park Service, *Underground Railroad*, 56.
14. Mayer, *All on Fire*, 112.
15. Siebert, *The Underground Railroad from Slavery to Freedom*, viii.
16. Dumond, *Antislavery*, 343.
17. Muelder, *Fighters for Freedom: The history of Anti-Slavery Activities of Men and Women Associated with Knox College*, 119.
18. See National Park Service, *Underground Railroad*, 9.
19. Boies, *History of DeKalb County*, 414.
20. National Park Service, *Exploring a Common Past*, 10.
21. Ibid., 45.
22. *Population Schedules of the Seventh Census of the United States: 1850*.
23. Norton, *Henrietta*, 80.
24. Ibid., 87.
25. Ibid., 77.
26. Boies, *History of DeKalb County*, 47.
27. Ibid.
28. Ibid., 109.
29. *The History of Five Points*, 12.
30. Eaklor, *American Antislavery Songs: A Collection and Analysis*, 371–372.
31. Gara, *The Liberty Line*, 3.
32. Ibid., 4.

Chapter 3

1. Anonymous, *Biographical Record of DeKalb County, Illinois*, 318.
2. Ibid.
3. *Mayfield United Church of Christ: 115 Years of Service for the Lord*.
4. Gross, *Past and Present of DeKalb County*, Vol. I, 156.

5. Ibid.
6. *Sycamore True Republican*, July 28, 1894.
7. Muelder, *Fighters for Freedom: The History of Anti-Slavery Activities of Men and Women Associated with Knox College*, 14.
8. *Sycamore City Weekly*, obituary of David West, February 13, 1890.
9. Waterman, "Letter from Phocian Hoffman," December 20, 1840.
10. Ibid.
11. Ibid.
12. Ibid.
13. Chapman, *Portrait and Biographical Album of DeKalb County, Illinois*, 315.
14. *Republican Sentinel*, August 2, 1854.
15. Miller, *The Larger Hope: The First Century of the Universalist Church in America 1770–1870*, 704.
16. *Sycamore True Republican*, January 22, 1896, obituary of Sylvanus Holcomb.
17. Gross, *Past and Present of DeKalb County*, Vol. I, 61.
18. *Sycamore True Republican*, September 4, 1880.
19. Chapman, *Portrait and Biographical Album of DeKalb County, Illinois*, 439.
20. Ibid.
21. Ibid., 440.
22. Ibid.
23. Ibid.
24. Ibid., 61.
25. Gross, *Past and Present of DeKalb County*, Vol. I, 60.
26. *The Sycamore True Republican*, December 8, 1909.
27. Siebert, *The Underground Railroad from Slavery to Freedom*, 28, ref. to Wilson, Henry, *History of the Rise and Fall of the Slave Power*, Vol. II, 63. Wilson was U.S. vice-president after changing his name from Jeremiah Colbath when he entered politics. He is related to author Nancy M. Beasley.
28. Ibid.
29. Eastman, "Letter from A.B. Thomas," January 3, 1883.
30. Eastman, "Letter from H. Brown, Jr.," January 15, 1883.
31. McLoughlin, transcriber, Matson, *Reminiscences of Bureau County, Illinois*.
32. See also Chapman, *History of Knox County, Illinois*, 201–215.
33. *Sycamore True Republican*, December 8, 1909.
34. Siebert, *The Underground Railroad from Slavery to Freedom*, 51
35. Ibid., 50.
36. *The DeKalb Chronicle Illustrated Souvenir Edition*, 1899, 72.
37. Boies, *History of DeKalb County*, 414.
38. *Sycamore True Republican*, October 1, 1902, obituary of Ann Denman Townsend.

Chapter 4

1. Douglass, "Letter to the Abolitionist Reunion, June 9–13, 1874," Chicago, Illinois.
2. Patten and Graham, *History of the Somonauk United Presbyterian Church*, 59.
3. Ibid., 47.
4. Ibid.
5. Ibid., 59.
6. Ibid.
7. Ibid.
8. Ibid., 59–60.
9. Gross, *Past and Present of DeKalb County*, Vol. I, 98.
10. Chapman, *Portrait and Biographical Album of DeKalb County, Illinois*, 672.
11. Switala, *Underground Railroad in Pennsylvania*, 9.
12. Scott, "Abolition as a Sacred Vocation," Perry and Fellman, eds., *Antislavery Reconsidered: New Perspectives on the Abolitionists*, 51.
13. Warren and Eastman, *The Genius of Liberty Extra: Slave Code of the State of Illinois*, 4.
14. Ibid.
15. Wiecek, "Latimer: Lawyers, Abolitionists, and the Problem of Unjust Laws," Perry, and Fellman, eds., *Antislavery Reconsidered: New Perspectives on the Abolitionists*, 221.
16. Siebert, *The Underground Railroad from Slavery to Freedom*, 44.
17. Willging, "Citizens for a Free West: Antislavery Advocates in DeKalb County, Illinois, 1843–1855," 10–13.
18. Chapman, *Portrait and Biographical Album of DeKalb County, Illinois*, 672.
19. U.S. Government Land Office, Bureau of Land Management, Accession/Serial #IL0920__.220.
20. Chapman, *Portrait and Biographical Album of DeKalb County, Illinois*, 672.
21. *Sycamore True Republican*, January 29, 1873, obituary of John Nelson Maxfield.
22. Elijah P. Lovejoy, *Alton Observer*, July 20, 1837.
23. Butterfield, *The American Past: A History of the United States from Concord to Hiroshima, 1775–1945*, 97.
24. Smith, *The Lovejoy Shrine: Home of Owen Lovejoy and Station on Underground Railroad*, 10.
25. Ibid., 12.
26. *Sycamore True Republican*, November 30, 1880, "40 years ago," reprinted from the *Earlville Gazette*.
27. Moore, "The Early Republicans and the Formation of the Republican Party in Illinois," Lovejoy, *Free West*, April 5, 1854.
28. Moore, "The Early Republicans and the Formation of the Republican Party in Illinois."
29. Smith, *The Lovejoy Shrine: Home of Owen Lovejoy and Station on Underground Railroad*, 9, attributed to the U.S. Congressional Record, 1859.
30. Ibid.
31. *Sycamore True Republican*, November 30, 1880.
32. Ibid.
33. Gross, *Past and Present of DeKalb County*, 659.
34. *Sycamore City Weekly*, February 13, 1890.
35. Ibid.
36. Chapman, *Portrait and Biographical Album of DeKalb County, Illinois*, 669.
37. Ibid., 660.
38. Gross, *Past and Present of DeKalb County*, Vol. 1, 98.
39. Ibid.
40. Obituary of David West submitted to *Sycamore City Weekly*, February 13, 1890.
41. Chapman, *Portrait and Biographical Album of DeKalb County, Illinois*, 661.
42. Gross, *Past and Present of DeKalb County*, Vol. I, 97.
43. Wood, "Memoirs of Women's Fellowship," 1890, 12.
44. Whitmore, "My DeKalb Chronicle," c. 1885. Alice Whitmore was David West's great granddaughter.
45. *Daily Chronicle*, "Lovell's Crossing was Stop on Way to Freedom," April 27, 1986. DeKalb County Historian Phyllis Kelley interview with Grace Lydig Johnson. The Lydig family owned the West farm from 1918 to 1936.
46. Ibid.
47. *Sycamore City Weekly*, obituary of David West, February 13, 1890.
48. Nason, *A Gazetteer of the State of Massachusetts*, 257.
49. Boies, *History of DeKalb County*, 451.
50. Ibid., 383.
51. *Sycamore True Republican*, February 27, 1918.
52. Boies, *History of DeKalb County*, 435.
53. Gross, *Past and Present of DeKalb County*, Vol. I, 440
54. Hossack, "Speech of John Hossack, Convicted of Violation of the Fugitive Slave Law; before Judge Drummond, of the U.S. District Court of Chicago."
55. Ibid.
56. Ibid.
57. Ibid.
58. Ibid.
59. Ibid.
60. Ibid.
61. Douglass, "Letter to the Abolitionist Reunion of June 9–13, 1874," Chicago, Illinois.

Chapter 5

1. Stowe, *Uncle Tom's Cabin*, 1852 Preface.
2. Sutherland, *The Expansion of Everyday Life*, 79.
3. Isaiah 58:7–8.
4. Leisch, *An Introduction to Civil War Civilians*, 1.
5. Boies, *History of DeKalb County*, 354.
6. Ibid.
7. Waterman, "Letter from Mary Hadley, February 24, 1842."
8. Kellogg, *Minutes of Church Meetings of the Congregational Church in Sycamore*, 17.
9. Scott, "Abolition as a Sacred Vocation," Perry and Fellman, eds., *Antislavery Reconsidered: New Perspectives on the Abolitionists*, 67.
10. Kellogg, *Minutes of Church Meetings of the Congregational Church in Sycamore*, 74.
11. Luke 1:15.
12. Kellogg, *Minutes of Church Meetings of the Congregational Church in Sycamore*, 75.
13. Ibid., 76.
14. Ibid.
15. Ibid.
16. Deuteronomy 23:15–16.

Chapter 6

1. Kellogg, *Minutes of Church Meetings of the Congregational Church in Sycamore*, Book C-1, 30–31.
2. Ibid., 38.
3. Ibid., 44.
4. Ibid.
5. Ibid., 46.
6. Ibid., 48.
7. Hope United Church of Christ, "A Brief History of the United Church of Christ."
8. Stephenson, *The Puritan Heritage*, 34.
9. Spinka, *A History of Illinois Congregational and Christian Churches*, 139.
10. Ibid.
11. Ibid.
12. *Population Schedules of the Seventh Census of the United States: 1850*.
13. Anonymous notes, "Church Meetings of the Congregational Church in Sycamore."
14. *Sycamore True Republican*, July 1, 1899.
15. *Manual of the First Congregational Church*.
16. *Manual of the Fox River Association with a Historical Sketch, 1835–1890*.
17. Boies, *History of DeKalb County*, 476.
18. *DeKalb Chronicle Illustrated Souvenir, 1899*, 114.
19. Wood, "Memoirs of Women's Fellowship, 1890," 2.
20. Spinka, *A History of Illinois Congregational and Christian Churches*, 141.
21. Ibid.
22. Kellogg, *Minutes of Church Meetings of the Congregational Church in Sycamore*, Book C-1, 12.
23. Ibid., 2.
24. Exodus 21:16.
25. Harris, "History of Negro Slavery in Illinois and of the Slavery Agitation in that State," 142.
26. Kellogg, *Minutes of Church Meetings of the Congregational Church in Sycamore*, Book C-1, 7.
27. Ibid., 16. The West family was not officially received into membership until April 14, 1844.
28. See Scott, "Abolition as a Sacred Vocation," Perry and Fellman, eds., *Antislavery Reconsidered: New Perspectives on the Abolitionists*, 51.
29. Sorin, *The New York Abolitionists: A Case Study of Political Radicalism*, 111.
30. Ibid., 97.
31. Isaiah 16:3.
32. *Western Citizen*, June 5, 1845.
33. Chapman, *Portrait and Biographical Album of DeKalb County, Illinois*, 258.
34. Kellogg, *Minutes of Church Meetings of the Congregational Church in Sycamore*, Book C-1, 17.
35. Ibid.
36. Sernett, *Abolition's Axe: Beriah Green, Oneida Institute, and the Black Freedom Struggle*, 45–46.
37. Green, "Things for Northern Men to Do: A Discourse Delivered Lord's Day Evening, July 17, 1836, in the Presbyterian church, Whitesboro, NY."
38. Muelder, *Fighters for Freedom: The History of Anti-Slavery Activities of Men and Women Associated with Knox College*, 23.
39. Ibid., 85.
40. Ibid., 75.
41. Ibid., 89.
42. Kellogg, *Minutes of Church Meetings of the Congregational Church in Sycamore*, Book C-1, 18.
43. Ibid.
44. United Church of Christ, "Congregationalism from Plymouth to the American Revolution."
45. Kellogg, *Minutes of Church Meetings of the Congregational Church in Sycamore*, Book C-1, 19.
46. Boies, *History of DeKalb County*, 386.
47. Ibid., 387.
48. Kellogg, *Minutes of Church Meetings of the Congregational Church in Sycamore*, Book C-1, 29.
49. Ibid., 26.
50. Ibid., 25.
51. Ibid., 41–42.
52. Ibid., 18.
53. Ibid., 29.
54. Ibid., 37.
55. Gross, *Past and Present of DeKalb County*, Vol. I, 330.
56. Kellogg, *Minutes of Church Meetings of the Congregational Church in Sycamore*, Book C-1, 28.
57. Boies, *History of DeKalb County*, 402.
58. Ibid., 382–383.
59. *Sycamore Illinois Illustrated Prospectus, 1906*, 6.
60. United Church of Christ, *The New Century Hymnal*, "Amazing Grace, How Sweet the Sound," 486. Newton captained a slave ship and was spiritually saved in a violent storm. He wrote this hymn to commemorate his experience and devoted his remaining life to the antislavery movement. See Rogers, "Amazing Grace: The Story of John Newton."
61. Kellogg, *Minutes of Church Meetings of the Congregational Church in Sycamore*, Book C-1, 128.
62. Ibid., 130.
63. Mark 12:31.

Chapter 7

1. Spinka, *A History of Illinois Congregational and Christian Churches*, 94.
2. Ibid.
3. Ibid., 94–95.
4. *Sycamore True Republican*, "Sixty Years Ago," April 14, 1900.
5. Scott, "Abolition as a Sacred Vocation." Perry and Fellman, eds., *Antislavery Reconsidered: New Perspectives on the Abolitionists*, 51.
6. *Sycamore True Republican*, February 28, 1912.
7. *Sycamore True Republican*, April, 1930, "90th Anniversary of First Congregational Church."
8. Chapman, *Portrait and Biographical Album of DeKalb County, Illinois*, 315.
9. Norton, Letter to sister, Augusta, January 25, 1848, *Henrietta*, 89.
10. *Sycamore Tribune*, April 15, 1940.
11. Norton, *Our Norton Family Story*, 26.
12. Kellogg, *Minutes of Church Meetings of the Congregational Church in Sycamore*, Book C-1, 50.
13. Ibid., 52.
14. Ibid., 53–54.
15. Ibid.
16. Deuteronomy 23:15–16.
17. Kellogg, *Minutes of Church Meetings of the Congregational Church in Sycamore*, Book C-1, 55–56.
18. Ibid., 56.
19. Norton, *Our Norton Family Story*, 42–44.
20. Kellogg, *Minutes of Church Meetings of the Congregational Church in Sycamore*, Book C-1, 82–83.
21. Ibid.

22. Siebert, *The Underground Railroad from Slavery to Freedom*, 44.
23. Kellogg, *Minutes of Church Meetings of the Congregational Church in Sycamore*, Book C-1, 115–116.
24. Ibid., 116–117.
25. *Amherst College Biographical Record*.
26. Gore, "Letter to the American Missionary Association, December 15, 1856."
27. Duncan, ed. *History of First Congregational Church: United Church of Christ, DeKalb, Illinois 1854–1984*, 8.
28. Switala, *Underground Railroad in Pennsylvania*, 3–4.
29. See Hagedorn, *Beyond the River: The Untold Story of the Heroes of the Underground Railroad*.
30. See Peters, *The Underground Railroad in Floyd County, Indiana*.

Chapter 8

1. Willard, "My Recollections of Curtis Smith, Pioneer," *Sycamore True Republican*, May 6, 1916.
2. Ibid.
3. Ibid.
4. Ibid.
5. Miller, *The Larger Hope: The First Century of the Universalist Church in America 1770–1870*, 704.
6. Bailey, John C.W., *Kane County, Illinois, Directory for 1859–1860*, "City of Aurora," 27.
7. Le Baron, *The Past and Present of Kane County, Illinois*, 344.
8. Davy, *From Oxen to Jets: A History of DeKalb County, 1835–1963*, 159.
9. *Sycamore True Republican*, "Report of 70th Anniversary of Universalist Church," October 2, 1915.
10. Ralph, *Parish and Church Record of the Universalist Church*, 6.
11. Litvin, "A Journal of Julia Abigail Fletcher, Commenced April 6th, 1846," 44.
12. *Western Citizen*, Fletcher, "The Neglected Opportunity," August 29, 1844, reprinted from the *Social Monitor*.
13. Litvin, "Julia Abigail Fletcher Carney papers."
14. Litvin, "A Journal of Julia Abigail Fletcher," 13.
15. Ibid., 14.
16. Ibid., 13.
17. Litvin, "Correspondence of Julia A. Fletcher Carney to Tom Carney, 1848–1850"; Carney, Julia A. Fletcher, "Letter to Tom Carney, July 14, 1848."
18. "Knox County, Illinois Genealogy & History."
19. Chapman, *Portrait and Biographical Album of DeKalb County, Illinois*, 857.
20. Ralph, *Parish and Church Record of the Universalist Church*, 32.
21. Harris, *Unitarian Universalist Origins: Our Historic Faith*.
22. Miller, *The Larger Hope*, 574.
23. Ibid.
24. Ibid.
25. Harris, *Unitarian Universalist Origins*.
26. Judy Deutsch, "What We Were and Are," *Unitarian Universalism: An Extremely Brief Overview for an Orientation Session*.
27. Miller, *The Larger Hope*, 576.
28. Ibid.
29. *Sycamore True Republican*, "Report of 70th Anniversary of Universalist Church," October 2, 1915.
30. Dutton, "Letter to Sister Jane, April 8, 1940."
31. Miller, *The Larger Hope*, 583.
32. Ibid., 585.
33. Ibid., 589–605.
34. Ibid., 589.
35. Ibid., 592.
36. Lewis, *The United States Biographical Dictionary, Kansas Volume*, 386.
37. Ibid.
38. Ibid.
39. Ibid.
40. Anonymous, *The Biographical Record of DeKalb County, Illinois*, 229.
41. Lewis, *The United States Biographical Dictionary, Kansas Volume*, 386.
42. Ibid.
43. Anonymous, *The Biographical Record of DeKalb County, Illinois*, 230.
44. Lewis, *The United States Biographical Dictionary, Kansas Volume*, 386.
45. *The Sycamore True Republican*, January 22, 1896.
46. Chapman, *Portrait and Biographical Album of DeKalb County, Illinois*, 710.
47. Ibid., 710–711.
48. Boies, *History of DeKalb County*, 477.
49. Chapman, *Portrait and Biographical Album of DeKalb County, Illinois*, 710.
50. Gross, *Past and Present of DeKalb County, Illinois*, Vol. 1, 98.
51. Ibid.
52. Ibid.
53. Gore, "Letter to the American Missionary Association," December 15, 1856.
54. Ibid.
55. Litvin, "Correspondence of Julia A. Fletcher Carney to Tom Carney, 1848–1850," September 6, 1847.
56. *Sycamore True Republican*, August 15, 1877, obituary of Rufus S. Sanborn.
57. Gross, *Past and Present of DeKalb County*, Vol. I, 170.
58. Sanborn, handwritten notes.
59. *Sycamore True Republican*, August 15, 1877, obituary of Rufus S. Sanborn.
60. United States Patent Office, July 17, 1866.
61. Sanborn, *Unitarian Universalist Inactive Minister Files*.
62. *Sycamore True Republican*, August 15, 1877, obituary of Rufus S. Sanborn.
63. *Sycamore True Republican*, May 6, 1916.
64. Ibid.
65. Ibid.

Chapter 9

1. Hossack, "Speech of John Hossack, Convicted of Violation of the Fugitive Slave Law; before Judge Drummond, of the U.S. District Court of Chicago."
2. Patten and Graham, *History of the Somonauk United Presbyterian Church*, 60.
3. Baker, Ed. *The Works of William H. Seward*, 23.
4. Ibid.
5. Wisconsin Historical Society, microfilm P01-848, Ohio Historical Society, *Underground Railroad in Illinois*, Vols. I and II.
6. Patten and Graham, *History of the Somonauk United Presbyterian Church*, 60.
7. Ibid., 61.
8. Ibid.
9. Boies, *History of DeKalb County*, 522.
10. Ibid.
11. Ibid.
12. Ibid., 522–523.
13. Patten and Graham, *History of the Somonauk United Presbyterian Church*, 5.
14. Ibid., 60.
15. Ibid.
16. *Western Citizen*, December 3, 1850.
17. Ibid.
18. Ibid.
19. Patten and Graham, *History of the Somonauk United Presbyterian Church*, 62.
20. *Western Citizen*, December 3, 1850.
21. Patten and Graham, *History of the Somonauk United Presbyterian Church*, 60.
22. Ibid.
23. *Western Citizen*, September 19, 1844.
24. Ibid.
25. Ibid.
26. Ibid.
27. American Presbyterian Church.
28. Hossack, "Speech of John Hossack, Convicted of Violation of the Fugitive Slave Law; before Judge Drummond, of the U.S. District Court of Chicago."

29. Patten and Graham, *History of the Somonauk United Presbyterian Church*, 2.

Chapter 10

1. Education 2000 Inc., *Landmarks of Faith: Methodist Camp Meetings*.
2. *Sycamore True Republican*, December 8, 1909.
3. *Western Citizen*, June 5, 1845.
4. Ibid.
5. *Sycamore True Republican*, December 8, 1909.
6. Ibid.
7. Education 2000 Inc., *Landmarks of Faith: Methodist Camp Meetings*.
8. *Western Citizen*, June 5, 1845.
9. Kellogg, *Minutes of Church Meetings of the Congregational Church in Sycamore*, Book C-1, 34.
10. Brawley, *Lorenzo Dow*, 267.
11. Ibid.
12. Dow, *The Book of Dow*, 511.
13. Dow, "An Old Diary."
14. *Sycamore True Republican*, June 10, 1935, commemorating the 100th anniversary of the first Methodist church in Sycamore.
15. Ibid., April 8, 1916.
16. Gross, *Past and Present of DeKalb County*, Vol. I, 155.
17. Ibid.
18. Boies, *History of DeKalb County, Illinois*, 109.
19. Siebert, *The Underground Railroad from Slavery to Freedom*, 405.
20. *Sycamore True Republican*, March 12, 1884.
21. Ibid.
22. *The History of Five Points, 1847–1937*, 12.
23. Ibid.
24. Ibid.
25. Ibid.
26. *Sycamore True Republican*, July 28, 1894.
27. Ibid.
28. Boies, *History of DeKalb County*, 465.
29. *The History of Five Points, 1847–1937*, 12.
30. Gross, *Past and Present of DeKalb County*, Vol. I, 101.
31. Gross and Congdon, "History of DeKalb County, Ill.," *Standard Atlas of DeKalb County, Illinois*, 83.
32. Ibid.
33. Ibid.
34. Ibid.
35. Gross, *Past and Present of DeKalb County*, Vol. I, 98.
36. Ibid.
37. Ibid.
38. Ibid., 156.
39. Ohio Wesleyan University, Charter.
40. Gross, *Past and Present of DeKalb County*, Vol. I, 155
41. Baker, ed., *The Works of William H. Seward*, Vol. I, 2.3

Chapter 11

1. Eastman Collection, Box 14, Manuscript Notebook, 2.
2. *Western Citizen*, January 5, 1845.
3. Ibid.
4. *Chicago Tribune*, June 15, 1883.
5. Lincoln to Washburne, December 11, 1854.
6. Washburne to Eastman, December 19, 1854.
7. *Chicago Tribune*, June 15, 1883.
8. Ibid.
9. Eastman Collection, Box 14, Manuscript Notebook, 2.
10. Ibid., 4.
11. Willging, "Citizens for a Free West: Antislavery Advocates in DeKalb County, Illinois, 1843–1855," 3.
12. Hagedorn, *Beyond the River*, 47.
13. Willging, "Citizens for a Free West," 6.
14. Gara, *The Liberty Line: The Legend of the Underground Railroad*, 90.
15. Spinka, *A History of Illinois Congregational and Christian Churches*, 136.
16. Gross, *Past and Present of DeKalb County*, Vol. I, 98.
17. Mahoney, "Black Abolitionists," *Chicago History: The Magazine of the Chicago Historical Society*, 28.
18. Ibid.
19. Dyer to Eastman, April 20, 1842.
20. Mahoney, "Black Abolitionists," 29.
21. *Chicago Tribune*, March 4, 2003, Section 2, 3.
22. Mahoney, "Black Abolitionists," 29.
23. Ibid.
24. Ibid., 29.
25. Ibid., 33.
26. Dyer to Eastman, January 29, 1884, Zebina Eastman collection, 13.
27. *Western Citizen*, March 6, 1845.
28. Ibid.
29. *Illinois Constitution of 1818*, Article VI, Section I.
30. *Laws of Illinois, Approved February 1, 1831*, Section I.
31. *Western Citizen*, March 6, 1845.
32. Ibid.
33. Ibid.
34. Ibid.
35. Ibid.
36. Ibid.
37. Ibid.
38. Ibid.
39. *Harper's Weekly*, "The Black Laws," February 11, 1865, 82.
40. Gross, *Past and Present of DeKalb County*, Vol. I, 66.
41. Ibid., 96.
42. Ibid.

Chapter 12

1. Lowance, ed., *Against Slavery: An Abolitionist Reader*, Emerson, "Lecture on Slavery," Boston, January 25, 1855, 305.
2. *Sycamore True Republican*, January 6, 1915.
3. Ibid.
4. Kellogg, "Letter to the American Home Missionary Society," March 24, 1841.
5. Ibid.
6. Ibid.
7. Ibid.
8. Ibid.
9. *Sycamore True Republican*, April 10, 1915, Hosea W. Willard retrospective.
10. Ibid.
11. Chapman, *Portrait and Biographical Album of DeKalb County, Illinois*, 692.
12. Kellogg, "Letter to the American Home Missionary Society," November 8, 1841.
13. Perry, "Letter to the American Home Missionary Society," April 1, 1842.
14. Ibid.
15. Ibid.
16. Ibid.
17. Perry, "Letter to the American Home Missionary Society," August 4, 1842.
18. *Western Citizen*, July 4, 1844.
19. Ibid., April 13, 1843.
20. Ibid.
21. Ibid.
22. Ibid.
23. Ibid., February 29, 1844.
24. Ibid., April 11, 1844.
25. Ibid., May 15 and May 22, 1845.
26. Ibid., May 15, 1845.
27. Ibid.
28. Ibid., May 29, June 5, June 12 and June 19, 1845.
29. Ibid., July 10, 1845.
30. Patten and Graham, *History of the Somonauk United Presbyterian Church*, 284.
31. Moore and Moore, eds., *Owen Lovejoy: His Brother's Blood, Speeches and Writings 1838–64*, xx.
32. Strong, *Perfectionist Politics: Abolitionism and the Religious Tensions of American Democracy*, 1.
33. *Western Citizen*, August 28, 1845.
34. Ibid.
35. Ibid., July 13, 1847.
36. Ibid., May 9, 1844.
37. Cavanagh, "Antislavery Sentiment and Politics in the Northwest 1844–60," 2.
38. *Western Citizen*, July 4, 1844.
39. Harris, "History of Negro Slavery in Illinois and of the Slavery Agitation in that State," 152.
40. *Western Citizen*, October 10, 1844.
41. Ibid.

42. Ibid. William Morgan, a presumed member of the Masonic order, was murdered in 1827.
43. Ibid.
44. Patten and Graham, *History of the Somonauk United Presbyterian Church*, Elizabeth Miller, "Letter to Ann Beveridge, October 12, 1844," 264.
45. Ibid., 57.
46. *Western Citizen*, September 12, 1844.
47. Ibid., August 1, 1844.
48. Ibid., September 12, 1844.
49. Ibid., November 14, 1844.
50. Patten and Graham, *History of the Somonauk United Presbyterian Church*, 94.
51. *Republican Sentinel*, August 2, 1854.
52. Applegate, *The Most Famous Man in America: The Biography of Henry Ward Beecher*, 278.
53. *Republican Sentinel*, August 2, 1854.
54. *Edited Appleton's Encyclopedia*.
55. *Republican Sentinel*, August 2, 1854, "Resolutions of the Anti-Nebraska Meeting."
56. Ibid.
57. Ordinance of 1787, adopted by Congress August 7, 1789; Lowance, *Against Slavery: An Abolitionist Reader*, 332.
58. *Republican Sentinel*, August 2, 1854, "Resolutions of the Anti-Nebraska Meeting."
59. Ibid.
60. Ibid.
61. Cavanagh, "Antislavery Sentiment and Politics in the Northwest 1844–60," 5.
62. Boies, *History of DeKalb County, Illinois*, 414.
63. Gross, *Past and Present of DeKalb County*, Vol. I, 194.
64. Ibid., 102.
65. Gross, *Past and Present of DeKalb County*, Vol. I, 102.
66. Perry and Fellman, eds., *Antislavery Reconsidered: New Perspectives on the Abolitionists*, Introduction, xv.
67. Spinka, ed., *A History of Illinois Congregational and Christian Churches*, 136.
68. Gross, *Past and Present of DeKalb County*, Vol. I, 102.
69. Boies, *History of DeKalb County, Illinois*, 414.
70. *True Republican*, October 27, 1857.
71. Applegate, *The Most Famous Man in America*, 278.
72. Cavanagh, "Antislavery Sentiment and Politics in the Northwest 1844–60," 2.
73. *True Republican*, October 27, 1857.
74. Ibid.
75. *True Republican*, October 20, 1857.
76. Gross, *Past and Present of DeKalb County*, Vol. I, 96.
77. *Republican Sentinel*, August 16, 1858.
78. Applegate, *The Most Famous Man in America*, 124.
79. *The Republican Sentinel*, October 4, 1858.
80. Ibid.

Chapter 13

1. *True Republican*, January 31, 1894.
2. Kett, *The Voters and Tax-Payers of DeKalb County, Illinois*, 148.
3. *Western Citizen*, July 26, 1842.
4. Ibid.
5. *True Republican*, January 31, 1894.
6. *True Republican*, November 7, 1857, reprinted from the *Washington Investigator*.
7. Kett, *The Voters and Tax-Payers of DeKalb County, Illinois*, 148.
8. *Sycamore True Republican*, January 17, 1941, 1.
9. Boies, *History of DeKalb County*, 414.
10. *True Republican*, October 23, 1907, Reprinted 1867 column by Henry L. Boies reflecting on the first ten years of the newspaper's history.
11. *Sycamore True Republican*, January 17, 1941, 6.
12. Kett, *The Voters and Tax-Payers of DeKalb County, Illinois*, 148.
13. *True Republican*, January 31, 1894.
14. Ibid.
15. *Sycamore True Republican*, January 17, 1941.
16. Beasley, ed., "A Compilation of the Early Membership Lists of the First Congregational Church in Sycamore."
17. United States General Land Office, Bureau of Land Management, Documents nos. 23085, 26613, 27150, 27739 and 28292.
18. Ibid., Document nos. 11426, 11427, 24667 and 29287.
19. *Sycamore True Republican*, September 9, 1899.
20. Chapman, *Portrait and Biographical Album of DeKalb County, Illinois*, 325.
21. Ibid., 786.
22. *Western Citizen*, December 3, 1850.
23. Patten and Graham, *History of the Somonauk United Presbyterian Church*, 38.
24. Ibid.
25. Chapman, *Portrait and Biographical Album of DeKalb County, Illinois*, 786.
26. Ibid., 326.
27. Ibid., 786.
28. Ibid., 778.
29. Ibid.
30. Boies, *History of DeKalb County*, 401.
31. Gross, *Past and Present of DeKalb County, Illinois*, Vol. I, 170.
32. Ibid.
33. *Sycamore True Republican*, "Recollections from 1852," February 28, 1912.
34. Ibid., 405.
35. David D. Brown later married Alice J. Ellwood, daughter of Hiram Ellwood of the famed DeKalb County barbed wire family; Brown became mayor of the city of DeKalb.
36. *Sycamore True Republican*, August 12, 1914.
37. Gross, *Past and Present of DeKalb County, Illinois*, Vol. I, 405.
38. *True Republican*, 1860; reprinted in *True Republican*, October 31, 1900.
39. Ibid.
40. Ibid.
41. Gross, *Past and Present of DeKalb County, Illinois*, Vol. I, 405.
42. *True Republican*, 1867; reprinted in the *Sycamore True Republican*, October 23, 1907.
43. *Sycamore True Republican*, obituary of Betsy M. Bassett, January 27, 1897.
44. *Sycamore True Republican*, "30 Years Ago," February 27, 1895.
45. *Sycamore True Republican*, obituary of Betsy M. Bassett, January 27, 1897.
46. Lincoln, "House Divided" speech, June 16, 1858.
47. Ibid.
48. Lincoln, "House Divided" speech, June 16, 1858.
49. Ibid.
50. Ibid.
51. *True Republican*, June 29, 1858.
52. Angle, *Four Lincoln Firsts*, paper presented to the Bibliographical Society of America, December 30, 1941, 5.
53. Ibid.
54. *Sycamore True Republican*, obituary of Betsy M. Bassett, January 27, 1897.
55. *DeKalb County Sentinel*, July 26, 1858.
56. Donald, *Lincoln*, 220.
57. Ibid.
58. Lincoln, "Mr. Lincoln's Reply in the Jonesboro Joint Debate"; Nicolay and Hay, eds., "Third Joint Debate at Jonesboro, Illinois, September 15, 1858," *The Complete Works of Abraham Lincoln*, v. 4, 51–52.
59. Ibid.
60. *Sycamore True Republican*, February 17, 1904, obituary of Campbell W. Waite.
61. *True Republican*, October 23, 1907, reprinted 1867 column by Henry L. Boies reflecting on the first ten years of the newspaper's history.

Chapter 14

1. Stowe, quote from *Old Town Folks*, in *Three Novels: Uncle Tom's Cabin,*

The Minister's Wooing, Old Town Folks, 1371.
2. Gore and Kellogg, *Report of Clerk, Congregational Church,* Book C-2, September 17, 1854–October 7, 1860, last pages, unnumbered.
3. United States Census, 1850, DeKalb County, Illinois, Social Statistics.
4. *Sycamore True Republican,* December 8, 1909.
5. Ibid.
6. Stowe, quote from *Old Town Folks,* 1371.
7. Chapman, *Portrait and Biographical Album of DeKalb County, Illinois,* 315.
8. *DeKalb County Sentinel,* August 9, 1858.
9. Ibid.
10. *Sycamore True Republican,* December 17, 1924.
11. Ibid., February 21, 1941.
12. Ibid., December 17, 1924.
13. Ibid.
14. Gross, *Past and Present of DeKalb County, Illinois,* Vol. I, 63.
15. *Sycamore True Republican,* March 18, 1939, reprinted from September 19, 1876.
16. Ibid.
17. Ibid.
18. Gross, *Past and Present of DeKalb County, Illinois,* Vol. I, 103.

Chapter 15

1. Douglass, "Letter to the Abolitionist Reunion, June 9–13, 1874, Chicago, Illinois."
2. See Peters, *The Underground Railroad in Floyd County, Indiana.*
3. Virga, *Eyes of the Nation: A Visual History of the United States,* 135.
4. Boies, *History of DeKalb County, Illinois,* 113–346.
5. Virga, *Eyes of the Nation,* 135.
6. *Sycamore True Republican,* September 19, 1877
7. *Chicago Tribune,* February 17, 2003.
8. Douglass, "Dred Scott Decision, Speech Delivered, in Part, at the Anniversary of the American Abolition Society, Held in New York, May 14, 1857," 40.
9. *Madison Magazine,* Pferdehirt, "Freedom Trail," March, 1999, 42.
10. Siebert, *The Underground Railroad from Slavery to Freedom,* 358.
11. *Sycamore True Republican,* December 8, 1909.
12. Bennett, from Macon, *Wade in the Water* (video), 2002.
13. Eastman Collection, Box 1, Folder 4, 140.
14. *Sycamore True Republican,* December 8, 1909.
15. Ibid., January 6, 1915.
16. Douglass, "Letter to the Abolitionist Reunion, June 9–13, 1874, Chicago, Illinois."

Biographical Dictionary

1. Chapman, *Portrait and Biographical Album of DeKalb County, Illinois,* 185.
2. Sorin, *The New York Abolitionists: A Case Study of Political Radicalism,* 106.
3. Ibid., 107.
4. Chapman, *Portrait and Biographical Album of DeKalb County, Illinois,* 515.
5. Beers and Leggett, *Biographical and Historical Record of Kane County, Illinois,* 250–251.
6. *True Republican,* January 31, 1894.
7. Angle, Presentation to the Bibliographical Society of America, December 30, 1941.
8. Gross, *Past and Present of DeKalb County,* Vol. II, 98.
9. Boies, *History of DeKalb County, Illinois,* 109, 522.
10. Chapman, *Portrait and Biographical Album of DeKalb County, Illinois,* 325.
11. Boies, *History of DeKalb County, Illinois,* 414.
12. *Republican Sentinel,* August 2, 1854.
13. Gross, *Past and Present of DeKalb County,* Vol. 1, 380.
14. *Sycamore True Republican,* September 14, 1901.
15. *Western Citizen,* December 3, 1850.
16. Boies, *History of DeKalb County, Illinois,* 414.
17. *True Republican,* June 24, 1931.
18. Chapman, *Portrait and Biographical Album of DeKalb County, Illinois,* 481.
19. *Sycamore True Republican,* February 18, 1885, obit for Benjamin P. Brown.
20. Gross, *Past and Present of DeKalb County,* Vol. I., 405.
21. Chapman, *Portrait and Biographical Album of DeKalb County, Illinois,* 481.
22. *Sycamore True Republican,* March 12, 1884.
23. Boies, *History of DeKalb County, Illinois,* 414.
24. Ibid.
25. Ibid., 95–105.
26. Ibid., 414.
27. *Delphos Herald,* July 28, 1894.
28. Chapman, *Portrait and Biographical Album of DeKalb County, Illinois,* 892.
29. Ibid., 591.
30. Boies, *History of DeKalb County, Illinois,* 414.
31. Gross, *Past and Present of DeKalb County,* Vol. I, 98.
32. *Sycamore True Republican,* July 28, 1894.
33. Ibid., July 21, 1886.
34. *Western Citizen,* April 13, 1843.
35. Dow, *The Book of Dow,* 491.
36. Clarke, *The Biographical Record of DeKalb County, Illinois,* 10.
37. Gross, *Past and Present of DeKalb County,* Vol. I, 393.
38. Clarke, *The Biographical Record of DeKalb County, Illinois,* 229.
39. DeKalb County Archives, Joiner History Room, Sycamore, Illinois.
40. Boies, *History of DeKalb County, Illinois,* 414.
41. *Sycamore True Republican,* November 30, 1880.
42. *DeKalb Chronicle Illustrated Souvenir, 1899,* 209.
43. Boies, *History of DeKalb County, Illinois,* 414.
44. Ibid., 579.
45. *Republican Sentinel,* August 2, 1854.
46. Patten and Graham, *History of the Somonauk United Presbyterian Church,* 22.
47. Chapman, *Portrait and Biographical Album of DeKalb County, Illinois,* 275.
48. Gore, "Letter to the American Missionary Association, December 15, 1856."
49. Boies, *History of DeKalb County,* 465.
50. Chapman, *Portrait and Biographical Album of DeKalb County, Illinois,* 481.
51. *Western Citizen,* April 13, 1843.
52. Boies, *History of DeKalb County,* 414.
53. Gross, *Past and Present of DeKalb County,* Vol. I, 326.
54. Boies, *History of DeKalb County, Illinois,* 414.
55. Ibid., 191.
56. Chapman, *Portrait and Biographical Album of DeKalb County, Illinois,* 370.
57. Rasmusen, *LaSalle County Lore,* 61.
58. *True Republican,* October 10, 1857.
59. Gross, *Past and Present of DeKalb County,* Vol. I, 98.
60. Boies, *History of DeKalb County,* 109.
61. *Republican Sentinel,* August 2, 1854.
62. Boies, *History of DeKalb County, Illinois,* 414.
63. *Shabbona Museum Scrapbook,* obituary of William W. Irwin, 121.
64. Clarke, *Biographical Record of DeKalb County, Illinois,* 319.
65. Chapman, *Portrait and Biographical Album of DeKalb County, Illinois,* 481.
66. Gross, *Past and Present of DeKalb County,* Vol. I, 170.

67. Chapman, *Portrait and Biographical Album of DeKalb County, Illinois*, 711.
68. Boies, *History of DeKalb County*, 414.
69. Kett, *The Voters and Tax-Payers of DeKalb County, Illinois*, 225.
70. Chapman, *Portrait and Biographical Album of DeKalb County, Illinois*, 481.
71. Gross, *Past and Present of DeKalb County*, Vol. I, 101.
72. *Sycamore True Republican*, November 25, 1903.
73. Chapman, *Portrait and Biographical Album of DeKalb County, Illinois*, 692.
74. *Sycamore True Republican*, July 21, 1886.
75. Chapman, *Portrait and Biographical Album of DeKalb County, Illinois*, 481.
76. Boies, *History of DeKalb County*, 95–105.
77. Ibid.
78. *Sycamore True Republican*, April 8, 1916.
79. *Western Citizen*, December 3, 1850.
80. *Republican Sentinel*, August 2, 1854.
81. Ibid.
82. Chapman, *Portrait and Biographical Album of DeKalb County, Illinois*, 672.
83. *Sycamore True Republican*, January 29, 1873.
84. *Western Citizen*, July 13, 1847.
85. Gross, *Past and Present of DeKalb County*, Vol. I, 152.
86. Ibid., 351.
87. Boies, *History of DeKalb County*, 465.
88. Ibid.
89. Joiner History Room. "Scrapbook of Lavina Haller Ault," Latin Nichols obituary.
90. Gross, *Past and Present of DeKalb County*, Vol. I, 351.
91. Ibid., 155.
92. Boies, *History of DeKalb County*, 465.
93. Gross, *Past and Present of DeKalb County*, Vol. I, 155.
94. *Sycamore True Republican*, December 8, 1909.
95. Gross, *Past and Present of DeKalb County*, Vol. I, 173.
96. Clarke, *Biographical Record of DeKalb County, Illinois*, 524.
97. Chapman, *Portrait and Biographical Album of DeKalb County, Illinois*, 481.
98. *Western Citizen*, July 13, 1847.
99. Boies, *History of DeKalb County*, 414.
100. *Sycamore True Republican*, November 30, 1880.
101. Gross, *Past and Present of DeKalb County*, Vol. I, 98.
102. Chapman, *Portrait and Biographical Album of DeKalb County, Illinois*, 252.
103. Cutler, *History of the State of Kansas*.
104. *The History of Five Points, 1847–1937*, 12.
105. *Paw Paw Centennial Book, 1982*, 67.
106. Boies, *History of DeKalb County*, 414.
107. *Sycamore True Republican*, July 21, 1886.
108. Ibid., July 1, 1899.
109. Ibid.
110. *Western Citizen*, April 13, 1843.
111. Gross, *Past and Present of DeKalb County*, Vol. II, 570.
112. Ibid., 204.
113. Boies, *History of DeKalb County, Illinois*, 414.
114. *Sycamore True Republican*, July 21, 1886.
115. Ibid., March 21, 1894.
116. Gross, *Past and Present of DeKalb County*, Vol. I, 155.
117. Willard, "My Recollections of Curtis Smith, Pioneer," *Sycamore True Republican*, May 6, 1916.
118. Gross, *Past and Present of DeKalb County*, Vol. I, 31.
119. Chapman, *Portrait and Biographical Album of DeKalb County, Illinois*, 368.
120. Ibid., 430.
121. Boies, *History of DeKalb County*, 109.
122. Gross, *Past and Present of DeKalb County*, Vol. I, 430.
123. Boies, *History of DeKalb County*, 109.
124. Ibid., 414.
125. Gross, *Past and Present of DeKalb County*, Vol. I, 430.
126. Boies, *History of DeKalb County*, 109.
127. *Sycamore True Republican*, March 28, 1883.
128. Angle, presentation to the Bibliographical Society of America, December 30, 1941.
129. Chapman, *Portrait and Biographical Album of DeKalb County, Illinois*, 315.
130. *Republican Sentinel*, August 2, 1854.
131. Clarke, *Biographical Record of DeKalb County, Illinois*, 545.
132. Kellogg, *Minutes of Church Meetings of the Cong Church in Sycamore*, Book C-1, 17.
133. *Western Citizen*, April 21, 1844.
134. Ibid., April 13, 1843.
135. Ibid., April 21, 1844.
136. Boies, *History of DeKalb County*, 414.
137. Gross, *Past and Present of DeKalb County*, Vol. I, 101.
138. Ibid., 99.
139. Clarke, *Biographical Record of DeKalb County, Illinois*, 448.
140. Chapman, *Portrait and Biographical Album of DeKalb County, Illinois*, 441.
141. *Western Citizen*, April 13, 1843.
142. Clarke, *Biographical Record of DeKalb County, Illinois*, 276.
143. *Sycamore True Republican*, April 13, 1895.
144. *Western Citizen*, April 13, 1843.

Bibliography

Primary Sources: Manuscript

UNPUBLISHED

Abstract of Title No. 12656 for Lot eight (8) in block Nineteen (19) in the Original Town of Sycamore, DeKalb County, Illinois. Sycamore, Illinois: Chicago Title and Trust Company. Owned by Nancy M. Beasley.

Anonymous Notes. *Church Meetings of the Congregational Church in Sycamore.* Sycamore, Illinois: First Congregational Church.

Beasley, Nancy M., transcriber. "A Compilation of the Early Membership Lists of First Congregational Church in Sycamore." From *Minutes of Church Meetings of the Congregational Church in Sycamore*, Book C-1 and Book C-6.

Dutton, William P. "Letter to Sister Jane, April 8, 1940." Sycamore, Illinois: Universalist Church.

Dyer, Charles V. "Letter to Zebina Eastman, April 20, 1842." Zebina Eastman Collection, Box XB 107a (1 of 2), Folder 1841–1861. Chicago: Chicago History Museum.

Dyer, Edward G. "Letter to Zebina Eastman, January 29, 1884." Zebina Eastman Collection, Box 2, Folder 8. Chicago: Chicago History Museum.

Eastman, Zebina. "1876 Invitation List to Chicago Abolitionist Reunion." Zebina Eastman Collection, Boxes 3–5, Vols. 1–13. Chicago: Chicago History Museum.

_____. *Mailbooks of The Western Citizen and Free West.* Zebina Eastman Collection, Boxes 3–5, Vols. 1–13. Chicago: Chicago History Museum.

_____. "Miscellaneous Abolitionists' Letters." Zebina Eastman Collection, Boxes 3–5, Vols. 1–13. Chicago: Chicago History Museum.

Elmer, Irving A. "Letter to C.F. Allen, January 2, 1925." Sycamore, Illinois: DeKalb County Archives, Joiner History Room.

Gore, Darius. "Letter to the American Missionary Association, December 15, 1856." New Orleans: American Missionary Association Archives, Amistad Research Center at Tulane University.

_____, and Jesse C. Kellogg. *Report of Clerk, Congregational Church, Sept 17, 1854 – October 7, 1860*, Book C-2. Sycamore, Illinois: First Congregational Church.

Hopkins, Dr. Rufus. "Daily Record of Patient Visits, 1848." Sycamore, Illinois: DeKalb County Archives, Joiner History Room.

Johnson, William Lucas. "Letter to Elizabeth Johnson, February 24, 1862." Jim Woodworth, ed. Baldwin, Kansas.

Kellogg, Jesse C. "Letters to the American Home Missionary Society." Sycamore, Illinois: First Congregational Church.

_____. *Minutes of Church Meetings of the Congregational Church in Sycamore*, Book C-1. Sycamore, Illinois: First Congregational Church.

Litvin, Martin, ed. "Correspondence — Julia A. (Fletcher) Carney to Tom Carney, 1848–1850," bMS 669/12. Andover-Harvard Theological Library, Harvard Divinity School, Cambridge, Massachusetts.

_____. "Correspondence — Julia A. (Fletcher) Carney to Tom Carney, 1848–1850," bMS 669/13. Andover-Harvard Theological Library, Harvard Divinity School, Cambridge, Massachusetts.

_____. "A Journal of Julia Abigail Fletcher," bMS 669/16. Andover-Harvard Theological Library, Harvard Divinity School, Cambridge, Massachusetts.

Manual of the Fox River Association with a Historical sketch, 1835–1890. Ottawa, Illinois: Republican-Times Printing House, 1890. Zebina Eastman Collection, Boxes 3–5, Vols. 1–13, Chicago History Museum.

Moore, William F. "The Early Republicans and the Formation of the Republican Party in Illinois." Presented to the Illinois Historic Preservation Conference, Springfield, Illinois, October 5, 2001.

Perry, The Rev. David I. "Letters to the American Home Missionary Society." Sycamore, Illinois: First Congregational Church.

Ralph, Walter S. *Parish and Church Record of the Universalist Church, Sycamore, Illinois, 1853–1903*, Book U-1. Sycamore, Illinois: Sycamore Universalist Church.

Shabbona Museum Scrapbook. Shabbona, Illinois: DeKalb County Archives, Joiner History Room.

Unitarian Universalist Inactive Minister Files. bMS 1446.

Andover-Harvard Theological Library, Harvard Divinity School, Cambridge, Massachusetts.
Washburne, Elihu B. "Letter to Zebina Eastman, December 19, 1854." Zebina Eastman Collection, Box XB 107a, Folder #1 1841–1861. Chicago: Chicago History Museum.
Waterman, Charlotte F. Letters, 1840–1842. Sycamore, Illinois: First Congregational Church.
Whitmore, Alice Barber. "My DeKalb Chronicle, written after 1885." Sycamore Illinois: DeKalb County Archives, Joiner History Room.
Willging, Peter J. "Citizens for a Free West: Antislavery Advocates in DeKalb County, Illinois, 1843–1855." Master's Thesis Submitted to the Faculty of the Department of History, Northern Illinois University, 1994. Sycamore, Illinois: DeKalb County Archives, Joiner History Room.
Wood, Elizabeth. "Memoirs of Women's Fellowship, 1890." Sycamore, Illinois: First Congregational Church.

Published

Angle, Paul M. *Four Lincoln Firsts*. New York: Bibliographical Society of America, 1942.
Cavanagh, Helen M. "Antislavery Sentiment and Politics in the Northwest 1844–60." Part of a Dissertation submitted to the Faculty of the Division of the Social Sciences in Candidacy for the Degree of Doctor of Philosophy, University of Chicago, Department of History, 1938. Chicago: University of Chicago Libraries, 1940. Newberry Library, Chicago, Illinois.
Douglass, Frederick. "Letter to the Abolitionist Reunion of June 9–13, 1874." Zebina Eastman Collection, Box 2, Folder 9. Chicago: Chicago History Museum.
Dow, Roswell. "An Old Diary" (Diary of E. Camp Joiner's great grandfather). Sycamore, Illinois: DeKalb County Archives, Joiner History Room.
Eastman, Zebina, and Hooper Warren. *The Genius of Liberty Extra, Slave Code of the State of Illinois*. The Illinois Anti-Slavery Society, 1839.
Harris, Norman Dwight. "History of Negro Slavery in Illinois and of the Slavery Agitation in that State." A Dissertation Submitted to the Faculty of the Graduate School of Arts and Literature in Candidacy for the Degree of Doctor of Philosophy, University of Chicago, Department of History. Chicago: A.C. McClurg & Co., 1904.
Hossack, John. *Speech of John Hossack, convicted of violation of the Fugitive Slave Law; before Judge Drummond, of the U.S. District Court of Chicago*. Rare Collections [1 broadside; Call letters: * oversize Ruggles 422]. Chicago: Newberry Library.
Norton, Arlene. *Henrietta*. Sun City, Arizona: Arlene Norton, 1986.

Repositories

American Missionary Association Archives, Amistad Research Center, Tulane University, New Orleans, Louisiana.
Chicago History Museum, Chicago, Illinois.
DeKalb County Archives, Joiner History Room, Sycamore, Illinois.
DeKalb Public Library, DeKalb, Illinois.
The Federated Church, Sycamore, Illinois.
Founders Memorial Library, Rare Book Room, Northern Illinois University, DeKalb, Illinois.
Illinois State Historical Library/Abraham Lincoln Presidential Library, Springfield, Illinois.
Library of Congress, Washington, D.C.
National Archives, Washington, D.C.
Newberry Library, Chicago, Illinois.
Ohio Historical Society Archives/Library, Wilbur H. Siebert Collection Microfilm Edition, MIC 192, Columbus, Ohio.
Sycamore Public Library, Sycamore, Illinois.
Wisconsin Historical Society, Madison, Wisconsin.

Primary Sources: Newspapers and Periodicals

Alton Observer, July 20, 1837. Alton, Illinois.
Chicago History, The Magazine of the Chicago Historical Society 20, Numbers 1 and 2 (Spring and Summer 1991): Chicago.
Chicago Tribune. Chicago.
Daily Chronicle. DeKalb, Illinois.
DeKalb Chronicle Illustrated Souvenir, 1899. DeKalb, Illinois.
DeKalb County Republican Sentinel. DeKalb, Illinois. Sycamore, Illinois: microfilm, Sycamore Public Library.
National Geographic 166, No. 1, July 1984. Washington, D.C.
Pferdehirt, Julia. "Freedom Trail." *Madison Magazine*. March 1999. Madison, Wisconsin.
Republican North Western. June 28, 1910. Belvidere, Illinois. Excerpt from the *Ottawa Republic*. June 1910, Ottawa, Kansas. Sycamore, Illinois: DeKalb County Archives, Joiner History Room.
Republican Sentinel. Sycamore, Illinois: microfilm, Sycamore Public Library.
"Sixty Years Ago." *Sycamore True Republican*, April 14, 1900. Sycamore, Illinois: DeKalb County Archives, Joiner History Room.
Sycamore City Weekly. February 13, 1890. Sycamore, Illinois: DeKalb County Archives, Joiner History Room.
Sycamore Tribune. Sycamore, Illinois: DeKalb County Archives, Joiner History Room.
Sycamore True Republican. Sycamore, Illinois: DeKalb County Archives, Joiner History Room.
Sycamore True Republican. Sycamore, Illinois: microfilm, Sycamore Public Library.
Sycamore True Republican Souvenir Edition,1897. Sycamore, Illinois: DeKalb County Archives, Joiner History Room.
True Republican. Sycamore, Illinois: DeKalb County Archives, Joiner History Room.
Western Citizen. Chicago, July 26, 1842, through March 14, 1848, Microfilm Roll A-9159, #109, Springfield, Illinois: Illinois State Historical Library.
Western Citizen. Chicago, March 21, 1848, through July 19, 1855, Microfilm Roll A-9160, Springfield, Illinois: Illinois State Historical Library.
Willard, Hosea W. "My Recollections of Curtis Smith,

Pioneer." *Sycamore True Republican,* May 6, 1916. Sycamore, Illinois: DeKalb County Archives, Joiner History Room.

Primary Sources: Other Printed Materials

The History of Five Points, 1847–1937, Vol. III, No. 2, Winter 1936–37. Mayfield, Illinois: Five Points Rural Training School, 1937.
Lincoln, Abraham. "House Divided" speech, June 16, 1858. Sycamore, Illinois: True Republican Office, 1858.
Lovell Crossing, Sycamore, Illinois, 1836–1940. Sycamore, Illinois: True Republican, 1940.
Manual of the First Congregational Church, Sycamore, IL. Sycamore, Illinois: True Republican Press, 1876.
Mayfield United Church of Christ: 115 Years of Service for the Lord. Mayfield, Illinois, 1976.
Paw Paw Centennial Book. Paw Paw, Illinois, 1982.
Population Schedules of the Census of the United States, 1840, 1850, 1860, 1870.

Secondary Sources: Books

Allen, William Francis, with Charles Pickard Ware and Lucy McKim Garrison. *Slave Songs of the United States.* Baltimore: 1867. Reprint Baltimore: Clearfield Co., Inc., 2004.
Applegate, Debby. *The Most Famous Man in America: The Biography of Henry Ward Beecher.* New York: Doubleday, 2006.
Baker, George E., ed. *The Works of William H. Seward,* Vol. I. New York: Redfield, 1853.
Ball, Edward. *Slaves in the Family.* New York: Farrar, Straus and Giroux, 1998.
Balme, The Rev. J.R. *American States, Churches, and Slavery.* Edinburg: William P. Nimmo, 1862. Reprint New York: Negro Universities Press, 1969.
Bartholomew, Marshall, Mabel E. Bray, Otto Meissner, and James L. Mursell. *New Music Horizons.* New York: Silver Burdett Company, 1945.
Berlin, Ira. *Many Thousands Gone: The First Two Centuries of Slavery in North America.* Cambridge: Belknap Press of Harvard University Press, 1998.
Beveridge, James Hoy. *The Church of the Pioneers: Somonauk United Presbyterian Church.* Somonauk, Illinois: United Presbyterian Church, 1971.
Bial, Raymond. *The Underground Railroad.* Boston: Houghton Mifflin, 1995.
Blockson, Charles L. *The Underground Railroad: Dramatic Firsthand Accounts of Daring Escapes to Freedom.* New York: Berkley, 1987.
Boies, Henry L. *History of DeKalb County, Illinois.* Chicago: O.P. Bassett, 1868.
Butterfield, Roger. *The American Past: A History of the United States from Concord to Hiroshima, 1775–1945.* New York: Simon & Schuster, 1947.
Carson, Clayborne. *Civil Rights Chronicle: The African-American Struggle for Freedom.* Lincolnwood, Illinois: Legacy, 2003.

Chadwick, Bruce. *Traveling the Underground Railroad.* Secaucus, New Jersey: Citadel Press, 1999.
Chapman Brothers. *Portrait and Biographical Album of DeKalb County, Illinois.* Chicago: Chapman Brothers, 1885.
Chapman, Charles C. *History of Knox County, Illinois.* Chicago: Blakely, Brown and Marsh, 1878.
Clark, George W. *The Liberty Minstrel.* Utica, New York: Jackson and Chaplin, 1845.
Clarke, S.J., ed. *The Biographical Record of DeKalb County, Illinois.* Chicago: S.J. Clarke Publishing Co., 1898.
Clinton, Catherine. *Harriet Tubman: The Road to Freedom.* New York: Little, Brown, 2004.
Combined Atlas Maps of DeKalb County, Illinois, 1871, 1892, 1905, 1929. Reprint Evansville, Indiana: Unigraphic, 1975.
Davy, Harriet Wilson, ed. *From Oxen to Jets: A History of DeKalb County, 1835–1963.* Dixon, Illinois: DeKalb County Board of Supervisors, 1963.
DeGregorio, William A. *The Complete Book of U.S. Presidents.* New York: Wings Books, 1993.
The DeKalb Chronicle Illustrated Souvenir Edition, 1899–1900. Reprint Evansville, Indiana: Unigraphic, Inc., 1981.
Dixon, Chris. *Perfecting the Family: Antislavery Marriages in Nineteenth-Century America.* Amherst: University of Massachusetts Press, 1997.
Donald, David Herbert. *Lincoln.* New York: Simon & Schuster, 1995.
Dorsey, James. *The Underground Railroad: Northeastern Illinois and Southeastern Wisconsin.* Zion, Illinois: Sons of Thunder Ministry, 2000.
Douglass, Frederick. *Narrative of the Life of Frederick Douglass.* New Haven: Yale University Press, 2001.
Dow, Robert P. *The Book of Dow.* Vermont: Tuttle Co., 1929.
Dumond, Dwight Lowell. *Anti-Slavery: The Crusade for Freedom in America.* Ann Arbor: University of Michigan Press, 1961.
Duncan, Don V., ed. *History of First Congregational Church, United Church of Christ, DeKalb, Illinois 1854–1984.* DeKalb, Illinois: First Congregational Church, 1984.
Eaklor, Vicki L. *American Antislavery Songs: A Collection and Analysis.* Westport, Connecticut: Greenwood Press, 1988.
Everett, Susanne. *History of Slavery.* Leicester, England: Magna Books, 1978.
Frank, Beryl. *Pictorial History of the Republican Party.* N.p.: Ottenheimer, 1988.
Franklin, John Hope, and Loren Schweninger. *Runaway Slaves, Rebels on the Plantation.* New York: Oxford University Press, 1999.
Gara, Larry. *The Liberty Line: The Legend of the Underground Railroad.* Lexington: University Press of Kentucky, 1996.
Gross, Lewis M. *Past and Present of DeKalb County,* Vol. I and Vol. II. Chicago: Pioneer, 1907.
_____, and G.E. Congdon. "History of DeKalb County, Ill." *Combined Atlas Maps of DeKalb County, Illinois, 1871, 1892, 1905, 1929.* Reprint Evansville, Indiana: Unigraphic, 1975.

Hagedorn, Ann. *Beyond the River: The Untold Story of the Heroes of the Underground Railroad.* New York: Simon & Schuster, 2002.

Hambrick-Stowe, Charles E. *Charles G. Finney and the Spirit of American Evangelicalism.* Grand Rapids, Michigan: William B. Eerdmans, 1996.

Harrold, Stanley. *American Abolitionists.* Essex, England: Pearson Education, 2001.

Henson, Josiah. *The Life of Josiah Henson, Formerly a Slave, Now an Inhabitant of Canada, as Narrated by Himself.* Boston: Arthur D. Phelps, 1849. Reprint Ontario: Uncle Tom's Cabin Museum, 1984.

The Holy Bible, The King James Version. New York: American Bible Society, 1951.

Howard, Victor B. *Conscience and Slavery: The Evangelistic Calvinist Domestic Missions, 1837–1861.* Kent, Ohio: Kent State University Press, 1990.

Hudson, J. Blaine. *Encyclopedia of the Underground Railroad.* Jefferson, North Carolina: McFarland, 2006.

Hunt, John Gabriel, ed. *The Essential Abraham Lincoln.* New York: Gramercy Books, 1993.

Kashatus, William C. *Just Over the Line: Chester County and the Underground Railroad.* University Park: Penn State University Press, 2002.

Kett, H.F., & Co. *The Voters and Tax-Payers of DeKalb County, Illinois.* Chicago: H.F. Kett & Co., 1876.

King, Roger A. *The Silent Rebellion: The Underground Railroad in Orange County, New York.* Monroe, New York: Library Research Associates, 1999.

Kraut, Alan M. "The Forgotten Reformers, A Profile of Third Party Abolitionists in Antebellum New York." Lewis Perry and Michael Fellman, eds. *Antislavery Reconsidered: New Perspectives on the Abolitionists.* Baton Rouge: Louisiana State University Press, 1979.

Le Baron, Jr., William. *The Past and Present of Kane County, Illinois.* Chicago: William LeBaron, Jr. and Co., 1878.

Leisch, Juanita. *An Introduction to Civil War Civilians.* Gettysburg: Thomas, 1994.

Litvin, Martin. *Black Angel.* Galesburg, Illinois: Log City Books, 1973.

Lowance, Mason. *Against Slavery: An Abolitionist Reader.* New York: Penguin Books, 2000.

Matson, N. *Reminiscences of Bureau County, Illinois.* Princeton, Illinois: Republican Book & Job Office, 1872.

Mayer, Henry. *All on Fire: William Lloyd Garrison and the Abolition of Slavery.* New York: St. Martin's Press, 1998.

McKay, Ernest. *Practical Radical: Portrait of a Politician.* Port Washington, New York: Kennikat Press, 1971.

McLagan, C.R. "Luke." *Nostalgia & Glee.* Sycamore, Illinois: D.C. Lithographers, 1960.

Miller, Russell E. *The Larger Hope: The First Century of the Universalist Church in America 1770–1870.* Boston: Unitarian Universalist Association, 1979.

Monk, Linda R. *The Words We Live By: Your Annotated Guide to the Constitution.* New York: The Songstone Press, 2003.

Moore, William F., and Jane Ann Moore, eds. *Owen Lovejoy: His Brother's Blood, Speeches and Writings 1838–64.* Urbana: University of Illinois Press, 2004.

Muelder, Hermann R. *Fighters for Freedom: A History of Anti-Slavery Activities of Men and Women Associated with Knox College.* New York: Columbia University Press, 1959.

Muelder, Owen W. *The Underground Railroad in Western Illinois.* Jefferson, North Carolina: McFarland & Company, Inc., 2008.

Nason, Elias. *A Gazetteer of the State of Massachusetts.* Boston, 1874.

National Park Service. *Exploring a Common Past: Researching and Interpreting the Underground Railroad.* Washington, D.C.: U.S. Department of the Interior, 1998.

_____. *Underground Railroad, Publication #156.* Washington, D.C.: U.S. Department of the Interior, 1990.

Norton, Arlene. *Our Norton Family Story.* Sun City, Arizona: Arlene Norton, 1984.

Patten, Jennie M., with Andrew Graham. *History of the Somonauk United Presbyterian Church.* Chicago, 1928.

Peters, Pamela R. *The Underground Railroad in Floyd County, Indiana.* Jefferson, North Carolina: McFarland, 2001.

Pirtle, Carol. *Escape Betwixt Two Suns: A True Tale of the Underground Railroad in Illinois.* Carbondale: Board of Trustees, Southern Illinois University, 2000.

Rasmusen, Marilyn, ed. *LaSalle County Lore.* LaSalle, Illinois: LaSalle County Historical Society, 1985.

Scott, Anne Firor. *The Southern Lady from Pedestal to Politics 1830–1930.* Chicago: University of Chicago, 1970. Reprint Charlottesville: University Press of Virginia, 1995.

Scott, Donald M. "Abolition as a Sacred Vocation." Lewis Perry and Michael Fellman, eds. *Antislavery Reconsidered: New Perspectives on the Abolitionists.* Baton Rouge: Louisiana University Press, 1979.

Sernett, Milton C. *Abolition's Axe: Beriah Green, Oneida Institute, and the Black Freedom Struggle.* Syracuse: Syracuse University Press, 1986.

Siebert, William H. *The Underground Railroad from Slavery to Freedom.* New York: Macmillan, 1898; Reprint Arthur W. McGraw, 1997.

Smith, George Owen. *The Lovejoy Shrine: Home of Owen Lovejoy and Station on Underground Railroad.* Tiskilwa, Illinois: Bureau Valley Chief, 1987.

Sorin, Gerald. *The New York Abolitionists: A Case Study of Political Radicalism.* Westport, Connecticut: Greenwood, 1971.

Spinka, Matthew, ed. *A History of Illinois Congregational and Christian Churches.* Chicago: Congregational and Christian Conference of Illinois, 1944.

Stampp, Kenneth M. *America in 1857: A Nation on the Brink.* New York: Oxford University Press, 1990.

Stephenson, George M. *The Puritan Heritage.* New York: Macmillan, 1952.

Stewart, James Brewer. *Holy Warriors: The Abolitionists and American Slavery.* New York: Hill and Wang, 1976.

Stowe, Harriet Beecher. *Three Novels: Uncle Tom's Cabin, The Minister's Wooing, Old Town Folks.* New York: Viking Press, 1982.

_____. *Uncle Tom's Cabin, or Life Among the Lowly.* New York: Hurst & Co., 1850. Reprint, New York: Penguin Putnam, 1998.

Strong, Douglas M. *Perfectionist Politics: Abolitionism and the Religious Tensions of American Democracy.* Syracuse: Syracuse University Press, 1999.

Sutherland, Daniel E. *The Expansion of Everyday Life.* New York: Harper and Row, 1989.

Switala, William J. *Underground Railroad in Delaware, Maryland, and West Virginia.* Mechanicsburg, Pennsylvania: Stackpole Books, 2004.

_____. *Underground Railroad in Pennsylvania.* Mechanicsburg, Pennsylvania: Stackpole Books, 2001.

Tilley Turner, Glennette. *The Underground Railroad in DuPage County, Illinois.* Glen Ellyn, Illinois: Newman Educational Publishing Co., 1986.

_____. *The Underground Railroad in Illinois.* Glen Ellyn, Illinois: Newman Educational, 2001.

The True Republican Souvenir Edition, 1897 and Sycamore, Illinois Illustrated Prospectus, 1906. Reprint DeKalb, Illinois: DeKalb County Historical Society, 1980.

United Church of Christ. "Amazing Grace, How Sweet the Sound." *The New Century Hymnal.* Cleveland: Pilgrim Press, 1995.

Urch, Gloria J. *Contributors to the Cause.* Hebron, Illinois: Yore Heritage Books, 2000.

Virga, Vincent, and Curators of the Library of Congress, eds. *Eyes of the Nation: A Visual History of the United States.* New York: Alfred A. Knopf, 1997.

Wiecek, William M. "Latimer: Lawyers, Abolitionists, and the Problem of Unjust Laws." Lewis Perry and Michael Fellman, eds. *Antislavery Reconsidered: New Perspectives on the Abolitionists.* Baton Rouge: Louisiana State University Press, 1979.

The World Book Multimedia Encyclopedia. Chicago, 1997.

Wyatt-Brown, Bertram. *Lewis Tappan and the Evangelical War Against Slavery.* Cleveland: Press of Case Western Reserve University, 1969.

Secondary Sources: Articles, Websites, Documentaries

American Presbyterian Church. The North-South Schism of 1861. February 2003. <http://www.americanpresbyterianchurch.org>.

Amherst College Biographical Record, Centennial Edition (1821–1921). March 2001. <http://www3.amherst.edu/~rjyanco94/genealogy/acbiorecord/1839.html#gored>.

Bailey, John C. W., ed. *Kane County, Illinois, Directory for 1859–1860,* "City of Aurora." June 2003. <http://www.litrails.org/Kane/1859directory.html>.

Beers and Leggett, ed. *Biographical and Historical Record of Kane County, Illinois.* Chicago: Beers, Leggett & Co., 1888. February 2010. <http://search.ancestry.com/browse/bookview.aspx?dbid=18487&iid=dvm_LochHist005442-00131-0&rc=2498,813,2748,875;2824,816,3092,863;548,2204,779,2252;1236,2207,1611,2256;3082,2301,3366,2364;2612,2463,2846,2525;2922,2465,3203,2513;954,2867,1218,2914;623,3194,882,3242;622,3359,887,3406;1989,4108,2213,4158&pid=172&ssrc=&fn=joseph&ln=bartlett&st=g>.

Brawley, Benjamin Griffith. *Lorenzo Dow.* Washington, D.C.: The Association for the Study of Negro Life and History, 1916. From *The Journal of Negro History* 1, no. 3, July 1916. March 15, 2004. <http://docsouth.unc.edu/church/brawleyld/brawley.html>.

The Christian Courier. April 29, 2012. <http://www.christiancourier.com/articles/780-the-significance-of-small-things>.

Cutler, William G. *History of the State of Kansas.* July 2003. <http://www.kancoll.org/books/cutler/>.

Delphos Daily Herald. July 28, 1894, Delphos, Ohio. April 21, 2008. <http://search.ancestry.com/search/db.aspx?dbid=7414>.

Deutsch, Judy. "What We Were and Are." *Unitarian Universalism: An Extremely Brief Overview for an Orientation Session.* Medfield, Massachusetts: First Parish Unitarian Universalist Church. November 6, 2000. <http://www.firstparishmedfield.org/unitarian_universalism.html>.

Douglass, Frederick. "Dred Scott Decision, Speech Delivered, in Part, at the Anniversary of The American Abolition Society, Held in New York, May 14, 1857." Library of Congress, Manuscript Division. March 2012. <http://memory.loc.gov/cgi-bin/ampage?collId=mfd&fileName=21/21039/21039page.db&recNum=38&tempFile=./temp/~ammem_wjaU&filecode=mfd&prev_filecode=mfd&itemnum=2&ndocs=2>.

Edited Appleton's Encyclopedia. January 2002. <http://www.famousamericans.net/ichabodcodding/>. <http://virtualology.com/apichabodcodding>, March 2012.

Education 2000 Inc. *Landmarks of Faith: Methodist Camp Meetings.* Video, Ft. Lauderdale, Florida: The Odyssey Channel, 2000.

Green, Beriah. "Things for Northern Men to Do: A Discourse Delivered Lord's Day Evening, July 17, 1836, in the Presbyterian church, Whitesboro, NY." New York: Published by Request, 1836. <http://medicolegal.tripod.com/green1836.htm>, March 21, 2002.

Harper's Weekly. "The Black Laws." February 11, 1865. <http://www.sonofthesouth.net/leefoundation/civil-war/1865/february/black-laws.htm>, April 29, 2012.

Harris, Mark W. *Unitarian Universalist Origins: Our Historic Faith.* May 2002. <http://archive.uua.org/info/origins.html>.

Illinois Constitution, 1818, Adopted at Kaskaskia in Convention, August 26, 1818. May 5, 2009. <http://tippecanoe.tripod.com/cl818.html>.

"Knox County, Illinois, Genealogy and History." April 29, 2012. <http://www.usgennet.org/usa/il/county/knox/knox_cemetery_default.html>.

Laws of Illinois, Approved February 1, 1831, Section I. Curriculum materials. April 19, 2008. <http://www.lib.niu.edu/1996/iht329602.html>.

Lewis, S. *The United States Biographical Dictionary, Kansas Volume.* Chicago, 1879. February 4, 2004. <http://search.ancestry.com/search/db.aspx?dbid=7709>.

Lincoln, Abraham. "Mr. Lincoln's Reply in the Jonesboro Joint Debate"; "Third Joint Debate at Jonesboro, Illinois, September 15, 1858." In *The Complete Works of Abraham Lincoln, v. 4,* John G. Nicolay and John Hay, eds. New York: Francis D. Tandy Company, 1894, 1858. Abraham Lincoln Historical Digitization Project, Northern Illinois University Libraries. April 6, 2009. <http://lincoln.lib.niu.edu>.

Lincoln, Abraham, to Elihu B. Washburne, December

11, 1854. Abraham Lincoln Papers, Library of Congress, Manuscript Division. Washington, D.C.: American Memory Project, 2000-02. March 23, 2009. <http://memory.loc.gov/cgi-bin/query/r?ammem/mal:@field(DOCID+@lit(d0058200))>.

Litvin, Martin, ed. "Julia Abigail Fletcher Carney Papers." Andover-Harvard Library, Harvard Divinity School. May 2002. <http://oasis.lib.harvard.edu/oasis/deliver/deepLink?_collection=oasis&uniqueId=div00669>.

Macon, James. "Wade in the Water: the Underground Railroad and DeKalb County, Illinois." Video, DeKalb, Illinois: Northern Illinois University Department of Communication, 2002.

Moore, William F., ed. *Lovejoy Society Newsletter, Vol. 2, No. 1, March 1997.*

Mahoney, Olivia. "Black Abolitionists." *Chicago History, The Magazine of the Chicago Historical Soci-ety, Spring and Summer 1991, Vol. XX, Numbers 1 and 2.* Chicago, Illinois: Chicago Historical Society, 1991.

Matson, N., and Denise McLoughlin, transcriber. *Reminiscences of Bureau County, Illinois.* Princeton, Illinois: Republican Book & Job Office, 1872. September 7, 2007. <www.tampicohistoricalsociety.citymax.com>.

Microsoft Encarta Encyclopedia 2000. Microsoft Corporation, 2001.

Ohio Wesleyan University. *Charter.* August 20, 2007. <http://about.owu.edu/>.

Rogers, Al. "Amazing Grace: The Story of John Newton." *Away Here in Texas*, July-August, 1996. March 10, 2002. <www.flash.net/~gaylon/jnewton.htm>.

Unchained Memories: Readings from the Slave Narratives. Home Box Office documentary. New York: AOL Time Warner Book Group, 2002.

United Church of Christ. "Congregationalism from Plymouth to the American Revolution." January 2002. <www.ucc.org>.

United Church of Christ. "Short Course in the History of the United Church of Christ." April 29, 2012. <http://www.ucc.org/about-us/short-course/>.

United States General Land Office Records, Bureau of Land Management. 2005–2009. <http://www.glorecords.blm.gov/>.

United States Patent Office. "*Annual Report of The Commissioner of Patents, Vol. II.*" Washington, D.C.: Government Printing Office, 1866. <www.google.com/patents/USRE2390.pdf>.

Index

Page numbers in ***bold italics*** indicate illustrations.

Abbott, Abiel, and family 176
Abbott, Bryant, and family 176
Abbott, Sylary 176
Adams, Alida 183, 51
Adams, Amos 176
Adams, Asher, and family 176
Adams, Betsy 187
Adams, Emily 47, 202
Adams, John 141
Adams, John Quincy 141
Adams, Pamelia, and family 176
Adams, Paulina 200
Adee, Jane 179
Adee, Mary Ann 119, 179
Alabama 116, 161
Albany, Illinois 34, 161
Albany, New York 26
Aldrich/Aldridge, Deborah 201
Alexander, Elizabeth, and family 177
Alexander, George 177
Alexander, James 177
Alexander, Mary 110, 187
Alexandria, Virginia 152
Allen, Catherine 203
Allen, Mary 202
Alton, Illinois 6, 21, 34, 44, 66, 137, 161
Alton Observer 44
*Amazing Grace **74***
Ambler, Mary Ann 202
Ambler, Ruth 179
American Antislavery Songs: A Collection and Analysis 23
American Home Missionary Society (A.M.H.S.) 8, 79, 80, ***85***, 86, 87, 132, 133
American Missionary Society (A.M.S.) 8, 86, 87, 99
Ames, Lydia 180
Amherst College 86
Amsden, Noah, and family 177
Anderson, Ann 186
Anderson, David, and family 177
Angle, Paul 158
Anglican Episcopal 29, 73, 104
Anti-Nebraska 8, 29, ***93***, 97, 108, 143–146, 153, 167
antislavery societies 27; DeKalb County 41, 93, 115, 117, 135–137; Illinois 45, 137; Kane County 63; Marion, Illinois 109; Philadelphia 18
antislavery songs 13, 15, 23, 171; *see also The Liberty Minstrel*
Arbuckle, Amanda 177
Arbuckle, Joseph 42; family 177
Arkansas 128
Arland, Elizabeth 177
Armstrong, David, and family 177
Armstrong, Elizabeth 180
Arnold, Mary 188
Associate Presbyterian Church *see* Somonauk Associate Presbyterian Church
Atkinson, Nancy 189
Attix/Atticks, James 177
Attix/Atticks, Sophronia, and family 177
Auburn Theological Seminary 77
Aurora, Illinois 8, 22, 33, 51, 90, 108, 115, 143, 146, 147, 153
Austin, Charles, and family 177
Avery, Harriet 184

Badger, Milton 133
Bailey/Bayley, Mary 177
Bailey, Pamelia 203
Bailey/Bayley, William, and family 177
Baker, Joseph, and family 177
Baker, Mary 183
Ballard, Esther, and family 177
Ballard, James 177
Baltimore, Maryland 173
Bannister, Daniel 42; family 177
Bannister, Lucinda 192
Bannister, Mary Elizabeth 177
Banniter, Sarah 183
Baptist 100, 115
barbed wire 129, 166
Barber, Amelia 188
Barber, Hannah 177
Barber, Henry, and family 42, 177
Barber, Levi 42; family 177
Barber, Mary 200
Barber, Pamelia 176
Barber, Rhoda 183
Barber, Sally 177
Barber, Wanton, and family 177
barnburner 143
Barnes, Ann "Lucy" 190
Barnes, Captain Eli ***70***
Barnes, Elizabeth 177
Barnes, Erastus 42, 133; family 177
Barrett, Harriet 193
Barringer, Gertrude 177
Barringer, John, and family 177
Barringer, William, and family 177
Bartholomew, George, and family 177
Bartholomew, Peninnah 177
Bartlett, Elizabeth 177, 196
Bartlett, Joseph, Jr., and family 177
Bartlett, Joseph P. 15; family 177
Bartlett, Julia 177
Bartlett, Marcus, and family 177
Bartlett, Martha (Harper) 177
Bartlett, Martha P. 197
Bartlett, Mary Ann 177
Bartlett, Moses, and family 177
Bartlett, Sarah 177
Bartlett, Temperance 177
Bartlett, Theodore, and family 177
Bascome, Flavel 127, 132
Bassett, Betsy 156, 177
Bassett, Orlando P. 8, 152, 156, ***157***, 158–160; family 177
Bathwick, Sophronia 181
Baxter, Ruth 196
Beard, Henry 168–170
Beavers, Caroline 188
Beavers, Mary, and family 178
Beavers, Theodore 178
Becker, Agnes 182
Becker, Edward 121; family 178
Becker, Harriet 186
Becker, Mary 178
Beecher, Rev. Henry Ward 83
Beecher, Lyman 26
Beers, Isabella 179
Beeson, Phoebe 181
Beitel, Emma 178
Beitel, Julius, and family 178
Bell, Jane 192
Bell, Lydia 182

Belles, Charles 178
Belles, Margaret, and family 178
Belles, Mary "Mollie," and family 178
Belles, Mathius 178
Benedict, Betsey Ann 178
Benedict, James, and family 178
Bennett, Lerone 173
Benton, John, and family 178
Benton, Julia 178
Beveridge, Agnes 106
Beveridge, Andrew 104–105; family 178
Beveridge, Ann 103–106, 112, 140, 153, 178
Beveridge, Elizabeth 108, 152–153, 178
Beveridge, George 6, 36, 42, 103–106, 110, 112, 130, 140, 153; family 178
Beveridge, Helen 178
Beveridge, James Hoy 8, 105, 108–109, 130, 138, 142–144, 147, 151–153, 156, 160; family 178
Beveridge, Jane 178
Beveridge, Jennette/Sarah 186
Beveridge, John Lourie 104, 108, 174; family 178
Beveridge, Thomas 105, 108, 153; family 178
Bigelow, Annie 187
Bigham/Brigham, Julia 199
Bill, J.A. 135
Billington, Emiline 178
Billington, Thomas, and family 178
Birdsall, George 178
Birdsall, Mariah/Maria 195
Birdsall, Sarah, and family 178
Birney, James G. 6, 7, 21, 45, 141, 153
Black, Roxana 181
Black Hawk, Chief 27
Black Laws 8, 23, 39, 128
Blacklidge, Sarah 192
Blackledge, Delilah/Della 178
Blackman, Nancy 178
Blackman, Philena 187
Blackman, Seth, and family 178
Blanchard, Catharine 190
Blanchard, Jonathan 86
Blee, Margaret 187
bleeding Kansas 97, 143
Bliss, Charlotte 178
Blood, Elizabeth 182
Blood, Lucinda 183
Bloomington, Illinois 144
Boardman, Corena/Corrina "Cora" 187
Boardman, Cyrus, and family 178
Boardman, Harriet 178
Boies, Henry 4–5, 23, **42**, 105–106, 119, 147
Bond, Eliza 191
Boone County, Illinois 29, 138
border ruffians 97
Boston, Mary Ann 178
Boston, Thomas, and family 178
Boston, Massachusetts 22, 52, 91–92, 100
Bowen, Ione 200
Bowers, Charlotte 193
Bowker, Sophronia 177
Boyd, Daniel, and family 178
Boyd, John, and family 178
Boyd, Margaret 178
Boyd, Mary 178
Boyd, Nancy 178
Braddock, John 147; family 178
Braddock, Sarah 178

Branch, Charles 42; family 178
Branch, Esther 178
Brayton, Horatio, and family 178
Brayton, Janette/Jeanette 178
Brewer, Hannah 180
Brigham, Anna 203
Brook, Charlotte 178
Brook, Clement, and family 178
Brook, Martha 178
Brook(s), Charlotte 179
Brook(s), Thomas 142; family 179
Brooks, Amos 122; family 179
Brooks, Rev. Jonas 12
Brooks, Laura 177
Brooks, Mary 179
Broughton, Caroline 179
Broughton, Chauncey, and family 179
Broughton, Isabella 179
Broughton, Mary 179
Brown, Arnold 42; family 179
Brown, Benjamin Putney 42; family 179
Brown, Caleb M. "Jersey" 8, 26, 57, 130, 151–152, 155–156, 157, 160; family 179
Brown, Catherine 152, 155, 179
Brown, Charlotte 179
Brown, David DePue 155, 212n35
Brown, Eben, and family 179
Brown, Rev. Ebenezer 63
Brown, Eliza 155, 179
Brown, Hannah 183
Brown, Jane 185
Brown, Jeremiah Libby 26, 42, 138; family 179
Brown, John 65, 164
Brown, Judith 179
Brown, Lepha 179
Brown, Louise/Louisa 179
Brown, Lydia 179, 189
Brown, Margaret 106, 187
Brown, Morris, and family 179
Brown, Phebe 193
Brown, Thankful 179
Brown, William 42; family 179
Brownell, Hannah 177
Browning, Clarinda 183
Browning, Mr. 9, 161
Bruce, Charlotte 185
Brush Point, Illinois 30, 41, 62, 113–115, 117–120, 122
Brush Point School 118
Brush Point Wesleyan Methodist Church see Wesleyan Methodist Church (Mayfield, Illinois)
Bryan, Jane, and family 179
Bryan, Orlando 179
Buchanan, James 8
Buckingham, Ann 179
Buckingham, Mary/Margaret 179
Buckingham, Nathan, and family 179
Buell, Syvil 188
Buffalo, New York 26
Bundy, Emily 197
Burchim, Joshua, and family 179
Burchim, Mary 179
Bureau County, Illinois 34, 37, 43, 52, 66, 138
Burnett, Eliza 196
Burr, Mabellia/Marilla 189
Butterfield, Benjamin 166; family 179
Butterfield, Daniel 73
Butterfield, Elena/Ellen/Eleanor 179

Butterfield, George 166; family 179
Butterfield, Matilda 166, 179
Butterfield, Nancy 166, 179
Butterfield, William, and family 179
Byers, Jane 179
Byers, Mary Ann 119, 179
Byers, William 119–120, 147; family 179
Byron, Illinois 83, 119; Congregational Church 63, 83

Cady, Maria 187
California 20, 29, 39, 104, 154
Calkins, Asa, and family 179
Calkins, Mary 179
Calkins, Melissa 186
Calkins, Ruth 179
Call, Alfred, and family 179
Call, Elvira 183
Call, Esther, and family 177
Call, Lydia 195
Call, Sabrina 179
Calvinistic 55, 104, 113
Cambridge, Massachusetts 84
Cameron, Alexander, and family 179
Cameron, Lucy 179
Camp, Eliza/Elizabeth 179
Camp, Franklin, and family 179
camp meetings 7, 114–117
Campbell, Amanda 180
Campbell, Barbara 179
Campbell, Daniel/Donald, and family 179
Campbell, Hannah 180
Campbell, Hugh, and family 180
Campbell, James 128
Campbell, John, and family 180
Campbell, Sarah 180
Canada 5, 11, 13, 15, 17, 23–24, 33–35, 66, 103, 118–121, 127, 130, 150, 155, 161, 163–164
Card, Amanda 180
Card, Eliza 182
Card, Louisa 180
Card, Orson, and family 180
Cardinal, Mary 187
Carney, Julia 52, 91–92, 95–96, 99, 180
Carney, Rev. Thomas 8, 52, 91–92, **93**, 95–96, 99, 101; family 180
Carpenter, Laura 202; family 180
Carpenter, Lucretia 193
Carpenter, Philo 127
Carpenter, William 180
Carr, Elizabeth 199; family 180
Carr, Lydia 180
Carr, Nancy 180
Carr, Thurston 142, 147; family 180
Carr, William 180
Carrier, Emily 197
Carter, Jared, and family 180
Cartwright, James 42; family 180
Cartwright, Nancy 190
Cartwright, Ruth 180
Case, Charles, and family 180
Case, Martha 180
Castle, Almira 181
Catholic 8, 44, 104
Caverly, Mercy 193
Cayuga County, New York 150
Champlin, Abigail 180
Champlin, David 100, 154; family 180
Champlin, Hiram, and family 180
Champlin, Hod, 100
Champlin, Lorinda 180

Champlin's Hall 100, 154
Chapin, Sarah 202
Chapman, Julius, and family 180
Chapman, Lucy 190
Chapman, Sarah/Sally 180
Chappell, Louisa 197
Chatfield, John, and family 180
Chatfield, Julia 180
Cheasbro, Abigail 180
Cheasbro, Antoinette 180
Cheasbro, Enos, and family 180
Cheasbro, John, and family 180
Cheasbro, Joseph, and family 180
Cheasbro, Mary Ann 194
Cheasbro, Patience 180
Cheever, Ezra 180
Cheever, Mary, and family 180
Chester, Illinois 34, 161
Chicago, Illinois 4, 6, 15, 18, 22, 26, 28, 30, 31, 33–34, 41, 43, 53, 57, 62, 66, *67*, 68, 100, 104–105, 107–108, 115, 121–124, *125*, 126–127, 132–133, 139–141, 150, 152–153, 159, 161, 173
Chicago Tribune 108, 123, 152, 173
Chief Black Hawk 27
Chief Shabbona 28
Chittenden, Betsy 187
Christy, Mary 177
Church, Calista 180
Church, Charles, and family 180
Church, Sally 180
Church of the Pioneers 105, 108
Churchill, Almira 181, 186
Churchill, Angeline 185
Churchill, Caroline 179, 180
Churchill, Castle 42; family 180
Churchill, David 42; family 180
Churchill, Maria 180
Churchill, Marilla 189
Churchill, Mary 179
Churchill, Patty 180
Churchill, Zenas 42; family 181
Cincinnati, Ohio 21, 45
circuit rider 66, 116–117, 122
Civil War Regiments: 8th Illinois Cavalry 152, 172, 178; 52nd Illinois Infantry 180, 184, 199; 57th Illinois Infantry 203; 92nd Illinois Infantry 195; 105th Illinois Infantry 37, 96, 168, 170, 172; 156th Illinois Infantry 195
Clark, Amelia 181
Clark, Eunice 193
Clark, Fanny 191
Clark, George, and family 181
Clark, George W. 7, 13
Clark, Horace 190
Clark, Rev. James Linneus/Limon 122; family 181
Clark, Martha 181
Clark, Rev. Nathaniel 63
Clay, Henry 7, 141–142
Clinton Township 6, 45, 102, 107, 117, 130, 147
Cobb, Charles 181
Cobb, Eliza, and family 181
Cochran, Merinda/Melinda 195
Codding, Ichabod 53, 137, 144
Coffin, Phebe 193
Colby, Elizabeth 188
Cole, Anna 181
Cole, Elizabeth 181
Cole, Tobias Britt, and family 181

Coleman, Adeline 192
Coles, Edward, Gov. 1
College of New Jersey 79
Collins, James 141
Collins, New York 46
Collins, Sarah "Sally" 196
Colton, Abigail 180
Colton, Calvin 147, 181
Colton, Caroline 62, 181
Colton, Clarissa 197
Colton, Gustavus, and family 181
Colton, Harriet, and family 181
Colton, Phoebe 181
Colton, Rufus 43, 133; family 181
Coltonville, Illinois 50, 52, 133; road 62
Comins, Elizabeth 186
Compromise of 1820 6, 8, 19, 96, 146, 159
Compromise of 1850 7–8, 20, 39, 97, 143; *see also* fugitive slave laws
Cone, Elizabeth 183
Congregational 1, 6–9, 13, 15–16, 22, 26, 29–30, *32*, 33, 40–41, 44–47, *48*, 49–50, 52, 55–57, 59–66, *67*, 68–69, 72, *73–74*, 75–77, *78*, 79, *81*, 82–84, *85*, 86–89, 91, 95–97, 99, 101, 108, 111, 116–117, 120, 122, 126, 130–137, 142–144, 146–147, 152, 154–155, 161–162, 173
Congregational Church (Sandwich, Illinois) 87
conscience Whig 8, 143
contraband 168, 170
Cook, Mary 186
Cook, Randolph 181
Cook County, Illinois 53, 84, *125*, 138
Coonfare/Coonfair, Daniel, and family 181
Coonfare/Coonfair, Elizabeth 181, 189
Cooper, Elizabeth 181, 195
Cooper, George, and family 181
Cooper, Mary 197
Cooper, Sarah 191
Corser, Hiram, and family 181
Corser, Roxana 181
Cortland Township 154
Cory, Catharine 181
Cory, Jesse, and family 181
Cossayuna, New York 138
Coster, Joseph, and family 181
Coster, Keziah 181
Coster, Marfia 181
Coster, Mary 181
Coster, Sophronia 181
cotton Whig 8, 143
Cowden, Anna 180
Cowen, Marilla, and family 181
Cowen, Theodore 181
Crandall, Susan 183
Crandle, Betsy 181
Crandle, Phineas, and family 181
Crawford, Alexander, Jr., and family 181
Crawford, Alexander, Sr. 43; family 181
Crawford, Laura 181
Crawford, Rachel 181
Crawford, Sarah 181
Creighton, Elizabeth 177
Crill, Almina/Elmira 194
Crill, Sarah 194
Crocker, Mary 191
Cross, Rev. John 34–35
Crossett, Abigail 181

Crossett, Jacob "Royal" 147; family 181
Crossett, Patty 180
Cutler, Silas, and family 181

Daily, Mary 200
Darling, Margaret 178
Davids, Tice 17
Davis, Eliza 181
Davis, Ellen 181
Davis, Mary "Polly" 181
Davis, Nancy 190
Davis, Ruel, and family 181
Davis, William 43, 109; family 181
Dawalt, Elizabeth 181
Dayton, Susan 186, 204
Dean, Lucretia 185
Dean, Moses 41
Dean, Sybil 185
Decker, Demmon 122; family 182
Decker, Hannah 182
Decker, Pamelia 187
Deitz/Deets, David, and family 182
DeKalb County Democrat 152
DeKalb County Medical Society 50, 71–72
DeKalb County Sentinel 8, 100, 148, 151, 156, 159–160, 167
DeLand, Saray 188
DeLong, Sarah 183
Democrat Party *93*, 97, 128, 141
DeMorest, Elizabeth 189
Denman, Ann 35, 200
Dennis, Amanda 177
Dennis, Charlotte 179
Dennis, Eliza 181
Dennis, Lurena/Lurana 185
Dennis, Major 43; family 182
Dennis, Mary 182
Dennis, Sarah 177
Densmore, Clarissa 187
Depp, Stephen 8, 170
DePue, Catherine 179
DeWolf, Calvin 127
Deyoe, Agnes 121, 182
Deyoe, Elizabeth 182
Deyoe, Emeline 182
Deyoe, Peter, and family 182
Deyoe, Rachel 193
Deyoe, William 121; family 182
Dick, Eliza 121, 182
Dick, John 27, 120–121; family 182
Dickson, John 182
Dietz/Deets Gertrude 182
Disbrow, Elizabeth 152, 178
Disbrow, Flora 192
Dixon, Mary 199
Dixon, Sarah "Sally" 198
Dobbin, Ann 106, 110, 200
Dobbin, Charity 182
Dobbin, David 103, 106; family 182
Dobbin, Eliza 182
Dobbin, Jane "Jennie" 191
Dobbin, Margaret 200, 201
Dobbin, Mary Jane 106, 182
Donald, Henry 169–170
Doty, Elizabeth 198
Douglas, Stephen 8, 9, 96, 124, 142, 143, 144, 145, 148, 151, 152, 156, 157, 159, 160
Douglass, Cyrena 118, 182
Douglass, Frederick 17, 36, *42*, 170–171, 173–174
Douglass, Hannah 182

Index

Douglass, Ira 43, 118; family 182
Dow, Agrippa 13, *93*, 117; family 182
Dow, Aristeen 182
Dow, Eliza/Elizabeth 179
Dow, Euphrasia 182
Dow, Kimball 92, *93*, 117, 129, 135–138; family 182
Dow, Levias/Lavius 43; family 182
Dow, Lorenzo 116–117
Dow, Nancy 188
Dow, Polly 182
Dow, Sophronia 184
Dow Academy 4, *93*, 154
Drake, Helen/Ellen 193
Drake, Hiram, and family 182
Drake, Maria 182
Dred Scott decision 8
Dublin, Matilda 8, 166–167
Duffey, James, and family 182
Duffey, Lydia 182
Duffey, Martha 182
DuPage County, Illinois 7, 126, 138
Durham, Henry 43; family 182
Durham, Losina "Jane" 182
Durham, Sabrina 179
Durham, Sarah/Sally 180
Dustin, Daniel 154; family 182
Dustin, Elmira 182
Dustin, Isabelle 182
Dutton, Elizabeth 182
Dutton, Everell 95–96; family 192
Dutton, Henry, and family 182
Dutton, Lucinda 183
Dutton, Mary 96
Dutton, Rosina 96, 182
Dutton, Sally 180
Dutton, Sarah 183
Dutton, William Paine 95–96
Dutton, William Parker 8, 96–98, 120; family 183
Dyer, Charles 126, 127, 141
Dyer, Edward 127
Dyer, George 127

Earl, Lawson 183
Earl, Rhoda, and family 183
Eastabrooks, Clarinda 183
Eastabrooks, Decatur 43; family 183
Eastabrooks, Elizabeth 183
Eastabrooks, Elvira 183
Eastabrooks, James, and family 183
Eastabrooks, John 43, 105; family 183
Eastabrooks, Mary 183
Eastman, Lucy 190
Eastman, Zebina 6, 34, 39, 43, *78*, 113, 123–124, *125*, 126–127, 136, 144, 150, 154, 173, 174
Easton, Agnes 183
Easton, Henry/Harvey, and family 183
Eaton, Charlotte 188
Eaton, John 100; family 183
Eaton, Prudence 198
Eaton, Roxanna 51, 183
Eaton, Susan 183
Eddy, Eunice 183
Eddy, William 109; family 183
Edgar, Ann 184
Edwards, Miranda/Myranda 183
Edwards, Pierpont 46, 142, 147; family 183
Eells, Richard 105–106
Elizabeth, Illinois 166
Elliott, Joshua 183

Elliott, Margaret 195
Elliott, Minerva, and family 183
Elliott, Nancy 189
Elliott, Sarah 189
Ellis, Betsey 183
Ellis, John, and family 183
Ellwood, Abraham 8, 166; family 183
Ellwood, Alida 129, 204
Ellwood, Alonzo, and family 183
Ellwood, Angeline 183
Ellwood, Chauncey 154, 166, 183
Ellwood, Isaac 129
Ellwood, James "Edmund," and family 183
Ellwood, Lodeski 183
Ellwood, Mary 183
Ellwood, Melinda 198
Ellwood, Sarah "Sally" 166, 183
Elmer, Lucinda 183
Elmer, Nathan, and family 183
Elmer, Tamar 183
Elmwood Cemetery *174*
Emancipation Proclamation 9, 34, 16; *see also* 13th Amendment (U.S. Constitution)
Emerick, Marcella, and family 183
Emerick, Warren 183
Emerson, Ralph Waldo 90, 131, 135
Emerson, Susan 203
Epsom, New Hampshire 100
Erie Canal 22, 26, 47, 62, 132
Erie County, New York 7, 46, 64, 72, 76
Erwin/Irwin, Samuel, and family 183
Evans, Mary 181

Fairbanks, Joseph, and family 183
Fairbanks, Mary Ann 183
Fairclo, Maria 198
Fairclo, Melissa 184
Fairfield, New York 28–29, 31
Farewell/Farwell, Alice 183
Farewell/Farwell, George, and family 183
Farley, Sarah 186
Farnsworth, David 154; family 183
Farnsworth, Hannah 183
Favor, Sarah 191
Fay, Alida 183, 51
Fay, Harriet 183
Fay, Horrace Wright 51, 147; family 183
Fay, Margaret 51, 183
Fay, Roxanna 51, 183
Fay, Wells 43; family 183
Fellows, Lodeski 183
Fenton, Eliza 183
Fenton, Merritt, and family 183
Ferguson, Elizabeth 184
Ferguson, James, and family 184
Ferguson, Martha 203
Ferguson, Nancy 184
Ferguson, Robert, and family 184
Fillmore, Millard 7
Fillmore, Phoebe 188
Finley, David, and family 184
Finley, Mary 184
Finney, Charles 26, 65
Firkins, Asahel, and family 184
Firkins, Harriet 184
First Congregational Church (Aurora, Illinois) 146; *see also* Aurora, Illinois
First Congregational Church (DeKalb, Illinois) 8, 87–88

First Congregational Church (Sycamore, Illinois) 1, 6–9, 13, 15, 22, 29–30, 40–41, *48*, 49–50, 56, 59–66, *67*, 68–69, *70*, 71–72, *73*, *74*, 75–77, *78*, 79, *81*, 82–84, *85*, 86–89, 96, 99, 116, 126, 132–134, 137, 142–144, 152–154, 161–162, 173
Five Points 120; road 62; school 120
Fletcher, Eunice 188
Fletcher, Julia 52, 91–92, 95–96, 99, 180
Fletcher, Thomas, Gov. 152
Flick, Anna 190
Flint, John 184
Flint, Mary, and family 184
Floyd County, Indiana 171
Ford, Thomas, Gov. 133–134
Fordham, Caroline 184
Fordham, Fitz Henry 184
Fordham, Melissa, and family 184
Fordham, William 144–146; family 184
Fort Scott 168
Fort Sumter 172
Foster, Clarissa 185
Foster, Moses 43; family 184
Foster, Thankful 179
Fowler, Mary Ann 177
Fox River, Illinois 33, 56, 63, 115
Fox River Union 56
Franklin County, Massachusetts 49
Franklin Township 117
free blacks 5, 39, 71, 88, 163, 170–171
Free West 40, 65, 123, *125*, 150
Free-Democrat 129, 147
Freeland Corners, Illinois 30, 153
Freeman, Edward 8, 165–168
Free-Soil Party 7, 21, 22, 35, 65–66, 108, 141–142, 147, 151, 153
Freesoilers 38, 107, 142–143, 147, 153
Freewill Baptist 100, 154
French, Alexander, and family 184
French, Ann 184
French, Avery, and family 184
French, Betsey 184
French, Eliza 184
French, Ellen 186
French, Isabel 184
French, James, and family 184
French, Jonathan 106; family 184
French, Mary 192
French, Mary Ann 184
French, Mary Jane 106, 182
French, Nancy 102, 184
French, Rensselaer 7, 102, 106–107, 110; family 184
French, William 105; family 184
fugitive slave laws 2, 8, 11, 18–20, 39–40, 44, 53, 83, 96–98, 102–103, 105, 107, 109, 143–146, 155, 171, 173
Fuller, Sarah 178
Fullerton, Jane 184
Fulton County, Illinois 76, 150
Furman/Firman/Freeman, John 43; family 184
Furman/Firman/Freeman, Mary 184
Furness, Herman 129–130; family 184
Furness, Sophronia 184
Furrey, Margaret 200

Gale, George 68
Galena, Illinois 104–105, 153
Galesburg, Illinois 38, 69, 86, 92, 99
Gallaher, Benjamin, and family 184

Gallaher, Jane 184
Gallano, Elizabeth 203
Gamble, Alexander, and family 184
Gamble, Henrietta/Euretta 184
Gammon, Ansel, and family 184
Gammon, Maria 184
Gammon, Sophia 184
Gandy, George 43, 92, 118; family 184
Gandy, Henry 43, 92, 96; family 184
Gandy, Lucinda 184
Gandy, Mary 184
Gardner, Catharine 185
Gardner, George, and family 184
Gardner, Harriet 184
Gardner, Ira, and family 185
Gardner, Mary Elizabeth 179
Garrison, William Lloyd 20–22, 30, 65, 94
Geneseo, Illinois 69
Geneva, Illinois 144, 168
Geneva, New York 55
Genius of Liberty 39, **125**
Genius of Universal Emancipation 124
Genoa, Illinois 6, 26, 49–50, **70**, 117, **125**, 147, 171–172
George, Ann 152, 154, 188
Gibson, Elizabeth 184
Giddings, Joshua 146
Gilbert, Eli, and family 185
Gilbert, Lois Anna 185
Gleason, Cynthia 185
Glidden, Clarissa 185
Glidden, Joseph 129; family 185
Glidden, Joshua "Willard" 129; family 185
Glidden, Mary 185
Gloucester, Massachusetts 94
Goble, Elizabeth 197
Goble, Lucy, and family 185
Good, William, and family 185
Goodrich, Cyrena 118, 182
Gore, Caroline 185
Gore, Charlotte 185
Gore, Chester, and family 185
Gore, Cynthia 185
Gore, Rev. Darius 86–87, 99; family 185
Gore, Lucretia 185
Gorton, Abigail 197
Graham, Charity 182
Graham, Houten 43; family 185
Graham, Isaac, and family 185
Graham, James, and family 1285
Graham, Margaret 185, 197
Graham, Mary 185
Graham, Mary Ann 191
Graham, Nancy 184, 195
Graham, Robert 43; family 185
Graham, Sarah 185
Graham, Thomas, and family 185
Grant Ulysses S. 52, 113, 114
Grason, Martha 180
Graves, Mary 28, 201
Gray, Mary 192
Great Lakes 19, 22, 26, 33, 47, 62, 66, 132, 150
Great Western (steamer) 127
Green, Alanson, and family 185
Green, Beriah 68, 75–76, 131
Green, Sybil 185
Gregory, Ezra "Starr" 43, 136, 142, 147, 153, 173; family 185
Gregory, Jane 185

Gregory, Mary Jane 195
Grey, Jim 53
Griggs, Charlotte 179
Guild, Harriet 199

Hagaman, Sarah 178
Hait, Esther 178
Half Day, Illinois 115
Hall, Amasa, and family 185
Hall, Angeline 185
Hall, Caroline 185
Hall, Charles 133
Hall, Ephraim 43; family 185
Hall, Jacob, and family 185
Hall, Lurana/Lurana 185
Hall, Marcenus 43; family 185
Hall, Marion 191
Hall, Mary 191
Hall, Mercy 185
Hall, Sina 196
Hamlin, Erastus 62, 80, 83, 134; family 185
Hamlin, Harriett 62, 83, 185
Hamlin, Joseph, and family 185
Hamlin, Mercia "Mercy" 185
Hammond, Rebecca 186
Hammond, Adelia 185
Hammond, Elias, and family 185
Hammond, Jacob, and family 186
Hammond, James "Monroe," and family 186
Hammond, Melissa 186
Hanchett, Diana 189
Hanchett, Eunice 113, 194
Hanchett, Phoebe 187
Hannah, Augusta 187
Harmon, Mary 182
Harmon, Rachel 195
Harnard, Angeline 159, 186
Harned, Edmund, and family 186
Harper, Ann 186
Harper, Betsey 203
Harper, Elizabeth 186
Harper, Harriet 186
Harper, James, and family 186
Harper, Margaret 188
Harper, Martha 177
Harper, Mary 192
Harper, Nancy 166, 179
Harper, Nancy/Agnes 194
Harper, Robert, and family 186
Harper, Sarah 186
Harper, Thomas, and family 186
Harper, William, and family 186
Harpers Ferry, Virginia 164
Harper's Weekly 128
Harrington, Caroline, and family 186
Harrington, Charlotte 186
Harrington, James **93**, 129, 138, 147; family 186
Harrington, Martha 196
Harrington, Ruffus 186
Harrington, Susan 186
Harrison, Abagail/Abagale 186
Harrison, Elizabeth 186
Harrison, George, and family 186
Harrison, John, and family 186
Harrison, William Henry 6, 142
Harsh, Levi, and family 186
Harsh, Mary 186
Hartman, Almira 186
Hartman, Elias 43; family 186
Haskell, Parthenia 190

Hatch, Harriet 181
Hatch, Lucy 177
Hatfield, Albert, and family 186
Hatfield, Amelia 186
Hatfield, Margaret 186
Hathaway, Caroline 180
Hathaway, John, and family 186
Hathaway, Maria 186
Hazlett, Maria/Mariah 196
Heath, Marietta 194
Heckman, Esther 190
Heckman, Philip, and family 186
Heckman, Sarah 186
Heckman, Susan 192
Hedges, Thomas, and family 186
Henderson, Elizabeth 186
Henderson, John 141; family 186
Henderson, Martha 181
Hennepin, Illinois 124
Henry, Chester, and family 186
Henry, Ellen 186
Henry, James 105; family 186
Henry, Jeannette/Sarah 186
Henry, John Vetch 36–37, 186
Herbert, David 160
Herkimer County, New York 28–29, 166
Herrick, Mary 198
Higby, Mary 198
higher law 103, 109, 122, 135
Hiland/Hyland/Highland, Hannah 88, 186
Hiland/Hyland/Highland, Joseph 88; family 186
Hill, George 138, 139, 147; family 187
Hill, Sarah 187
Hills, Mary 187
Hills, Steven, and family 187
Hinds, Tamar 183
Hinsdale, Illinois 33
Hinsdale, New Hampshire 100
Hiscock, Harriet 200
Hiscox, Euphrasia 182
History of DeKalb County, Illinois 4, **42**, 63, 105–106, 119, 147
History of Five Points 120
History of the Somonauk United Presbyterian Church 105, 108
Hitchcock, Pluma 198
Hix, Louisa 187
Hix, Seymour, and family 187
Hoag, Augustus 187
Hoffman, Phocion 28–29, 51
Hogeboom, Elizabeth 182
Holcomb, Betsy 187
Holcomb, Corena/Corrina "Cora," and family 187
Holcomb, Julia 98, 187
Holcomb, Reuben 168, 187
Holcomb, Sylvanus 43, 92, 98–99; family 187
Holderness, Philena 187
Holderness, William, and family 187
Holdredge/Holdridge, Wayne/Duane, and family 187
Holdredge/Holdridge, Clarissa 187
Hollembeak/Hollenbeck, Aramont, and family 187
Hollembeak/Hollenbeck, Pamelia 187
Hollister, Hugh, and family 187
Hollister, Maria 187
Hollister, Phoebe 187
Holmes, Julia 180

Holroyd, Adelia "Delia" 187
Holroyd, Augusta 187
Holroyd, James, and family 187
Holroyd, Mary 187
Holroyd, William, and family 187
Holt, Sarah 186
Hoover Betsy 181
Horning, Anna 201
Horton, Annie 187
Horton, Caroline 187
Horton, Dexter, and family 187
Horton, Hannah 187
Horton, Julius, and family 187
Horton, Miles, and family 187
Horton, Phebe 187
Hosford, Rebecca 191
Hossack, John 1, *14*, 53, 102, 173
Hough, Burage/Burrage 43, 110; family 187
Hough, Elizabeth 187
Hough, George, and family 187
Hough, Hester 187
Hough, John, and family 187
Hough, Margaret 187
Hough, Mary 110, 187
Hough, Matthew, Jr., and family 187
Hough, Nancy 187
Houghland, Mary "Mollie" 178
Hovey, Mary 179
Howard, Alma 190
Howard, Emily 100, 197
Howison, Alexander, and family 187
Howison, Catharine 188
Howison, Hannah 188
Howison, James, and family 187
Howison, Margaret 106; family 187
Howison, Robert, and family 187
Howison, William 109; family 188
Hoy, Ann 104–106, 153, 178
Hoyt, Benjamin, and family 188
Hoyt, Caroline 167, 201
Hoyt, Catherine "Arna" 188
Hoyt, Mary 190
Hubbard, John, and family 188
Hubbard, Livona/Livonia 188
Hubbard, Nelson, and family 188
Hubbard, Rachel 188
Hubbert, Sarah 177
Hudson, Charles 84, *85*; family 188
Hunt, Caroline 188
Hunt, John 188
Hunt, William 144, 146–147; family 188
Huntley, Amelia 188
Huntley, Luman 43; family 188
Huntly, Rebecca 195
Hyatt, Alvin 43; family 188
Hyatt, Jerusha 188
Hyatt, Katherine 188
Hyde, Eunice 188
Hyde, Jonathan, and family 188
Hyde, Marion 188
Hyde, Phoebe 188
Hyde, Sarah "Eliza" 199
Hyde, Simeon, and family 188

Ide, Harvey 43; family 188
Ide, Sarah 188
Illinois (steamer) 127
Illinois Canal *51*
Illinois Constitution 6, 7, 88, 128, 138–139
Illinois State Normal School 69

Indiana 19, 27, 84, 88, 145, 171
Indignation Meeting 8, 107, 109, 143
Ingersoll, Betsey 178
Iowa 27, 122, 163–165
Irvin, Mary 178
Irwin, Elizabeth 178, 188
Irwin, Jane 192
Irwin, Margaret 188
Irwin, Sarah 186
Irwin, William, and family 188
Ismon, George, and family 188
Ismon, Harriet "Hattie" 188
Ismon, Mary 188

Jackman, Abner 25, 43, 135, 155; family 188
Jackman, Armena 25, 155, 193
Jackman, Eliza 155, 179
Jackman, Louisa "Mary," and family 25, 155, 188
Jackman, Louise/Louisa 179
Jackson, Almina 189
Jackson, Andrew 141, 142
Jackson, Sarah 198
Jacocks, Diana 192
James, Ann 152, 154, 188
James, Daniel 8, 151–152, 154–155, 160; family 188
James, Harriet 193
Jankins, Lucinda 195
Jefferson, Thomas 141, 145, 146
Jefferson, Ohio 146
Jefferson, Wisconsin 82
Jenness, Richard, and family 188
Jenness, Sybil 188
Jennings, Prudence 193
Jo Davies County, Illinois 166
Johnson, Isaac, and family 188
Johnson, Nancy 188
Johnson, Sarah 180
Joiner, Beulah, and family 188
Joiner, Charlotte 188
Joiner, Henry, and family 188
Joiner, Sylvanus 188
Jones, Diana 189
Jones, Elizabeth 189
Jones, Harvey, and family 189
Jones, Henry, and family 189
Jones, John 127
Jones, Julia/Judy 168
Jones, Lucinda 189
Jones, Malden, and family 189
Jones, Margaret 186
Jones, Mary 189
Jones, Mary Ann 178
Jones, Owen, and family 189
Jonesboro, Illinois 8, 160
Jordan, Betsy 189
Jordan, Martha 182
Jordan, Moses, and family 189
Joslyn, Albert, and family 189
Joslyn, Antoinette 180
Joslyn, Aristeen 182
Joslyn, Harry 92, 147; family 189
Joslyn, Julia 98, 187
Joslyn, Lorinda 180, 189
Joslyn, Lucy 189
Joslyn, Mabellia/Marilla 189
Joslyn, Phineas 43, 92, 100; family 189
Judd, Amanda 199
Judd, John 43; family 189
Judd, Mary "Ariel" 189
Judson, Helen 178

Kalamazoo, Michigan 166
Kane County, Illinois 6–7, 15, 33–34, 63, 68, 90, 96, 98, 114, 126, 138, 144, 150, 168
Kansas-Nebraska Act 8, 20, 96–97, 142, 145–146, 159
Kaskaskia, Illinois 27
Keefe, Lucy 196
Kellogg, Elizabeth 49
Kellogg, Emily "Jennie" 195
Kellogg, Hiram 11, 15, 168; family 189
Kellogg, Jesse 6, 15, *32*, 43, 49, 57, 62–63, *73*, 76–77, *78*, 80, 82–84, 98, 130–134, 144, 162, 168; family 189
Kellogg, Mary, and family 189
Kellogg, Orlando 189
Kellogg, Phoebe 32, 49, 62–63, 132, 189
Kelly, Lucinda 189
Kelsey, Hannah 203
Kemp, James, and family 189
Kemp, Sarah 189
Kempton, Mahala 198
Kendall, Louisa "Mary" 155, 188
Kendall County, Illinois 126, 128, 138
Kentucky 17, 23, 39, 52, 115, 165–166, 168–169
Kerns, S.H., and family 189
Kidd, Rachel 181
Kilcup, Mary 198
Kincade, Betsy 194
King, Almina 189
King, Elizabeth 189
King, Gideon 43; family 189
King, Harriet 178
King, Lydia 189
King, Lyman, and family 189
King, Rev. Martin Luther, Jr. 40
King, Philip, and family 189
Kingsley, Eben/Elon, and family 189
Kingsley, Elizabeth 189
Kingsley, Margaret 189
Kingsley, Mason, and family 189
Kingston, Illinois 122, 170, 166
Kinney, Rachel 188
Kinyon, George, and family 189
Kinyon, Marilla 189
Kinyon, Nancy 189
Kirkpatrick, Hannah 188
Kirkpatrick, Hezekiah, and family 189
Kirkpatrick, Isaac, and family 189
Kirkpatrick, Jesse, and family 190
Kirkpatrick, Julia 190
Kirkpatrick, Nancy 189
Kirkpatrick, Richard, and family 190
Kirkpatrick, Ruth 909
Kirkpatrick, Sarah 189
Kishwaukee River 25, 30, 66, 69, 71, 133
Knapp, Julia 194
Knapp, Ruth 198
Knight, Amanda 180
Knight, Mary 190
Knight, Samuel, and family 190
Knox College 69, 86
Knox County, Illinois 4, 34, 37
Kretsinger, George 190
Kretsinger, Mary, and family 190

Lackey, Nancy 180
Lake County, Illinois 7
Lake Michigan 19, 22, 33, 66, *67*, 121, 127

Lamb, Curtis, and family 190
Lamb, Fanny 190
Lamb, Hester 190
Lancaster, Massachusetts 91
Lander, Joseph 43, 129–130; family 190
Lander, Rachel 129, 190
Langdon, Henry, and family 190
Langdon, Mary 190
LaSalle County, Illinois 13, 31, 53, 66, 102, 111, *125*, 126, 138, 141
Latham, Ann "Lucy" 190
Latham, Anna 190
Latham, Benjamin, and family 190
Latham, Hubbard, and family 190
Lathrop, Chandler 190
Lathrop, Lucy, and family 190
Lattin, Carlos 43, 84, 118; family 190
Lattin, Nancy 190
Lavergne, Tennessee 168
Laverty, Caroline 190
Laverty, Hamilton, and family 190
Laverty, Nancy 190
Laverty, Selennia 190
law of God 53, 135, 145
Lawrence, Mary 190
Lawrence, William, and family 190
Lawyer, David 190
Lawyer, Maria, and family 190
Lay, Emily 190
Lay, Harriet 183
Lay, Janette/Jeanette 178
Lay, Samuel 43, 108, 144; family 190
Lee, Alma 190
Lee, Catharine 190
Lee, Charles, and family 190
Lee, Cyrus, and family 190
Lee, Mary 193
Lee County, Illinois 61
Lemoin/Lamoin, Anna 190
Lemoin/Lamoin, Lucius, and family 190
Leonard, Minerva 183
Leyson, John, and family 190
Leyson, Mary 190
The Liberator 20
The Liberty Minstrel 7, 13, *14*
Liberty Party 6, 7, 21, 22, 38, 45, *93*, 107, 123, *125*, 131, 136, 137, 138, 139, 140, 141, 142, 144, 147, 153
Lincoln, Abraham 8–9, 34, 124, 143, 150–151, 156, *157*, 158–161, 173
Little, Abijah, and family 190
Little, Alvira 190
Little, Amanda 195
Little, Eleanor 190
Little, Esther 190
Little, Henry, and family 190
Little, Lucy 190
Littlefield, Sarah 197
Livingston, Nancy 185
Lloyd, Artemas 190
Lloyd, Margaret 189
Lloyd, Parthenia, and family 190
Lockerby, Catharine 194
Lord, Frances 191
Lord, Samuel, and family 191
Love, Alice, and family 191
Love, Frederick 191
Lovejoy, Elijah 6, 44–46, 52, 124, 127, 137, 173
Lovejoy, Owen 6, 43, 45–46, 52, 173
Lowrie, Mary 184
Lucas, Lucinda 198
Lundy, Benjamin 124, *125*

Lykens County, Kansas 98
Lyman, Loretta "Lettie" 200
Lyndon, Vermont 154
Lyon, Fanny 191
Lyon, George, and family 191

Mack, Emeline 182
Mackey/Mackie, Eliza 191
Mackey/Mackie, Mary 191
Mackey/Mackie, William "Henry" 43; family 191
Mackie, James 43; family 191
Mackie, Margaret 200
Mackie, Susan 62, 191
Madden, Eliza 191
Madden, Henry 43, 109, 133, 138, 144–146; family 191
Mallows, Abigail, and family 191
Mallows, George 191
Malta, Illinois *51*
Maltby, Eliza 191
Maltby, Joseph, and family 191
Maltby, Sarah 191
manual labor school 68–69
Marshall, Eveline 196
Marshall, Mary 203
Martin, Betsey 184
Martin, Harry 43, 57, 59–60, 77; family 191
Martin, Jane 178, 191
Martin, John, and family 191
Martin, Sarah 191
Mason, Experience 191
Mason, Henry, and family 191
Mason, Jarvis, and family 191
Mason, Lucretia 185
Mason, Lucy 191
Massachusetts 28, 49, 50, 71, 72, 84, 91, 94, 95, 100, 124, 165
Massingham, Elizabeth 186
Matteson, Benjamin, and family 191
Matteson, Christina 191
Matteson, Marion 191
Matteson, Miriam 191
Matteson, Oscar 191
Matteson, Silvia 193
Maxfield, Clarissa 192
Maxfield, Elizabeth 196
Maxfield, JoAnna "Anna" 41, 191
Maxfield, John 6, 37, 41, *42*, 43, 46, 50; family 191
Maxfield, John "Nelson" 41, 43; family 191
Maxfield, Mary 191
Maxfield, Rebecca 191
Maxfield, William 41, 43; family 191
Mayfield, Illinois 7, 25, 26, 30, 33, 34–35, 62, 109, 113–115, 117122, *125*, 126, 144, 146–147, 162–163, 171–173
Mayo, Edward 154, 159–160, 167
McAffee, Martha 194
McAllister, James, and family 191
McAllister, James, Jr., and family 191
McAllister, Jane "Jennie" 191
McAllister, Mary 177
McAllister, Mary Ann 191
McAllister, Sarah 185, 191
McAllister, William, and family 191
McArthur, Caroline 185
McBride, Rebecca 192
McBride, Samuel, and family 192
McCleery, Elizabeth 194
McCleery, Margaret 187

McCleery/McCleary/McClary, Adeline 192
McCleery/McCleary/McClary, James, and family 192
McCleery/McCleary/McLeary, Edward, and family 192
McCleery/McCleary/McLeary, Jane 192
McCleland, Mary 192
McCleland, Mason, and family 192
McClellan, Emeline "Emma" 192
McClellan, James, and family 192
McConnell, Mary 185
McCormick, Charles, and family 192
McCormick, Clarissa 192
McCormick, Lucinda 192
McCoy, Addison 192
McCoy, Sarah 192
McDonald, Sarah 192
McDonald, Susan 192
McDonald, Wallace "William," and family 192
McDonnal, Mary 185
McFarland, James, and family 192
McFarland, Mary 192
McFarland, Robert, and family 192
McFarland, Sarah 192
McFarland, William, and family 192
McGaughey, Nancy "Agnes" 199
McGilvra, Francis 192
McGilvra, Jacob 122; family 192
McGilvra, Mary 192
McGue, Jane 193
McHenry County, Illinois 126
McKechnie/McGeachie, Barbara 179
McKee, Mary 192
McKee, Sarah 192
McKee, William, and family 192
McKillup/McKellup, Hannah 186
McMillan, Elizabeth 181
McNeal, Mary 190
McNorton, Eleanor 190
McQuarie/McCuiry, Diana 192
McQuarie/McCuiry, John, and family 192
McQuestin, Julia 177
Meacham, Lucinda 184
Meacham, Mary 184
Mead, Mercy 185
Mendenhall, Geraldine 192
Mendenhall, James, and family 192
Mercer, David "Smith," and family 192
Mercer, Margaret 192
Merrick, Betsey 196
Merriman, Almira 192
Merriman, Mary 192
Merriman, Peter, and family 192
Merritt, Charles, and family 192
Merritt, Flora 192
Mesquakie (Indians) 27
Metcalf, Eunice 183
Methodist Episcopal Church (Sycamore, Illinois) 25, 113–114, 117–118
Meyers, Catharine "Kate" 203
Michigan 19, 27, 124, 145, 166
Michigan Canal 19, *51*
Middlebury, Vermont 32
Miles, Sarah 194
Miller, Andrew 192
Miller, Cynthia 163
Miller, Daniel, and family 192
Miller, Dinah 195
Miller, Elizabeth 140, 192
Miller, Gilley 192

Miller, Harriet 184
Miller, Jane 192
Miller, Jeannette 192
Miller, Lyndia 198
Miller, Margaret, and family 192
Miller, Mary 163, 164
Miller, Peter, and family 192
Miller, Robert 163
Miller, Samuel 43; family 192
Miller, William 43; family 192
Milne, Allen, and family 193
Milne, Laurinda 193
Mississippi 38, 44, *51*, 52, 61, 116, 128, 161, 164–165
Mississippi River 19, 27–28, 34, 61, 66, 161, 165–166
Missouri Compromise *see* Compromise of 1820
Moline, Illinois 34
Moore, Elizabeth 181, 187
Moore, James, and family 193
Moore, Mariah/Maria 193
Moore, Phebe 193
Moore, Silvia 193
More, Voranus "Emory" 43; family 193
Moreland, Hugh, and family 193
Moreland, Prudence 193
Morgan, William 140, 212*ch*12*n*42
Mormon 7, 26, 141
Morrison, Jane 193
Morrison, John, and family 193
Morse, Isaac, and family 193
Morse, Sophia 193
Moses, Charlotte 193
Mulford, Gertrude 177
Mulford, Jeremiah, and family 193
Mulford, Mary 193
Mullen, Esther 121, 193
Mullen, John 33, 43, 121; family 193
Mullen, Mary 193
Mullen, Phebe 193
Mullen, Rachel 193
Mullen, Sarah "Ann" 193
Mumford, Louisa 187
Mumford, Sarah 193
Mumford, Thomas, and family 193
Munsell/Munsall, Laura 196
Munt, Amelia 181
Murray, Elizabet "Betsey" 193
Murray, John, and family 193
Muscatine, Iowa 164

Needham, Benjamin, and family 193
Needham, Charlotte 193
Needham, Harriet 193
Needham, Lois Anna 185
New Hampshire 96, 100, 117, 130, 139
New Jersey 79, 155
Newburg, Illinois 144
Newell, Harriet 200
Newman, Huldah 196
Newton, Adeline, and family 193
Newton, Clarissa "Clara," and family 193
Newton, David 193
Newton, John *74*, 209*n*60, 220
Newton, Liberty 193
Nichols, Abigail 196
Nichols, Armena 25, 155, 193
Nichols, Charlotte 193
Nichols, Ephraim 43; family 193
Nichols, Esther 121, 193
Nichols, Hannah 182

Nichols, Helen/Ellen 193
Nichols, Ira 43, 118, 121–122; family 193
Nichols, John 43, 118; family 193
Nichols, Latin 26, 43, 121; family 193
Nichols, Lepha 179
Nichols, Lucretia 193
Nichols, Mary Ann 193
Nichols, Mercy 193
Nichols, Peter 43, 118, 121; family 193
Nichols, Phebe 200
Nichols, Reuben 43, 122; 193
Nichols, Sarah "Ann" 193
Nichols, Stephen, and family 193
Nicholson, Catharine 181
Nicholson, Eunice, and family 193
Nicholson, Thomas 193
Nickerson, Eunice 113, 194
Nickerson, Mulford 113, 118
Nickerson, Roxana 194
Nickerson, William 34, 113–114, 118–122, 130, 147, 162–163, 165, 173–174; family 194
Nind, Sarah 189
Nisbet, Matthew, and family 194
Nisbet, Nancy/Agnes 194
Norcutt, Norman, and family 194
Norcutt, Sarah 194
Norcutt, Winslow 43
Norfolk, Virginia 163–164
North Star 24, 37
Northern Illinois University 69
Northwest Ordinance 6, 19–20, 145
Northwest Territory 6, 19, 27, 29, 47, 61–62, 64, 98, 113, 123, 145
Norton, Eliza 198
Norton, Hamilton 63
Norton, Henrietta 22–23, 52, *78*, 79, 194
Norton, Henry/Harvey 194
Norton, Oliver 1, 7, 22–23, 52, *78*, 79–80, *81*, 82–84, 142, 194

Oak Mound Cemetery 52
Oberton/Overton, Isabella 194
Oglesby, Richard, Gov. 144, 154
Ohio 3–5, 6, 17, 19, 27, 31, 34, 41, 45, 52, 61, 72, 84, 88, 96, 122–123, *125*, 129, 145–146, 159, 169
Ohio River 17, 19, 61, 66, 145
Ohio State University 3
Ohio Wesleyan University 122
Olds, Elizabeth 183
Olmstead, Catharine 194
Olmstead, Eleanor 194
Olmstead, Helen 194
Olmstead, Isaac "Lewis," and family 194
Olmstead, Julia 194
Olmstead, Marietta 194
Olmstead, Mary 194
Olmstead, Mathew "William," and family 194
Olmstead, Miriam 191
Olmstead, Nathan, and family 194
Olmstead, Parthenia 203
Olmstead, William, and family 194
Ordinance of 1787 *see* Northwest Ordinance
Ormsby, Betsy 194
Ormsby, Hannah 194
Ormsby, John, and family 194
Orput, Almina/Elmira 194
Orput, James, and family 194
Orput, John 43; family 194

Orput, Lucy 191
Orput, Sarah 194
Orr, David, and family 194
Orr, Elizabeth 194
Orr, Martha 1294
Osterhout/Osterhoud, Mary 192
Oswald, Ann 186
Ottawa, Illinois 15, 31, 133, 144, 153, 159, 173
Ousterhout, Elizabeth 198
Owen(s), Eleanor 194

Page, Austin 50, 72, 194
Page, Elizabeth "Eliza" 50, 194
Page, Horatio 6–8, 43, 49–50, 62–63, *70–73*, *78*, 130, 134, 163, 165, 171, *174*; family 194
Page, Sarah 194
Paine, Chester 194
Paine, Clarinda, and family 194
Paine, Rosina 96, 182
Pampas Township 23, 118, 147
Paola, Kansas 98
Park, Sophia 193
Parker, Ann 122, 201
Parker, Eliza 200
Parker, Maria 180
Parker, Mary Ann 194
Parker, Sarah "Sally" 202
Parker, Silas "Smith" 194
Parsons, Caroline 187
Parsons, Geraldine 192
Partridge, Lucy 185
Past and Present of DeKalb County, Vol. I *48*, 121
Patten, Agnes 106, 194
Patten, Alexander 36, 106, 153; family 194
Patten, Catherine 195
Patten, Elizabeth 138, 195
Patten, James, and family 195
Patten, Jane 195
Patten, Mary, and family 195
Patten, Robert 106; family 195
Patten, William 103, 106, 109, 138; family 195
Patterson, John, and family 195
Patterson, Mary Jane 195
Pauly, Elmira 182
Paw Paw, Illinois 33, 46, 61, 86, 102, 147, 171
Pearsons, Sarah 201
Peavy, Nehemiah, and family 195
Peavy, Selinda 195
Peck, Harriet, and family 195
Peck, Lydia 195
Peck, Margaret 195
Peck, Nathan 92, 100; family 195
Peck, Timothy 195
Pennsylvania 18, 30, 38, 59, 88, 120, 130, 156
People's Party 148
Peoria, Illinois 124, 150
Peoria Evening Republican 150
Peoria Register 124, 150
Perce/Perse, Martha 202
Percival, Sarah 191
Perdy, Lucy 179
Perkins, Abigail 181
Perkins, Betsy 189
Perkins, Martha 195
Perkins, Moses, and family 195
Perkins, Sarah 195

Perry, David 63, 133–136; family 195
Perry, Delilah/Della 178
Perry, Margaret 201
Perry, Mariah/Maria 134, 195
Perry, Nancy 178
Peters, Luard, and family 195
Peters, Merinda/Melinda 195
Peters, Minerva, and family 195
Peters, Pamela 171
Peters, Warren 195
Phebus, Jeannette 192
Phelps, William 43, 130; family 195
Phillips, Mary "Ariel" 189
Phillips, Wendell 21
Picket, Thomas 150
Pierce, Charles, and family 195
Pierce, Emily "Jennie" 195
Pierce, Franklin 8, 143
Pierce, Ruth 180
Pierson, Ann 196
Pierson, Elizabeth 195
Pierson, Timothy, and family 195
Pike, Elizabeth 195
Pike, Silas, and family 195
Pilgrim 60–61, 139
Piper, David, and family 195
Piper, Margaret 195
Pittsfield, Massachusetts 49, 71
Place, Mary 189
Pleasant Hill 122; road 62; school 118
Plumb, Sophrona 203
Plymat, Ada 199–200
Polk, James 7, 141, 142
Pollock, Nancy 107, 184
Polo Press 119
Pomeroy, Temperance 177
Pond, JoAnna "Anna" 41, 191
Poplin, Rachel 109; family 195
Poplin, William 43, 109, 195
popular sovereignty 8, 20, 96, 142, 145, 159
Port Byron, Illinois 34, 161
Porter, Jedediah, and family 195
Porter, Mary Ann/Marian 195
Porter, Phebe 200
Porter, Selina 197
Portrait and Biographical Album of DeKalb 4, 37
Portsmouth, Virginia 163
Potawatomie (Indians) 27–28, 66, 133
Potter, Ann/Anna 195
Potter, Chester 43; family 195
Potter, Dinah 195
Potter, Henry, and family 195
Powell, Elizabeth 186
Powell, Hannah 182
Powell, Ruth 180
Powers, Amanda 195
Powers, Asa, and family 195
Powers, Lucinda 195
Powers, Mary "Polly" 195
Powers, Rebecca 195
Pratt, Almus 43; family 196
Pratt, Elizabeth 195, 196
Pratt, Elizabeth "Eliza" 50, 194
Pratt, Emily 190
Pratt, Mary/Margaret 179
Pratt, Sarah "Sally" 196
Prescott, Almira/Almina 196
Prescott, Mary "Polly" 196
Prescott, William, and family 196
Preston, Justus 43; family 196
Preston, Sina 196

Price, Mary 196
Price, Mathias, and family 196
Princeton, Illinois 34, 38, 43–46, 66, 150, 161, 173
Princeton University 79
Pritchard, Elotia 196
Pritchard, Reuben 6, **42**, 45–46, 147; family 196
Provincetown, Massachusetts 100
Pugsley, Katherine 188
Purcell, James 121; family 196
Purcell, Lucy 196
Purdun/Purdam, Amanda 196
Purdun/Purdam, John, and family 196
Puritan 1, 30, 40, 59–61, 71–72, **73**, **74**, 87, 95, 104, 126
Putnam, Elizabeth 196

Quaker 5, 18, 30, 34, 88
Quilhot, Elizabeth 192
Quincy, Illinois 34, 105, 141, 150, 161

Ralph, Justin 196
Rand, Aaron, and family 196
Rand, Elizabeth 197
Randall, Elvira 197
Randall, Mary 202
Rankin, John **125**
Ransom, Ann 196
Ransom, Elizabeth 196
Ransom, Thomas, and family 196
Rathbun/Rathbone, Edwin, and family 196
Rathbun/Rathbone, Laura 196
Raymond, Eveline 196
Raymond, Matilda 179
Raymond, Nichodemus, and family 196
Read, Abigail 196
Read, William, and family 196
Redfield, Amanda 180
Redfield, Sophronia 181
Reed, Celina 203
Reed, Sarah 181
Reese, Ella 202
Reeves, Huldah 196
Reeves, Michael, and family 196
Renwick, Eliza 196
Renwick, Herbert, and family 196
Republican Party 8, 22, 35, 38–39, 51, 65, 66, **78**, **93**, 97, 108, 109, 120, 125, 130, 131, 133, 135, 136, 143, 146–147, 128, 149, 151, 153–158, 160
Republican Sentinel 8, 124, 143, 148–149, 151, 154–156, 170
Rhermann, Lydia 179
Rich, Clarissa "Clara" 198
Richards, Emily 197
Richards, Nathaniel, and family 196
Richards, Rhoda "Elizabeth" 63, 203
Richards, Ruth 196
Richardson, Ann 196
Richardson, Asa, and family 196
Richardson, Betsey 196
Richardson, George, and family 196
Richardson, Joseph, and family 196
Richardson, Judith 179
Richardson, Lucinda 196
Richardson, Maria/Mariah 196
Richardson, Peter, and family 196
Richmond, Elisha, and family 196
Richmond, Lucina 196
Riddle, Enoch, and family 196
Riddle, Mary "Polly" 196

Ringer/Ranger, Catherine/Katherine 203
Ripley, Ohio 17, 31
Ripon, Wisconsin 8, 146
Rixon, Martha 195
Roberts, Robert, and family 196
Roberts, Susan 196
Robertson, Isabella 106, 197
Robertson, Margaret 197
Robertson, Mary Jane 202
Robertson, William 106; family 196–197
Robinson, Almon 43, 197
Robinson, Caroline 181
Robinson, Charles 59–60; family 197
Robinson, Clarinda 197
Robinson, Clarissa 197
Robinson, Elizabeth 197
Robinson, Ezra, and family 197
Robinson, Mercy 43; family 197
Rock Island, Illinois 34, 161, 164
Rock River, Illinois 69, 115
Rockford, Illinois 22, 69, 79, 100, 144
Roe, Joseph 167
Rogers, Amos 23; family 197
Rogers, Caroline M. 201
Rogers, Elizabeth 197
Rogers, Jacob, and family 197
Rogers, Louisa 197
Rood, Sally 177
Root, Eliza 203
Roscoe, Illinois 22
Rose, Abigail 197
Rose, Chauncey 56; family 197
Rose, Clarinda 197
Rose, Ellsworth 13, 49, 63, 72, 77, **78**, 147; family 197
Rose, Emily 49, 197
Rose, Francis 192
Rose, Jesse 56–57, 61–63, 84, 134–136; family 197
Rose, John, and family 197
Rose, Laura 180
Rose, Louisa 197
Rose, Lucinda 12, 202
Rose, Ruth, and family 197
Rose, Selina 197
Rosebrook, Lois 197
Rosebrook, William, and family 197
Ross, Caroline 202
Ross, Philinda/Philana "Polly" 201
Ross Grove, Illinois 102; Presbyterian Church 102
Rote, Mary Ann 120
Roundsville, Elvira 90, 197
Roundsville, Rev. William 30, 90–91, 96; family 197
Rowden, Mary "Polly" 195
Rowe, Harrison 186
Rowley, John 197
Rowley, Louisa, and family 197
Ruggles, Mabel 197
Ruggles, Martha 197
Ruggles, Stanley, and family 197

Sac (Indians) 27
Safford, Edward, and family 197
Safford, Henry 130; family 197
Safford, Sarah 197
St. Charles, Illinois 11, 15, 31, 33–34, 47, **48**, 68, 90–91, 96, 120–121, 150, 169
St. Louis, Missouri 44
St. Louis Democrat 152

Index

St. Louis Observer 44
Sanborn, Emily 100, 197
Sanborn, Rev. Rufus 99–101; family 197
Sandwich, Illinois 8, *51*, 87–88, 117, 172; Congregational church 8, 87
Sansworth, David, and family 197
Sansworth, Mary 197
Sauk (Indians) 27
Schryver/Schriver, Albert 197
Schryver/Schriver, Hannah, and family 197
Schryver, Rebecca 200
Scot 36, 38, 53, 103–106, 108–109, 111, 119, 120
Scotland 27, 53, 102–104, 109, 111
Scott, Keziah 181
Sears, Andrew, and family 197
Sears, Mary 197
Seavy/Seavey, Lucy 185
Seavy/Seavey, Samantha, and family 197–198
Seavy/Seavey, William 198
Sebree, Gilley 192
Seeley, Charlotte 198
Seeley, John, and family 198
Selders, Elizabeth 181
Selts, Mary 190
Settly, Maria 190
Setzer, Hannah 198
Seventh Day Adventist 26
Seventh Day Baptist 46
Seward, William H. 102, 122
Seyler, Annie 199
Shabbona, Chief 28
Shankland, John 106; family 198
Shankland, M. Ellen 198
Sharp, Margaret 192
Shaver, Solomon 119, 120
Shaw, George Bernard 10
Shaw, Sarah 195
Shaw, Sarah "Sally" 198
Shaw, William, and family 198
Sheffield, Joseph, and family 198
Sheffield, Sarah 198
Shelburn/Sherburn, Maranda 177
Sheldon, Abigail, and family 198
Sheldon, Betsy 177
Sheldon, Silas, Jr. 198
Sheley, Elena/Ellen/Eleanor 179
Sheley, Elizabeth 198
Sheley, Elizabeth "Betsy" 198
Sheley, John, and family 198
Shepard, Andrew 43; family 198
Shepard, Eliza 198
Shephard, Alvin 198
Shephard, Elizabeth, and family 198
Shepherd, John 7, 71, 165, 171
Shepherd/Shepard, Pluma 198
Shepherd/Shepard, Russell, and family 198
Sherburne, Hezekiah, and family 198
Sherburne, Mary 198
Sheridan, Harriet 188
Shillibeer/Sillibeer, Sarah 193
Sholes, Eliza 199
Shoudy, Hannah 187
Shurtleff, Albert, and family 198
Shurtleff, Clarissa "Clara" 198
Shurtleff, Davie, and family 198
Shurtleff, Ichabod, III, and family 198
Shurtleff, Laura 181
Shurtleff, Lyndia 198
Shurtleff, Mahala 198
Shurtleff, Mary 198
Shurtleff, Ruth 198
Sibley, Catherine 195
Siebert, Wilbur 3–4, 20, 35, 40, 66, 124, 173
Siglin, Hannah 198
Siglin, Jacob, and family 198
Silverthorn, Joannah 201
Simons, Jabez 59–61; family 198
Simons, Jacob 198
Simons, Laura, and family 198
Simons, Thirza 198
Sivwright, Alexander, and family 198
Sivwright, George, and family 198
Sivwright, James, and family 198
Sivwright, Lucinda 198
Sivwright, Maria 198
Sivwright, Mary 198
Sivwright, Nelson, and family 198
Sivwright, Prudence 198
Sixbury, Joseph 43, 147; family 198
Sixbury, Melinda 198
Skeels, Lavina/Lavonia 203
Skinner, Jerusha 188
Skinner, Mary Ann 184
Slack, Jane 191
Slade, Catherine 203
slavecatchers 33, 99, 103, 105
Sly, Joanna 198
Sly, Joseph 43, 110; family 198
Smiley, Elizabeth 186
Smiley, Ruth 190
Smith, Abigail 198
Smith, Albert V.L. 100; family 198
Smith, Anna/Emma 199
Smith, Annie 199
Smith, Beulah 188
Smith, Calista 180
Smith, Caroline 180
Smith, Catherine 177
Smith, Charles 13; family 199
Smith, Chester 199
Smith, Curtis 43, 90, 92, *93*, 95, 101, 138; family 199
Smith, David, and family 199
Smith, Eliza 199
Smith, Elizabeth 199
Smith, Elizabeth "Betsey" 193
Smith, Esther 199
Smith, Gerrit 121
Smith, Harriet 199
Smith, Joseph 7, 141
Smith, Lawrence, and family 199
Smith, Lucy 198, 199
Smith, Marcia 199
Smith, Maria 199
Smith, Martha 202
Smith, Mary 187
Smith, Oliver, and family 199
Smith, Phebe "Ann" 200
Smith, Rachel, and family 199
Smith, Spafford 43; family 199
Smith, Susan 196
Smith, William, and family 199
Snow, Abigail 199
Snow, Benjamin, and family 199
Snow, Elizabeth 199
Snow, Frederick, and family 199
Snow, John 43; family 199
Snow, Margaret 199
Snow, Mary 199
Somes, Jane 195
Somonauk, Illinois 4, 6, 8, 18, 33, 34, 36–37, 41, 52, 86, 102–112, 138, 140–144, 147, 153, 171–172; township 30, *125*, 153
Somonauk Associate Presbyterian Church 102–104, 106, 111, 153
Somonauk Corners, Illinois 153
Somonauk United Presbyterian Church 7, 40, 10, 109, 126, 152
Souter/Suiter, Agnes 202
South Grove Township 27, 119, 121
Sowers, Mary 199
Sowers, William, and family 199
Spencer, Henry, and family 199
Spinka, Mathew 76
Spring, Alpona/Aluna 199
Spring, George 92; family 199
Springfield, Illinois 109, *157*
squatter sovereignty 142
Squaw Grove Township *51*, 147
Squires, Experience 191
Stafford, Moses 43; family 199
Stafford, Sarah 199
Stanley, Abagail/Abagale 186
Stark, Amanda 199
Stark, David "Webster," and family 199
Stark, Louisa 199
Stark, Marshall 43, 118, 129–130; family 199
Starkey, Amanda 196
Stevens, Ann 179
Stevens/Stephens, Asa, Jr., and family 199
Stevens, Irene 199
Stevens, John, and family 199
Stevens, Lucina 196
Stevens, Marian/Mary/Marion 199
Stevens, Philena 199
Stevens, Rebuk 199
Stevens, Samuel 43; family 199
Stevens, Sarah "Eliza" 199
Stevens, William, and family 199
Steward, Emeline "Emma" 192
Steward, Mary 192
Stewart, Elijah 109; family 199
Stewart, Julia 199
Stewart, Mary 178
Stewart, Nancy "Agnes" 199
Stewart, Rebecca 192
Stiles, Aaron 147
Stillwell, Esther 199
Stipp, Margaret 51, 183
Storrs, Polly 182
Stott, Eliza 182
Stott, Margaret 200
Stowe/Stow, Asahel 56–57, 61; family 199
Stowe, Harriet Beecher 7, 26, 54, 83, 161
Stowe, Louisa 197
Stowe, Rebecca 186
Strong, Rachel 190
Strouse, Mary 199
Sugar Grove, Illinois 33
Sumner, Ada 1990299
Sumner, Ebenezer, and family 199–200
Swartwood, James, and family 200
Swartwood, Paulina 200
Sycamore True Republican 77, 119, *157*, 158, 172

Talbot, Charles, and family 200
Talbot, Harriet 200
Taplin, Isabelle 182

Tappan, Harriet 200
Tappan, Silas 130; family 200
Tappan, William, and family 200
Taylor, Frances 191
Taylor, Harriet 200
Taylor, Hugh, and family 200
Taylor, Margaret 185, 195
Taylor, Rev. 138
Taylor, Zachary 7, 142
Teeter, Christina 191
Telford, Ann 106, 110; family 200
Telford, Francis "Frankie" 106, 110, 200
Telford, Julia 110; family 200
temperance 7, 55–57, 59–60, 62, 68–69, 76–77, 80–*81*, 82–83, 88, 114–115, 131, 143, 153
Tennessee 127, 141, 161, 168–170
Texas 7, 141, 168
13th Amendment (U.S. Constitution) 9; see also Emancipation Proclamation
Thom, John, and family 200
Thom, Margaret 200
Thomas, Eliza 200
Thomas, Ellen, and family 200
Thomas, Marion 188
Thomas, R.B., and family 200
Thomas, William 200
Thompson, Agnes 183
Thompson, Eliza 184, 200
Thompson, Emily 201
Thompson, Joseph, and family 200
Thompson, Lorena 201
Thompson, Margaret 200
Thompson, Mariah/Maria 193
Thompson, Mathew, and family 200
Thompson, Milo 159, 200
Thompson, Rebecca 200
Thompson, William, and family 200
Thoreau, Henry David 11
Thornberg/Thornburg, Margaret 192
Thrall, Charles, and family 200
Thrall, Loretta "Lettie" 200
Thurston, Adelia "Delia" 187
Tibbets, Delila 200
Tibbets, William, and family 200
Tiffany, Hester 187
Timmerman, Ione 200
Timmerman, Marvin, and family 200
Tindall, Benjamin, and family 200
Tindall, Jesse, and family 200
Tindall, Mary 200
Tindall, Sarah 200
Toby, Harriett 185
Tower, David, and family 200
Tower, Mary 190, 200
Townsend, Ann 35, 200
Townsend, Charles 43, 118–121, 163; family 200
Townsend, George, and family 200
Townsend, Joshua 35, 43, 118–121, 163; family 200
Townsend, Mary Ann 193
Townsend, Nancy 202
Townsend, Phebe 35, 200
Townsend, Rachel 200
Townsend, Stephen 35, 43, 84, 118–120, 122, 142, 147, 163; family 200
Trask, Sarah 177
Trimble, Job, and family 200
Trimble, Margaret 200
Troeger, Emma 178
True Republican 8, 46, 77, 119, 147–148, 151–156, *157*, 158–160, 167, 172

Truesdale, Julia 199
Tubman, Harriet 171
Tucker, Ann 202
Turner, Eliza 183
Turner, Mary 96
Tuttle, Eliza 200
Tuttle, Phebe "Ann" 200
Tuttle, Philo, and family 200
Tyler, Louisa 199
Tyrell/Tyrrel, Mary 179
Tyrrell, Mercia "Mercy" 185

Uncle Tom's Cabin 7, 54, 83, 161
Underground Railroad from Slavery to Freedom 3, 34, 124
Underground Railroad routes 11, 18, 23, 33–34, 36, 38, 45, 62, 66, *67*, 68, 150, 161, 164–165
Union County, Illinois 160
Union Theological Seminary 79
United Presbyterian Church (Somonauk, Illinois) see Somonauk United Presbyterian Church
United States Constitution 6, 7, 9, 19–10, 45, 53, 88, 103, 107, 122, 141, 145, 173
Universalist Church (Sycamore, Illinois) 1, 7–8, 30, 40, 52, 64, *73*, 90–92, *93*, 94–101, 117, 122, 126, 166;; see also Universalists
Universalists 52, 64, *73*, 90–92, 94–95, 101, 111, 131, 135, 147;; see also Universalist Church

Van Buren, Martin 6, 7, 141, 142
Vandalia, Illinois 27
Vandeburg, Abram, and family 200–201
Vandeburg, Louisa 201
Van Deventer, Mary 197
Van Horn, Marcia 199
Van Tuyl, Thirza 198
Van Voorhees, Jane 179
Vermont 25, 26, 29, 32, 41, 64, 68, 90, 92, 96, 100, 124, 127, 131, 132, 154
Vicksburg, Mississippi *51*, 52
Voters and Tax-payers of DeKalb County, Illinois 4

Wadgen, Mary 8, 50, 163–165
Wager, Losina "Jane" 182
Wager, Philinda/Philana "Polly" 201
Wager, Reuben, and family 201
Wager, Sarah "Sally" 203
Waite, Campbell 8, 150–152, 156, *157*, 158, 160, 167; family 201
Waite, Daniel 150
Waldo, Mary 28, 201
Walker, Helen 194, 201
Walker, James 106; family 201
Walker, John 106, 110; family 201
Walker, Margaret 201
Walker, Mary 194
Walker, Nancy 106, 201
Wallace, Charlotte 198
Wallace, Margaret 178
Wallace, Sarah 187
Walls, Catharine 188
Walls, Nancy 106, 201
Walrod, Anna 201
Walrod, Charlotte 186
Walrod, Elizabeth "Eliza" 201
Walrod, Jonas, and family 201

Walrod, Maria 182
Walrod, Morris 43, 129; family 201
Ward, Jacob, and family 201
Ward, Margaret 201
Warner, Marcella 183
Warren, Anson/Ahneson 201
Warren, Hooper 39, *125*
Washburn, Elizabeth "Betsy" 198
Washington, George 25, 35, 36, 56, 141, 173
Washington County, New York 6, 36, 104, 138, 140, 153
Waterman, Caroline E. 129, 167, 201
Waterman, Caroline M. 201
Waterman, Caroline W. 129, 204
Waterman, Charles 169
Waterman, Charlotte 28–29, 31, 52, 56, *70*;, and family 201
Waterman, Deborah 201
Waterman, Eliza, and family 201
Waterman, Elizabeth 177
Waterman, Emily 201
Waterman, Illinois 8, *42*, 45, 86
Waterman, James 29, 201
Waterman, John 92; family 201
Waterman, John Aldrich/Aldridge 201
Waterman, John C. 8, 29, 43, *70*, 92–*93*, 100, 138, 144, 146, 167; family 201
Waterman, John D. 28, 201
Waterman, Judith 201
Waterman, Lucy 189
Waterman, Lyman 201
Waterman, Maria, and family 201
Waterman, Mary Graves 28; family 201
Waterman, Mary H. 29, 202
Waterman, Philander, and family 201
Waterman, Robert 29, 201
Watkins, Mary 165, 196
Wattermans, Abigail 180
Weber, Catharine 201
Weber, Philip, and family 201
Webster, Ann 122, 201
Webster, Calvin/Calvary 122; family 201
Webster, Louisa 201
Weeden, Frances 201
Weeden, George 92–*93*, 154; family 201
Weeden, Lorena 201
Weeden, Lucius, and family 201
Weeden, Lucy 203
Weeden, Martha 203
Weeden, Sarah 201
Weeden, Warren, and family 201
Weeks, Maria 181
Weld, Theodore Dwight 26
Wellington, Joannah 202
Wellington, Sparock/Sparoc, and family 202
Wells, Agnes 202
Wells, Caroline 202
Wells, Rev. Edwin 7, 77–*78*, 136; family 202
Wells, Ellen 200
Wells, Lucinda 12, 202
Wells, Mary H. 29, 202
Wells, Solomon 33, 43; family 202
Wells, Timothy 29, 43, 169; family 202
Wells, William, and family 202
Wentworth, John 53, 139, 140
Wesleyan Methodist 113–115, 117–118, 146–147; see also Wesleyan Methodist Church

Wesleyan Methodist Church (Mayfield, Illinois) 7, 25, 30, 35, 41, 113–114, 118, 120–122, 126
West, Aaron 47–*48*, 59, 68–69, 72, *78*, 80, 98, 136; family 202
West, Alice 12, 47, 64, 191
West, Asa "Porter" 12, 47; family 202
West, David 1, 7, 11, *12–14*, 15–17, 24, 30, 33, 46–*48*, 49, 57, 64–66, 68–69, 72–73, 75–76, *78*, 82, 84, 98–99, 120, 130–131, 139, 142, 147, 162, 168, 172; family 202
West, Elias 11–*12*, 15, 47–*48*, 168–168; family 202
West, Ella 202
West, Emily 47, 80, 202
West, Laura 198
West, Lucinda 12, 202
West, Minerva 195
West, Nancy 202
West, Orrin 12, 47; family 202
West, Sarah L., and family 202
West, Sarah "Sally" 202
West Liberty, Iowa 164
Western Citizen 2, 6, 18, 25, 33–35, 38, 40–41, *42*, 43, 45, 47, 56, 63, 65, 71–72, 76, *78*, 84, 87, 91–92, 97, 106–110, 113–115, 118, 121, 122–124, *125*, 126–127, 129–130, 134–139, 141, 144, 147, 150–155, 166, 169, 172–173
Western World 148
Westlake, Eliza 191
Wharry, Evans 117, 202
Wharry, Martha, and family 202
Wheeler, Mary Ann 202
Wheeler, Miranda/Myranda 183
Wheeler, Penelope 180
Wheeler, William, and family 202
Whig 6–9, 22, 38, 107, 120, 124, 138, 141–142, 144, 147, 152, 153
Whig Party 22, 142, 143, 157
White, Alexander, and family 202
White, Ann 202
White, Elizabeth 202
White, Jane 176
White, Joseph, and family 202
White, Mary 202
White, Mary Jane 202
White, Phebe 187
White, Thomas, and family 202
White, William 43; family 202

Whitford, Cyrus 43; family 202
Whitford, Laura 202
Whiting, Hiram, and family 202
Whitman, John, and family 203
Whitman, Mary 203
Whitman, Sarah "Sally" 203
Whitmore, Anna 203
Whitmore, Benjamin 43; family 203
Whitmore, Celina 203
Whitmore, Enos, and family 203
Whitmore, James, and family 203
Whitmore, Lavina/Lavonia 203
Whitmore, Susan 203
Whitney, Betsey 203
Whitney, James, and family 203
Whitney, Nancy 189
Whitney, Ruth 197
Whittemore, Catherine/Katherine 203
Whittemore, Hannah 203
Whittemore, Lorenzo, and family 203
Whittemore, Samuel, and family 203
Widgen, Abel 163–164
Widgen, Elizabeth 163
Wilbur, Sophia 184
Wilcox, Catharine "Kate" 203
Wilcox, Henrietta 79
Wilcox, William, and family 203
Wilkins, F. 151
Wilkinson County, Mississippi 164
Will County, Illinois 4, 29, *32*, 102, 132, 144
Willard, Hosea 92; family 203
Willard, Lucy 199, 203
Willard, Marcia 199
Willard, Martha 203
Willard, Oliver 92; family 203
Williams, Hester 190
Williams, Robert 159, 203
Williamson, Isabella 106, 197
Willmarth, Almira/Almina 196
Willoughby Medical College 72
Willson, George 43; family 203
Willson, Sarah 203
Wilmot Proviso 7, 142
Wilson, Henry 173, 208*ch3n*27
Wilson, John 8, 167–168
Wilson, Mary "Polly" 181
Wiltberger, Elizabeth "Ann" 199
Windsor, Canada 127
Winnebago (Indians) 27
Winnebago County, Illinois 122, 144

Wisconsin 8, 19, 27, 82, 118, 127, 129, 145, 146, 153
Wise, Maria 184
Witherspoon, Marietta 194
Wood, Catherine 203
Wood, Frances 201
Wood, Henry *12*, *32*–33, 49, 63, 132; family 203
Wood, Joseph, and family 203
Wood, Mary 183
Wood, Phoebe 32, 49, 62–63, 132, 189
Wood, Rhoda "Elizabeth" 49, 63, 181, 203
Wood, Selinda 195
Wood, Thomas 33, 132; family 203
Woodley, Selina, and family 203
Woodley, Thomas 203
Woodrough, Betsy 187
Woodruff, Baldwin 130; family 203
Woodruff, Felix, and family 203
Woodruff, Mary 204
Woodruff, Pamelia 203
Woodruff, Sophrona 203
Woodward, Charles 203
Woodward, Laura, and family 203
Woodworth, Lorinda 189
Woolsey, Parthenia 203
Woolsey, Thomas 43, 135–136; family 203
Worden, Benjamin, and family 203
Worden, Martha 203
Worf, Charles, and family 203
Worf, Susanna 203
Wright, Clark 43, 117; family 203
Wyandotte Constitution Convention 98
Wyman, Eliza 203
Wyman, Ellen 181
Wyman, James, and family 203
Wyman, Lucinda 196
Wyman, Ralph 43; family 204
Wyman, Susan 186, 204

Young, Alida 204
Young, Caroline 129, 204
Young, Ellzey/Elsey 129; family 204
Young, Mary 204
Young, Sabrie 176
Young, Simon, and family 204

Zubler, Susanna 203

www.ingramcontent.com/pod-product-compliance
Lightning Source LLC
Chambersburg PA
CBHW081552300426
44116CB00015B/2850